T0257879

# Current Progress in Multimedia

# Volume I

# Current Progress in Multimedia
# Volume I

Edited by **Alicia Witte**

**C**LANRYE
**I**NTERNATIONAL

New Jersey

Published by Clanrye International,
55 Van Reypen Street,
Jersey City, NJ 07306, USA
www.clanryeinternational.com

**Current Progress in Multimedia: Volume I**
Edited by Alicia Witte

© 2015 Clanrye International

International Standard Book Number: 978-1-63240-128-1 (Hardback)

This book contains information obtained from authentic and highly regarded sources. Copyright for all individual chapters remain with the respective authors as indicated. A wide variety of references are listed. Permission and sources are indicated; for detailed attributions, please refer to the permissions page. Reasonable efforts have been made to publish reliable data and information, but the authors, editors and publisher cannot assume any responsibility for the validity of all materials or the consequences of their use.

The publisher's policy is to use permanent paper from mills that operate a sustainable forestry policy. Furthermore, the publisher ensures that the text paper and cover boards used have met acceptable environmental accreditation standards.

**Trademark Notice:** Registered trademark of products or corporate names are used only for explanation and identification without intent to infringe.

Printed in the United States of America.

# Contents

**Permissions**

**List of Contributors**

# Preface

Multimedia refers to content that uses a combination of different content forms. It is concerned with the electronically controlled integration of graphics, text, drawings, video, animation, audio, and any other media where every type of information can be represented, stored, transmitted and processed digitally. This is in contrast with media that use only basic computer displays such as traditional forms of printed or hand-produced material. Multimedia combines a huge plethora of media forms that deal with interactivity like text, audio, still images, animation and video, as previously said. Multimedia as a field can be broadly divided into two categories- linear and non-linear. Linear active content is multimedia that usually advances mostly without any directional control for the viewer such as a cinema presentation. On the other hand non-linear multimedia uses interaction to monitor progress as with a self-paced computer based training or video game. Hypermedia is another example of non-linear content. Multimedia can be usually recorded and played, displayed, or accessed by information content processing devices, such as computerized and electronic devices, but can also be part of a live performance. Such a multiplicity of interactions and avenues for advancements that better our lives makes the field of multimedia crucial to human development.

I am grateful to those who put their hard work, effort and expertise into these research projects as well as those who were supportive in this endeavour.

**Editor**

# Enhancing Scalability in On-Demand Video Streaming Services for P2P Systems

**R. Arockia Xavier Annie,[1] P. Yogesh,[2] and A. Kannan[2]**

[1] Department of Computer Science and Engineering, College of Engineering, Anna University, Chennai 600025, India
[2] Department of Information Science and Technology, College of Engineering, Anna University, Chennai 600025, India

Correspondence should be addressed to R. Arockia Xavier Annie, annie@annauniv.edu

Academic Editor: Martin Reisslein

Recently, many video applications like video telephony, video conferencing, Video-on-Demand (VoD), and so forth have produced heterogeneous consumers in the Internet. In such a scenario, media servers play vital role when a large number of concurrent requests are sent by heterogeneous users. Moreover, the server and distributed client systems participating in the Internet communication have to provide suitable resources to heterogeneous users to meet their requirements satisfactorily. The challenges in providing suitable resources are to analyze the user service pattern, bandwidth and buffer availability, nature of applications used, and Quality of Service (QoS) requirements for the heterogeneous users. Therefore, it is necessary to provide suitable techniques to handle these challenges. In this paper, we propose a framework for peer-to-peer- (P2P-) based VoD service in order to provide effective video streaming. It consists of four functional modules, namely, Quality Preserving Multivariate Video Model (QPMVM) for efficient server management, tracker for efficient peer management, heuristic-based content distribution, and light weight incentivized sharing mechanism. The first two of these modules are confined to a single entity of the framework while the other two are distributed across entities. Experimental results show that the proposed framework avoids overloading the server, increases the number of clients served, and does not compromise on QoS, irrespective of the fact that the expected framework is slightly reduced.

## 1. Introduction

Today, Internet faces proliferation of social network groups that use advanced technology to transfer large commercial data such as image, audio, and video. This trend has led to the popular websites such as YouTube, Flickr, and Joost. As a result, the number of user requests for various video contents through the Internet has grown exponentially every year [1].

Even with reduction in cost on storage and connectivity, the Internet still faces problem in providing quality video to all its customers. Video server faces scalability problem to a large extent with millions of users added to the community every year. Therefore, serving heterogeneous clients efficiently is still an unsolved problem at the servers [2].

Video-on-Demand (VoD) is one such application that has large viewership. It is different from video live streaming.

In live video streaming systems, nodes request for data around a particular playback time [3], with ultimately no interactive request such as Fast-Forward (FF) or Back-Ward (BW), and hence become more or less like the broadcast service which is trivial. As number of users scale up, it is necessary to increase the buffer size. This helps to provide a shared frame so that the needed frame could be retrieved from among those peers. There are dedicated servers for different live streaming subjects that handle heterogeneous client groups by sending different streams satisfying the user's bit rate pattern [4]. Our work handles live streaming and goes a step further to handle applications such as e-learning and VoD with interactivity.

Emerging advancement in distributed systems such as peer-to-peer (P2P) systems with new challenges is becoming more complex. This is due to the challenges in (i) dealing with large scale systems, (ii) achieving real-time VCR (Video

Cassette Recorder) interactivity more effectively, and (iii) provision of video quality with less resources in distributed settings [5–7]. Solutions towards all the previously mentioned challenges lie in deploying appropriate systems in integration with (Quality of Service) QoS supportive system, resource management algorithms, protocols, and approaches in design. In this work, we provide a new solution by combining winning factors such as optimal multiversion and multilayer adaptive streaming [8] video server for the distributive sharing P2P clients and a proxy kind of tracker to reduce the load at the sever that manages peers. We compared this proposed work with existing P2P Gnutella and client server systems with relevant QoS and resource management techniques. Performance improvements for two important resources namely, quality and time towards the interactivity and scalability factors have been proved to be attractive with our proposed design. Moreover, latency is greatly reduced in our work compared with the existing works.

A typical video streaming system, as described in [1, 2], requires three major components: (1) a media-stream server that stores and retrieves video based on the available user bandwidth, (2) an intended proxy server called tracker which tracks the video content in the P2P systems, and (3) the designated heterogeneous P2P client group.

Currently, media servers use multicast streaming and serve the same video through multiple channels to satisfy heterogeneous end users. Here, the encoding rate differs based on the bit rates, and hence it is adaptive streaming [9]. Encoding is performed because the server needs different bit rates for the same video to be sent across for varied services like mobile phones, PCs, set-top boxes, ipads, and so forth; this creates additional workload at the server. This is overcome in [10] which uses same multicast group to serve variety of users by dropping few frames for lower bit rate users. This work has been later extended by yu et al. [10] to overcome the defect of reduction in bit rate with an average increase in frame rate of about 30% for better video quality.

However, close observation and analysis of yu et al's [10] work made us to think of combining other solutions for VoD provided through a proxy server called as tracker in this proposed work.

In order to improve the video quality even for a lesser advantageous end user (namely, users with lower bandwidth speed/bit rates), we propose a new solution that combines the features of all the above solutions. Hence, we achieved the user-perceived video, without quality deterrent from media server by proposing a new *Quality Preserving Multivariate Video Model (QPMVM)* for heterogeneous peer group. The term "multivariate" in this work means usage of either multilayered video streams or multiversioned video streamsor integrated video streams for optimal solution tosatisfy heterogeneous users.

Multiversion systems encode a video sequence into several independent streams at different rates [8, 11]. This requires dropping of frames of the higher bit rates to satisfy the lower bit rates. Moreover it helps to store multiple versions of the same video file with different bit rate as per the user requirement. It also streams the particular bit rate versioned file of the same video to requester. Though it

increases the storage cost, the quality provided is improved, and streaming latency is reduced. During transmission, the server switches among different versions to achieve the desired sending rate. Here, we have used multiple versions for providing better quality by storing minimal number of versions, which is as low as three versions permanently for the uploaded video by a client.

Multilayer systems encode a video sequence into several nonoverlapped, dependent streams [12, 13]. Multilayer systems work in par with the Scalable Video Encoding (SVC) with the difference that here the server provides input to the dropping of layers of frames on the fly to satisfy the requestor's bit rate. This is necessary because the contributions of Fine Grained (FG) layers to the overall video quality are different [14] which are handled by the server using the transcoder module of QPMVM.

Combining the two streaming pattern is termed as hybrid stream. Hybrid streams are generated when the multiversion streams switch to multilayered one for the required bit rate by dropping frame from the current multiversion stream. Multiversion cannot be combined with Scalable Video Coding since it contains multiple base layers and is more suitable to scale in three-dimension space [14].

When the video quality is conserved to certain extent, we move one step further for reducing the delay and latency. This is performed by sharing of peers and henceforth provides VCR interactivity in VoD application that is more desirable with this proposed model. The tasks concentrated within the peer groups include (i) apportioning cached content, (ii) value-based content placement at the peer cache for sharing, (iii) peer energizer (a sharing initiator), and (iv) heuristic-based scheduler at the tracker system for late joiners of the multicast group and interactive requestors. All these multifaceted functionalities have been combined, to scoop up the VoD system as per the user's satisfactory notion on quality of the perceived video [15].

The media server proposed in this work manages the video requests from heterogeneous clients and is also responsible for handling the scalability factors affecting the server.

The tracker present in this framework is situated at the edge router of the peer groups connecting to the backbone network. The tracker acts as message transmitter across the peers and services media streams that the peers have requested to and from the media server. The management of the peers, like the peer request scheduling, managing entry and exit of each peers, Look-Up-Table (LUT) management using Ant-Based optimized routing for the peer groups are handled at the tracker rather than by the server [16, 17]. The combination of the QPMVM at server and the tracker enhances the system as a whole and hence reduces the latency during scalability.

This work provides an optimal solution for video streaming by finding multiple views of the problem in terms of server, tracker, and peer clients. There are many significant contributions that are made in this work. First, the provision of QPMVM at the server reduces the load and improves the video quality. Second, the tracker proposed in this framework increases the streaming ability within the peer groups. Third, the peers are motivated to share the distributed video contents. Finally, the latency is reduced for normal playback as well as VCR operations.

The remainder of this paper is organized as follows: we discuss the related work in Section 2; our proposed video streaming system architecture is given in Section 3; the performance metrics used in the evaluation of the system are presented in Section 4; we discuss our results obtained and analyse them in Section 5. Finally in Section 6, we summarize our findings and suggest possible directions for future investigations.

## 2. Related Research

The Video-on-Demand (VoD) as portrayed in large number of systems involves the server component, the proxy or content distribution server along with huge number of clients who are end users of the VoD systems [16, 18, 19]. At the server side, the existing literature has extensively discussed numerous solutions to optimize the storage/retrieval of video files [8, 10, 20]. Any server, which maintains video files in its database with a single version pertaining to a particular bit rate, cannot serve multiple heterogeneous clients with ease and without degrading the quality. In order to serve these heterogeneous clients, the server adopts two methods according to the literature available in this area. Each method has its own advantages and disadvantages. For instance, the multiversioning avoids the cost of encoding/decoding during video streaming with the help of independent stored video file. But this produces frequent switches among stored versions that result in low reference locality and hence incur additional I/O cost. Furthermore, storing multiple versions requires a lot of storage when the number of requested video for different content is tremendously large during concurrent user access.

In multilayered system, each multilayer video can be stored as Coarse Grained (CG), Fine Grained (FG), or a combination of both. Here, the base layer is the most basic version of the video stored, and the subsequent layers are built on top of them. Hence, it is not necessary to waste storage for storing maximum number of different versions of the same video. Instead, only three different layers are used in our work. This, however, has indirect impact on time as the transcoding is performed in real time based on the current bit rate pattern of the peers [14]. Moreover, adaptation is implemented by introducing an extra layer. If there is any problem in transmitting the base layer itself, then the end video's quality is reduced drastically. The hierarchical encoding is more suitable for multicast to heterogeneous clients while the switching streams can be used in both unicast and multicast [20]. But when a video is played at client side, the user may wish to fast forward (FF), rewind (RW), and so forth. This requires the video to be played at an increased speed. In short, the client needs an interactive server, which responds immediately as per the client request. This becomes quite difficult, if the server has a single large file, because, to play the video at an increased speed, the frames must be identified and transcoded at run time [10]. It becomes easier when the server maintains a special copy

of video, which gives the client a fast version of the same video. In this work, we achieve higher performance using the proposed Quality Preserving Multivariate Video Model (QPMVM).

Today, as the cost of storage has come down, we effectively constructed the server by combining both multiversion as well as multilayered approaches and tested the system for heterogeneous P2P group. P2P client pattern is the most accepted among the many VoD system solutions. P2P media streaming is becoming popular rapidly for the reason that the streaming service of client/server model takes up too much server resource and could not meet the increasing demand of scalability [7]. CoopNet, PALS, PROP, Toast, and Zebroid provide on-demand streaming using P2P networks. Each of these systems seeks to support an infrastructure-based system with P2P networks and thus achieves scalability to some extent [20, 21]. However, all these existing solutions are not sufficient to provide effective services in the current scenario. Therefore, it is necessary to provide new store and retrieval techniques to meet the current demands. In this work, we achieve scalability through multiversions. Moreover, this work has been implemented in P2P technology and shows the advantages of serving on a large scale that has already been introduced to the media streaming systems. VCR (Video Cassette Recorder) functionality is one of the most used features in real-world streaming applications [22] which operates for FF, BW, seek, pause, and so forth. Also, the problem of scalability to a large user population in media streaming systems is only mitigated to a certain degree in the past but not solved.

Optimal methods for video file storage are becoming increasingly important owing to the rising numbers of video server populations. Adaptations that optimize playable frame rate by storing minimal number of configurations require intensive computation through loading of processor [23, 24]. Storing all possible configurations for a single video file for all the bit rates a client can have during internet connectivity requires tremendous amount of storage. Only when the memory used is sparse and the processor load is reduced [25], video servers would find it appealing. To meet these apparently conflicting demands, this work proposes a system for optimizing video server storage.

## 3. Video Streaming System Architecture

The video streaming system proposed in the paper possesses the media server which services the client requests for the videos stored in its database. A proxy, called as tracker in this work, lies between the media server and the P2P clients. The proxy is implemented in one of the peer nodes or at the edge router of the network connecting the media server and the P2P client systems. Here, it is implemented at the edge router of the system so that it conveniently tracks the client requests that passes through it, as well as the network condition at the peer end. Figures 1(a) and 1(b) show the high-level setup of the video streaming system architecture proposed in this paper which comprises of all the three main components of

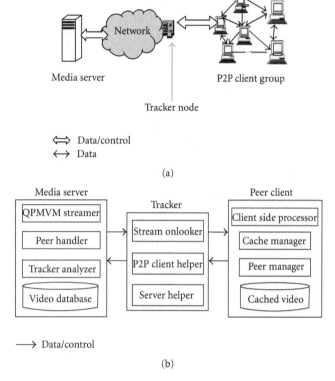

Media server

Tracker node

P2P client group

$\Longleftrightarrow$ Data/control
$\longleftrightarrow$ Data

(a)

(b)

Figure 1: (a) System architecture; (b) High level system.

the VoD system, namely, the media server, tracker, and the peer clients.

*3.1. Media Server.* A video server, which is connected to the Internet, may have diverse client populations and hence is very difficult for the server to respond to multiple clients with varied user profiles. The situation of multiple video requests by heterogeneous clients is handled in Napster server and few other VoD servers by having multiple versioned streaming systems [26–28]. But the same can be achieved using multilayered approach as well. In this approach, though the same stream is sent to both the users, it requires dropping of some frames. In such a scenario, few very important frames such as "I" and "P" frames might also be dropped depending on the overflow of the buffer at client end and the transmission speed at the server/client network. In such a case, the quality at the user end would not be commendable.

By considering the advantages of both the systems proposed by Yu et al. [10] and Cheng-Hsin and Mohamed [8], we propose a hybrid approach in this paper for providing effective VoD using multiversioning with multilayering. In addition, we propose a new proxy called tracker deployed at the edge routers of each client networks in order to reduce the delay in searching and forwarding from the server. From the experiment conducted with this new model, it has been observed that this multiversioned system provides better quality than the multilayered system [12, 29]. On one hand, when a channel experiences network congestion, a multiversioned system which has a precomputed version file, sends the correct frame based on the bandwidth availability

at that time. On the other hand, during such congestion, the only possible option for the multilayered system is to drop frame(s) irrespective of its priority. Therefore, in this research work, the features of both multiversioning and multilayering are integrated, and a tracker with local user profile database and decision-making capability has been proposed.

*3.1.1. Quality Preserving Multivariate Video Model (QPMVM).* As mentioned earlier both multiversioning and multilayering systems have both advantages as well as disadvantages. The choice depends on various factors that arise from the exact user profile details known to the server at the start of a streaming request. Moreover, the packet receiving details from the network side which are received at the server via probing the network to know about the congestion and slow delivery helps to analyze the reasons for congestion and delay. This challenge is addressed in this work by introducing the QPMVM at the server as one of the modules in order to manage the server by providing consistent throughput without overloading the server even during peak number of requests. Figure 2 shows the architecture of the proposed QPMVM model at the server. We do not make any assumption about the format of layered video. Any scalable or layered video coding scheme can be incorporated into our framework. This can work on lower-end codec such as MPEG-2, MPEG-4, MPEG-21 as well as higher end codec such as MPEG-4 Part 10/H.264 AVC (Advanced Video Coding). As H.264 SVC (Scalable Video Coding) is delay intense with respect to computational complexity than the other codec forms [30], this work is better off with H.264 AVC with single-base layer. Hence, in this work, we have considered all MPEG video formats with the intent that most of the videos used in the Internet fall into this category. QPMVM has the advantage of identifying through the seed estimator, a way of holding lesser number of multiple versions for a video which is encoded by the transcoder. From the stored multiversions, the multilayering is done on the fly through the Decider module.

Generally, whenever the server detects any network change, it drops a layer of frames, in order to achieve the desired bit rate for the given video. Dropping "B" frames allows protection of more important "I" and "P" frames for the same amount of bandwidth [29, 31]. The data size for the three frames is known to be I > P > B. Also, dropping "B" frames sparsely does not affect much of the user's perception of the video [32–34]. But dropping multiple layers of frames, without keeping in mind the frame priorities with respect to its Group of Picture's (GOP) can affect the received video quality at the client to a great extent. In such a scenario, due to bit error and packets loss it is not possible for the receiver to recover all the frames. For example, the first B frame can be recovered only if the first I frame and the first P frame are successfully recovered. The loss of P frame will cause subsequent P and B frames to be unrecoverable, affecting the quality of the video. To increase the expected number of frames successfully reconstructed, the server can adapt to the network condition by changing the amount of redundant

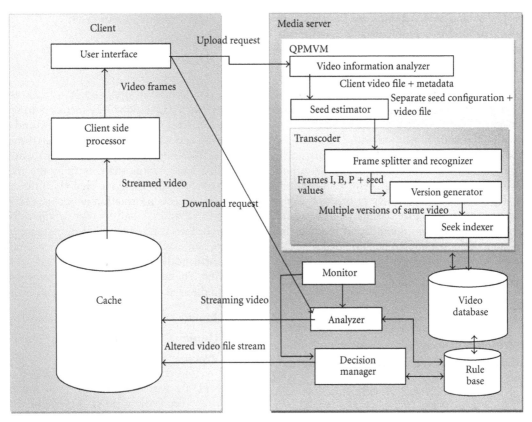

FIGURE 2: Media Server.

information sent to protect the video against different packet loss rates [4, 7, 9]. The system must alter the bit pattern in the frames' Group of Pictures (GOP) to improve the efficiency.

This is because of the fact that when a video is being played at an increased speed, "$n$" number of frames may be dropped per GOP (of "$m$" frames). When receiving the video file, the receiver will expect "$m$" frames when actually only "$m - n$" frames are received. This reduction in frames must be set in the GOP's bit pattern so that the receiver expects only "$m - n$" frames. This is done by supplying the end user with Forward Error Correction (FEC) code as done in Jiangchuan [13] within the MPEG frame header. Block diagram of QPMVM subsystem and the important activities of the subsystem are shown in Figure 4.

The QPMVM system in media server can be logically divided into two components, namely, upload and download video streaming. The uploading component uses Transmission Control Protocol (TCP), and the video streaming is performed using Real Time Protocol (RTP). When the system is executing in an upload scenario, it takes a video as input from the client side. As video sent from the server is implemented using RTP, it gives added advantage in determining video streaming metrics that are more appropriate to the real world scenario that combine Real Time Streaming Protocol (RTSP) as well as Real Time Control Protocols (RTCP) in a connection-oriented network. Next, based on the client side's profile which includes details such as IP address, bandwidth, and user preference category (i.e., high priority user, medium

priority user, low and very low priority), the server decides its video streaming method to be either the layered approach or the versioned approach for a video request to a particular client based on the user profile and details from the network. Once these details are available at the server side, the video is analysed to decide on the seed configuration of the video that is to be streamed. Once the seed configurations are identified, based on the information gathered from the video file the versions are generated. The process of generating versions involves identifying the frames based on the information gathered. The versions are then stored in the database.

When the QPMVM system is executing in a video streaming scenario, multiple components work at the same time. First of all, the client request for a particular file is received at the server which triggers a check for the availability of the file in the database. Further, a check for a compatible version is done. Once both the checks get completed, the users' connection profiles are now taken into account, and if an exact version has not been found amongst the existing versions, then transcoding is done at run time and the video is streamed across and played on the client side.

Throughout the entire process of streaming the video file, the network conditions are monitored, and when a change in the network condition is detected, communication with the client is activated to check how many frames of the video have already been played at the client. This frame information coupled with the change in the network bandwidth information is used to identify which part of the video must be played and in which version. Basically our pattern of evolving around user profile data does not mean that very often communication through message transfer is made to acquire knowledge of the current situation, rather only when the network causes reduction in data flow do we make the server change its stand from multiversion to multilayering. This is beneficial immensely as the time for deciding is reduced.

In other works, the communication with the client to know about the details of frames played (current situation) is not done periodically rather only when the situation demands. This obviously helps during client VCR request pattern where, for a medium or a lower prioritized client the layered versions are sent for that specific VCR requests. The following subsections explain the different modules in the QPMVM system with their implementation details.

*QPMVM Algorithm:*

**Request Type I**

**Input:** Request to upload a video into the server database from a client

**Output:** Server stores the uploaded video into the database

**Process:**

(1) Video information extracted from the uploaded video
(2) Seed configurations identifier to create versions
(3) Frames split and stored

**Request Type II**

**Input:** Request a video to the server by a client

**Output:** Client receives the video

**Process:**

(1) Based on client network priority

(2a) If same video version is present in database it is retrieved and sent to client

Else

(2b) Multilayered video is sent to the client

**Request Type III**

**Input:** Video VCR request to the server by a client

**Output:** client receives the video part

**Process:**

(1) Based on client network priority

(2) Appropriate video part with required version is layered to client.

The QPMVM is a major module in the server side which extracts the video metadata, splits frames, creates versions, and successfully stores it as indexed version in the video database. It uses the aspects like bit rate control, buffer control, and frame positioning control methods from the javax.media classes of Java Media Framework (JMF). It encompasses three modules:

(i) Video Information Analyser,

(ii) Seed Estimator,

(iii) Transcoder.

*(i) Video Information Analyser.* It receives the video file from the client and analyses the metadata to separate useful information like Group of Pictures (GOPs) and so forth. This is done by extracting the MPEG header from every video file. The upload operation from the client sends a video file. The video information analyzer splits the metadata apart from the video part of the received video file. The metadata is parsed, and the information about the client is gathered such as its IP address and its user profile as being high or medium or low. The video information is also gathered from the metadata like frame rate, GOP, video duration, bit rate, and so forth, both these information is then stored for future processing. The output from the video information analyzer is sent to the seed estimator and peer handler modules.

**Input:** Client uploaded video metadata

**Output:** Client information and video information

**Process:**

(1) By extracting data on the uploaded client's connectivity, the client is categorized as:

If the connecting bandwidth is

(a) up to 52 Kbps then, very low priority client

(b) between 52 Kbps and 112 Kbps then, low priority client

(c) between 112 Kbps and 256 Kbps then, medium priority client

(d) between 256 Kbps and 512 Kbps then, high priority client

(2) Video metadata is extracted from the video file.

*(ii) Seed Estimator.* As the name suggests the seed estimator receives the metadata and decides upon the seed values that we intend to make the uploaded video into several versions. The seed values here mean the relative number of versions that is required for a particular video file to be stored in the database. It is the seed values generated that decide upon the version numbers. This is intended for client nodes with Internet connections ranging from 16 Kbps through a telephone dial up networks to 512 Mbps through DSL networks.

In order to arrive at the seed values, we calculate them by analyzing the bit rate of the video; subsequently we reduce the given bit rate by just half the bit rates and figure seed versions that equal these halved rates. We stop factoring the bit rate by two until the bit rate reached is greater than or equal to 16 kbps because it is known that user's connection setup speed cannot be slower than this. The reason we go in for halving the bit rates without doubling it is we signify the uploaded video version as it is with its provided quality and go in for supporting the lower end clients with almost the same quality by storing versions with lesser bit rates. Most importantly, these subversions (means lower bit rate versions of the given video file) are each arrived through the generated seeds, and hence each video version is stored expressing the seed values. This paves in for storing only very few versions for the overall vast difference in the number of client bit rate pattern, thereby reducing the storage space at the server enormously.

**Input:** Video bit rate of the uploaded video file by a client

**Output:** Number of seeds for the input video file

**Process:**

(1) Uvbr = video bit rate of the uploaded video file by a client

(2) seed_count = 0

(3) while (Uvbr ! = 16 Kbps)

Uvbr = Uvbr/2

If Uvbr generated is within the priority limit of the client group, then

seed_count = seed_count + 1.

Else

No change in seed_count.

*(iii) Transcoder.* The transcoder is another major submodule within the processor. This module uses the input from the other two submodules within the processor and performs transcoding operation. This ensures different layers exist upon these base versions. Transcoder includes (a) frame splitting and recognizing I, P, and B frames, (b) version generation, and (c) seeking the frames in the video.

*(a) Frame Splitting and Recognizing I, P, and B Frames.* Frame splitting module identifies the Intra (I), Bidirectional interpolated (B), and Prediction (P) frames and splits them. GOP gives us information that says how many frames are present between consecutive I frames. Each frame of the video has a separate header which is called the picture header. This is essential because it contains information which tells us about I, P, and B frames. The picture header has the frame information in byte 5 of the MPEG header. The bits set at 3rd, 4th, and 5th position are checked, and the following are inferred: "001" is I frame; "010" is a P frame; "011" is a B frame. The seed values provided by the Seed Estimator module and the video received from client are used here as references to generate multiple versions of the same video to accommodate heterogeneous client bit rate pattern. The realization of I, P, and B frames from all the GOPs is done. Here, information from the video file's hint track called the *video track,* is used to include streaming information. A video file usually contains multiple *tracks.* Individual tracks can have metadata, such as the aspect ratio of a video track, title of the video, episode numbers, and variable bit rate/constant bit rate [35, 36]. The track information set at the MPEG header of the uploaded video file provides more information

which is hinted in the video file per data unit of the stream. This will help in extracting the GOP during sending the video for requests. The information of the current frame being processed from the uploaded video file lends it to being I, P. or B frame.

**Input:** Video frames

**Output:** Recognize and Split Frames as I or P or B

**Process:**

(1) For each instance of the Track-information or hint tracks from the metadata of the uploaded video file

(1a) Store images in Image-control.

(1b) Extract data units from the hint tracks

(2) while (!Reached end of the Frameset)

{ I = track_no $*$ GOP

P = track_no + $(k + 1) * j$

B = all other frames }

Where-"track_no" is the nth I frame encountered at that time, "$k$" is the number of B frames between the consecutive I and P frames "$j$" is P frame counter.

*(b) Version Generation.* The user video needs to be morphed to the lower versions. This is done with the help of the seed values that have been identified. Based on the property that dropping of B frames does not affect the quality of the video that much, the system proceeds to drop B frames at first to accommodate to the lower bit rate versions. We use the information obtained from frame splitting and recognizing for the seed value from the seed estimator to generate versions for the users with lower bit rate pattern. In this work when creating multiversions, the frame rate is not affected much, because the bit rate has no impact on the frame rate of a video. It is with respect to a codec [23, 35]. Also, the aim is to fit the multiversion file into any possible client bit rate without losing quality. Different versions of same video file are generated using the following algorithm.

**Input:** Client uploaded video file, seed_count from seed estimator

**Output:** Video versions generated

**Process:**

(1) Read video as bit stream

(2) Check for GOP header and picture header, if (match found)

(a) Read nth bit and obtain whether I, B or P frame

(b) For each seed obtained from seed estimator, drop every 5th B frames subjected to the required bit rate (information from Monitor).

If (no more B frames to drop) drop no frames.
Generate versions.
Every 5th B frame is dropped, since it is not very difficult to generate one, as it might lie between two B frames and/or

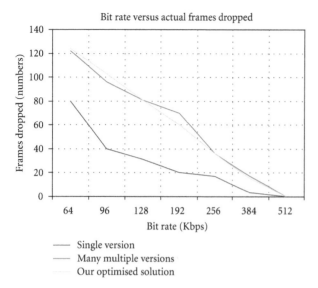

FIGURE 3: Bit rate (kbps) versus actual no. of packets dropped.

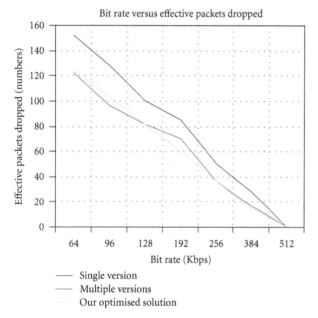

FIGURE 4: Bit rate (kbps) versus actual no. of packets dropped.

an I and a P frame as well. This is better than dropping consecutive B frames [34]. Any GOP under consideration would have the probability that based on this information it would speed up the encoding/decoding process to a greater extent. This is better than to scan the frames of importance before dropping, which is time consuming or not to scan at all which is unfavourable when quality is perceived [37]. This is supported by our simulation result as well from Figures 3 and 4.

*(c) Seeking the Frames in the Video.* When a client prefers to play a video file, he selects it and starts to view the video file. Sometimes, after the client has started to view the file, and

when the video is still being played, the same client's network condition may change for the worse. Congestion may throw up, and video frames may get clogged at the bottleneck link which may not be able to transfer the high bit rate frames that the client is currently viewing. But the link might allow few frames of lower bit rates to pass through it. Our system is designed to adapt to such changes and provide the next best available video version for that condition. In order to achieve this, the seek indexer traverses the video file after every nth frame to avoid retrieving the entire video file in the new version to be played for the client. The inputs to this module are video frames played by the client, and the seed value corresponding to the bit rate change needed to be placed on the incoming video due to the change in the network condition.

**Input:** link strength, video version

**Output:** frame to be played is identified in stored video version

**Process:**

(1) Extract the video version file to be played for bit rate given by "i" at the client.

(2) while (not end of file )

{     Check frame rate;

    if (frame_no mod GOP = = 0)

        i = frame_no / GOP;

    if (frame_no is a multiple of GOP)

        Timestamp = frame_no_i / n;

}

Where "i" is the indication of the frame we try to determine as the one to be played at the client.

*3.1.2. Monitor and Analyser.* The input to the monitor is from the client side. Output is the identified network conditions from the RTSP protocol. The functionality of the analyzer is simple. It merely searches for the client compatible version, and if it is not found, it sends the nearest compatible lower version. This is understood from the following

The output from monitor module gives the network configuration details of the client's download request, and this input query is sent to the database, to search for the client compatible version.

**Input:** link strength, video viewed by the client

**Output:** video to be played is identified in stored video version as per the link strength

**Process:**

(1) If the queried file is found, search for version

(a) if version not found, extract immediate lower version file and send

(b) Else, send the version matched file.

*3.1.3. Decision Manager* . In a video streaming application, after a client has partly downloaded a file, if the video is still being played, the same client's network configuration may change. Our system is designed to adapt to such a change and provide the next best available video version. Here, it becomes important that we do not retransmit the frames that have already been played on the client side. The decision manger predicts and decides which frames can be skipped and which frames should be sent.

The process dealt at the decision manager can be explained with the following example: If a client-A is connected to the system for some "$t_x$" seconds, during which "Y" number of frames is received at that client. If the network configurations change at the some "$t_{X+1}$th" second, and if we analyze and send the new version video, it would be meaningless to send the first "Y" frames. The decision manager thus transmits the video from the "Y + 1th" frame after analyzing the current GOP and its associated frame streamed recently. For instance, if the "Y" frame is an "I" frame, thus decoding and reencoding are needed to search for the new version starting from the "Y + 1" frame. Therefore, the current GOP helps out in the delivery of required stream.

Here, the usage of RTP protocol helps in achieving this pattern of skipping frames and sending the current frame from the stored multiversion video file. This is one of the novel techniques used in our work that reduces both time to select the frame from stored video version and send or to generate them to the current bit rate level of the connected client through the already sending stream on the fly [8], by dropping packets which is multilayering done in adaptive streaming method. Client side communication is also done through this module.

The selection of stored video version or dropping of frames to match the limited bandwidth is decided here.

The input given is video file that client has requested along with the monitor's output as to which frame has been viewed recently. The output to this module generates a new compilation of video with dropped frames

**Input:** Identified video version from Server

**Output:** Frame to be played at the client

**Process:**

(1) If current bit rate of client matches stored video version then check frame number, seek to that frame and send from that frame onwards.

(2) Else, drop layers of B frames from the current video stream, seek to the requested frame number and send from that frame onwards.

*3.2. Tracker.* The cooperation provided by the peers by uploading to the fellow peers with incentivized pattern as seen in [18, 19, 38] is added to motivate the peers as jubilant uploaders. This further achieves better focus on servicing requesters rather than spending time in identifying providers at the tracker. In our system, we consider all peers are cheerful in providing as they are serviced with greater download speed for each completed (100% data received by

the peer requester) or partially completed (40% to 90% data received by the peer requester) uploads. The combination of these destined methods at the tracker provides novelty to this approach with which we deem to achieve far more than that was intended with great impact on client satisfaction. The basic processes at the tracker for all the combined effort to be put into the router or a separate dedicated peer node for this tracking should include the following modules: (1) Stream Onlooker, (2) P2P Client helper, and (3) Server-side Helper.

*3.2.1. The Stream Onlooker.* The Stream Onlooker (SO) is quite similar in a way to the analyzer module of the QPMVM. This keeps a watch on the incoming requests from the client to the media server which notes down the request information in the tracker table (LUT). Also, it saves the video segment information stored by the media server during push stream which is used for managing further requests among the peer groups. Among all the other things, it keeps watch on the stream request generated within the peer group, by looking for further requests to be made by the same requester after assigning another peer to serve for the request currently made by the requesting peer.

For example if peer "A" has requested a video segment "i," then the tracker could receive only two more request, for the same video segment from the same peer "A." By this we guarantee that the request has either been serviced by another providing peer for the better or the request has not been served by the provider peer to whom the request was directed to, for the worse. In which case, the tracker manages to route it to another peer and the media server simultaneously. By this way the tracker fixes the servicing time for the requesting peer and looks on for another reliable provider with options open within the local peers of high profile range groups.

This part of the work at the tracker to look for capable service providers in the peer group satisfies the requesting peer to get serviced before the exhaustion of its buffered video content. Moreover the agreed peer provider who would not serve the requesting peer client would get less benefit in terms of speed and video quality as the agreement has been futile with no services at the client end. After agreement, the nonproviding peer node's information could be captured with the same request generated by the requesting client who has timed out its earlier request. This information on the nonprovider becomes fruitful at the same time to look for any further requests from the non-provider as such to look in for network-related problems like link congestion, attack-driven malicious nodes and so on, and if there are no such problems, the information would be used for negative incentives.

**Input:** Streaming requests to the server/tracker from the peer clients

**Output:** Manage client uploading/downloading pattern send information to tracker

**Process:**

(1) Maintain database

(1a) Requested video file, user id of the requester, number of requests by same user for the same content and/or different content, servicer details and so forth,

(1b) For uploading within peer groups and the rate of upload.

(1c) For downloading within peer groups or from server and the rate of upload.

(1d) Place the most uploading peer at the top and the remaining in consecutive order of their sharing ability.

(2) Update tracker with the managed database for every request serviced.

(3) Provide entity on the PM and CM to PCH.

*3.2.2. P2P Client Helper.* The P2P Client Helper (PCH) manages and provides information for Ant-based routing at the tracker. The Stream Onlooker (SO) updates and sends the information on each peer based on the services required as well as services provided among peers to PCH. The PCH holds the latest information on the clips cached at each peer in all the peer nodes as a table.

**Input:** From Stream Onlooker

**Output:** Analyzed video segments and policies

**Process:**

(1) Places the pushed video segments from the media server into the peers, by queue maintained by the SO.

(1a) The top of the queue has the maximal provider and the rear the least provider in the peer group-This data subjectively used for pushing data as well as incentive at the peer.

(1b) Identifies and updates route for Ant based optimization. (Any peer node is not selected for an optimal route but with the information from the maximal queued.)

This achieves high delivery to the client side by combining these several solutions put together.

*3.2.3. Server-Side Helper.* The Server-side Helper (SH) mainly concerns with scheduling the peer group requests mostly at the tracker and very few at the Media server. The Server-side Helper maintains hash table to provide the requesting peer map with video segment needed from the various peers stored across peer group. The PCH and SO input the SH with the needed information for managing the admission control dynamically altering the choice when the provider or the receiver is no more worthy of doing any of it due to network-related problems. The topology of the peer group connected and maintained as Earliest Reachable Merge Tree (ERMT) with Static Full Stream Scheduling (SFSS) [11, 16, 39] gains more momentum in multicast streaming for the peers as scheduled by the SH. The SH provides another most prominent work to server that helps it to place the pushed video content at the peers based on the ability of each peer of its bandwidth speed and buffering size

which is to serve others. This is to identify the best supplier (peer) for the current request. By best suppliers we mean those peer nodes that can stream the requested video as fast as possible which is achieved by tracking the reduced load at those peers to serve the requester.

**Input:** Split video segments

**Output:** Place video segments among the clients

**Process:**

$m$: total number of peers in the system

$N$: total number of segments a video is split.

$A$: average bandwidth of all $m$ peers

bi: bandwidth of ith peer "Pi".

ph: high bandwidth peers

pl: low bandwidth peers

Npl: Total number of segments to be allocated for low bandwidth peers.

Nph: Total number of segments to be allocated for high bandwidth peers.

Categorize the $m$ peers into

ph where, bandwidth $> A$ for all nodes in this set and

pl where, bandwidth $< A$ for all nodes in this set

for i = P1 to Pm

$Nph = (N * (bi) \text{ PeerHigh}) / (A * m)$

$Npl = N - Nph$

$Ni = (N * bi) / (A * m)$

Ni video segments are distributed to Pi.

The video segments that have been obtained by splitting the video file are distributed among the various peers in the system based upon their utility bandwidth. More precisely, the peers having more bandwidth receive more segments and vice versa. It is also possible for the end user to view a specified segment in the video. This improves user interactivity of the system by providing for random-seek option.

*3.3. Peer Node.* Distributed P2P network is more advantageous in the setup of VOD system [17, 40]. Each peer node is equipped to handle a factor of the overall load from the server by serving with its buffered content. Peers are henceforth clients with mini version of the server. The requests arise from the clientpart of the peer node, and the streaming service comes from the server part of the peer. Here, we call it as service provider. Not only does the service provider is quite complicated but then it needs to have the current information on the video segments held at each peer and also needs to combine with existing multicast streams to service in a better way. The user interface at each peer contains the Audio Video receiver (AV receiver) which is used for Real Time Protocol (RTP) video reception. Processing at each Peer node comprises of the (i) Client Side Processor (CSP) (ii) Cache Manager, and (iii) Peer Manager which we detail in the following sections.

*3.3.1. Client Side Processor.* The Client Side Processor (CSP) acts as the heart of every peer node in the network. Because, it keeps track as well as informs the most important matters happening within the peer to the tracker as well as neighbor peers. CSP attends to the various tasks that take place at the peers.

The most important of all and several other individual peer subtasks like decoding the video and connecting with Cache Manager and Peer Manager. The various factors leading to proper uploading and henceforth the incentives maintenance very much depends on CSP's informed data. Here, the sender does not magnify the sending details but the receiver notifies it to the tracker. Which means in the normal sense as the sender might not fulfill or rather provide to the custom peer node but inform to the tracker that it had completed its service; this magnification by the sender is clarified by the receiver's CSP information. The components of the CSP meticulously work with the Media server, tracker and other peers to provide them with optimized content delivery. The Cache Manager (CM) and the Peer Manager (PM) also inputs content stored to the CSP.

**Input: Various tasks at the peers**

//∗ multicast stream upload, multicast stream download, buffer scanner, network bandwidth connectivity, video segments buffered, services provided and services received, services disrupted, subtasks like decoding the video and connecting with Cache Manager for knowing high priority task and Peer Manager and so forth, ∗//

**Output:** Information supplied to tracker and neighbor peers

**Process:**

(1) Inform on each task performed at a peer to the tracker.

(2) The stream shift that takes place for the different version of the same video file, is also provided by the CSP during uploading to fellow peers.

(3) CSP maps the tracked frame number when rewind, fast forward and pause buttons are clicked.

   (i) It uses the aspects like bit rate control, buffer control and frame positioning method.

   (ii) It induces request appropriate to the Cache Manger's data on the cached content within the playback time.

*3.3.2. Cache Manager.* Video content buffered at the peer is managed by Cache Manager (CM). The importance of cache manager towards bringing out efficient working of peer groups sharing is explained in this subsection. There are two cache, used in each peer. Ones completely dedicated for the server to push its video content called the *serve-cache* is and the other is used by the peer for its client application called the *playback cache/buffer*. In our work, we presume there is enough cache to hold at the client so there is no need for cache replacement policy.

The serve-cache would also slowly accustom to fill in the user's/client's interest. The user's interest is expected to lie within any two of all the videos at hand. The Cache Manager acts as a monitor of the playback system wherein the playback time of the current clip is used to fill in the playback cache. If the cache is almost empty and does not get filled up within the stipulated playback time,

**Input:** Playback time indicator from the player.

**Output:** CM raises high priority issue to the CSP.

**Process:**

(1) CM does not wait until the last bit of the cached content is viewed rather as in several of the Media players' cache warning takes place at half of 1/4th of the cached content [28] which is fixed as the threshold here too

(2) Sets high priority bit.

(3) Halt all other services that it was carrying out and perform for getting the next needed video segment.

(4) For normal play back, the cached content in the playback buffer is managed to hold the viewer's interest through (1)–(3) steps.

(5) For VCR requests, if the server-push content is different from the interest of the user it would not benefit from the cached content.

(6) % of cache hit is required to be greater than the cached content at each client. Hence, the non-interest cached content would alter its position from *serve-cache* to another of the interest filled *serve-cache* peer node.

For any VCR request like seek Fast-forward generated within the client, the playback buffer keeps playing the latest video segment that it is currently viewing for 20 msecs and immediately switches over to the kth video segment held in the playback cache. Here, $k$ is the random number generated that lies within the currently viewing clip number to half of the maximum segment number. The maximum segment number lies as the last clip in the limit of the existing playback buffer content [40].

If the VCR request is for seek Fast-backward, the same as Fast-forward with reverse action carries on here. But, if the currently viewing clip is the first clip in the playback cache, this particular seek request grabs the clip segment previously to currently viewing clip minus kth (any integer value for $k$ that matches the *serve-cache* content) clip from the *serve-cache* if present (which is highly possible); else it grabs the clip within next hop of its neighbors processed by CSP within 2 secs (maximum).

For any other VCR actions like pause, continue lies within the previously explained two types. For request of any new video, while the currently viewing video is different, CM searches for video in *serve-cache* instantly without looking in the *playback cache*. It then accepts clips from a different multicast stream through CSP and retains the currently viewed clip in the *serve-cache*.

*3.3.3. Peer Manager.* Communication between other peer nodes to receive and to send video streams happens through this Peer Manager (PM).

The speed at which the receiver receives the video streams gets increased by few kbps based on the incentivized value prescribed by the tracker; the senders have minimal upload bandwidth in which the receiver combines channels as it receives from many nodes at the same time quantifying the incremental speed for its service already provided.

> **Input:** Tracker information and bandwidth correlation map.
>
> **Output:** communication and incentives by interacting with the groups intimated by the tracker through CSP in order to supply at incentive sufficed speed.
>
> **Process:**
>
> (1) For each video shared among a group, it maintains a leader (higher bandwidth within group);

The PM accurately maps with all other servicing peer nodes at the same time and balances upload among this specific group for the specified client.

*Incentive Algorithm*

*Peer Up-Loaders*

> (1) Tracker stores the up-loader's peer information for incentive management.
>
> (2) Critical case-exhaustion of buffer content,
>
> > (i) Uploading peers can agree on uploading for critical case.
> >
> > (ii) Once agreed,
> >
> > > (a) No more high priority bit is set by the requestor
> > >
> > > (b) Else, look for Congestion, Malicious nodes. If found, then do not mark the agreed up-loader for negative incentive (reduce download speed by 10 kbps per negative score per agreed peer)
> > >
> > > (c) Else, mark the agreed up-loader for negative incentive
> > >
> > > (d) Else, uploaded successfully (100%) or partially (40–90% may happen due to external failures), provide positive incentive counter set (increase download speed by 25 kbps per positive score by combining multiple agreed up-loaders)

*Peer Down-Loaders*

> (1) Incentivized peers are tracked by the tracker. PM present at each peer verifies the incentive received.
>
> (2) Achieving incentives (at tracker, Peer):
>
> > (i) If Incentive queue managed at the tracker has counter set and if the counter is not more than can be serviced then provide full incentive.

> > (ii) Else, divide the counter by half and check whether half the incentive can be serviced by individual Up-loader or by combining multiple up-loaders,
> >
> > (iii) Repeat the above step until incentive serviceable.
> >
> > (iv) If Negative incentive, update incentive queue per peer basis at tracker and that peer.

*Combining Multiple Up-Loaders*

This is done as one of the group member say "Pi'" who has maximal bandwidth say at "$q$" kbps, but currently provides at the rate of "$q$-$x$" kbps (since it in reality, complete bandwidth is underutilized) this "$x$" kbps would be compensated by another peer in the group by sending at its current bit rate "plus" the left out bit rate that is, if supposedly it sends at "$r$" kbps and its maximal is below "$r + x$" kbps it compensates the complete streaming rate. If not, the "$x$" kbps would be shared among the existing group to provide incremental support bandwidth which is obtained by adding current sending rate plus 2 kbps by all until receiver is fulfilled with the added bit rate. This requires enormous client communication management to support the incentive set. Hence, with PM the feasibility to provide to peers with ultimate caution and care has been obtained.

## 4. Performance Study (METRICS) and Experimental Setup

The experimental setup for the simulation run is shown in Table 1. The simulation is done using Java code for the entire system. Here, the simulated system is compared with Bittorrent-based Gnutella system and the normal client-server system and we call the Gnutella system, as the traditional P2P system as they form the base for any P2P network system for file sharing. In traditional P2P system, the segments are equally distributed among the peers without the tracker scheme. The components of a social network are simulated as our peer network groups.

Firstly, we evaluate the main subsystem in VoD setup, which is our QPMVM that ensures video quality does not gets deteriorated as the user bandwidth reduces below the video bit rate. We evaluate this subsystem present at the server by calculating the loss of packets and compare the loss of effective frames in packets to the existing multiversion and multilayer systems. We consider this as the parameter for QoS. Normally, when frame drop occurs, the receiver's capacity is lesser than the senders. A simulation setup that performs for the frame drops in three different systems are handled here. It shows, I and P frames lost with single version and many multiple version system is relatively high than our QPMVM system. Though it stores very few multiple version it rarely drops effective frames. In QPMVM we look for B frames that are to be dropped first, and lastly we drop the P frames and finally I frames during the packet transmission. This of course is not handled in both multilayered as well as multiversion systems where the frames in a packet are

TABLE 1: Experimental values.

| Simulation setup | |
| --- | --- |
| Total number of peers | 100 |
| Total number of videos | 5 |
| Min-Segment size | 1 sec |
| Max-Segment size | 25 secs |
| Serve-cache size of each peer | 200 secs or 180 segments |
| Play buffer size | 30 segments |
| Upload bandwidth | 32 kbps–512 kbps |
| Download bandwidth | 32 kbps–512 kbps |
| Video bit rate | 64–512 kbps |
| Length of video | 180 secs |
| Tracker bandwidth | 32 kbps–512 kbps |
| Simulation time | 3600 secs |
| Reservation buffer size | 4 segments |
| Incentive increment per count | 25 kbps |

TABLE 2: Video Samples.

| S. no | Video name | Time length (min:sec) | Data rate (kbps) |
| --- | --- | --- | --- |
| 1 | v_1 (Core) | 0:50 | 4086 |
| 2 | v_2 (Bodyguard) | 3:30 | 4971 |
| 3 | v_3 (3idiots) | 4:40 | 4209 |
| 4 | v_4 (Magadheera) | 5:40 | 5204 |
| 5 | v_5 (Inception) | 6:40 | 3466 |

TABLE 3: Segment split.

| S. no. | Storage peers | Sample 1 | | Sample 2 | |
| --- | --- | --- | --- | --- | --- |
| | | Bandwidth (kbps) | No. of segments | Bandwidth (kbps) | No. of Segments |
| 1 | P_B | 100 | 5 | 115 | 6 |
| 2 | P_C | 90 | 5 | 58 | 3 |
| 3 | P_D | 70 | 4 | 45 | 2 |
| 4 | P_E | 80 | 4 | 95 | 5 |
| 5 | P_F | 20 | 1 | 30 | 2 |
| 6 | P_G | 60 | 3 | 25 | 1 |
| 7 | P_H | 40 | 2 | 65 | 4 |
| 8 | P_I | 60 | 3 | 75 | 4 |
| 9 | P_J | 50 | 3 | 55 | 3 |

dropped without its relevance consideration as studied in [12].

Secondly, we evaluate the proposed work by considering the entire system as a whole with the server and the tracker along with 100 peer nodes. The simulation run for one hour with request arrival rate using random distribution and its corresponding factors such as start-up latency, seek latency, network throughput, simultaneous peers in action, and media server load are studied. Finally, every peer that contributes to our VoD system that increases its upload bandwidth as a profit has provided added multicast strength reducing load at server and solving penalized sending peer. The experimental study with the other two systems has been done with same peers reacting inefficiently to the same setup.

Table 2 describes the various video samples used for testing and its properties like time length and data rate. The number of segments for each video is fixed for the traditional system, whereas it is dynamically calculated for the proposed system with the available set of peer nodes formed in a group with its heterogeneous ability such as bandwidth rate and cache size as explained earlier. Dynamic splitting a video is done until the request for that video remains within the group. Table 3 provides the dynamic split of the same video v_1 stored at the same peer node at different bandwidth strength indicated as Sample 1 and Sample 2.

Table 3 gives the number of segments stored in each peer according to the algorithm present in the Server Helper (SH) which distributes segments based on peer's capacity.

## 5. Results and Discussion

In this section, we put forth a test copy of the system that is suited for application such as VoD, based on set-top boxes as well as the multimedia content sharing at the social network systems. The fundamental approach to the reduction in service latency as well as providing optimal quality than any feasible solution is our concern. We prove this here with the several graphs and tables which provide proof to the system with the tracker and our QPMVM which is more advantageous than the systems that have very few factors working at the server end or the client end or at the proxy end. Since we combined all the factors from different viewpoint, this creates elements where the client side perception has more impact towards the betterment of the system as a whole. There are several results in the form of graphs and tables, but here we provide only a few of them to highlight our works aim.

Frames dropping is one concept to check for, in any service provider, such as our media server which services for video requests. On requests that come from peer clients, the sender's video bit rate should match that of the receiver's bit rate. If there is no match, frame dropping occurs when the sender's bit rate is more than the receiver's receiving capacity which happens due to congestion at the client network, and the bandwidth is clogged with the sender's data which the user could not process. This is present in all the server technology to drop frames and progress with streaming until it is uniformly completed in all multicast clients.

Here, in Figure 7, we see that the average number of frames dropped for video streams at 316 bits per second to 5 clients that receive at 56 kbps to 512 kbps. At 64 kbps, the client reception is very poor, and the loss of packets is comparatively more than that of 512 kbps reception, at which point all the clients receive the data packets without frames being lost. In Figure 7 it can be noted that the choking level is for lesser bit rate at client as seen from the graph. The table shows the difference in the three technologies discussed so far. Single version storage of video files drops few frames because it would be a lower version video with reduced picture quality that suffices even the least set of clients with very low connectivity. Also, it is seen that the

TABLE 4: Amount of memory used by different systems for different versioned files.

| Single version | Traditional multiple version | Our optimal solution |
|---|---|---|
| 609 KB | 2416 KB | 1403 KB |
| 10453 KB | 42113 KB | 22874 KB |

TABLE 5: Segment distribution in proposed P2P.

| Peer groups | Bandwidth (kbps) | No. of videos | Segments |
|---|---|---|---|
| A | 100 | 3 | v_1, v_2, v_3 |
| B | 80 | 3 | v_2, v_5, v_6 |
| C | 60 | 2 | v_1, v_4 |
| D | 45 | 1 | v_1 |
| E | 30 | 1 | v_5 |

TABLE 6: Segment distribution in t raditional P2P.

| Peer groups | Bandwidth (kbps) | No. of videos | Segments |
|---|---|---|---|
| A | 100 | 2 | v_1, v_2 |
| B | 80 | 2 | v_3, v_4 |
| C | 60 | 2 | v_1, v_3 |
| D | 45 | 2 | v_5, v_2 |
| E | 30 | 2 | v_4, v_5 |

TABLE 7: Total view time.

| No. of simultaneous users (name of peers) | Total viewing time(s) | | |
|---|---|---|---|
| | Proposed P2P | Client server | traditional P2P |
| 1 (B) | 481 | 469 | 640 |
| 2 (B,D) | 543 | 481 | 764 |
| 3 (A,B,D) | 584 | 806 | 1199 |
| 4 (A,B,D,E) | 723 | 1015 | 1254 |
| 5 (A,B,C,D,E) | 923 | 2634 | 1867 |

number of frames dropped by a single version is much less when compared to other multiple version systems. This is contrary to the fact that maintaining multiple versions is an optimal solution. The effectiveness of multiversioning is evident when we observe that the actual packets dropped are not the effective packets which we describe in the following paragraph.

In a single version system I, B, or a P frame could be dropped. But each one has a different level of importance. If the system drops a single I frame, then the corresponding full GOP is deemed to be useless. An important detail to note in Figure 3's graphical representation of the table is that the number of frames dropped is almost the same between the traditional multiversion scheme (that maintains every possible version for the client pattern) and our optimal solution. This indicates our optimal solution drops almost the same number of frames but it uses minimal storage as compared to the traditional scheme by setting a base version and few higher versions. It is also seen in Figure 3 that the frame drop in single version is less. To understand that the I, P, and B frames' corresponding priorities are taken into account in multiversioning, we plot a second graph as shown in Figure 4, which gives the effective number of packets dropped.

To understand the impact of the effective frame drop we must compare Figures 3 and 4. In Figure 3, we take the example where 3 frames are dropped in the single version (384 kbps file); we note that the corresponding effective frame rate is 28 frames. This is explained as follows:

Total no. of frames dropped: 3

Total no. of I frames dropped: 2

Total no. of P frames dropped: 1

Total no. of B frames dropped: —-

GOP : 12

If an I frame is dropped, none of the other frames can be decoded in the GOP, that is, dropping a single I frame effectively drops 12 frames. If a P frame is dropped, dependant B frames cannot be decoded. Hence,

No. of frames dropped because of I frames lost:

$2 \times 12 = 24$

No. of frames dropped because of P frames lost:

4 B frames

Total no. of effective frames dropped: 29 frames

Moreover, it is clear from Table 4 that a single version file requires lesser memory, but at the expense of video quality. Using all possible versions that satisfy the different client abilities in terms of its receiving minimal capacity, we find that this consumes enormous storage size for a single video file. Our optimized storage reduces the size for a single video content by approximately half of it and provides more or less same video quality similar to the multiversioned system. This is a major advantage of using the higher-versioned video at times of congestion to serve a slightly lower capacity client that is managed by our QPMVM system to drop off ineffective frames on the fly.

In traditional P2P system, the segments are equally distributed among the peers without the tracker system as shown in Table 4, and the proposed system has the distribution of clips based on the peer ability as shown in Table 5. For proposed, traditional, and client server systems, we measured the evaluation parameters given in Table 1.

*The Total Viewing Time of the Video for Peer Group B Is Observed as Follows.* From Tables 5 and 6, we have analyzed the total viewing time for 5 peer groups. As the number of simultaneous peers increases the time for viewing, the entire video increases. The variations among the three models are explained in the following section.

Table 7, we have analyzed the total viewing time for 5 peer groups.

*Total Viewing Time.* From the graph in Figure 5, we observe that when the percentage of simultaneous users at a point of time is very low (i.e., less than 40 users in this case),

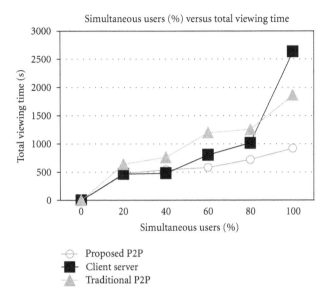

Simultaneous users (%) versus total viewing time

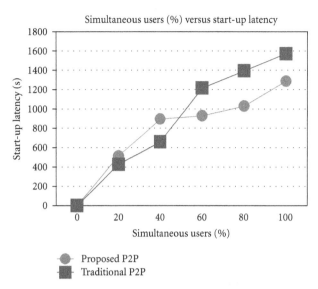

Simultaneous users (%) versus start-up latency

FIGURE 5: Percentage of simultaneous users versus total viewing time.

FIGURE 6: Percentage of simultaneous users versus start-up latency.

accessing all the segments from the server itself is preferable. This is because to access the segments from various peers, the user has to divide its bandwidth among the peers in the system. This initial joining time could be used to push video streams among the connected peers. In case of the client server model the entire bandwidth is dedicated to user. But as the number of users (simultaneous access) grows, the P2P model that we have proposed proves to be better. This can be explained as follows. As an example, 4 users request for viewing the video. (a) In client-server model, the server has to satisfy requests of all the clients in the network. This would obviously require more time. And also, the load on the server increases drastically. (b) Looking into the Proposed P2P model, the segments are shared among all the peers available. In this model, the bandwidths of all the peers are utilized. Thus, there is no overload problem in this case. This proves better for proposed system in comparison to the Traditional P2P in a way, because the segments are split according to the peer capacities the time for serving the requests for viewing is drastically reduced here.

*(1) The Start-Up Latency for % of Simultaneous Users Is Observed as Follows.* From the measured values, we observed that the start-up is comparatively less for our system than the traditional P2P model. Comparing the first two values, it is seen that there is decrease in the latency in the case of traditional P2P model. This is because the server has a bandwidth rate that is comparatively greater than a single peer in the network. Thus the time for serving a system decreases. This is the same with the startup latency as well. Figure 6 shows the startup latency for the various users occurring simultaneously.

*(2) The Seek Latency for % of Simultaneous Users Is Observed as Follows.* While measuring the seek latency, firstly, the proposed P2P (all users accessing different segments), we

have peers from peer P_B request for the segment wk_7 from peer P_C. All other peers request for segments that are not in peer P_C. Secondly, the proposed P2P (2 users accessing same segments), peer P_B, and peer P_D request for the segment wk_7 from peer C simultaneously. All other peers request segments that are not in peer C. We could infer that seek latency is comparatively less for our system at the peak time. We efficiently offload the server at the peak time request for seek. The other peers have requests generated for various other clips that are not in sequence similar to P_B and P_D requests. Figure 7 shows the greater improvement of having tracker to manifest the VCR-based requests to locate and retrieve effectively in the proposed system.

Further, for explanations by looking at this case from a slightly different perspective, we have the users/clients requesting for a segment (same or each different) that is spatially ahead, and we find this method of combining multiple subsystems working together is more efficient for VCR (seek) than that given in [20, 29].

When the P2P Groups access different segments, multiple end users put forth seek requests simultaneously. But each end user request for a unique segment located at different peers. Thus, in this case the entire bandwidth of the storage peer that contains the requested segment is dedicated to that single requesting end user.

When the P2P Groups access different segments, multiple end users put forth seek requests simultaneously. But each end user request for a unique segment located at different peers. Thus, in this case the entire bandwidth of the storage peer that contains the requested segment is dedicated to that single requesting end user.

When the P2P groups access same segments, all the VCR requesting clients are made for the same segment at the same time. Thus the storage peer holding that requested segment has to share its bandwidth to serve the multiple end users. Utilizing the bandwidth of the many peers in the system model improves the performance when compared

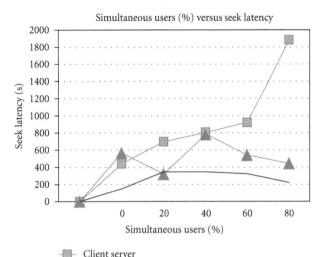

Figure 7: % of simultaneous users versus seek latency.

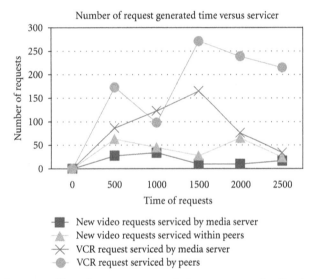

Figure 8: No. of request generated time versus service for the proposed system.

to dedicating (by dividing/sharing) the entire bandwidth of Server (Client-Server model) to all requesters (with others requests as well) [40].

In the traditional P2P system, the entire set of requests is sent to the server. This later identifies the clips present in the peer groups and reroutes them accordingly [29]. Be it requests for same segment or multiple segments, they have to be satisfied by the single system. Hence, there is a heavy increase in terms of load on the server. This in turn increases the seek time. In a nutshell, it deteriorates the performance of the complete model.

Figure 8, shows the overall requests as handled by our work which we mention here as the proposed system. The requests here are the requests for new video and VCR requests. The ability of this system to handle most of the

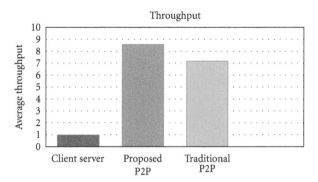

Figure 9: Throughput comparison.

requests with ease shows the utilization factor of the proposed work with the tracker and the optimized distribution at hand among the peers. The same when working with the traditional system showed 45% of the requests were handled by the media server whereas the proposed system made only 17% of the requests handled by the media server.

*Throughput Measure.* Performance tests for measuring throughput have been conducted, and the throughputs for the various models have been found to be as shown in Figure 9.

The graph in Figure 9 shows that the throughput of proposed P2P system is much better than a client server model and more similar to the traditional model. In client server model, since all requests are served only by the server, the other peers in the system are idle most of the time. In the proposed system, all the peers actively serve the requesting end user with the segments stored in it. Thus our system achieves high throughput and hence efficiently utilizes most of the peer resources. This is slightly greater than the proposed one as it leaves certain peers underutilized and several others overutilized. Hence the traditional P2P suffers a slight lower throughputthan our proposed P2P.

## 6. Conclusion and Future Work

Our proposed system with QPMVM, tracker in P2P VOD environment, has shown performance which utilizes various resource management techniques. It also understands performance limits in order to deploy adaptive QoS effectively in larger scaling systems.

*Major Contributions from This Work Are as Follows*

(i) A novel workable solution QPMVM for video streaming systems, especially for a VoD system, in place where there is provision of limited system resources and infrastructure. For example, systems that are possible only with lower bandwidth, less neighbor support and so on, could perform much better by employing our system (namely, e-learning with limited users).

(ii) Optimized usage of server bandwidth, reduced server load, storage, and prevalent better quality video at client by combining multiversion and multilayer system for videos at the server.

(iii) Stressing the video segment distribution combined with incentive mechanism solves idleness among peer sharers is another major advantage. This increases the usage of available distributed bandwidth among the social network groups with incentive benefits.

(iv) Design and integration of the entire system with performance study over various scenarios highlight the coordination and management rules provided by the various subsystems at the server, tracker, and the P2P nodes.

*Limitations of This Work*

(i) As this system is to provide better utilities for low profile consumers, sufficient video files that fit this category were considered for simulation. Hence, use of H.264 (SVC) is avoided/omitted.

(ii) If all the consumers request different videos at the same instant, then the peer structure would perform poorly, because there would be no possibility for initial sharing and thereby increasing the seek latency.

(iii) The cache store and replacement policies worked with are optimal in their usage but could further be altered to suit the peer sharing ability with their profiles in mind. Peer churns must be handled for real time efficiency.

This work supports all MPEG file formats including MPEG-4 part 10 (AVC); future enhancements could include usage of H.264 (SVC) files that could provide remarkable solutions that can be studied. Advanced caching policies could be fitted into the framework to upgrade the system.

# References

[1] C. Zhijia, L. Chuang, and W. Xiaogang, "Enabling on-demand internet video streaming services to multi-terminal users in large scale," *IEEE Transactions on Consumer Electronics*, vol. 55, no. 4, pp. 1988–1996, 2009.

[2] A. Raghuveer, N. Kang, and D. H. C. Du, "Techniques for efficient streaming of layered video in heterogeneous client environments," in *Proceedings of the IEEE Global Telecommunications Conference (GLOBECOM '05)*, vol. 1, pp. 245–250, December 2005.

[3] Y. Yang, A. L. H. Chow, L. Golubchik, and D. Bragg, "Improving QoS in BitTorrent-like VoD systems," in *Proceedings of the IEEE International Conference on Computer Communications (IEEE INFOCOM '10)*, San Diego, Calif, USA, March 2010.

[4] B. Giovanni, S. Thomas, and A. Luigi, "Theoretical models for video on demand services on peer-to-peer networks," *International Journal of Digital Multimedia Broadcasting*, vol. 2009, Article ID 263936, 8 pages, 2009.

[5] A. G. Nemati and M. Takizawa, "Application level QoS in multimedia peer-to-peer (P2P) networks," in *Proceedings of the 22nd International Conference on Advanced Information Networking and Applications Workshops/Symposia (AINA '08)*, pp. 319–324, March 2008.

[6] L. Bo, C. Yanchuan, C. Cui Yi, X. Yuan, Q. Fan, and L. Yansheng, "Minimizing service disruption in peer-to-peer streaming," in *Proceedings of the IEEE Computer Communications and Networking Conference (CCNC '11)*, pp. 1066–1071, 2011.

[7] Y. Lingjie, G. Linxiang, Z. Jin, and W. Xin, "SonicVoD: a VCR-supported P2P-VoD system with network coding," *IEEE Transactions on Consumer Electronics*, vol. 55, no. 2, pp. 576–582, 2009.

[8] H. Cheng-Hsin and H. Mohamed, "Optimal coding of multi-layer and multiversion video streams," *IEEE Transactions on Multimedia*, vol. 10, no. 1, pp. 121–131, 2008.

[9] G. M. Muntean, G. Ghinea, and T. N. Sheehan, "Region of interest-based adaptive multimedia streaming scheme," *IEEE Transactions on Broadcasting*, vol. 54, no. 2, pp. 296–303, 2008.

[10] H. Yu, E. C. Chang, W. T. Ooi, M. C. Chan, and W. Cheng, "Integrated optimization of video server resource and streaming quality over best-effort network," *IEEE Transactions on Circuits and Systems for Video Technology*, vol. 19, no. 3, pp. 374–385, 2009.

[11] L. Jiangchuan, B. Li, and Z. Ya-Qin, "Adaptive video multicast over the internet," *IEEE Multimedia*, vol. 10, no. 1, pp. 22–33, 2003.

[12] S. McCanne, M. Vetterli, and V. Jacobson, "Low-complexity video coding for receiver-driven layered multicast," *IEEE Journal on Selected Areas in Communications*, vol. 15, no. 6, pp. 983–1001, 1997.

[13] L. Jiangchuan, B. Li, and Y. Q. Zhang, "Optimal stream replication for video simulcasting," *IEEE Transactions on Multimedia*, vol. 8, no. 1, pp. 162–169, 2006.

[14] T. C. Thang, J. W. Kang, J. J. Yoo, and Y. M. Ro, "Optimal multilayer adaptation of SVC video over heterogeneous environments," *Advances in Multimedia*, vol. 2008, Article ID 739192, 8 pages, 2008.

[15] C. Yan, F. Toni, and Y. Nong, "QoS requirement of network applications on the Internet," *Proceedings of Information, Knowledge, Systems Management*, vol. 4, no. 1, pp. 55–76, 2004.

[16] R. A. X. Annie and P. Yogesh, "VoD system: providing effective peer-to-peer environment for an improved VCR operative solutions," *Communications in Computer and Information Science*, vol. 106, no. 2, pp. 127–134, 2010.

[17] F. V. Hecht, T. Bocek, and B. Stiller, "B-Tracker: improving load balancing and efficiency in distributed P2P trackers," in *Proceedings of the 11th IEEE International Conference on Peer-to-Peer Computing (P2P '11)*, pp. 310–313, 2011.

[18] C. Liang, Z. Fu, Y. Liu, and C. W. Wu, "Incentivized peer-assisted streaming for on-demand services," *IEEE Transactions on Parallel and Distributed Systems*, vol. 21, no. 9, pp. 1354–1367, 2010.

[19] T. Guo and Y. Zhang, "Research of incentive mechanisms in P2P-based Video on Demand System," in *Proceedings of the 2nd International Conference on Networking and Distributed Computing (ICNDC '11)*, pp. 340–343, 2011.

[20] J. M. Dyaberi, K. Kannan, and V. S. Pai, "Storage optimization for a peer-to-peer video-on-demand network," in *Proceedings of the ACM SIGMM Conference on Multimedia Systems (MMSys '10)*, pp. 59–70, February 2010.

[21] D. Tursun and W. Liejun, "Adaptive stream multicast for video in heterogeneous networks," *Information Technology Journal*, vol. 8, no. 2, pp. 246–249, 2009.

[22] D. Wang and J. Liu, "Peer-to-peer asynchronous video streaming using skip list," in *Proceedings of the IEEE International*

*Conference on Multimedia and Expo (ICME '06)*, pp. 1397–1400, July 2006.

[23] E. Tan and C. T. Chou, "Frame rate control for video streaming," in *Proceedings of the 36th Annual IEEE Conference on Local Computer Networks (LCN '11)*, pp. 163–166, 2011.

[24] S. F. Chang and A. Vetro, "Video adaptation: concepts, technologies, and open issues," *Proceedings of the IEEE*, vol. 93, no. 1, pp. 148–158, 2005.

[25] F. Takaya, E. Rei, M. Kei, and S. Hiroshi, "Video-popularity-based caching scheme for P2P video-on-demand streaming," in *Proceedings of the 25th IEEE International Conference on Advanced Information Networking and Applications (AINA '11)*, pp. 748–755, March 2011.

[26] S. Saroiu, K. P. Gummadi, and S. D. Gribble, "Measuring and analyzing the characteristics of Napster and Gnutella hosts," *Multimedia Systems*, vol. 9, no. 2, pp. 170–184, 2003.

[27] H. Byun and M. Lee, "A tracker-based P2P system for live multimedia streaming services," in *Proceedings of the 13th International Conference on Advanced Communication Technology: Smart Service Innovation through Mobile Interactivity (ICACT '11)*, pp. 1608–1613, February 2011.

[28] C. Jia Ming, L. Jenq Shiou, C. Yen Chiu, W. Hsin Wen, and S. Wei Kuan, "MegaDrop: a cooperative video-on-demand system in a Peer-to-Peer environment," *Journal of Information Science and Engineering*, vol. 27, no. 4, pp. 1345–1361, 2011.

[29] I. Radulovic, P. Frossard, and O. Verscheure, "Adaptive video streaming in lossy networks: versions or layers?" in *Proceedings of the IEEE International Conference on Multimedia and Expo (ICME '04)*, vol. 3, pp. 1915–1918, Taipei, Taiwan, June 2004.

[30] P. Seeling and M. Reisslein, "Video transport evaluation with H.264 video traces," *IEEE Communications Surveys and Tutorials*, no. 4, pp. 1–24, 2011.

[31] L. Tionardi and F. Hartanto, "The use of cumulative inter-frame jitter for adapting video transmission rate," in *Proceedings of the Confernce on Covergent Technologies for the Asia-Pacific Region (IEEE TENCON '03)*, pp. 364–368, October 2003.

[32] R. Mahindra, R. Kokku, H. Zhang, and S. Rangarajan, "MESA: farsighted flow management for video delivery in broadband wireless networks," in *Proceedings of the 3rd International Conference on Communication Systems and Networks (COMSNETS '11)*, pp. 1–10, January 2011.

[33] D. Gangadharan, H. Ma, S. Chakraborty, and R. Zimmermann, "Video quality-driven buffer dimensioning in MPSoC platforms via prioritized frame drops," in *Proceedings of the IEEE 29th International Conference on Computer Design (ICCD '11)*, pp. 247–252, 2011.

[34] A. A. Sofokleous and M. C. Angelides, "DCAF: an MPEG-21 dynamic content adaptation framework," *Multimedia Tools and Applications*, vol. 40, no. 2, pp. 151–182, 2008.

[35] J. Annesley, G. Bäse, J. Orwell, and H. Sabirin, "An extension of the AVC file format for video surveillance," in *Proceedings of the 3rd ACM/IEEE International Conference on Distributed Smart Cameras (ICDSC '09)*, pp. 1–8, September 2009.

[36] P. Amon, T. Rathgen, and D. Singer, "File format for scalable video coding," *IEEE Transactions on Circuits and Systems for Video Technology*, vol. 17, no. 9, pp. 1174–1185, 2007.

[37] T. L. Lin, J. Shin, and P. Cosman, "Packet dropping for widely varying bit reduction rates using a network-based packet loss visibility model," in *Proceedings of the Data Compression Conference (DCC '10)*, pp. 445–454, March 2010.

[38] C. Hu and C. Tu, "Research on P2P incentive mechanism," in *2010 International Forum on Information Technology and Applications (IFITA '10)*, vol. 1, pp. 47–50, July 2010.

[39] Y. W. Wong, J. Y. B. Lee, V. O. K. Li, and G. S. H. Chan, "Supporting interactive video-on-demand with adaptive multicast streaming," *IEEE Transactions on Circuits and Systems for Video Technology*, vol. 17, no. 2, pp. 129–141, 2007.

[40] Q. Wei, T. Qin, and S. Fujita, "A two-level caching protocol for hierarchical peer-to-peer file sharing systems," in *Proceedings of the IEEE 9th International Symposium on Parallel and Distributed Processing with Applications (ISPA '11)*, pp. 195–200, 2011.

# 2

# QoE-Based Performance Evaluation for Adaptive Media Playout Systems

**Mingfu Li**

*Department of Electrical Engineering, Chang Gung University, 259 Wen-Hwa 1st Road, Kwei-Shan, Tao-Yuan 33302, Taiwan*

Correspondence should be addressed to Mingfu Li; mfli@mail.cgu.edu.tw

Academic Editor: George Ghinea

To improve the playout quality of video streaming services, several adaptive media playout (AMP) mechanisms were proposed in literature. However, all performance evaluations and comparisons for AMPs were made in terms of quality of service (QoS) metrics. As one knows, there may exist a trade-off between QoS metrics, such as buffer underflow and overflow performance. Thus, it is not sufficient to only evaluate the performance of AMPs in terms of QoS metrics. In this paper, we will evaluate and compare the performance of several AMPs from the aspect of quality of experience (QoE). Numerical results will show that some existing AMP systems do not perform better than the nonadaptive playout system from the point of view of overall QoE.

## 1. Introduction

Recently, multimedia streaming applications such as IPTV [1] have been increasing rapidly due to the significant growth of bandwidth in access networks, such as xDSL, FTTH, 3G/4G, and WiMAX. However, due to the random delay/jitter encountered in Internet, at the client side the video playout interruption, block distortions, and nonpredictive preroll time may occur during a playout session. To counteract the effects of network jitter on the quality of video streaming, adaptive media playout (AMP) techniques, which can control the media playout rate dynamically, have emerged [2–10]. Some AMP schemes, such as [2–7], adjust the media playout rate dynamically according to the buffer fullness. Another AMP based on buffer variation rather than buffer fullness was proposed in [8]. The other content-aware AMPs that take into account the content of a video sequence and motion characteristics of different scenes were presented in [9, 10]. The content-aware AMP only slows down the low-motion scenes such that the perceived effect is lower.

The quality of service (QoS) refers to several related aspects of telephony and computer networks that allow the transport of traffic with special requirements. QoS metrics belong to quantitative metrics that can be measured objectively by using network equipment. Therefore, they are usually called objective QoS metrics. Several objective QoS metrics, such as underflow probability, overflow probability, variance of distortion of playout (VDoP) [3, 7], initial playout delay, playout curve, and mean playout rate have been used for evaluating the performance of AMP mechanisms. Detailed definitions of most of these objective metrics can be found in [7]. Several works had shown that there may exist a trade-off among these metrics mentioned above [4, 7]. For example, there exists a trade-off between underflow and overflow performance. Thus, it is sometimes difficult to definitely judge whether an AMP scheme is better than the other one in terms of QoS metrics. Most importantly, these objective QoS metrics cannot directly reflect the users' perception on the playout quality of an AMP system. Accordingly, it is necessary to develop another effective method for evaluating the performance of AMP schemes from the aspect of users' perception.

The users' perception of a service is expressed by the quality of experience (QoE) which is a subjective measure of a customer's experiences with a service. Generally, the schemes of assessing the user's perception are called QoE techniques [11–18] and measured in terms of MOS (mean opinion score) [19]. The MOS is expressed as a single number in the range 1 to 5, where 1 is the lowest perceived quality and 5 is the highest perceived quality. However, the average MOS of measurements can range from 0 to 5 in real applications. QoE assessment includes three different approaches: subjective, objective, and hybrid. Subjective QoE assessment is the most accurate method to get the user's perception. However, subjective approach is time consuming and has a high evaluation cost. Objective QoE assessment [15, 16] may be performed in real time but the accuracy of the user's perception could be a problem. As to the hybrid approach, it combines the subjective and the objective methods to obtain the QoE [13, 14]. The hybrid scheme can assess the QoE in real time while reducing the cost in the subjective test. However, all the QoE evaluation methods mentioned above do not consider the effects of AMP schemes. Therefore, a real time and cost-effective QoE assessment scheme which takes the impact of AMP into account was proposed in [20]. In [20], several QoS-QoE mapping functions for individual QoS metrics were derived based on subjective tests. The considered QoS metrics include the initial playout delay, packet loss rate, underflow time ratio, and playout rate. These objective QoS metrics can be obtained by using network measurement equipment. In addition, in [20] an integrated multivariate QoS-QoE mapping function was presented to evaluate the overall QoE of a video streaming service. In this paper, the QoE evaluation method proposed in [20] will be utilized for assessing the QoE performance of AMP systems.

The rest of this paper is organized as follows. Section 2 gives the overview of AMP schemes. In Section 3, the QoE evaluation method in [20] will be summarized. Section 4 evaluates the QoE performance of various AMP systems. Finally, Section 5 makes the concluding remarks.

## 2. Overview of Adaptive Media Playout Schemes

In [2, 3], several different playout rates are allowed for the AMP system to compensate for the effects of network delay jitters and reduce underflow events. If the number of buffered packets exceeds a given threshold, the AMP system uses a normal playout rate $\mu_0$. Otherwise, the AMP system employs proportionally reduced rates. We call such an AMP scheme the linear slowdown scheme. Its playout rate function $\mu(n)$ is depicted in Figure 1. Another novel AMP based on buffer variation for determining the playout rate was proposed in [8]. The scheme proposed in [8] can keep the video playout as smooth as possible while adapting to the network conditions. The playout rate adjustment is based on the buffer variation $\Delta F$ (in frames) and the parameter $\tau$. When $|\Delta F| \geq \tau$, a playout adjustment order is issued and the playout interval is adjusted linearly with time. For the AMPs mentioned above [2, 3, 8], the playout rates cannot be faster than the normal playout rate $\mu_0$. When only slowing down the playout rate is allowed, the playout latency of the whole video stream may be extended significantly. In addition, slowing down the playout rate may increase the overflow probability when the client buffer size is finite. To eliminate the additional playout latency and reduce the overflow probability, speeding up the playout rate is possible in [4, 6]. The paper [6] proposed an algorithm to dynamically calculate a slow or a fast playout factor based

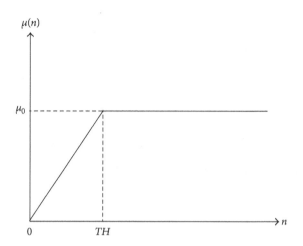

FIGURE 1: The playout rate function of linear slowdown playout system (smoother) [2, 3].

on the current buffer state, target buffer level, past history of media data reception, estimate of future data arrival, and the estimated network conditions.

Most AMP schemes do not take the buffer overflow issue into consideration. To improve this drawback, the AMP with multiple thresholds, the slowdown threshold $L$, the speedup threshold $H$, and the dynamic playback threshold $P_n$, were presented in [7]. In addition to the conventional slowdown threshold $L$, a dynamic playback threshold $P_n$ and a speedup threshold $H$ were designed. Whenever the buffer fullness exceeds the speedup threshold $H$, the playout rate must increase to reduce the buffer fullness for avoiding buffer overflow. The dynamic playback threshold algorithm (DPTA) in [7] is designed for dynamically adjusting the playback threshold $P_n$, which determines the initial playout delay under various network conditions. The proposed AMP in [7] is called DPTA+APTA and is summarized as follows. DPTA estimates the network jitter from the most recent frame arrivals to decide the proper playout delay. First, $J_n$, the cumulative average jitter of the first $n$ arrivals during a preroll period, is updated at each frame arrival as follows:

$$
\begin{aligned}
J_n &\equiv \frac{\sum_{i=1}^{n-1} |X_i - T|}{n-1} \\
&= \left(1 - \frac{1}{n-1}\right) J_{n-1} + \frac{|X_{n-1} - T|}{n-1}, \quad \text{for } n > 1,
\end{aligned}
\tag{1}
$$

where $X_i$ is the frame interarrival time between the $i$th and the $(i + 1)$st video frames and the time $T$ is the normal playout duration of each video frame. Then the dynamic playback threshold $P_n$ is computed according to the following piecewise linear equation

$$
P_n = L_0 + (L - L_0) \cdot \min\left\{1, \frac{J_n}{cT}\right\},
\tag{2}
$$

where $L_0$ and $c$ are design parameters. According to our experiments in [7], there exist larger fluctuations for $J_n$ at smaller values of $n$. Thus, to increase the estimation reliability of $P_n$, a lower bound $L_0$ is set for $P_n$ so that the false start of playback can disappear at $n < L_0$. Also, the value of $L_0$ must not be set too large, or the initial playout delay cannot be reduced. According to our experiments in [7], $L_0 = 10$ is an appropriate setting. The parameter $c$ relates $J_n$ to $P_n$ linearly. Based on our experiments in [7], the value of $c$ should be set within the range of 1.5 to 2.5 so that the initial playout delay can be acceptable for most cases.

Whenever the current buffer fullness $n$ surpasses or equals $P_n$, the playback can start immediately with the proper playout rate which is determined by the following equation

$$\mu(i,n) = \begin{cases} R_L(n) & \text{if } n < L, \\ R_S(i) & \text{if } L \leq n \leq H, \\ R_H(n) & \text{if } n > H, \end{cases} \tag{3}$$

where $R_S(i)$ is a random process and is determined by the arrival process tracking algorithm (APTA) presented in [7]. That is, $R_S(i)$ is dependent on the frame arrival process at the client buffer and is limited between $(1 - r)\mu_0$ and $(1 + r)\mu_0$, as shown in Figure 2. Anyone interested in the detailed derivation of $R_S(i)$ can refer to [7]. $R_H(n)$ and $R_L(n)$ are defined as follows:

$$R_H(n) = (1 + r_2)\mu_0 - \left(\frac{N - \min\{n, N\}}{N - H}\right)^2 (r_2 - r)\mu_0,$$
$$R_L(n) = (1 - r_1)\mu_0 + \left(\frac{n}{L}\right)^2 (r_1 - r)\mu_0, \tag{4}$$

where $N$ is the uppermost threshold correlated to the client buffer size. Notably, the playout rates should be limited such that rate variations are unnoticeable or acceptable by users. And the perception of a slowdown video is usually different from that of a speedup video for users. Therefore, two different restricted deviation ratios, denoted by $r_1$ and $r_2$ for $R_L(n)$ and $R_H(n)$, respectively, are set for playout rates. The corresponding playout rate function of DPTA+APTA is given by Figure 2.

## 3. QoE Evaluation Method for AMP Systems

According to the experiences on video streaming applications (e.g., YouTube videos) over Internet, nonpredictive buffering time before playout, playback interruptions due to buffer underflow, and video block distortions owing to packet losses are frequently encountered phenomenons during watching a video streaming session. Hence, in this work, the objective QoS metrics, such as the initial playout delay, loss rate, and buffer underflow time, are selected for assessing the QoE of video streaming services. Additionally, if the AMP scheme that can dynamically adjust the playout rate is employed in the media player for improving the video playout quality, the impact of AMP on the QoE must also be considered. Thus, the playout rate metric must be included in the QoE evaluation as well. The definitions and illustrations of these aforementioned QoS metrics are given as follows.

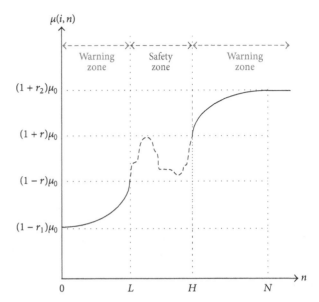

FIGURE 2: The playout rate function of DPTA+APTA playout system [7].

(i) *Initial playout delay*: in order to compensate for the effects of network jitters, a playout buffer is usually allocated at the client. For alleviating the jitter effect on the video playout quality, a streaming video can start playback only when the buffer fullness exceeds a certain threshold. For a video stream, at the start of streaming, the time duration between the first frame arrival at the client buffer and its displaying is defined as the initial playout delay. Nonpredictive or long initial playout delay is annoying to users.

(ii) *Loss rate*: video packets may be discarded in the network or at the client buffer due to buffer overflow. Such packet losses can lead to block distortions in the video playout and degrade the users' perception.

(iii) *Underflow time ratio*: the case that no frame exists in the client buffer for display is called buffer underflow. The occurrence of buffer underflow will intermit the video playout so that the streaming quality is seriously degraded. Therefore, the incidence of buffer underflow is a key metric for evaluating the quality of video streaming services. The ratio of total underflow duration to the overall playback time of a video streaming is defined to be the underflow time ratio.

(iv) *Playout rate*: the playout rate may vary in the media player with AMP. When the playout rate variation is over a threshold, such as 25%, it may be easily perceived by users. So the effects of playout rate variation on the QoE must also be considered and evaluated.

The QoS parameters mentioned above can be obtained by using network measurement equipment. How to assess the overall QoE of a video streaming service from these measured QoS parameters, however, becomes an issue. To solve this problem, in [20], a product form is utilized to create an integrated multivariate QoE function for evaluating the overall QoE of a video streaming service. According to our previous work [20], the overall QoE of a video streaming service can be assessed based on these four QoS metrics mentioned above as follows:

$$f_I \left( QoS_u, QoS_l, QoS_d, QoS_r \right)$$

$$= 5 \cdot \frac{f_u \left( QoS_u \right)}{5} \cdot \frac{f_l \left( QoS_l \right)}{5} \cdot \frac{f_d \left( QoS_d \right)}{5} \cdot \frac{f_r \left( QoS_r \right)}{5},$$

(5)

where $QoS_u$, $QoS_l$, $QoS_d$, and $QoS_r$ represent the underflow time ratio ($0 \le QoS_u \le 1$), loss rate ($QoS_l$%), initial playout delay ($QoS_d$ seconds), and normalized playout rate ($QoS_r \ge 0$) metrics, respectively. In other words, the normalized integrated QoE or MOS, $f_I(QoS_u, QoS_l, QoS_d, QoS_r)/5$, equals the product of all normalized QoEs of individual QoS metrics. Note that since the QoE ranges from 0 to 5, the normalized QoE must be divided by 5. The individual QoS-QoE mapping functions in (5) are given as follows:

$$f_u \left( x \right) = 5e^{-5.71x},$$

(6)

$$f_l \left( x \right) = 5e^{-1.607x},$$

(7)

$$f_d \left( x \right) = 5e^{-0.0416x},$$

(8)

$$f_r \left( x \right) = 5x^{8.94} e^{-8.94(x-1)}.$$

(9)

All equations (6) to (9) are derived based on subjective tests conducted in [20] and the nonlinear regression approach. The resulting mapping functions for the underflow time ratio, loss rate, and initial playout delay metrics conform to exponentially decaying functions, while the mapping function for the normalized playout rate metric follows the probability density function of Gamma distribution. Since the maximum value of QoE is 5, the maximum values of individual QoEs in (6) to (9) cannot be larger than 5 for all $x \ge 0$. Thus, in (6) to (9) the coefficients before the exponential functions must be set to 5. Other constants in these mapping functions are determined by using the nonlinear regression approach. Related subjective tests and detailed derivations of these QoS-QoE mapping functions can be found in [20]. Next, (5) will be used for evaluating the integrated QoE performance of an AMP system.

## 4. QoE Assessment Results of AMP Systems

In this section, we will use simulations to obtain the QoS performance of different AMP mechanisms. Next, (5) will be employed to compute the QoEs of different media playout systems, including nonadaptive, linear slowdown [2, 3], linear slowdown+speedup, DPTA+APTA($r = 0.25$) [7], and buffer variation [8] schemes. These playout systems are described briefly as follows:

(i) *Nonadaptive*: the normal playout rate $\mu_0$ is always employed by the media player.

(ii) *Linear slowdown*: it is similar to the scheme presented in [2, 3]. However, the media player will reduce the playout rate linearly between $\mu_0$ and $(1 - r_1)\mu_0$ only when the buffer fullness is less than the threshold $L$, as shown in Figure 3(a).

(iii) *Linear slowdown+speedup*: this AMP will slow down or speed up the playout rate linearly when the buffer fullness is below $L$ or over $H$, respectively. Its playout rate function is depicted in Figure 3(b).

(iv) DPTA+APTA($r = 0.25$): it is the AMP presented in [7] with parameter $r = 0.25$ and has the playout rate function shown in Figure 2.

(v) *Buffer variation scheme*: it is the AMP scheme presented in [8]. In our simulations, the adjustment algorithm for this scheme follows the method described in [8] except that the initial buffer reference level is set to $L$ rather than half of the buffer size. In addition, after an underflow event, the playout can resume only when the buffer fullness is accumulated up to $L$ again. The parameter $\tau$ defined in [8] equals 12 in our simulations.

Notably, all the startup playback thresholds of the above media playout systems except DPTA+APTA ($r = 0.25$) are fixed at $L$. Additionally, the playout rates are limited between $(1 - r_1)\mu_0$ and $(1 + r_2)\mu_0$ for all considered AMP mechanisms, as shown in Figures 2 and 3.

First, we adopt NS2 network simulator [21] to generate jittered video traffic patterns. Then the jittered video traffic patterns are employed as the arrival process of various media playout systems which are implemented using the C++ programs developed by ourselves. The network architecture for simulations is shown in Figure 4. In our simulations, we use the MPEG-4 encoded video, Jurassic Park I [22], as the video streaming source. This MPEG-4 video is VBR and has average bit rate 770 kbps, and its total playback time is one hour. The frame rate of this MPEG-4 video is 25 fps. Thus, the normal playout duration of each frame, $T$, equals 40 ms. Moreover, the average frame size of this video is about 3800 bytes. Since the encoded frame size is variable in reality, the buffer size in our simulations will be set in number of bytes. But the playout rate adaptation is still based on the number of frames. In our simulations, the client buffer size is set to 2 Mbytes. Since the average frame length is close to 4000 bytes, the corresponding uppermost threshold $N$ in Figure 2 is set to about 500. All video frames are transmitted from the server (node 0) to the receiver (node 5) and are jittered by the cross-traffic when they traverse the network. The Pareto ON-OFF traffic type with parameters (burst time, idle time) = (400 ms, 600 ms) is chosen as the cross-traffic. In all our simulations, the cross-traffic rates of all links in Figure 4 are set to be equal. At the receiver node, all the frame arrival times of the simulated video stream are saved in a file to be the video frame arrival process for media playout systems. Various cross-traffic loads are conducted in our simulations. And under each traffic load, 10 distinct jittered video traffic patterns are produced by starting streaming at different times. In addition, no frame loss in the network is assumed in our simulations, that is, in this study the frame losses are only

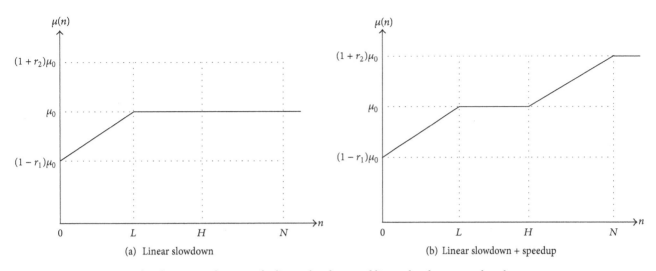

(a) Linear slowdown

(b) Linear slowdown + speedup

FIGURE 3: The playout rate functions for linear slowdown and linear slowdown+speedup playout systems.

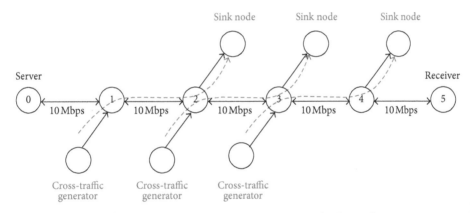

FIGURE 4: The network architecture for generating jittered video traffic patterns.

induced by the buffer overflow at the client buffer. Related parameter settings in our simulations are listed in Table 1.

Subsequently, the QoS parameters, including initial playout delay ($QoS_d$), underflow time ratio ($QoS_u$), loss rate ($QoS_l$), and normalized playout rate ($QoS_r$) of each media playout system are measured. The measurements of these QoS values are similar to those in [7]. After obtaining these QoS parameters, we apply the QoE mapping functions in (6)–(9) to transform each QoS value into its corresponding QoE/MOS. The mapped QoE/MOS of each playout system in the individual QoS metric is shown in Figure 5. Finally, using (5) one can find the overall QoE of each media playout system. The results are presented in Figure 6.

According to Figure 5, if only the QoE of an individual QoS metric is compared among different media playout systems, then it is very difficult to judge which playout scheme is the best. This is because there exists a trade-off among different QoS metrics. Therefore, it is not feasible to only use QoS values for performance comparisons among various playout systems. However, when the overall QoEs of different media playout systems are derived by using (5), as shown in Figure 6, performance comparisons among various playout systems become easy.

TABLE 1: Parameter settings for simulations.

| Parameters | Value |
| --- | --- |
| Client buffer size | 2 Mbytes |
| $L_0$ | 10 |
| $L$ | 100 |
| $H$ | 150 |
| $N$ | 500 |
| $c$ | 2.0 |
| $r_1$ | 0.4 |
| $r_2$ | 0.4 |

From Figure 5, we find that the linear slowdown AMP can only improve the QoE in underflow time ratio metric $QoS_u$, while it degrades the QoE in normalized playout rate metric $QoS_r$ when compared with the nonadaptive playout system. And the overall QoE of the linear slowdown AMP, as shown in Figure 6, is nearly improved as compared to the nonadaptive playout system. As to the buffer variation AMP, the QoE performance in underflow time ratio metric $QoS_u$ is the best, while the QoE performance in loss rate metric

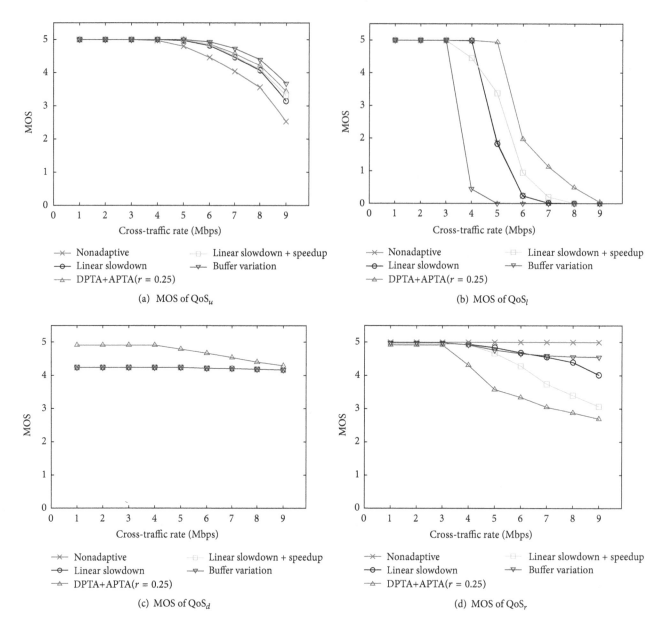

(a) MOS of QoS$_u$

(b) MOS of QoS$_l$

(c) MOS of QoS$_d$

(d) MOS of QoS$_r$

FIGURE 5: Corresponding QoEs of individual QoS metrics for different playout systems.

QoS$_l$ becomes the worst, as shown in Figure 5. The overall QoE of the buffer variation AMP, as presented in Figure 6, becomes even worse than that of the nonadaptive playout system. However, in Figure 6 DPTA+APTA($r = 0.25$) can significantly improve the overall QoE of a streaming service under various traffic load conditions. According to Figure 5, since DPTA algorithm can adapt the initial playout delay to network traffic conditions, DPTA+APTA($r = 0.25$) achieves the best QoE in initial playout delay metric QoS$_d$. Although the QoE of DPTA+APTA($r = 0.25$) in normalized playout rate metric QoS$_r$ is the worst, DPTA+APTA($r = 0.25$) significantly improves the QoEs in underflow time ratio and loss rate metrics. This is because APTA can adjust the playout rate based on the frame arrival process to stabilize the buffer fullness so that buffer underflow and overflow probabilities are

significantly reduced. Finally, DPTA+APTA($r = 0.25$) achieves the best overall QoE. Therefore, it is worthy for DPTA+APTA($r = 0.25$) to effectively adapt the playout rate for improving the QoE of a video streaming service.

## 5. Conclusions

This study introduces a QoE-based evaluation method for AMP systems. The overall QoE of an AMP system can be computed according to the proposed integrated QoE function with multivariate QoS metrics. The obtained QoE can indicate the performance of an AMP system from the aspect of users' perception. Thus, the knotty trade-off problem among various QoS metrics is resolved in the performance

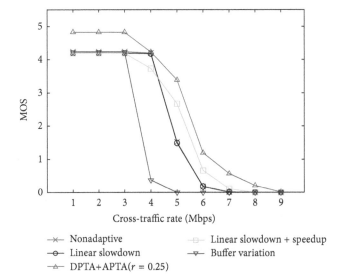

FIGURE 6: Overall QoEs of different playout systems.

comparison of AMP systems. Numerical results show that some AMP mechanisms, such as linear slowdown and buffer variation schemes, do not perform better than the nonadaptive playout system from the viewpoint of users' perception. But DPTA+APTA($r = 0.25$) scheme can really improve the QoE of a video streaming service. In addition to the performance evaluation of AMP systems, we believe that the presented QoE-based evaluation approach can also be applied to the performance assessment of other multimedia service systems.

## Acknowledgments

This work was supported by National Science Council of Republic of China under Grant NSC101-2221-E-182-004. The authors would also like to thank all reviewers for their valuable comments and suggestions.

## References

[1] Y. Xiao, X. Du, J. Zhang, F. Hu, and S. Guizani, "Internet protocol television (IPTV): the killer application for the next-generation internet," *IEEE Communications Magazine*, vol. 45, no. 11, pp. 126–134, 2007.

[2] M. C. Yuang, S. T. Liang, and Y. G. Chen, "Dynamic video playout smoothing method for multimedia applications," *Multimedia Tools and Applications*, vol. 6, no. 1, pp. 47–60, 1998.

[3] N. Laoutaris and I. Stavrakakis, "Adaptive playout strategies for packet video receivers with finite buffer capacity," in *Proceedings of International Conference on Communications (ICC '01)*, pp. 969–973, June 2001.

[4] M. Kalman, E. Steinbach, and B. Girod, "Adaptive media playout for low-delay video streaming over error-prone channels," *IEEE Transactions on Circuits and Systems for Video Technology*, vol. 14, no. 6, pp. 841–851, 2004.

[5] Y. Li, A. Markopoulou, N. Bambos, and J. Apostolopoulos, "Joint power-playout control for media streaming over wireless

links," *IEEE Transactions on Multimedia*, vol. 8, no. 4, pp. 830–843, 2006.

[6] S. Deshpande, "Underflow prevention for AV streaming media under varying channel conditions," in *Multimedia on Mobile Devices 2007*, vol. 6507 of *Proceedings of the SPIE*, January 2007.

[7] M. Li, T. W. Lin, and S. H. Cheng, "Arrival process-controlled adaptive media playout with multiple thresholds for video streaming," *Multimedia Systems*, vol. 18, no. 5, pp. 391–407, 2012.

[8] Y. F. Su, Y. H. Yang, M. T. Lu, and H. H. Chen, "Smooth control of adaptive media playout for video streaming," *IEEE Transactions on Multimedia*, vol. 11, no. 7, pp. 1331–1339, 2009.

[9] H. C. Chuang, C. Huang, and T. Chiang, "Content-aware adaptive media playout controls for wireless video streaming," *IEEE Transactions on Multimedia*, vol. 9, no. 6, pp. 1273–1283, 2007.

[10] Y. Li, A. Markopoulou, J. Apostolopoulos, and N. Bambos, "Content-aware playout and packet scheduling for video streaming over wireless links," *IEEE Transactions on Multimedia*, vol. 10, no. 5, pp. 885–895, 2008.

[11] A. Takahashi, D. Hands, and V. Barriac, "Standardization activities in the ITU for a QoE assessment of IPTV," *IEEE Communications Magazine*, vol. 46, no. 2, pp. 78–84, 2008.

[12] B. Wang, X. Wen, S. Yong, and Z. Wei, "A new approach measuring users' QoE in the IPTV," in *Proceedings of Pacific-Asia Conference on Circuits, Communications and System (PACCS '09)*, pp. 453–456, May 2009.

[13] K. Piamrat, C. Viho, A. Ksentini, and J. M. Bonnin, "Quality of experience measurements for video streaming over wireless networks," in *Proceedings of the 6th International Conference on Information Technology: New Generations (ITNG '09)*, pp. 1184–1189, April 2009.

[14] A. Khan, L. Sun, and E. Ifeachor, "QoE prediction model and its application in video quality adaptation over UMTS networks," *IEEE Transactions on Multimedia*, vol. 14, no. 2, pp. 431–442, 2012.

[15] M. H. Pinson and S. Wolf, "A new standardized method for objectively measuring video quality," *IEEE Transactions on Broadcasting*, vol. 50, no. 3, pp. 312–322, 2004.

[16] Z. Wang, A. C. Bovik, H. R. Sheikh, and E. P. Simoncelli, "Image quality assessment: from error visibility to structural similarity," *IEEE Transactions on Image Processing*, vol. 13, no. 4, pp. 600–612, 2004.

[17] H. J. Kim, D. H. Lee, J. M. Lee, K. H. Lee, W. Lyu, and S. G. Choi, "The QoE evaluation method through the QoS-QoE correlation model," in *Proceedings of the 4th International Conference on Networked Computing and Advanced Information Management (NCM '08)*, pp. 719–725, September 2008.

[18] H. J. Kim and S. G. Choi, "A study on a QoS/QoE correlation model for QoE evaluation on IPTV service," in *Proceedings of the 12th International Conference on Advanced Communication Technology: ICT for Green Growth and Sustainable Development (ICACT '10)*, pp. 1377–1382, February 2010.

[19] ITU-T Rec., "P. 800, Mean Opinion Score (MOS) Terminology," March 2003.

[20] M. Li and C.-Y. Lee, "A cost-effective and real-time QoE evaluation method for multimedia streaming Services," *Telecommunication Systems, Special Issue on Innovations in Emerging Multimedia Communication Systems*. In press.

[21] The Network Simulator (NS2), http://www.isi.edu/nsnam/ns/.

[22] http://www2.tkn.tu-berlin.de/research/trace/trace.html.

# 3

# Protecting H.264/AVC Data-Partitioned Video Streams over Broadband WiMAX

**Laith Al-Jobouri, Martin Fleury, and Mohammed Ghanbari**

*School of Computer Science and Electronic Engineering, University of Essex, Colchester CO4 3SQ, UK*

Correspondence should be addressed to Martin Fleury, fleum@essex.ac.uk

Academic Editor: Martin Reisslein

Broadband wireless technology, though aimed at video services, also poses a potential threat to video services, as wireless channels are prone to error bursts. In this paper, an adaptive, application-layer Forward Error Correction (FEC) scheme protects H.264/AVC data-partitioned video. Data partitioning is the division of a compressed video stream into partitions of differing decoding importance. The paper determines whether equal error protection (EEP) through FEC of all partition types or unequal error protection (UEP) of the more important partition type is preferable. The paper finds that, though UEP offers a small reduction in bitrate, if EEP is employed, there are significant gains (several dBs) in video quality. Overhead from using EEP rather than UEP was found to be around 1% of the overall bitrate. Given that data partitioning already reduces errors through packet size reduction and differentiation of coding data, EEP with data partitioning is a practical means of protecting user-based video streaming. The gain from employing EEP is shown to be higher quality video to the user, which will result in a greater take-up of video services. The results have implications for other forms of prioritized video streaming.

## 1. Introduction

Portable devices are proliferating, as the era of the wired Internet draws to a close and 4G wireless systems, and their successors [1] bring greater bandwidth capacity to access networks. User-based video-streaming applications are anticipated to be a key to the success of broadband wireless access networks such as IEEE 802.16e (mobile WiMAX) [2]. WiMAX itself is proving to be attractive in many areas where existing cell phone coverage is sparse or nonexistent. However, the migration of Internet applications to 4G wireless access presents a problem for video-streaming applications. This is because wireless channels are fundamentally error prone, whereas compression, for most of its coding gain, depends upon predictive coding. Consequentially, because of source-coding data dependencies, errors can disrupt a compressed video bitstream, and these errors can subsequently propagate in space and time. In the multimedia research world, unequal error protection (UEP) through

channel coding or forward error correction (FEC) has proved to be a rich area of investigation. Many schemes (some of which are reviewed in Section 2) have been proposed that map differential protection onto prioritized coded video data. However, there are strong signs that, in the commercial world, video service providers, in the interests of video content integrity, have opted for reliable streaming protocols, which simply resend data found to be corrupted or lost. This approach is not possible for all types of service but equal error protection (EEP) up to a sufficient level is possible. At the heart of this paper's investigation is a rather fundamental question, which is whether UEP gains in reducing bitrate are worth the extra complexity involved. One can go further and suggest that EEP will, for a relatively small increase in bitrate, bring significant gains in video quality. It can also avoid computationally intense optimization procedures that may prove unattractive to commercial providers. The current paper demonstrates these ideas in the context of prioritized data-partitioned video streams. As the research community has naturally investigated UEP procedures, we believe that advocating EEP is a relatively novel approach.

For two-way, interactive applications and user-to-user streaming, the problem of wireless errors cannot be overcome by the currently popular Dynamic Adaptive HTTP Streaming (DASH) [3]. DASH employs reliable TCP transport. However, mobile devices do not have storage capacity for multiple representations of a video stream, as required at DASH servers. For example, in [4] the DASH server storage was found for 90-minute videos encoded at up to 16 bitrates, in steps of 500 kbps starting at 500 kbp. The storage costs were 5 streams at 5 GB, 10 streams at 18 GB, and 16 streams at 46 GB. With current server storage costs [4] as low as 0.125 USD per month per 1 GB, multiple videos can be stored on a server in this way. Unfortunately, even short video clips stored in this way on a mobile device can pose an extra burden on memory capacity, which also has other calls on its capacity. Consequently, the streaming of video sequences with significant source-coding complexity remains particularly at risk, because of increased predictive data dependencies between packets and because of increased packet sizes. Such videos will be temporally or spatially active or a mixture of both.

In previous research by the authors [5], data-partitioned video streaming was employed as a means of separating out the more important source-coded data. In such data-partitioned video, the compressed video bitstream is split into up to three partitions before packetization, according to the importance of the content type to the decoding of the video. In general, smaller, less error-prone, packet sizes result and, for broadcast quality video, the more important data are carried in the smallest packets. In our previous work [5], all such packets were protected against errors with EEP, irrespective of their size. However, it is also possible [6] to apply UEP by duplicating one or more of the higher-priority segments but not duplicating the less important packets. Additionally, it is feasible [7] to protect higher-priority segments through the differential use of scalable channel coding, namely, by means of Raptor rateless coding [8]. However, it is unclear to what extent lower-priority segments can be left unprotected without an adverse effect on video quality or, indeed, whether lower complexity EEP is preferable at a small increase in bitrate. Consequently, the current paper directly compares EEP with UEP by carefully selecting appropriate configurations for data-partitioned video streams.

In work in [9], UEP of data-partitioned video was compared with EEP for single-layer video. Thus, EEP was not applied to data partitioning, as the intention of the work [9] was to show the potential advantage of the limited layering that data-partitioning represents. In [9], UEP was found to provide lower average quality than EEP but it had a greater probability of providing good quality video, despite adverse channel conditions. This leads to the question of why not apply EEP to a data-partitioned video stream.

In [9], differential protection was achieved by selecting from a set of discrete channel coding rates, through punctured convolutional codes. However, in order to determine the protection level, an optimization procedure was necessary to minimize potential distortion. This procedure depended on the quantization parameter (QP) and the coding rate for each partition. The wireless channel characteristics also had to be known in advance by the encoder. However, leaving aside the computational complexity of the optimization search in [9], there is another key difference between the system of [9] and that of [5] and this paper. In [9] no feedback occurs, so that it is not possible to request additional redundant data. In fact, when using punctured convolutional codes in [9] (rather than the rateless codes used herein), it is not possible to generate additional redundant data. In fact, as discussed in Section 3, rateless channel coding has a number of other advantages over conventional codes, apart from the ability to dynamically generate additional redundant data. We have demonstrated the scheme for WiMAX. The frame structure of WiMAX includes a send and receive subframe, making it convenient to immediately send a single request for additional redundant data. However, for two-way conversational video services such as videophone, the feedback channel is automatically available anyway.

Data partitioning in this paper can be viewed as a simplified form of SNR or quality layering [10]. Extended quality layering can also be applied to video streaming across WiMAX. In [11], adaptive multicast streaming was proposed using the Scalable Video Coding (SVC) extension for H.264 [12]. Fixed WiMAX channel conditions were monitored in order to vary the bitrate accordingly. Unfortunately, the subsequent decision of the JVT standardization body for H.264/AVC *not* to support fine-grained scalability (FGS) implies that it will be harder to respond to channel volatility in the way proposed in [11]. Other works have also investigated combining scalable video with multiconnections in [13] and in comparison with H.264/AVC in [14]. However, the data dependencies between layers in H.264/SVC medium-grained scalability are a concern. Unlike in FGS, enhancement layer packets may successfully arrive but be unable to be reconstructed if key pictures also fail to arrive. Besides, for commercial one-way streaming, simulcast is now likely to be preferred to H.264/SVC for the reasons outlined in [4]. In [4], it was found that the extra overhead from sending an SVC stream compared to an H.264/AVC stream meant that the cost of bandwidth consumption outweighed the reduced storage cost of SVC once more than 64 sessions had occurred (assuming 16 simulcast streams or 16 video layers per session). In another comparison [15], it was proposed that scalable video with UEP cannot provide any advantage over H.264/AVC with EEP in a wireless environment, due to the overhead of scalable video coding compared to that of single-layer coding.

In an H.264/AVC (Advanced Video Coding) codec, when data partitioning is enabled, every slice is divided into three separate partitions, and each partition is located in either of type-2 to type-4 Network Abstraction Layer Units (NALUs). (A slice is a subdivision of a picture or video frame, and an NALU is output as a virtual packet by an H.264/AVC codec, as part of its network-friendly approach [16].) For simplicity of interpretation just one slice per frame was employed in the current paper. It is then optionally possible to divide each slice into up to three data partitions. For purely intracoded video frames, I-frames, just two data partitions occur. However, in streaming over wireless it is common to avoid periodic I-frames, as they result in an increased data rate due to the inefficiency of intracoding. Consequently, an IPPPP... frame coding structure (i.e., one I-frame followed by all P-frames) is used with some form of distributed intrarefresh [17]. Then, apart from the first frame, all slices are divided into three.

In such a stream, a packet bearing an NALU of type 2, also known as data-partition-A, contains the most important information, including the Macroblock (MB) types and addresses, motion vectors, and essential header information. If any MBs in these frames are intracoded, their frequency transform coefficients are packed into a type-3 NALU, also known as data-partition-B. Intracoded block patterns (CBPs) are also included, as these specify in compact form which blocks within an MB contain nonzero coefficients. Type-4 NALs, also known as data-partition-C, carry the transform coefficients of the motion-compensated inter-picture coded MBs along with inter-CBPs. These three partitions, types A, B, and C, form segments of the video bitstream. They are subsequently each output as Real-Time Transport Protocol (RTP) packets by the codec in RTP mode, prior to dispatch as Internet Protocol (IP)/User Datagram Protocol (UDP) packets. (It is assumed that header compression over a broadband wireless link will greatly reduce the header overhead [18] from 40 B to one or two B on average.)

Because the evaluation in this current paper uses distributed intrarefresh rather than periodic intracoded frames, delay arising from the sudden dispatch of multiple packets forming I-frames is avoided. As no B-frames are used, the schemes are suitable for the low-complexity processors on mobile devices, though there is an issue over the need for a hardware implementation of data partitioning. Then, by adopting Constant Bit-Rate (CBR) streaming in tests, a comparison between different schemes is fair. In fact, CBR streaming allows commercial providers to plan storage capacity and bandwidth utilization, at a cost in some fluctuations in video quality. From [19], when using data-partitioned video streaming, it is important to set constrained interprediction (CIP), as otherwise partition-B cannot be made completely independent of partition-C. When CIP is set, intraprediction can only be performed by referencing other intracoded MBs. If no suitable MBs are available, then intraprediction is not possible. As CIP prevents predictive reference to inter-coded MBs, the information in partition-C is no longer required, thus allowing partition-B to become independent of partition-C. In the Joint Model (JM) reference software for H.264/AVC, CIP is actually set in the input parameter file. In [20] it is revealed that, even when data partitioning is not in use, setting CIP is effective in combating higher packet loss rates. However, whenever CIP is set, there is a limited loss of compression efficiency, whose loss is quantified in [20]. On the other hand, it is not possible to make partition-C independent of partition-B without breaking the codec's compatibility with

the H.264/AVC standard. Reconstruction of all partitions is dependent on the survival of partition-A, though that partition remains independent of the other partitions.

The remainder of this paper is organized as follows. Section 2 describes physical and software approaches to UEP. Physical (PHY-) layer UEP avoids bitrate overhead but is inflexible compared to software UEP. Section 2 also reviews application-layer EEP in wireless video streaming. Section 3 goes on to consider rateless channel coding, which is employed in adaptive fashion for EEP and UEP alike. Unlike conventional channel coding, in rateless coding, the redundant data to information data ratio can be dynamically scaled, making it suitable for application-layer protection. Then, before a comparative evaluation, Section 4 examines the simulation model and its validity. Section 5 is our comparison of UEP with EEP for data-partitioned video. Section 6 concludes the paper, with some recommendations for future research.

## 2. Related Research

The idea of UEP for segmented video bitstreams has taken various forms prior to the H.264/AVC codec standard (otherwise known as MPEG-4 part 10). In an MPEG-4 Part 2 codec, partitioning was internal to a packet with just two partitions. The first contained header, motion, and other shape information. The second contained the texture (transform coefficients), with decoder resynchronization headers placed internally at the start of each partition. In [21], PHY-layer FEC was enhanced for a fixed-sized part at the start of each packet. Unfortunately, as the size of the first MPEG-4 partition may vary in size, some motion vectors could receive less protection. Besides, each network traversed by the video stream would need to have special arrangements for this type of traffic. Finally, by placing both partitions in one packet, no account is taken of the risk of decoder desynchronization when packet loss occurs.

To avoid these problems, the authors of [22] proposed that MPEG-4 part 2 internal partitions should be split between packets, forming two different streams. Headers would be needed to allow partitions from the same video frame to be identified. This is what now occurs within an H.264/AVC codec; except three rather than two streams are formed. In [22], UEP was implemented by placing each of the MPEG-4 part 2 streams in different General Packet-Radio Service (GPRS) channels, with different channel coding rates for each stream. However, in our scheme we prefer application-layer protection, in addition to any PHY-layer protection that may be present. This makes a solution more amenable to end-to-end control.

In [23], another approach for broadcast video was taken in which hierarchical modulation favored those H.264/AVC partitions containing more important data for the reconstruction of the video frame. One reason H.264/AVC data partitioning was chosen, rather than other forms of layering, was that it does not significantly increase the bitrate of the composite stream. In fact, this is the same reason that Hierarchical Quadrature Amplitude Modulation (HQAM) was chosen rather than channel coding: that it does not increase the bitrate. However, in extensions to the scheme, Turbo channel coding was additionally required for poor wireless channel conditions. The proposed scheme [23] was intended to be flexible, altering the QAM symbol constellation according to the desired bitrates.

HQAM is not the only form of PHY-layer prioritization, and in [24] data partitions were mapped onto different antennas in a space-time block coding. Two segments were employed with high-priority bits (those separated more in the coding) for partition-A and low-priority bits for the partitions-B and -C. The prioritization is different from the arrangement in the current paper, because herein partition-A and -B are grouped as a high-priority segment. However, this is explained by the different picture coding structures in each paper, that is, in [24] and the current paper. In the current paper, the use of distributed intrarefresh MBs rather than periodic intracoded pictures (I-pictures) means that it is important to protect partition-B packets, as they contain intracoded transform coefficients.

Software approaches to UEP may combine prioritized channel encoding of video with interleaving across packets. (Interleaving is employed to counter long error bursts during deep wireless channel fades.) In Priority Encoding Transmission (PET) [25], parity symbols of a systematic code are included in successive packets such that high-priority segments can be recovered, even if a large number of packets are erased. On the other hand, lower priority segments will be lost if a few packets amongst the interleaved group are erased. PET is capable of refinement in a rate-distortion manner [26] but, with just three partitions, the relevance of such refinements to the current scheme appears restricted. Besides, a problem with all packet-interleaving methods is the impact of increased latency when the decoder has to wait for all the packets in an interleaved group to arrive before reconstruction can take place.

Turning to EEP, application-layer EEP leads to an increase in overall bitrate. In return, EEP can result in gains in flexibility and in the ability to address the special needs of compressed video arising from the risk of temporal error propagation. Application-layer Raptor code has been applied [27] to a number of error-prone network environments, because of the stringent anticipated requirements for IPTV [28]. In these realizations all packets are protected against erasure, while bit errors are assumed to be protected at the physical layer. The Digital Video Broadcast (DVB) project has specified [29] optional application-layer rateless coding, as has 3rd Generation Partnership Project (3GPP) [30]. However, in these standards the potential for dynamic adaptation of the protection level was not exploited.

## 3. Rateless Channel Coding

In this paper, rateless coding is employed to protect data-partitioned video. Rateless coding is employed in an adaptive manner [5] by retransmission of additional redundant data, as and when required. However, notice that rateless codes are a probabilistic channel code, in the sense that reconstruction

is not guaranteed. Raptor coding [8], as used herein, is a systematic variety of rateless code that does not share the high error floors of prior rateless codes. It also has $O(n)$ decoder computational complexity. Systematic codes allow packets without any reported errors to be treated separately to those without them. Thus, processing can be sped up by splitting processing into two processing streams if systematic coding is used.

It is the ability to easily generate new symbols that makes rateless codes to be rateless. Decoding will succeed with small probability of decoder failure if any of $k(1 + \varepsilon)$ symbols are successfully received, where $k$ is the number of source symbols originally present and $\varepsilon$ is a low percentage of coding overhead. In its simplest form, the symbols are combined in an exclusive OR (XOR) operation according to the order specified by a randomized, low-density generator matrix, and, in this case, the probability of decoder failure is $\partial = 2^{-k\varepsilon}$, which for large $k$ approaches the Shannon limit. The random sequence must be known to the receiver but this is easily achieved through advance knowledge of the sequence seed.

In general, encoding of rateless codes is accomplished as follows. Choose $d_i$ randomly from some distribution of degrees, where $\rho_{di} = \Pr (\text{degree } d_i)$; Pr is the probability of a given event. Choose $d_i$ random information symbols $R_i$ from amongst the $k$ information symbols. These $R_i$ symbols are then XORed together to produce a new composite symbol, which forms one symbol of the transmitted packet. Thus, if the symbols are bytes, all of the $R_i$ byte's bits are XORed with all of the bits of the other randomly selected bytes in turn. It is not necessary to specify the random degree or the random symbols chosen if it is assumed that the (pseudo-)random number generators of sender and receiver are synchronized.

Symbols are processed at the decoder as follows. If a symbol arrives with degree greater than one, it is buffered. If a clean symbol arrives with degree one, then it is XORed with all symbols in which it was used in the encoding process. This decrements the degree of each of the symbols to which the degree-one symbol is applied. When a symbol is eventually reduced to degree one, it too can be used in the decoding process. Notice that a degree-one symbol is a symbol for which no XORing has taken place. Notice also that for packet erasure channels a clean degree-one symbol (a packet) is easily established as such. For byte-erasures, the PHY-layer FEC can be reasonably expected to isolate clean symbols or blocks of clean symbols.

In the decoding process, the robust Soliton distribution [31] is employed as the degree-distribution, as this produces degree-one symbols at a convenient rate for decoding. It also avoids isolated symbols that are not used elsewhere. Two tuneable parameters $c$ and $\delta$ serve to form the expected number of useable degree-one symbols. Set

$$S = c \ln\left(\frac{k}{\delta}\right)\sqrt{k}, \tag{1}$$

where $c$ is a constant close to 1 and $\delta$ is a bound on the probability that decoding fails to complete. Now define

$$
\begin{aligned}
\tau(d) &= \frac{S}{k}\frac{1}{d} \quad \text{for } d = 1, 2, \ldots \left(\frac{k}{S}\right) - 1 \\
&= \frac{S}{k}\ln\left(\frac{S}{\delta}\right) \quad \text{for } d = \frac{k}{S} \qquad (2) \\
&= 0 \quad \text{for } d > \frac{k}{S}
\end{aligned}
$$

as an auxiliary positive-valued function to give the robust Soliton distribution:

$$
\mu(d) = \frac{\rho(d) + \tau(d)}{z}, \qquad (3)
$$

where $z$ normalizes the probability distribution to unity and is given by

$$
z = \sum_d (\rho(d) + \tau(d)). \qquad (4)
$$

## 4. Simulation Model

*4.1. Wireless Configuration.* To establish the behavior of rateless coding under WiMAX, the ns-2 simulator was augmented with a module from the Chang Gung University, Taiwan [32] that has proved an effective way of modeling IEEE 802.16e's behavior. Ten runs per data point were averaged (arithmetic mean), and the simulator was first allowed to reach steady state before commencing testing.

In the evaluation, transmission over WiMAX was carefully modeled. The PHY-layer settings selected for WiMAX simulation are given in Table 1. The antenna heights are typical ones taken from the standard [33]. The antenna is modeled for comparison purposes as a half-wavelength dipole, whereas a sectored set of antenna on a mast might be used in practice to achieve directivity and, hence, better performance. The IEEE 802.16 Time Division Duplex (TDD) frame length was set to 5 ms, as only this value is supported in the WiMAX forum simplification of the standard. The data rate results from the use of one of the mandatory coding modes [2, 33] for a TDD downlink/uplink subframe ratio of 3:1. The WiMAX base station (BS) was assigned more bandwidth capacity than the uplink to allow the BS to respond to multiple mobile subscriber stations (MSs). Thus, the parameter settings in Table 1 such as the modulation type and PHY-layer coding rate are required to achieve a datarate of 10.67 Mbps over the downlink. Notice also that there is 1/2 channel coding rate at the PHY-layer of IEEE 802.16e, in addition to the application-layer channel coding that we add. However, as discussed in Section 2, application-layer coding for compressed video stream is frequently used in wireless systems because of the high packet losses and error rates that can occur.

A two-state Gilbert-Elliott channel model [34] simulated the channel model for WiMAX. Though this model does not reproduce the physical characteristics that give rise to noise and interference, it does model the error bursts [35]

TABLE 1: IEEE 802.16e parameter settings.

| Parameter | Value |
| --- | --- |
| PHY | OFDMA |
| Frequency band | 5 GHz |
| Bandwidth capacity | 10 MHz |
| Duplexing mode | TDD |
| DL/UL subframe ratio | 3 : 1 |
| Frame length | 5 ms |
| Max. packet length | 1024 B |
| Raw data rate (downlink) | 10.67 Mbps |
| IFFT size | 1024 |
| Modulation | 16-QAM 1/2 |
| Guard band ratio | 1/16 |
| MS transmit power | 245 mW |
| BS transmit power | 20 W |
| Approx. range to SS | 1 km |
| Antenna type | Omni-directional |
| Antenna gains | 0 dBD |
| MS antenna height | 1.2 m |
| BS antenna height | 30 m |

OFDMA: orthogonal frequency division multiple access.

commonly experienced by an application. It is such bursts that are particularly harmful to compressed video data. In the Gilbert-Elliott model, PGG is the probability of remaining in the good state, while PG is the probability of byte error in the good state, which was modelled internally by a Uniform distribution. PBB and PB are the corresponding parameters for the bad state.

*4.2. Video Configuration.* Two video clips with different source-coding characteristics were employed in the tests in order to judge the dependency of the results upon video source-coding complexity. The first test sequence was *Paris*, which is a studio scene with two upper body images of presenters and moderate motion. The background is of moderate-to-high spatial complexity leading to larger slices. The other test sequence was *Football*, which has rapid movements and consequently has high temporal coding complexity. Both sequences were CBR encoded at Common Intermediate Format (CIF) ($352 \times 288$ pixel/picture). CIF resolution was used for ready comparison with the prior work of others on video communication with mobile devices.

Clearly if one of the high-definition (HD) resolutions were to be used, as processing within H.264/AVC is on an MB-basis, the number of packets output would normally be scaled up linearly. However, because viewers are more sensitive to visual artefacts at higher resolutions, the frame rate is usually increased from as low as 24 frame/s to as much as 90 frame/s. The fidelity extension to H.264/AVC [36] extended the sample bit depth to ten bits and introduced a new $8 \times 8$ transform block size for increased sensitivity to texture detail. An increased frame rate and bit depth will lead to more than just a linear increase in the number of packets, as would adoption of one of the new chroma formats [36]. This increase requires redimensioning of the buffer at the mobile device to avoid excess packet loss but to not result in an increase in latency at the same time. As streaming rates of greater than 2.5 Mbps for 1280 × 720 pixels/frame progressively scanned (720p) HD video [37] will put considerable strain on deployed WiMAX networks, a study of the proposed system for HD over WiMAX is reserved for future work. Short sequences such as *Paris* and *Football* were also selected for comparison with the work of others. These sequences are standard reference sequences chosen by the codec designers for their typicality and as a test of coding performance. Future work should also consider longer video streams or even carousels formed by a set of reference sequences to investigate further the effect of WiMAX network factors.

As previously mentioned, it is common for mobile devices to avoid the need for the more complex processing involved in bipredictive B-frames by using an IPPPP... Group of Pictures (GOP) structure. This arrangement also avoids sudden increases in latency [38] when periodic I-frames are employed. The frame rate was 30 Hz. It was necessary to protect against spatiotemporal error propagation in the event of inter-coded P-picture slices being lost. To ensure higher quality video, 2% intracoded MBs (randomly placed) were included in each frame (apart from the first I-picture) to act as anchor points in the event of slice loss. The JM 14.2 version of the H.264/AVC codec software was utilized to assess the objective video quality (Peak Signal-to-Noise Ratio (PSNR)) after packet loss, relative to the input YUV raw video. (YUV is not an acronym but the name of a color space that takes human perception of color into account.) In general, the configuration of the JM software is by a parameter file that acts as input to the decoder. Thus, this is how the percentage of randomly inserted intracoded MBs is specified.

Lost partition-C slice packets were compensated for by error concealment using the motion vectors in partition-A at the decoder to identify candidate replacement MBs in the last previously correctly received frame. Intra error concealment was also employed, as described below. In general, in the H.264/AVC codec standard, error concealment is a nonnormative feature, that is, a feature which is not needed for compliance with the standard. Nevertheless, in [39] a number of nonnormative error concealment algorithms for H.264/AVC were recommended, as, though error concealment is outside the scope of the standard, it is nevertheless needed. An attempt is made to conceal any lost slices. Error concealment within a lost slice is on an MB basis. Previously concealed MBs can be used to conceal missing MBs. Concealment proceeds from the edges of a lost slice inwards. For intracoded concealment of a missing MB, spatially adjacent pixels to a missing MB, if available, are interpolated to form the pixels of a missing MB. For inter-coded MBs within a lost slice, if very little motion has occurred, replacement by the matching MB in the previous frame occurs (known as error concealment by previous frame replacement). Otherwise, it is recommended [39] to

use one of the motion vectors of the surrounding MBs to identify a replacement MB. An algorithm to choose that motion vector is detailed in [39]. In the case of an MB split into subblocks, an average of the MVs of the subblocks within the MB is taken to form a candidate MV. The H.264/AVC algorithms will work even if only one correctly received slice is available within a frame.

A detailed guide to reconstruction of data-partitioned video by an H.264/AVC decoder is given in [40]. If partition-B is lost, missing MBs can be concealed by employing motion vectors from partition-A, and intra error concealment is optionally employed. In this sense, optional has a similar meaning to nonnormative, and in fact in the JM implementation used herein, intra error concealment is included. The procedure for lost partition-C packets has already been described. If both partition-B and partition-C go missing, then they are replaced by the MBs pointed to by the motion vectors in partition-A. If partition-A is lost, it is recommended to use the motion vectors of adjacent MB rows, that is, MBs from adjacent slices if these are available. Other ways of partitioning H.264/AVC coding data were also considered at the time of standardization such as splitting low and high transform coefficients normally present in partition-C and placing them in partition-A [41] or duplicating slice header and MB type information present in partition-A and placing it in partition-B [42]. The former [41] was recommended in certain circumstances when zigzag scanning of the transform coefficients is replaced by double scanning but, in terms of standardization, this recommendation appears to introduce "needless design variation" [43]. The latter [42] may introduce extra overhead [43] as the default case. Hence, [42] was also excluded from the standard.

It should also be remarked that others have conducted performance tests on using data partitioning. In [37] it was observed that it is possible to drop partitions B and C, while at the same time decreasing the quantization parameter (QP) to increase the video quality for an equivalent file size to retain the two partitions with a higher QP (lower video quality). However, this strategy was reported to only be worth trying for bipredictive B-frames, which in this current paper were not used. In [16], partition-A was repeated twice at low packet loss rates (3%), and three times at higher error rates (5, 10 and 20%) with competitive results compared to other forms of error resilience. In [44], in an approach that bears some resemblance to earlier work in [7], UEP was applied in an overlapping or sliding window fashion. In one experiment, each of the three partition types was aggregated from the frames in a GOP to form three segments. In another experiment, partition-As were combined with partition-Bs and accumulated as one segment, while the other segment was formed by aggregating all the partition-C NALUs within a GOP. Data from the anchor frame within the GOP was also included in the higher priority segment. The authors of [44] concluded that placing each data-partition type in its own segment was preferable to single-layer coding. It was also preferable to combine partition-A and partition-B, in terms of controlling the desired video data rate and erasure protection level.

Notice also that the JM implementation of random intracoded MBs does not duplicate placements of such MBs in previous frames, which was a defect identified in [45] of previous implementations of this form of intra placement. In fact, when all MB positions have been occupied over a sequence of frames, the random placement pattern is then repeated so that all MBs are refreshed in each cycle of the placement pattern. Therefore, the JM scheme, as it is a cyclic replacement one, can be compared to the use of a cyclic line of intracoded MBs. At best at the end of each cycle, all data is refreshed, and in that respect the use of randomly placed intracoded MBs acts just like the insertion of a periodic I-frame; that is, it provides a point of random access. However, the cyclic line procedure in CIF resolution frames refreshes at a quicker rate than the 2% of random intracoded used herein, as a horizontal line is equivalent to 5.5% of the MBs. For data-partitioned video this will lead to an increase in the size of partition-B and an increased bit-rate as a result. On the other hand, quality will on average be increased, not just due to the extra intracoded MBs but due to the fact that CIP will not restrict coding gain to such an extent. The latter gain arises as there are always adjacent intracoded MBs in a cyclic intra-refresh line. Therefore, future work can investigate the trade-offs between the different ways of inserting intracoded MBs.

### 4.3. Rateless Decoder Modelling.

We used the following statistical model [46] to model the performance of the rateless decoder:

$$P_f(m, k) = 1 \quad \text{if } m < k$$
$$= 0.85 \times 0.567^{m-k} \quad \text{if } m \geq k, \tag{5}$$

where $P_f(m, k)$ is the decode failure probability of the code with $k$ source symbols if $m$ symbols have been successfully received (and $1 - P_f$ is naturally the success probability). Notice that the authors of [46] comment and show that for $k > 200$ the model of (5) almost perfectly models the performance of the code. This implies that if blocks are used approximately, 200 blocks should be received before reasonable behavior takes place. This observation also motivated the choice of bytes within a packet as the symbols, to reduce latencies. Upon receipt of the correctly received data, decoding of the information symbols is attempted, which will fail with a probability given by (5) for $k > 200$.

## 5. Evaluation

Tests evaluated various metrics, especially video quality for EEP and UEP alternatives. As mentioned in Section 3, in the UEP alternative partitions-A and -B form one segment with rateless coding applied, while partition-C was unprotected. The size of per-packet redundant data [5] was adaptively found from

$$R = \frac{L}{1 - BL} - L, \tag{6}$$

where $L$ is the payload length and $BL$ is the instantaneous probability of byte loss (a byte within a packet is the rateless

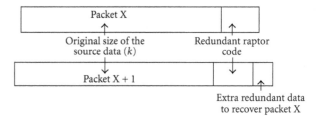

FIGURE 1: Division of payload data in a packet between source data, original redundant data, and extra redundant data for a previous erroneous packet.

code symbol). Up to 5% zero-mean Gaussian noise was additively included to distort the channel estimate in order to account for estimation inaccuracy. The rateless code belief propagation decoding algorithm has a small probability of failure and in which case extra redundant data were sent in the next packet. Only one retransmission over the WiMAX link is allowed to avoid increasing latency. However, as a retransmission request can be sent in the return TDD subframe, the additional delay is restricted to one WiMAX frame transmission time, that is, a minimum of 5 ms. Thus, if it turns out that the packet cannot be reconstructed, despite the provision of redundant data, extra redundant data are added to the next packet. In Figure 1, packet X is corrupted to such an extent that it cannot be reconstructed. Therefore, in packet X + 1 some extra redundant data is included up to the level that its failure is no longer certain. It is implied from (5) that if less than $k$ symbols (bytes) in the payload are successfully received, then further $k - m + e$ extra redundant bytes can be sent to reduce the risk of failure. In the evaluation tests, $e$ was set to four, resulting in a risk of failure of 8.7% (from (5)) in reconstructing the original packet if the extra redundant data successfully arrives. This reduced risk arises because of the exponential decay of the risk that is evident from (5) and which gives rise to Raptor code's low error probability floor [47].

To see the effect of channel conditions, the Gilbert-Elliott parameters were varied to produce a poor Channel 1 and a somewhat better Channel 2. The settings were CH1 = (PGG = 0.95, PBB = 0.96, PB = 0.02, PB = 0.165) and CH2 = (PGG = 0.97, PBB = 0.94, PB = 0.01, PB = 0.05). Similarly, the CBR data rate was tested both at 500 kbps and 1 Mbps for the two video clips of Section 4, *Football* and *Paris*. To ensure independence between partitions B and C, CIP was turned on, and 2% intra-refresh MBs were randomly added to the P-picture slices (refer to Section 4). Though a visual representation might pick out more clearly some results, for reasons of compactness and because some data representations are not helped by using charts, the presentation in this paper is through a set of tables.

### 5.1. Results.

Tables 2 and 3 show EEP and UEP protection modes, respectively. No outright packet loss occurs in these and subsequent tables, except due to internal packet corruption, when attempts at packet repair have failed. Though the percentage of corrupted packets is high under

TABLE 2: Metrics for channel 1 with EEP.

| With EEP | Football 2% IR CIP 500 kbps IPPP... | Football 2% IR CIP 1 Mbps IPPP... | Paris 2% IR CIP 500 kbps IPPP... | Paris 2% IR CIP 1 Mbps IPPP... |
|---|---|---|---|---|
| Dropped packets (%) | 0 | 0 | 0 | 0 |
| Packet end-to-end mean delay (s) | 0.0068 | 0.0084 | 0.0068 | 0.0087 |
| Mean PSNR (dB) | 33.54 | 39.00 | 35.88 | 40.58 |
| Corrupted packets (%) | 24.61 | 30.64 | 21.77 | 30.55 |
| Corrupted packet mean delay (s) | 0.0170 | 0.0183 | 0.0166 | 0.0171 |

IR: intrarefresh, CIP: constrained intrarefresh.

TABLE 3: Metrics for channel 1 with UEP.

| With UEP | Football 2% IR CIP 500 kbps IPPP... | Football 2% IR CIP 1 Mbps IPPP... | Paris 2% IR CIP 500 kbps IPPP... | Paris 2% IR CIP 1 Mbps IPPP... |
|---|---|---|---|---|
| Dropped packets (%) | 11.02 | 10.38 | 12.77 | 15.11 |
| Packet end-to-end mean delay (s) | 0.0068 | 0.0083 | 0.0066 | 0.0080 |
| Mean PSNR (dB) | 30.56 | 30.5 | 28.3 | 28.02 |
| Corrupted packets (%) | 13.58 | 20.25 | 9.00 | 15.44 |
| Corrupted packet mean delay (s) | 0.0164 | 0.0183 | 0.0161 | 0.0170 |

IR: intrarefresh, CIP: constrained intrarefresh.

TABLE 4: Mean per frame overhead in bytes from rateless coding for the *Football* sequence.

| | Football 2% IR CIP 500 kbps IPPP... | Football 2% IR CIP 1 Mbps IPPP... |
|---|---|---|
| EEP/CH1 | 41 | 84 |
| UEP/CH1 | 28 | 51 |
| EEP/CH2 | 10 | 20 |
| UEP/CH2 | 7 | 12 |

IR: intrarefresh, CIP: constrained intraprediction.

TABLE 5: Mean per frame overhead in bytes from rateless coding for the *Paris* sequence.

| | Paris 2% IR CIP 500 kbps IPPP... | Paris 2% IR CIP 1 Mbps IPPP... |
|---|---|---|
| EEP/CH1 | 42 | 82 |
| UEP/CH1 | 19 | 25 |
| EEP/CH2 | 10 | 19 |
| UEP/CH2 | 5 | 6 |

IR: intrarefresh, CIP: constrained intraprediction.

EEP, because extra redundant data for all partitions can be requested, it was possible to reconstruct all packets after one retransmission. However, under UEP, reconstruction of the longer partition-C packets was no longer possible, leading to an increase in the percentage of dropped packets to over 10% and a decrease in the percentage of corrupted packets, that is, packets that could be repaired. The main impact in terms of objective video quality (PSNR) is a drop in quality when UEP is employed.

Clearly, Table 3 shows the maximum drop in quality due to UEP, as it would also be possible to protect partition-C with a reduced percentage of rateless redundant data (rather than the zero percentage used). In contrast, gains from UEP are twofold. Firstly, because the percentage of corrupted packets is significantly reduced, the overall delay arising from the need to resend redundant data is reduced though mean corrupted packet delay is greater at 1 Mbps, as packets are longer. Secondly, under UEP there is an increase in the overall video bitrate arising from the reduction in rateless code overhead.

The mean per-frame overhead is given in Tables 4 and 5 for the *Football* and *Paris* sequences, respectively. The overhead from using UEP, in that respect, is about half of that of EEP. However, the maximum overhead for EEP at 500 kbps

(42 B at 30 Hz) is a rate of $42 \times 8 \times 30 = 10$ kbps or 2% of the CBR rate. For EEP at 1 Mbps the maximum overhead is $84 \times 8 \times 30 = 20$ kbps or again 2% of the CBR rate. Therefore, the relative bitrate saving from using UEP rather than EEP is about 1% of the overall bitrate, which is obviously a small percentage. For this small gain in bitrate the drop in video quality is severe.

To investigate wireless channel dependency, results were taken for the channel 2 characteristics given in the introduction to this section. From Table 6, under EEP the performance metrics essentially remain the same as for channel 1, except for a reduction in the number of corrupted packets arising from the improved channel conditions. This will cause overall delay to be reduced but, as no packets are lost outright, there is no loss in video quality. When UEP is employed in Table 7, there is also a reduction in the percentage of dropped packets, in most cases to below 10%. This has the effect of improving the objective video quality by several dB but the quality is still well below the level of the EEP streams.

These results imply that in both types of channel conditions tested there is a significant negative impact on video quality from reducing protection of partition-C. As previously mentioned, motion-copy (MC) error concealment [39] is employed at the decoder to compensate for loss of partition-C. However, the gains from using MC error concealment to compensate for the loss of partition-C are not strongly apparent in the results. That observation can be applied to both the types of video content tested. This does not mean that there is no gain from data partitioning, as it has been long known that MC error concealment can significantly improve video quality in all but highly active video sequences. For example, in [21] there was a 5 dB improvement in quality from applying error concealment to MPEG-4 Part 2 data partitioning. In [48],

TABLE 6: Metrics for channel 2 with EEP.

| With EEP | Football 2% IR CIP 500 kbps IPPP... | Football 2% IR CIP 1 Mbps IPPP... | Paris 2% IR CIP 500 kbps IPPP... | Paris 2% IR CIP 1 Mbps IPPP... |
|---|---|---|---|---|
| Dropped Packets (%) | 0 | 0 | 0 | 0 |
| Packet end-to-end mean delay (s) | 0.0067 | 0.0084 | 0.0068 | 0.0082 |
| Mean PSNR (dB) | 33.54 | 39.00 | 35.88 | 40.58 |
| Corrupted packets (%) | 11.41 | 20.51 | 12.33 | 18.00 |
| Corrupted packet mean delay (s) | 0.0172 | 0.0180 | 0.0163 | 0.0169 |

IR: intrarefresh, CIP: constrained intraprediction.

TABLE 7: Metrics for channel 2 with UEP.

| With UEP | Football 2% IR CIP 500 kbps IPPP... | Football 2% IR CIP 1 Mbps IPPP... | Paris 2% IR CIP 500 kbps IPPP... | Paris 2% IR CIP 1 Mbps IPPP... |
|---|---|---|---|---|
| Dropped packets (%) | 3.71 | 6.79 | 7.55 | 11.11 |
| Packet end-to-end delay (s) | 0.0067 | 0.0081 | 0.0065 | 0.0079 |
| Mean PSNR (dB) | 32.22 | 34.9 | 30.76 | 30.16 |
| Corrupted packets (%) | 7.69 | 13.71 | 4.77 | 6.88 |
| Corrupted packet mean delay (s) | 0.0159 | 0.0179 | 0.0156 | 0.0164 |

IR: intrarefresh, CIP: constrained intraprediction.

the gain after whole frame loss from refining motion-copy (RMC) error concealment (through recursive estimation of motion vectors over multiple frames) was found to improve over previous frame replacement (PFR) and MC error concealment.

In [49], for a 5% packet loss rate, MC of the motion vectors of the last reference frame improved upon PFR by at least 2 dB in PSNR, and a further 2 dB at least if RMC was used. Conversely, the availability of the correct motion vectors from protected partition-A (rather than estimated ones) will significantly benefit video quality. It should also be added that, for broadcast quality video, the smaller partition-A packet sizes [6] are an additional form of protection relative to larger partition-C packets, even when EEP is applied.

## 6. Conclusion

As user expectations of mobile video streaming increase, video quality becomes an important determinant of the take-up of a service. In this paper, it was shown that equal error protection can result in several dBs gain in video quality over unequal error protection of data-partitioned video. The overhead from using EEP rather than UEP was about 1% of the overall constant bit rate. Consequently, as data-partitioning already brings advantages in terms of smaller packet sizes for more important data and the ability to compensate if texture data is lost, equal error protection is preferable, except when there is a severe shortage of available bandwidth. As the recent trend is towards much greater bandwidth capacity for mobile systems, then the bitrate savings from UEP may no longer be worth pursuing.

There are a number of avenues for future research. Section 4.2 mentioned the need for testing the scheme with the emerging HD and 3D (stereoscopic) resolutions that will eventually migrate to broadband wireless streaming. That section also mentioned alternative ways of partitioning H.264/AVC coding data, which was not standardized but nevertheless was worth considering. It is also possible to propose still other ways of subpartitioning partitions B and C, which have been investigated by some of the authors. The merits of these schemes and different forms of packetization are worthy of investigation. In Section 4.2 also, it was mentioned that there are many alternatives for insertion of intracoded MBs, which will each have their effect on the resulting video quality. This paper has considered CBR video but Variable Bit Rate (VBR) video is often preferred by researchers, because, despite time-varying data rates and unpredictable storage requirements, it results in an even quality. By virtue of open-loop coding, it also results in a simpler codec. In particular, CBR is unsuitable for HD video as quality variations are more apparent. This suggests that at a cost in delay the impact of the protection scheme for smoothed HD video streaming should be investigated. For VBR video streams, varying the QP will impact on the distribution of coding data between partitions. Therefore, the impact of QP dependency on the robustness of the scheme can also be investigated.

## References

[1] D. Raychaudhuri and N. B. Mandayam, "Frontiers of wireless and mobile communications," *IEEE Proceedings*, vol. 100, no. 4, pp. 824–840, 2012.

[2] J. G. Andrews, A. Ghosh, and R. Muhammed, *Fundamentals of WiMAX: Understanding Broadband Wireless Networking*, Prentice Hall, Upper Saddle River, NJ, USA, 2007.

[3] T. Stockhammer, P. Fröjdh, I. Sodagar, and S. Rhyu, "Information technology—MPEG systems technologies—Part 6: Dynamic adaptive streaming over HTTP (DASH)," ISO/IEC MPEG Draft International Standard, 2011.

[4] H. Kalva, V. Adzic, and B. Furht, "Comparing MPEG AVC and SVC for adaptive HTTP streaming," in *Proceedings of the IEEE International Conference on Consumer Electronics*, pp. 160–161, 2012.

[5] L. Al-Jobouri, M. Fleury, and M. Ghanbari, "Adaptive rateless coding for data-partitioned video streaming over a broadband wireless channel," in *Proceedings of the 6th Conference on Wireless Advanced (WiAD '10)*, p. 6, June 2010.

[6] L. Al-Jobouri, M. Fleury, and M. Ghanbari, "Error-resilient IPTV for an IEEE 802.16e channel," *Wireless Engineering and Technology*, vol. 2, no. 2, pp. 70–79, 2011.

[7] R. Razavi, M. Fleury, M. Altaf, H. Sammak, and M. Ghanbari, "H.264 video streaming with data-partitioning and growth

codes," in *Proceedings of the IEEE International Conference on Image Processing (ICIP '09)*, pp. 909–912, November 2009.

[8] A. Shokrollahi, "Raptor codes," *IEEE Transactions on Information Theory*, vol. 52, no. 6, pp. 2551–2567, 2006.

[9] T. Stockhammer and M. Bystrom, "H.264/AVC data partitioning for mobile video communication," in *Proceedings of the International Conference on Image Processing (ICIP '04)*, pp. 545–548, October 2004.

[10] S. Mys, P. Lambert, and W. De Neve, "SNR scalability in H.264/AVC using data partitioning," in *Proceedings of the Pacific Rim Conference on Multimedia*, pp. 329–338, 2006.

[11] O. I. Hillestad, A. Perkis, V. Genc, S. Murphy, and J. Murphy, "Adaptive H.264/MPEG-4 SVC video over IEEE 802.16 broadband wireless networks," in *Proceedings of the 16th International Packet Video Workshop*, pp. 26–35, November 2007.

[12] H. Schwarz, D. Marpe, and T. Wiegand, "Overview of the scalable video coding extension of the H.264/AVC standard," *IEEE Transactions on Circuits and Systems for Video Technology*, vol. 17, no. 9, pp. 1103–1120, 2007.

[13] H. H. Juan, H. C. Huang, C. Huang, and T. Chiang, "Cross-layer mobile WiMAX MAC designs for the H.264/AVC scalable video coding," *Wireless Networks*, vol. 16, no. 1, pp. 113–123, 2008.

[14] J. Casasempere, P. Sanchez, T. Villameriel, and J. Del Ser, "Performance evaluation of H.264/MPEG-4 scalable video coding over IEEE 802.16e networks," in *Proceedings of the IEEE International Symposium on Broadband Multimedia Systems and Broadcasting (BMSB '09)*, pp. 1–6, May 2009.

[15] T. Stockhammer, "Is fine granular scalable video coding beneficial for wireless video applications?" in *Proceedings of the EEE International Conference on Multimedia and Expo*, vol. 1, pp. 193–196, 2003.

[16] S. Wenger, "H.264/AVC over IP," *IEEE Transactions on Circuits and Systems for Video Technology*, vol. 13, no. 7, pp. 645–656, 2003.

[17] M. M. Hannuksela, Y. K. Wang, and M. Gabbouj, "Isolated regions in video coding," *IEEE Transactions on Multimedia*, vol. 6, no. 2, pp. 259–267, 2004.

[18] C. Bormann, C. Burmeister, M. Degermark et al., "RObust Header Compression (ROHC): framework and four profiles: RTP, UDP, ESP, and uncompressed," IETF RFC 3095, 2001.

[19] Y. Dhondt, S. Mys, K. Vermeirsch, and R. Van de Walle, "Constrained inter prediction: removing dependencies between different data partitions," in *Advanced Concepts for Intelligent Visual Systems*, pp. 720–731, 2007.

[20] C. M. T. Calafate and M. P. Malumbres, "Evaluation of the H.264 codec," Tech. Rep. DISCA-UPV-2003, Universidad Politecnica Valencia, 2003.

[21] W. Rabiner, M. Budagavi, and R. Talluri, "Proposed extensions to DMIF for supporting unequal error protection of MPEG-4 video over H.324 mobile networks," in *ISO/IEC JTC 1/SC 29/WG 11, Doc. M4135, MPEG Atlantic City Meeting*, October 1998.

[22] S. T. Worrall, S. N. Fabri, A. H. Sadka, and A. M. Kondoz, "Prioritisation of data partitioned MPEG-4 video over mobile networks," *European Transactions on Telecommunications*, vol. 12, no. 3, pp. 169–174, 2001.

[23] B. Barmada, M. M. Ghandi, E. V. Jones, and M. Ghanbari, "Prioritized transmission of data partitioned H.264 video with hierarchical QAM," *IEEE Signal Processing Letters*, vol. 12, no. 8, pp. 577–580, 2005.

[24] G. H. Yang, D. Shen, and V. O. K. Li, "UEP for video transmission in space-time coded OFDM systems," in *Proceedings of the 23rd Annual Joint Conference of the IEEE Computer and Communications Societies (IEEE INFOCOM '04)*, pp. 1200–1210, March 2004.

[25] A. Albanese, J. Blömer, J. Edmonds, M. Luby, and M. Sudan, "Priority encoding transmission," *IEEE Transactions on Information Theory*, vol. 42, no. 6, pp. 1737–1744, 1996.

[26] A. E. Mohr, E. A. Riskin, and R. E. Ladner, "Unequal loss protection: graceful degradation of image quality over packet erasure channels through forward error correction," *IEEE Journal on Selected Areas in Communications*, vol. 18, no. 6, pp. 819–828, 2000.

[27] M. Luby, T. Stockhammer, and M. Watson, "IPTV systems, standards and architectures: part II—application layer FEC In IPTV services," *IEEE Communications Magazine*, vol. 46, no. 5, pp. 94–101, 2008.

[28] ITU-T Rec. Y.1541, "Internet Protocol Aspects—Quality of Service and Network Performance: Network Performance Objectives for IP-Based Services," 2002.

[29] ETSI TS 102 034 v1.3.1, "Transport of MPEG 2 Transport Stream (TS) Based DVB Services over IP Based Networks," DVB Blue Book A086rev5, October 2007.

[30] 3GPP TS26.346, "Multimedia Broadcast/Multicast Service (MBMS): Protocols and Codecs," December 2005.

[31] M. Luby, "LT codes," in *Proceedings of the 34rd Annual IEEE Symposium on Foundations of Computer Science*, pp. 271–280, November 2002.

[32] F. C. D. Tsai, J. Chen, C.-W. Chang, W.-J. Lien, C.-H. Hung, and J.-H. Sum, "The design and implementation of WiMAX module for ns-2 Simulator," in *Proceedings of the Workshop on ns2: The IP Network Simulator (WNS2 '06)*, article no. 5, 2006.

[33] IEEE, "802.16e-2005, IEEE Standard for Local and Metropolitan Area Networks. Part 16: Air Interface for Fixed and Mobile Broadband Wireless Access Systems," 2005.

[34] C. Jiao, L. Schwiebert, and B. Xu, "On modeling the packet error statistics in bursty channels," in *Proceedings of the IEEE Conference on Local Computer Networks*, pp. 534–541, 2002.

[35] Y. J. Liang, J. G. Apostolopoulos, and B. Girod, "Analysis of packet loss for compressed video: effect of burst losses and correlation between error frames," *IEEE Transactions on Circuits and Systems for Video Technology*, vol. 18, no. 7, pp. 861–874, 2008.

[36] D. Marpe, T. Wiegand, and S. Gordon, "H.264/MPEG4-AVC fidelity range extensions: tools, profiles, performance, and application areas," in *Proceedings of the IEEE International Conference on Image Processing (ICIP '05)*, vol. 1, pp. 593–596, September 2005.

[37] H. Bing, *3D and HD Broadband Video Streaming*, Artech House, Boston, Mass, USA, 2010.

[38] R. M. Schreier and A. Rothermel, "Motion adaptive intra refresh for low-delay video coding," in *Proceedings of the International Conference on Consumer Electronics (ICCE '06)*, pp. 453–454, January 2006.

[39] V. Varsa, M. Hannuksela, and Y. K. Wang, "Non-normative error concealment algorithms," in *Proceedings of the 14th Meeting of ITU-T Video Coding Experts Group*, 2001, doc.VCEG-N62.

[40] S. Wenger and T. Stockhammer, "H.26L over IP and H.324 framework," in *Proceedings of the 14th Meeting of ITU-T Video Coding Experts Group*, Santa Barbara, Calif, USA, 2001, doc. VCEG-N52.

[41] J. C. Ye and Y. Chen, "Flexible data partitioning mode for streaming video," in *Proceedings of the 4th Meeting of Joint Video Team (JVT '02)*, July 2002, doc. JVT-D136.

[42] T. Stockhammer, "Independent data partitions A and B," in *Proceedings of the 3rd Meeting of Joint Video Team (JVT '02)*, May 2002, doc. VT-C132.

[43] G. Sullivan, "Seven steps toward a more robust codec design," in *Proceedings of the 3rd Meeting of Joint Video Team (JVT '02)*, May 2002, doc. JVT-C117.

[44] S. Nazir, D. Vukobratovic, and V. Stankovic, "Expanding window random linear codes for data partitioned H.264 video transmission over DVB-H network," in *Proceedings of the IEEE International Conference on Image Processing*, pp. 2205–2208, 2011.

[45] G. Côté and F. Kossentini, "Optimal intra coding of blocks for robust video communication over the Internet," *Signal Processing: Image Communication*, vol. 15, no. 1, pp. 25–34, 1999.

[46] M. Luby, T. Gasiba, T. Stockhammer, and M. Watson, "Reliable multimedia download delivery in cellular broadcast networks," *IEEE Transactions on Broadcasting*, vol. 53, no. 1, pp. 235–246, 2007.

[47] R. Palanki and J. S. Yedidia, "Rateless codes on noisy channels," in *Proceedings of theIEEE International Symposium on Information Theory*, p. 37, July 2004.

[48] J. T. Chien, G. L. Li, and M. J. Chen, "Effective error concealment algorithm of whole frame loss for H.264 video coding standard by recursive motion vector refinement," *IEEE Transactions on Consumer Electronics*, vol. 56, no. 3, pp. 1689–1695, 2010.

[49] S. K. Bandyopadhyay, Z. Wu, P. Pandit, and J. M. Boyce, "An error concealment scheme for entire frame losses for H.264/AVC," in *Proceedings of the IEEE Sarnoff Symposium*, pp. 1–4, March 2006.

# 4

# Multiple Feature Fusion Based on Co-Training Approach and Time Regularization for Place Classification in Wearable Video

**Vladislavs Dovgalecs, Rémi Mégret, and Yannick Berthoumieu**

*IMS Laboratory, University of Bordeaux, UMR5218 CNRS, Bâtiment A4, 351 cours de la Libération, 33405 Talence, France*

Correspondence should be addressed to Vladislavs Dovgalecs; vladislavs.dovgalecs@gmail.com

Academic Editor: Anastasios Doulamis

The analysis of video acquired with a wearable camera is a challenge that multimedia community is facing with the proliferation of such sensors in various applications. In this paper, we focus on the problem of automatic visual place recognition in a weakly constrained environment, targeting the indexing of video streams by topological place recognition. We propose to combine several machine learning approaches in a time regularized framework for image-based place recognition indoors. The framework combines the power of multiple visual cues and integrates the temporal continuity information of video. We extend it with computationally efficient semisupervised method leveraging unlabeled video sequences for an improved indexing performance. The proposed approach was applied on challenging video corpora. Experiments on a public and a real-world video sequence databases show the gain brought by the different stages of the method.

## 1. Introduction

Due to the recent achievements in the miniaturization of cameras and their embedding in smart devices, a number of video sequences captured using such wearable cameras increased substantially. This opens new application fields and renews the problematics posed to the Multimedia research community earlier. For instance, visual lifelogs can record daily activities of a person and constitute a rich source of information for the task of monitoring persons in their daily life [1–4]. Recordings captured using wearable camera depict a view that is inside-out, close to the subjective view of the camera wearer. It is a unique source of information, with applications such as a memory refresh aid or as an additional source of information for the analysis of various activities and behavior related events in healthcare context. This often comes at the price of contents with very high variability, rapid camera displacement, and poorly constrained environments in which the person moves. Search for specific events in such multimedia streams is therefore particularly challenging. As was shown in [5, 6], multiple aspects of the video content and its context can be taken into account to provide a complete view of activity related events: location, presence of objects

or persons, hand movements, and external information such as Global Positioning System (GPS), Radio Frequency Identification (RFID), or motion sensor data. Amongst these, location is an important contextual information, that restricts the possible number of ongoing activities. Obtaining this information directly from the video stream is an interesting application in multimedia processing since no additional equipment such as GPS or RFID is needed. In some applications, this may be even be a constraint, since the access to such modalities is limited in practice by the available devices and the installation of any invasive equipment in the environment (such as home) may not be welcome.

Considering the high cost of labeling data for training when dealing with lifelogs, and therefore the low amount of such labeling, inferring place recognition information from such content is a particularly great challenge. For instance, in the framework presented in [7], video lifelog recordings are made in an unknown environment and ground truth location information is limited to small parts of the recording. In such setup, the information sources are short manual annotations and large unlabeled recording parts. The use of unlabeled data to improve recognition performance was up to now reserved to more generic problems and was not evaluated in within the context of wearable video indexing. Efficient usage of this information for place recognition in wearable video indexing therefore defines the problem of the present work.

In this paper, we propose a novel strategy to incorporate and take advantage of the unlabeled data for place recognition. It takes into account both unlabeled data, multiple features and time information. We present a complete processing pipeline from low-level visual data extraction up to the visual recognition. The principal contribution of this work constitutes a novel system for robust place recognition in weakly annotated videos. We propose a combination of the Co-Training algorithm with classifier fusion to obtain a single classification estimate that exploits both multiple features and unlabeled data. In this context, we also study a range of confidence computation techniques found in the literature and introduce our own confidence measure that is designed to reduce the impact of uncertain classification results. The proposed system is designed as such that each component is evaluated separately and its presence is justified. It will be shown that each component yields an increase in classification performance, both separately as well as in a combined configuration, as demonstrated on public and our challenging in-house datasets.

The system we propose in this paper is motivated by the need to develop a robust image-based place recognition system as a part of high-level activity analysis system developed within the IMMED project [7]. As a part of this project, a wearable video recording prototype (see Figure 1) video annotation software and activity recognition algorithms were developed as well but will be left out of the scope. More detail on the latter can be found in [7, 8].

The paper is organized as follows. In Section 2, we review related work from the literature with respect to visual recognition, multiple feature fusion, and semisupervised learning. In Section 3, we present the proposed approach and algorithms. In Section 4, we report the experimental evaluations done on two databases in real life conditions and show the respective gains from the use of (a) multiple features, (b) unsupervised data, and (c) temporal information within our combined framework.

## 2. Literature Review

### 2.1. Activity Monitoring Context

*2.1.1. Motivation.* With this subsection we aim to put our work in the context of activity detection and recognition in video. Several setups have been used for that matter: ambient and wearable sensors.

*2.1.2. Monitoring Using Ambient Sensors.* Activity recognition systems have emerged quickly due to recent advances in large video recording and in the deployment of high computation power systems. For this application field, most of proposed methods originated from scene classification where static image information is captured and categorized.

Authors in [9] use the SVM classifier to classify local events such as "walking" and "running" in a database consisting of very clean and unoccluded video sequences. Perhaps

FIGURE 1: Wearable camera recording prototype used in the IMMED project.

in a more challenging setup, human behavior recognition is performed in [10] by proposing specially crafted sparse spatiotemporal features adapted for temporal visual data description. Conceptually a similar approach is proposed in [11] where each event in a soccer game is modeled as a temporal sequence of Bag of Visual Words (BOVWs) features used in a SVM classifier, termed strings, which are then compared using the string kernel.

Detection and recognition of events in real-world industrial workflows is a challenging problem because of great intraclass variability (complex classifiers required), unknown event start/end moments, and requirement to remember the whole event history which violates Markovian assumptions of conditional independence (e.g., HMM-based algorithms). The problem is alleviated in [12], where authors propose an online worker behavior classification system that integrates particle filter and HMM.

*2.1.3. Monitoring Using Wearable Sensors.* Alternatively, activity information can be also obtained from simple on-body sensors (e.g., acceleration) and wearable video.

Authors in [13] investigated two methods for activity context awareness in weakly annotated videos using 3D accelerometer data. The first one is based on multi-instance learning by grouping sensor data into bags of activities (instead of labeling every frame). The second one uses a graph structure for feature and time similarity representation and label information transfer in those structures. Results favor label propagation based methods in multiple feature graphs.

Visual lifelog indexing by human actions [2, 3, 14, 15] is proposed recently in healthcare with expansion of the Alzheimer disease. Early attempts to answer the challenge was done in [1, 4] as a part of the SenseCam and IMMED projects proposing lightweight devices and event segmentation algorithms. A motion-based temporal video segmentation algorithm with HMM at the core [8] identified strong correlation between activities and localization. This study reveals the complexity of the issue which consists in learning a generative model from few training data, extension to larger scale, and in difficulty to recognize short and infrequent activities. These and related issues were addressed in [16] with Hierarchical HMM which simultaneously fusing complementary low-level and midlevel (visual, motion, location, sound, and speech) features and the contribution of an automatic audio-visual stream segmentation algorithm. Results validate the choice of two-level modeling of activities using Hierarchical HMM and reveal improvement in recognition performance when working with temporal segments. Optimal feature fusion strategies using the Hierarchical HMM are studied in [17]. The contributed intermediate level fusion at the observation level, where all features are treated separately, compares positively to more classic early and late fusion approaches.

This work is a part of an effort to detect and recognize person's activities from wearable videos in the context of health-care within the IMMED (http://immed.labri.fr/) project [7] and continued within the Dem@Care (http://www.demcare .eu/) project. Localization information is one of multiple possible cues to detect and recognize activities solely from the egocentric point of view of the recording camera. Amongst these location estimation is an important cue, which we now discuss in more detail.

### 2.2. Visual Location Recognition

*2.2.1. Motivation.* Classifying the current location using visual content only is a challenging problem. It relates to several problematics that have been already addressed in various contexts such as image retrieval from large databases, semantic video retrieval, image-based place recognition in robotics, and scene categorization. A survey [18] on image and video retrieval methods covers the paradigms such as semantic video retrieval, interactive retrieval, relevance feed-back strategies, and intelligent summary creation. Another comprehensive and systematic study in [19] that evaluates multimodal models using visual and audio information for video classification reveals the importance of global and local features and the role of various fusion methods such as ensembles, context fusion, and joint boosting. We will hereafter focus on location recognition and classification.

To deal with location recognition from image content only, we can consider two families of approaches: (a) from retrieval point of view where a place is recognized as similar to an existing labeled reference from which we can infer the estimated location; (b) from a classification point of view where the place corresponds to a class that can be discriminated from other classes.

*2.2.2. Image Retrieval for Place Recognition.* Image retrieval systems work by a principle that visual content presented in a query image is visually similar or related to a portion of images to be retrieved from database.

Pairwise image matching is a relatively simple and attrac-tive approach. It implies query image comparison to all annotated images in the database. Top ranked images are selected as candidates and after some optional validation procedures the retrieved images are presented as a result to the query. In [20] SIFT feature matching followed by voting and further improvement with spatial information is

performed to localize indoors with 18 locations with each of them presented with 4 views. The voting scheme determines locations whose keypoints were most frequently classified as the nearest neighbors. Additionally, spatial information is modeled using HMM bringing in neighbor location relationships. A study [21] for place recognition in lifelogs images found that the best matching technique is to use bi-directional matching which nevertheless adds computational complexity. This problem is resolved by using robust and rapid to extract SURF features which are then hierarchically clustered using the $k$-means algorithm in a vocabulary tree. The vocabulary tree allows the rapid descriptor comparison of query image descriptors to those of the database and where the tree leaf note descriptor votes for the database image.

The success of matching for place recognition depends greatly on the database which should contain a large amount of annotated images. In many applications, this is a rather strong assumption about the environment. In the absence of prior knowledge brought by completely annotated image database covering the environment, topological place recog-nition discretizes otherwise continuous space. A typical approach following this idea is presented in [22]. Authors propose the gradient orientation histograms of the edge map as image feature with a property that visually similar scenes are described by a similar histogram. The Learning Vector Quantization method is then used to retain only the most characteristic descriptors for each topological location. An unsupervised approach for robot place recognition indoors is adapted in [23]. The method partitions the space into convex subspaces representing room concepts by using approximated graph-cut algorithm with the possibility for user to inject can group and cannot group constraints. The adapted similarity measure relies on the 8-point algorithm constrained to planar camera motion and followed by robust RANSAC to remove false matches. Besides high computation cost, the results show good clustering capabilities if graph nodes representing individual locations are well selected and the graph is properly built. Authors recognize that at larger scale and more similarly looking locations, more false matching images may appear.

*2.2.3. Image Classification for Place Recognition.* Training visual appearance model and using it to classify unseen images constitutes another family of approaches. Image information is usually encoded using global or local patch features.

In [24] an image is modeled as a collection of patches, each of which is assigned a codeword using a prebuilt codebook, yielding a bag of codewords. The generic Bag of Word [25] approach has been quite successful as global features. One of its main advantages is the ability to represent possibly very complex visual contents and address scene clutter problem. It is flexible enough to accommodate both discrete features [25] and dense features [26], while letting the possibility to include also weak spatial information by spatial binning as in [27]. Authors in [6] argue that indoor scenes recognition require location-specific global features and propose a system recognizing locations by objects that are present in them. An interesting result suggests that the final recognition performance can be boosted even further as more object information is used in each image. A context-based system for place and object recognition is presented in [5]. The main idea is to use context (scene gist) as a prior and then use it as a prior infer what objects can be present in a scene. The HMM-based place recognition system requires a considerable amount of training data, possible transition probabilities, and so forth, but integrates naturally temporal information and confidence measure to detect the fact of navigating in unknown locations. Probabilistic Latent Semantic Analysis (pLSA) was used in [28] to discover higher level topics (e.g., grass, forest, water) from low-level visual features and building novel low dimensional representation used afterwards in $k$-Nearest Neighbor classifier. The study shows superior classification performance by passing from low-level visual features to high-level topics that could be loosely attributed to the context of the scene.

*2.2.4. Place Recognition in Video.* Place recognition from recorded videos brings both novel opportunities and information but also poses additional challenges and constraints. Much more image data can be extracted from video while in practice some small portion of it can be labeled manually. An additional information that is often leveraged in the literature is the temporal continuity of the video stream.

Matching-based approach has been used in [29] to retrieve objects in video. Results show that simple matching produces a large number of false positive matches but the usage of stop list to remove most frequent and most specific visual words followed by spatial consistency check significantly improves retrieval result quality. In [30] belief functions in the Bayesian filtering context are used to determine the confidence of a particular location at any time moment. The modeling involves sensor and motion models, which have to be trained offline with sufficiently large annotated database. Indeed, the model has to learn the model of allowed transitions between places, which require the annotated data to represent all possible transitions to be found in the test data.

An important group of methods performing simultaneous place recognition and mapping (SLAM) is widely used in robotics [31, 32]. The main idea in these methods is to simultaneously build and update a map in an unknown environment and track in real time the current position of the camera. In our work, the construction of such map is not necessary and may prove to be very challenging since the environment can be very complex and constantly changing.

### 2.3. Multiple Feature Learning

*2.3.1. Motivation.* Different visual features capture different aspects of a scene and correct choice depends on the task to solve [33]. To this end, even humans perform poorly when using only one information source of perception [34]. Therefore, instead of designing a specific and adapted descriptor for each specific case, several visual descriptors can be combined in a more complex system while yielding increased discrimination power in a wider range of applications. Following the survey [35], two main approaches can be identified for the fusion of multiple features, depending on whether the fusion is done in the feature space (early fusion), or in the decision space (late fusion).

*2.3.2. Early Fusion.* Early fusion strategies focus on the combination of input features before using them in a classifier. In the case of kernel classifiers, the features can be seen as defining a new kernel that takes into account several features at once. This can be done by concatenating the features into a new larger feature vector. A more general approach, Multiple Kernel Learning (MKL), also tries to estimate the optimal parameters for kernel combination in addition to the classifier model. In our work we evaluated the SimpleMKL [36] algorithm as a representative algorithm of the MKL family. The algorithm is based on gradient descent and learns a weighted linear combination of kernels. This approach has notably been applied in the context of object detection and classification [37–39] and image classification [40, 41].

*2.3.3. Late Fusion.* In the late fusion, strategy several base classifiers are trained independently and their outputs are fed to a special decision layer. This fusion strategy is commonly referred to as a stacking method and is discussed in depth in the multiple classifiers systems literature [42–46]. This type of fusion allows to use multiple visual features, leaving their exploitation to an algorithm which performs automatic feature selection or weighting respective to the utility of each feature.

It is clear that nothing prevents using an SVM as base classifier. Following the work of [47], it was shown that SVM outputs, in the form of decision values, can be combined the linearly using Discriminative Accumulation Scheme (DAS) [48] for confidence-based place recognition indoors. The following work evolved by relaxing the constraint of linearity of combination using a kernel function on the outputs of individual single feature outputs giving rise to Generalized DAS [49]. Results show a clear gain of performance increase when using different visual features or completely different modalities. Other works follow a similar reasoning but use different combination rules (max, product, etc.), as discussed in [50]. A comprehensive comparison of different fusion methods in the context of object classification is given in [51].

### 2.4. Learning with Unlabeled Data

*2.4.1. Motivation.* Standard supervised learning, with single or multiple features, is successful if enough labeled training samples are presented to the learning algorithm. In many practical applications, the amount of training data is limited while a wealth of unlabeled data is often available and is largely unused. It is well known that the classifiers learned using only training data may suffer from overfitting or incapability to generalize on the unlabeled data. In contrast, unsupervised methods do not use label information. They may detect a structure of the data; however, a prior knowledge and correct assumptions about the data is necessary to be able to characterize a structure that is relevant for the task.

Semisupervised learning addresses this issue by leveraging labeled as well as unlabeled data [52, 53].

*2.4.2. Graph-Based Learning.* Given a labeled set $L = \{(\mathbf{x}_i, y_i)\}_{i=1}^{l}$ and an unlabeled set $U = \{\mathbf{x}_j\}_{j=l+1}^{l+u}$, where $\mathbf{x} \in \mathcal{X}$ and $y \in \{-1, +1\}$, the goal is to estimate class labels for the latter. The usual hypothesis is that the two sets are sampled i.i.d. according to the same joint distribution $p(\mathbf{x}, y)$. There is no intention to provide estimations on the data outside the sets $L$ and $U$. Deeper discussion on this issue can be found in [54] and in references therein.

In graph-based learning, a graph composed of labeled or unlabeled nodes (in our case representing the images) and interconnected by edges encoding the similarities is built. Application specific knowledge is used to construct such graph in such a way that the labels of nodes connected with a high weight link are similar and that no or a few weak links are present between nodes of different classes. This graph therefore encodes information on the smoothness of a learned function $f$ on the graph, which corresponds to a measure of compatibility with the graph connectivity. The use of the graph Laplacian [55, 56] can then be used directly as a connectivity information to propagate information from labeled nodes to unlabeled nodes [57], or as a regularization term that penalizes nonsmooth labelings within a classifier such as the Lap-SVM [58, 59].

From a practical point of view, the algorithm requires the construction of the full affinity matrix $W$ where all image pairs in the sequences are compared and the computation of the associated Laplacian matrix $L$, which requires large amounts of memory in $O(n^2)$. While theoretically attractive, the direct method scales poorly with the size of the graph nodes which seriously restricts its usage on a wide range of practical applications working.

*2.4.3. Co-Training from Multiple Features.* The Co-Training [60] is a wrapper algorithm that learns two discriminant classifiers in a joint manner. The method trains iteratively two classifiers such that in each iteration the highest confidence estimates on unlabeled data are fed into the training set of another classifier. Classically two views on the data or two single feature splits of a dataset are used. The main idea is that the solution or hypothesis space is significantly reduced if both trained classifiers agree on the data and reduce the risk of overfitting since each classifier also fits the initial labeled training set. More theoretical background and analysis of the method is given in Section 3.3.2.

The algorithm of Co-Training was proposed in [60] as a solution to classify Web pages using both link and word information. The same method was applied to the problem of Web image annotation in [61, 62] and automatic video annotation in [63]. Generalization capacity of Co-Training on different initial labeled training sets was studied in [64]. More analysis on theoretical properties of Co-Training method can be found in [65] such as rough estimates of maximal number of iterations. A review on different variants of the Co-Training algorithm is given [66] together with their comparative analysis.

*2.4.4. Link between Graph and Co-Training Approaches.* It is interesting to note the link [67, 68] between Co-Training

method and label propagation in a graph since adding the most confident estimations in each Co-Training iteration can be seen as label propagation from labeled nodes to unlabeled nodes in a graph. This view of the method is further discussed and practically evaluated in [69] as a label propagation method on a combined graph built from two individual views.

Graph-based methods are limited by the fact that graph edges encode low-level similarities that are computed directly from the input features. The Co-Training algorithm uses a discriminative model that can be adaptive to the data with each iteration and therefore achieve better generalization on unseen unlabeled data. In the next section, we will build a framework based on the Co-Training algorithm to propose our solution for image-based place recognition.

In this work we attempt to leverage all available information from image data that could help to provide cues on camera place recognition. Manual annotation of recorded video sequences requires a lot of human labor. The aim of this work is to evaluate the utility of unlabeled data within the Co-Training framework for image-based place recognition.

## 3. Proposed Approach

In this section we present the architecture of the proposed method which is based on the Co-Training algorithm and then discuss each component of the system. The standard Co-Training algorithm (see Figure 2) allows to benefit from the information in the unlabeled part of the corpus by using a feedback loop to augment the training set, thus producing augmented performance classifiers. In the standard algorithm formulation, the two classifiers are still separate, which does not leverage their complementarity to its maximum. The proposed method addresses this issue by providing a single output using late classifier fusion and time filtering for temporal constrain enforcement.

We will present the different elements of the system in the order of increasing abstraction. Single feature extraction, preparation, and classification using SVM will be presented in Section 3.1. Multiple feature late fusion and a proposed extension to take into account the time information will be introduced in Section 3.2. The complete algorithm combining those elements with the Co-Training algorithm will be developed in Section 3.3.

*3.1. Single Feature Recognition Module.* Each image is represented by a global signature vector. In the following sections, the visual features $\mathbf{x}_i^{(j)} \in \mathcal{X}^{(j)}$ correspond to numerical representations of the visual content of the images where the superscript $(j)$ denotes the type of visual features.

*3.1.1. SVM Classifier.* In our work we rely on Support Vector Machine (SVM) classifiers to carry out decision operations. It aims at finding the best class separation instead of modeling potentially complex within class probability densities as in generative models such as Naive Bayes [70]. The maximal margin separating hyperplane is motivated from the

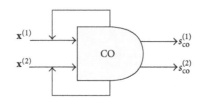

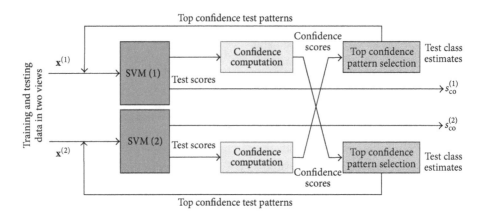

FIGURE 2: Workflow of the Co-Training algorithm.

statistical learning theory viewpoint by linking the margin width to classifier's generalization capability.

Given a labeled set $L = \{(\mathbf{x}_i, y_i)\}_{i=1}^{l}$, where $\mathbf{x} \in \mathbb{R}^d$, $y \in \{-1, +1\}$, a linear maximal margin classifier $f(\mathbf{x}) = \mathbf{w}^T\mathbf{x} + b$ can be found by solving

$$\min_{\mathbf{w},b,\xi} \sum_{i=1}^{l} \xi_i + \lambda \|\mathbf{w}\|^2 \tag{1}$$

$$\text{s.t. } y_i\left(\mathbf{w}^T\mathbf{x}_i + b\right) \geq 1 - \xi_i, \quad \xi_i \geq 0, \forall i, i = 1, \ldots, l$$

for hyperplane $\mathbf{w} \in \mathbb{R}^d$ and its offset $b \in \mathbb{R}$. In regularization framework, the loss function called Hinge loss is

$$\ell\left(\mathbf{x}, y, f\left(\mathbf{x}\right)\right) = \max\left(1 - y_i f\left(\mathbf{x}_i\right), 0\right), \quad \forall i, i = 1, \ldots, l \tag{2}$$

and the regularizer

$$\Omega_{\text{SVM}}\left(f\right) = \|\mathbf{w}\|^2. \tag{3}$$

As it will be seen from discussion, the regularizer plays an important role in the design of learning methods. In the case of an SVM classifiers, the regularizer in (3) reflects the objective to be maximized—maximum margin separation on the training data.

*3.1.2. Processing of Nonlinear Kernels.* The power of the SVM classifier owes its easy extension to the nonlinear case [71]. Highly nonlinear nature of data can be taken into account seamlessly by using kernel trick such that the hyperplane is found in a feature space induced by an adapted kernel function $k(\mathbf{x}_i, \mathbf{x}_j) = \langle \Phi(\mathbf{x}_i), \Phi(\mathbf{x}_j) \rangle$ in Reproducing Kernel Hilbert Space (RKHS). The implicit mapping $\mathbf{x} \mapsto \Phi(\mathbf{x})$ means that we can no longer find an explicit hyperplane $\{\mathbf{w}, b\}$

since the mapping function is not known and may be of very large dimensionality. Fortunately, the decision function can be formulated in so-called dual representation [71] and then the solution minimizing regularized risk according to the Representer theorem is

$$f_k\left(\mathbf{x}\right) = \sum_{i=1}^{l} \alpha_i y_i k\left(\mathbf{x}_i, \mathbf{x}\right) + b, \quad k = 1, \ldots, c, \tag{4}$$

where $l$ is the number of labeled samples.

Bag of Words descriptors have been used intensively for efficient and discriminant image description. The linear kernel does not provide the best results with such representations, which has been more successful with kernels such as the Hellinger kernel, $\chi^2$-kernel, or the intersection kernel [6, 27, 33]. Unfortunately, training with such kernels using the standard SVM tools is much less computationally efficient than using the linear inner product kernel, for which efficient SVM implementations exist [72]. In this work, we have therefore chosen to adapt the input features to the linear context, using two different techniques. For the BOVW (Bag of Visual Words) [25] and SPH (Spatial Pyramid Histogram) [27] features, a Hellinger kernel was used. This kernel admits an explicit mapping function, using a square root transformation $\phi([x_1 \cdots x_d]^T) = [\sqrt{x_1} \cdots \sqrt{x_d}]^T$. In this particular case, a linear embedding $\mathbf{x}' = \phi(\mathbf{x})$ can be computed explicity and will have the same dimensionality as input feature. For the CRFH (Composed Receptive Field Histogram) features [26], the feature vector has very large number of dimensions, but is also extremely sparse, with between 500 and 4000 nonzeros coefficients from many millions of features in total. These features could be transformed into a linear embedding using Kernel Principal Component Analysis [73], in order to reduce it to a 500-dimension linear embedding vector.

In the following, we will therefore consider that features are all processed into a linear embedding $\mathbf{x}_i$ that is suitable for efficient linear SVM. Utility of this processing will be evident in the context of the Co-Training algorithm, which requires multiple retraining and prediction operations of two visual feature classifiers. Other forms of efficient embedding, proposed in [38], could be also used to reduce learning time. This preprocessing is done only once, right after feature extraction from image data. In order to simplify the explanations, we will slightly abuse notation by denoting directly by $\mathbf{x}_i$ the linearized descriptors without further indication in the rest of this document.

### 3.1.3. Multiclass Classification.
Visual place recognition is a truly multiclass classification problem. The extension of the binary SVM classifier to $c > 2$ classes is considered in a one-versus-all setup. Therefore $c$ independent classifiers are trained on the labeled data, each of which learns the separation between one class and the other classes. We will denote by $f_k$ the decision function associated to class $k \in [| 1, \ldots c |]$. The outcome of the classifier bank for a sample $\mathbf{x}$ can be represented as a scores vector $\mathbf{s}(\mathbf{x})$ by concatenating individual decision scores:

$$\mathbf{s}(\mathbf{x}) = \left( f_1(\mathbf{x}), \ldots, f_c(\mathbf{x}) \right). \tag{5}$$

In that case, the estimated class of a testing sample $\mathbf{x}_i$ is estimated from the largest positive score:

$$\widehat{y}_i = \arg \max_{k=1,\ldots,c} f_k(\mathbf{x}_i). \tag{6}$$

### 3.2. Multiple Feature Fusion Module and Its Extension to Time Information.
In this work, we follow a late classifier fusion paradigm with several classifiers being trained independently on different visual cues and fusing the outputs for a single final decision. We motivate this choice compared to early fusion paradigm as it will allow easier integration at the decision level of augmented classifiers obtained by the Co-Training algorithm, as well as providing a natural extension to inject temporal continuity information of video.

### 3.2.1. Objective Statement.
We denote the training set by $L = \{(\mathbf{x}_i, y_i)\}_{i=1}^{l}$ and the unlabeled set of patterns by $U = \{\mathbf{x}_j\}_{j=l+1}^{l+u}$ where $\mathbf{x} \in \mathcal{X}$ and the outcome of classification is a binary output: $y \in \{-1, +1\}$.

The visual data may have $p$ multiple cues describing the same image $I_i$. Suppose that $p$ cues has been extracted from an image $I_i$:

$$\mathbf{x}_i \longrightarrow \left( \mathbf{x}_i^{(1)}, \mathbf{x}_i^{(2)}, \ldots, \mathbf{x}_i^{(p)} \right), \tag{7}$$

where each cue $\mathbf{x}_i^{(j)}$ belongs to an associated descriptor space $\mathcal{X}^{(j)}$.

Denote also by $p$ the decision functions $f^{(1)}, f^{(2)}, \ldots, f^{(p)}$, where $f^{(j)} \in \mathcal{F}^{(j)}$ are trained on the respective visual cues and are providing estimation $\widehat{y}_k^{(j)}$ on the pattern $\mathbf{x}_k^{(j)}$.

Then for a visual cue $t$ and $c$ class classification in one-versus-all setup, a score vector can be constructed:

$$\mathbf{s}^t = \left( f_1^t(\mathbf{x}), \ldots, f_c^t(\mathbf{x}) \right). \tag{8}$$

In our work we adopt two late fusion techniques: Discriminant Accumulation Scheme (DAS) [47, 48] and SVM-DAS [49, 74].

### 3.2.2. Discriminant Accumulation Scheme (DAS).
The idea of DAS is to combine linearly the scores returned by the same class decision function across multiple visual cues $t = 1, \ldots, p$. The novel combined decision function for a class $j$ is then a linear combination:

$$f_j^{\mathrm{DAS}}(\mathbf{x}) = \sum_{t=1}^{p} \beta_t f_j^t(\mathbf{x}), \tag{9}$$

where the weight $\beta$ is attributed to each cue according to its importance in the learning phase. The novel scores can then be used in decision process, for example, using max score criterion.

The DAS scheme is an example of parallel classifier combination architectures [44] and implies a competition between the individual classifiers. The weights $\beta_t$ can be found using a cross-validation procedure with the normalization constraint:

$$\sum_{t=1}^{p} \beta_t = 1. \tag{10}$$

### 3.2.3. SVM Discriminant Accumulation Scheme.
The SVM-DAS can be seen as a generalization of the DAS by building a stacked architecture of multiple classifiers [44] where individual classifier outputs are fed into a final classifier that provides a single decision. In this approach every classifier is trained on its own visual cue $t$ and produces a score vector as in (8). Then the single feature score vectors $\mathbf{s}_i^t$ corresponding to one particular pattern $\mathbf{x}_i$ are concatenated into a novel multifeatures scores vector $\mathbf{z}_i = [\mathbf{s}_i^1, \ldots, \mathbf{s}_i^p]$. A final top-level classifier can be trained on those novel features:

$$f_j^{\mathrm{SVMDAS}}(\mathbf{z}) = \sum_{i=1}^{l} \alpha_{ij} y_i k(\mathbf{z}, \mathbf{z}_i) + b_j. \tag{11}$$

Notice that the use of kernel function enables a richer class of classifiers modeling possibly nonlinear relations between base classifier outputs. If a linear kernel function is used,

$$k_{\mathrm{SVMDAS}}(\mathbf{z}_i, \mathbf{z}_j) = \langle \mathbf{z}_i, \mathbf{z}_j \rangle = \sum_{t=1}^{p} \langle \mathbf{s}_i^t, \mathbf{s}_j^t \rangle, \tag{12}$$

then the decision function in (11) can be rewritten by exchanging sums:

$$\begin{aligned}
f_j^{\mathrm{SVMDAS}}(\mathbf{z}) &= \sum_{i=1}^{l} \alpha_{ij} y_i k(\mathbf{z}, \mathbf{z}_i) + b_j \\
&= \sum_{i=1}^{l} \langle \mathbf{s}_i^t, \mathbf{s}_j^t \rangle \sum_{t=1}^{p} \alpha_{ij} y_i + b_j.
\end{aligned} \tag{13}$$

Denoting $\mathbf{w}_j^t = \sum_{i=1}^l \alpha_{ij} y_i \mathbf{s}^t$, we can rewrite the decision function using input patterns and the learned weights:

$$f_j^{\text{SVMDAS}}(\mathbf{z}) = \sum_{t=1}^p \sum_{k=1}^l \mathbf{w}_{jk}^t f_j^t(\mathbf{x}). \qquad (14)$$

The novel representation reveals that using a linear kernel in the SVMDAS framework renders a classifier with weights being learned for every possible linear combination of base classifiers. The DAS can be seen as a special case in this context but with significantly less parameters. Usage of a kernel such as RBF or polynomial kernels can result in even richer class of classifiers.

The disadvantage of such configuration is that a final stage classifier needs to be trained as well and its parameters tuned.

*3.2.4. Extension to Temporal Accumulation (TA).* Video content has a temporal nature such that the visual content does not usually change much in a short period of time. In the case of topological place recognition indoors, this constraint may be useful as place recognition changes are encountered relatively rarely with respect to the frame rate of the video.

We propose to modify the classifier output such that rapid class changes are discouraged in a relatively short period of time. This leads to lower the proliferation of occasional temporally localized misclassifications.

Let $s_i^t = f^{(t)}(\mathbf{x}_i)$ be the scores of a binary classifier for visual cue $t$ and $h$ a temporal window of size $2\tau + 1$. Then temporal accumulation can be written as

$$s_{i,\text{TA}}^t = \sum_{k=-\tau}^\tau h(k)\, s_{i+k}^t \qquad (15)$$

and can be easily generalized to multiple feature classification by applying it separately to the output of the classifiers associated to each feature $s^t$, where $t = 1, \ldots, p$ is the visual feature type. We use an averaging filter of size $\tau$, defined as

$$h(k) = \frac{1}{2\tau + 1}, \quad k = -\tau, \ldots, \tau. \qquad (16)$$

Therefore, input of the TA are the SVM scores obtained after classification and output are again the processed SVM scores with temporal constraint enforced.

*3.3. Co-Training with Time Information and Late Fusion.* We have already presented how to perform multiple feature fusion within the late fusion paradigm, and how it can be extended to take into account the temporal continuity information of video. In this section, we will explain how to additionally learn from labeled training data and unlabeled data.

*3.3.1. The Co-Training Algorithm.* The standard Co-Training [60] is an algorithm that iteratively trains two classifiers on two view data $\mathbf{x}_i = (\mathbf{x}_i^{(1)}, \mathbf{x}_i^{(2)})$ by feeding the highest confidence score $z_i$ estimates from the testing set in another view classifier. In this semisupervised approach,

the discriminatory power of each classifier is improved by another classifier's complementary knowledge. The testing set is gradually labeled round by round using only the highest confidence estimates. The pseudocode is presented in Algorithm 1 which could be also extended to multiple views as in [53].

The power of the method lies in its capability of learning from small training sets and grows eventually its discriminative properties on the large unlabeled data set as more confident estimations are added into the training set. The following assumptions are made:

(1) the two distinct visual cues bring complementary information;

(2) the initially labeled set for each individual classifier is sufficient to bootstrap the iterative learning process;

(3) the confident estimations on unlabeled data are helpful to predict the labels of the remaining unlabeled data.

Originally the Co-Training algorithm performs until some stopping criterion is met unless $N$ iterations are exceeded. For instance, a stopping criteria could be a rule that stops the learning process when there are no confident estimations to add or there have been relatively small difference from iteration $t - 1$ to $t$. The parameter-less version of Co-Training works till the complete exhaustion of the pool of unlabeled samples but requires a threshold on confidence measure, which is used to separate high and low confidence estimates. In our work we use this variant of the Co-Training algorithm.

*3.3.2. The Co-Training Algorithm in the Regularization Framework*

*Motivation.* Intuitively, it is clear that after a sufficient number of rounds both classifiers will agree on most of the unlabeled patterns. It remains unclear why and what mechanisms make such learning useful. It can be justified from the learning theory point of view. There are less possible solutions or classifiers from the hypothesis space that agree on unlabeled data in two views. Recall that every classifier individually should fit its training data. In the context of the Co-Training algorithm each classifier should be somehow restricted by another classifier. The two trained classifiers, that are coupled in this system, effectively reduce possible solution space. Each of those two classifier is less likely to be overfitting since each of them has been initially trained on its training while taking into account the training process of another classifier that is carried out in parallel. We follow the discussion from [53] to give more insights about this phenomena.

*Regularized Risk Minimization (RRM) Framework.* Better understanding of the Co-Training algorithm can be gained from the RRM framework. Let's introduce the Hinge loss

INPUT:
    Training set $L = \left\{ (\mathbf{x}_i, y_i) \right\}_{i=1}^{l}$;
    Testing set $U = \left\{ \mathbf{x}_i \right\}_{i=1}^{u}$;
OUTPUT:
    $\widehat{y}_i$—class estimations for the testing set $U$;
    $f^{(1)}, f^{(2)}$—trained classifiers;
PROCEDURE:
    (1) Compute visual features $\mathbf{x}_i = (\mathbf{x}_i^{(1)}, \mathbf{x}_i^{(2)})$ for every image $I_i$ in the dataset
    (2) Initialize $L_1 = \left\{ (\mathbf{x}_i^{(1)}, y_i) \right\}_{i=1}^{l}$ and $L_2 = \left\{ (\mathbf{x}_i^{(2)}, y_i) \right\}_{i=1}^{l}$
    (3) Initialize $U_1 = \left\{ \mathbf{x}_i^{(1)} \right\}_{i=1}^{u}$ and $U_2 = \left\{ \mathbf{x}_i^{(2)} \right\}_{i=1}^{u}$
    (4) Create two work sets $\widetilde{U}_1 := U_1$ and $\widetilde{U}_2 := U_2$
    (5) Repeat until the sets $\widetilde{U}_1$ and $\widetilde{U}_2$ are empty (CO)
        (a) Train classifiers $f^{(1)}, f^{(2)}$ using the sets $L_1, L_2$ respectively;
        (b) Classify the patterns in the sets $\widetilde{U}_1$ and $\widetilde{U}_2$ using the classifiers $f^{(1)}$ and $f^{(2)}$ respectively;
            (i) Compute scores $s_{\text{test}}^{(1)}$ and confidences $z^{(1)}$ on the set $\widetilde{U}_1$
            (ii) Compute scores $s_{\text{test}}^{(2)}$ and confidences $z^{(2)}$ on the set $\widetilde{U}_2$
        (c) Add the $k$ top confidence estimations $\overline{L}_1 \subset \widetilde{U}_1, \overline{L}_2 \subset \widetilde{U}_2$
            (i) $L_1 := L_1 \cup \overline{L}_1$
            (ii) $L_1 := L_1 \cup \overline{L}_1$
        (d) Remove the $k$ top confidence patterns from the working sets
            (i) $\widetilde{U}_1 := \widetilde{U}_1 \setminus \overline{L}_1$
            (ii) $\widetilde{U}_2 := \widetilde{U}_2 \setminus \overline{L}_2$
        (e) Go to step (5).
    (6) Optionally: perform Temporal Accumulation (TA) according to (15)
    (7) Perform classifier output fusion (DAS)
        (a) Compute fused scores $\mathbf{s}_{\text{test}}^{\text{DAS}} = (1 - \beta)\, \mathbf{s}_{\text{test}}^{(1)} + \beta \mathbf{s}_{\text{test}}^{(2)}$;
        (b) Output class estimations $\widehat{y}_i$ from the fused scores $\mathbf{s}_{\text{test}}^{\text{DAS}}$

ALGORITHM 1: The CO-DAS and CO-TA-DAS algorithms.

function $\ell(\mathbf{x}, y, f(\mathbf{x}))$ commonly used in classification. Let's also introduce empirical risk of a candidate function $f \in \mathcal{F}$:

$$\widehat{R}(f) = \frac{1}{l} \sum_{i=1}^{l} \ell\left(\mathbf{x}_i, y_i, f(\mathbf{x}_i)\right) \qquad (17)$$

which measures how well the classifier fits the training data. It is well known that minimizing only training error, the resulting classifier is very likely to overfit. In practice regularized risk (RRM), minimization is performed instead:

$$f^{\text{RRM}} = \arg \min_{f \in \mathcal{F}} \widehat{R}(f) + \lambda \Omega(f), \qquad (18)$$

where $\Omega(f)$ is a nonnegative functional or regularizer that returns a large value or penalty for very complicated functions (typically the functions that fit perfectly to the data). The parameter $\lambda > 0$ controls the balance between a fit to the training data and the complexity of the classifier. By selecting a proper regularization parameter, overfitting can be avoided and better generalization capability on the novel data can be achieved. A good example is the SVM classifier. The corresponding regularizer $\Omega_{\text{SVM}}(f) = (1/2)\|\mathbf{w}\|^2$ selects the function that maximizes the margin.

*The Co-Training in the RRM.* In semisupervised learning we can select a regularizer such that it is sufficiently smooth

on unlabeled data as well. Keeping all previous discussion in mind, indeed a function that fits the training data and is respecting unlabeled data will probably perform better on future data. In the case of the Co-Training algorithm, we are looking for two functions $f^{(1)}, f^{(2)} \in \mathcal{F}$ that minimize the regularized risk and agree on the unlabeled data at the same time. The first restriction on the hypothesis space is that the first function should not only reduce its own regularized risk but also agree with the second function. We can then write a two-view regularized risk minimization problem as

$$\left(\widetilde{f}^{(1)}, \widetilde{f}^{(2)}\right)$$

$$= \arg \min_{f^{(1)}, f^{(2)}} \sum_{t=1}^{2} \left( \frac{1}{l} \sum_{i=1}^{l} \ell\left(\mathbf{x}_i, y_i, f^{(t)}(\mathbf{x}_i)\right) \right.$$

$$\left. + \lambda_1 \Omega_{\text{SVM}}\left(f^{(t)}\right) \right) \qquad (19)$$

$$+ \lambda_2 \sum_{i=1}^{l+u} \ell\left(\mathbf{x}_i, f^{(1)}(\mathbf{x}_i), f^{(2)}(\mathbf{x}_i)\right),$$

where $\lambda_2 > 0$ controls the balance between an agreed fit on the training data and agreement on the test data. The first part of (19) states that each individual classifier should fit the

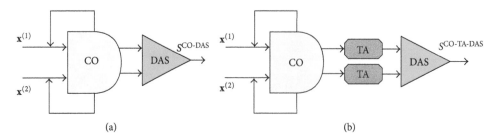

FIGURE 3: Co-Training with late fusion (a); Co-Training with temporal accumulation (b).

given training data but should not overfit, which is prevented with the SVM regularizer $\Omega_{\text{SVM}}(f)$. The second part is a regularizer $\Omega_{\text{CO}}(f^{(1)}, f^{(2)})$ for the Co-Training algorithm, which incurs penalty if the two classifiers do not agree on the unlabeled data. This means that each classifier is constrained both by its standard regularization and is required to agree with another classifier. It is clear that an algorithm implemented in this framework elegantly bootstraps from each classifiers training data, exploits unlabeled data, and works with two visual cues.

It should be noted that the framework could be easily extended to more than two classifiers. In the literature the algorithms following this spirit are implementing multiple view learning. Refer to [53] for the extension of the framework to multiple views.

### 3.3.3. Proposition: CO-DAS and CO-TA-DAS Methods.
The Co-Training algorithm has two drawbacks in the context of our application. The first drawback is that it is not known in advance which of the two classifiers performs the best and if complementarity properties had been leveraged to their maximum. The second drawback is that no time information is used unless the visual features are constructed to capture this information.

In this work we will use the DAS method for late fusion while it is possible to use the more general SVMDAS method as well. Experimental evaluation will show that very competitive performances can be obtained using the former, much more simpler method. We propose the CO-DAS method (see Figure 3(a)), which addresses the first drawback by delivering a single output. In the same framework, we propose the CO-TA-DAS method (see Figure 3(b)), which additionally enforces temporal continuity information. Experimental evaluation will reveal relative performances of each method with respect to baseline and with respect to each other.

The full algorithm of the CO-DAS (or CO-TA-DAS if temporal accumulation is enabled) method is presented in Algorithm 1.

Besides the base classifier parameters, one needs to set the threshold $k$ for the top confidence sample selection, temporal accumulation window width $\tau$, and the late fusion parameter $\beta$. We express the threshold $k$ as a percentage of the testing samples. The impact of this parameter is extensively studied in Sections 4.1.4 and 4.1.5. The selection of the temporal accumulation parameter is discussed in Section 4.1.3. Finally, discussion on the selection of the parameter $\beta$ is given in Section 4.1.2.

### 3.3.4. Confidence Measure.
The Co-Training algorithm relies on confidence measure, which is not provided by an SVM classifier out of the box. In the literature, several methods exist for computing confidence measure from the SVM outputs. We review several methods of confidence computation and contribute a novel confidence measure that attempts to resolve an issue which is common to some of the existing measures.

*Logistic Model (Logistic).* Following [75], class probabilities can be computed using the logistic model that generalizes naturally to multiclass classification problem. Suppose that in one-versus-all setup with $c$ classes, the scores $\{f^k(\mathbf{x})\}_{k=1}^c$ are given. Then probability or classification confidence is computed as

$$P(y = k \mid \mathbf{x}) = \frac{\exp\left(f^k(\mathbf{x})\right)}{\sum_{i=1}^c \exp\left(f^i(\mathbf{x})\right)} \tag{20}$$

which ensures that probability is larger for larger positive score values and sum to 1 over all scores. This property allows to interpret the classifier output as a probability. There are at least two drawbacks with this measure. This measure does not take into account the cases when all classifiers in one-versus-all setup reject the pattern (all negative score values) or accept (all positive scores). Finally, forced score normalization to sum up to one may not transfer all dynamics (e.g., very small or very large score values).

*Modeling Posterior Class Probabilities (Ruping).* In [76] a parameter-less method was proposed which assigns score value:

$$z = \begin{cases} p_+, & f(\mathbf{x}) > 1, \\ \dfrac{1 + f(\mathbf{x})}{2}, & -1 \le f(\mathbf{x}) \le 1, \\ p_-, & f(\mathbf{x}) < 1, \end{cases} \tag{21}$$

where $p_+$ and $p_-$ are the fractions of positive and negative score values, respectively. Authors argue that interesting dynamics relevant to confidence estimation happen in the region of margin and the patterns classified outside the margin have a constant impact. This measure has sound theoretical background in a two-class classification problem but it does not cover multiclass case as required by our application.

*Score Difference (Tommasi).* A method that does not require additional preprocessing for confidence estimation was proposed in [77] and thresholded to obtain a decision corresponding to "no action," "reject," or "do not know" situation for medical image annotation. The idea is to use the contrast between the two top uncalibrated score values. The maximum score estimation should be more confident if other score values are relatively smaller. This leads to a confidence measure using the contrast between the two maximum scores:

$$z = f^{k^*}(\mathbf{x}) - \max_{k=1,\dots,c,k\neq k^*} f^k(\mathbf{x}). \tag{22}$$

This measure has a clear interpretation in a two-class classification problem where larger difference between the two maximal scores hints for better class separability. As it is seen from equation, there is an issue with the measure if all scores are negative.

*Class Overlap Aware Confidence Measure.* We noticed that class overlap and reject situations are not explicitly taken into account in neither of confidence measure computation procedures. The one-versus-all setup for multiple class classification may yield ambiguous decisions. For instance, it is possible to obtain several positive scores or all positive or all negative scores.

We propose a confidence measure that penalizes class overlap (ambiguous decisions) at several degrees and also treats two degenerate cases. By convention, confidence should be higher if a sample is classified with less class overlap (fewer positive score values) and further from the margin (larger positive value of a score). Cases with all positive or negative scores may be considered as degenerate $z_i \leftarrow 0$.

The computation is divided in two steps. First we compute the standard Tommasi confidence measure:

$$z_i^0 = f^{j^*}(\mathbf{x}_i) - \max_{i=1,\dots,c,i\neq j^*} f^i(\mathbf{x}) \tag{23}$$

then the measure $z_i^0$ is modified to account for class overlap

$$z_i = z_i^0 \max\left(0, 1 - \frac{p_i - 1}{C}\right), \tag{24}$$

where $p_i = \text{Card}(\{k = 1,\dots,c \mid f^k(\mathbf{x}_i) > 0\})$ represents the number of classes for which $\mathbf{x}_i$ has positive scores (class overlap). In case of $\forall k, f^k(\mathbf{x}_i) > 0$ or $f^k(\mathbf{x}_i) < 0$, we set $z_i \leftarrow 0$.

Compared to the Tommasi measure, the proposed measure additionally penalizes class overlap which is more severe if the test pattern receives several positive scores. Compared to logistic measure, samples with no positive scores yield zero confidence, which allows to exclude them and not assign doubtful probability values.

Constructing our measure, we assume that a confident estimate is obtained if only one of binary classifiers return a positive score. Following the same logic, confidence is lowered if more than one binary classifiers return a positive score.

## 4. Experimental Evaluation

In this section we evaluate the performance of the methods presented in the previous section on two datasets. Experimental evaluation is organized in two parts: (a) on the public database IDOL2 in Section 4.1 and (2) on our in-house database IMMED in Section 4.2, respectively. The former database is relatively simple and is expected to be annotated automatically with small error rate, whereas the latter database is recorded in a challenging environment and is a subject of study in the IMMED project.

For each database, two experiment setups are created: (a) randomly sampled training images across all corpus and (b) more realistic video-versus-video setup. First experiment allows for the gradual increase of supervision which gives insights of place recognition performance for algorithms under study. The second setup is more realistic and is aimed to validate every place recognition algorithm.

On the IDOL2 database, we extensively assess the place recognition performance for each independent part of the proposed system. For instance, we validate the utility of multiple features, effect of temporal smoothing, unlabeled data, and different confidence measures.

The IMMED database is used for validation purposes on which we evaluate all methods and summarize their performances.

*Datasets.* The IDOL2 database is a publicly available corpus of video sequences designed to assess place recognition systems of mobile robots in indoor environment.

The IMMED database represents a collection of video sequences recorded using a camera positioned on the shoulder of volunteers and capturing their activities during observation sessions in their home environment. These sequences represent visual lifelogs, for which indexing by activities is required. This database presents a real challenge for image-based place recognition algorithms, due to the high variability of the visual content and the unconstrained environment.

The results and discussion related to these two datasets are presented in Sections 4.1 and 4.2, respectively.

*Visual Features.* In this experimental section, we will use three types of visual features that have been used successfully in image recognition tasks: Bag of Visual Words (BOVWs) [25], Composed Receptive Field Histograms (CRFHs) [26], and Spatial Pyramid Histograms (SPHs) [27].

In this work we used 1111 dimensional BOVW histograms which was shown to be sufficient for our application and feasible from the computation point of view. The visual vocabulary was built in a hierarchical manner [25] with 3 levels and 10 sibling nodes to speed up the search of the tree. This allows to introduce visual words ranging from more general (higher level nodes) to more specific (leaf nodes). The effect of overly frequent visual words is addressed with the use of common normalization procedure tf-idf [25] from text classification.

The SPH [27, 78] descriptor harnesses the power of the BOVW descriptor but addresses its weakness when it comes to spatial structure of the image. This is done by

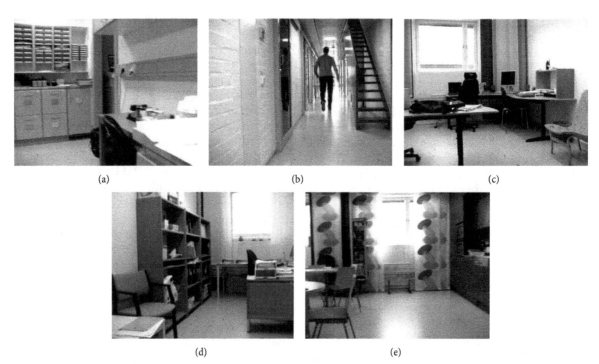

FIGURE 4: IDOL2 dataset sample images: (a) Printer Area, (b) Corridor, (c) Two-Person Office, (d) One-Person Office, and (e) Kitchen.

constructing a pyramid where each level defines coarse to fine sampling grid for histogram extraction. Each grid histogram is obtained by constructing standard BOVW histogram with local features SIFT sampled in a dense manner. The final global descriptor is composed of concatenated individual region and level histograms. We empirically set the number of pyramid levels to 3 with the dictionary size of 200 visual words, which yielded in 4200 dimensional vectors per image. Again, the number of dimensions was fixed such that maximum of visual information is captured while reducing computational burden.

The CRFH [26] descriptor describes a scene globally, by measuring responses returned after some filtering operation on the image. Every dimension of this descriptor effectively counts the number of pixels sharing similar responses returned from each specific filter. Due to multidimensional nature and the size of an image, such descriptor often results in a very high dimensionality vector. In our experimental evaluations, we used second order derivatives filter in three directions, at two scales with 28 bins per histogram. The total size of global descriptor resulted in very sparse up to 400 million dimension vectors. It was reduced to a 500-dimensional linear descriptor vector using KPCA with an $\chi^2$ kernel [73].

*4.1. Results on IDOL2.* The public database KTH-IDOL2 [79] consists of video sequences captured by two different robot platforms. The database is suitable to evaluate the robustness of image-based place recognition algorithms in controlled real-world conditions.

*4.1.1. Description of the Experimental Setup.* The considered database consists of 12 video sequences recorded with the

"minnie" robot (98 cm above ground) using a Canon VC-C4 camera at a frame rate of 5 fps. The effective resolution of the extracted images is 309 × 240 pixels.

All video sequences were recorded in the same premises and depict 5 distinct rooms—"One-Person Office," "Two-Person Office," "Corridor," "Kitchen," and "Printer Area". Sample images depicting these 5 topological locations are shown in Figure 4.

The annotation was performed using two annotation setups: random and video versus video. In both setup three image sets were considered: labeled training, validation set, and an unlabeled set. The unlabeled set is used as the test set for performance evaluation. The performance is evaluated using the accuracy metric, which is defined as the number of correctly classified test images divided by the total number of test images.

*Random Sampling Setup.* In the first setup, the database is divided into three sets by random sampling: training, validation, and testing. The percentage of training data with respect to the full corpus defines the *supervision level*. We consider 8 *supervision levels* ranging from 1% to 50%. The remaining images are split randomly in two halves and used, respectively, for validation and testing purposes. In order to account for the effects of random sampling, 10-fold sampling is made at each supervision level and the final result returned as the average accuracy measure.

It is expected that global place recognition performance raises from mediocre performance at low supervision to its maximum at high supervision level.

*Video-versus-Video Setup.* In the second setup, videos sequences are processed in pairs. The first video is completely annotated while the second is used for evaluation purposes.

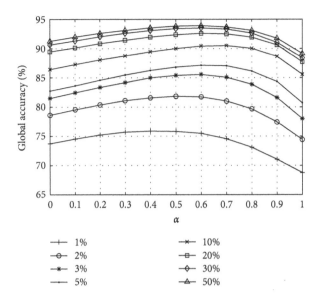

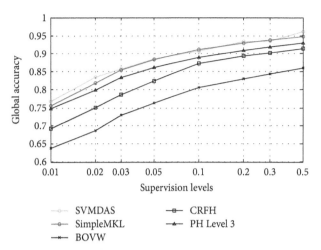

FIGURE 5: Effect of the DAS late fusion approach on the final performance, for various supervision levels. Plot of the accuracy as a function of the parameter $\alpha$ that balances the fusion between SPH features (3 levels) if $\alpha = 0$ and CRFH if $\alpha = 1$ (IDOL2 dataset, random setup).

FIGURE 6: Comparison of single (BOVW, CRFH, and SPH) and multiple feature (SVMDAS, SimpleMKL) approaches for different supervision levels. Plot of the accuracy as a function of the supervision level (IDOL2 dataset, random setup).

The annotated video is split randomly into training and validation sets. With 12 video sequences under consideration, evaluating on all possible pairs amount to $132 = 12 \times 11$ pairs of video sequences. We differentiate three sets of pairs: "EASY," "HARD," and "ALL" result cases. The "EASY" set contains only the video sequence pairs where the light conditions are similar and the recordings were made in a very short span of time. The "HARD" set contains pairs of video sequences with different lighting conditions or video sequences recorded with a large time span. The "ALL" set contains all the 132 video pairs to provide an overall averaged performance.

Compared to random sampling setup, the video-versus-video setup is considered more challenging and thus lower place recognition performances are expected.

### 4.1.2. Utility of Multiple Features.
We study the contribution of multiple features for the task of image-based place recognition on the IDOL2 database. We will present a complete summary of performances for baseline single feature methods compared to early and late fusion methods. These experiments were carried out using the random labeling setup only.

*The DAS Method.* The DAS method leverages two visual feature classifier outputs and provides a weighted score sum in the output on which class decision can be made. In Figure 5, the performance of DAS using SPH Level 3 and CRFH feature embeddings is shown as a function of fusion parameter $\alpha$ at different supervision levels. Interesting dynamics can be noticed for intermediary fusion values that suggest for feature complementarity. The fusion parameter $\alpha$ can be safely set to an intermediary value such as 0.5 and the

final performance would exceed that of every single feature classifier alone at all supervision levels.

*The SVMDAS Method.* In Figure 6, the effect of the supervision level on the performances of classification is shown for single feature and multiple features approaches. It is clear that all methods perform better if more labeled data is supplied, which is an expected behavior. We can notice differences in the performances on the 3 single feature approaches, with SPH providing the best performances. Both SVMDAS (late fusion approach) and SimpleMKL (early fusion approach) operate fusion over the 3 single features considered. They outperform the single feature baseline methods. There is practically no difference between the two fusion methods on this dataset.

*Selection of the Late Fusion Method.* Although not compared directly, the two late fusion methods DAS and SVMDAS deliver very comparable performances. Maximum performance comparison (at best $\alpha$ for each supervision) of the DAS (Figure 5) to those of the SVMDAS (Figure 6) confirms this claim on this particular database. Therefore, the choice of the DAS method for the following usage in the final system is motivated by this result and by simplified fusion parameter selection.

### 4.1.3. Effect of Temporal Smoothing

*Motivation.* Temporal information is an implicit attribute of video content which has not been leveraged up to now in this work. The main idea is that temporally close images should carry the same label.

*Discussion on the Results.* To show the importance of the time information, we present the effect of the temporal accumulation (TA) module on the performance of single feature SVM classification. In Figure 7, the TA window size is varied from no temporal accumulation up to 300 frames. The results

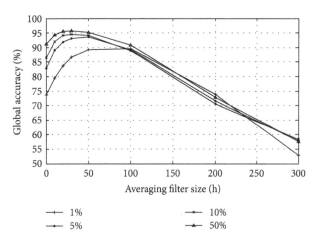

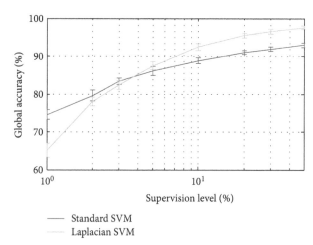

FIGURE 7: Effect of the filter size in temporal accumulation. Plot of the accuracy as a function of the TA filter size. (IDOL2 dataset, SPH Level 3 features).

FIGURE 8: Comparison of standard single feature SVM with semi-supervised Laplacian SVM with RBF kernel on SPH Level 3 visual features (IDOL2 dataset, random setup).

show that temporal accumulation with a window size up to 100 frames (corresponding to 20 seconds of video) increases the final classification performance. This result shows that some minority of temporally close images, which are very likely to carry the same class label, obtain an erroneous label and temporal accumulation could be a possible solution. Assuming that only a minority of temporal neighbors are classified incorrectly makes the temporal continuity a strong cue for our application and should be integrated in the learning process as will be shown next.

*Practical Considerations.* In practice, the best averaging window size cannot be known in advance. Knowing the frame rate of the camera and relatively slow room change, the filter size can be set empirically to a number of frames that are captured in one second, for example.

### 4.1.4. Utility of Unlabeled Data

*Motivation.* The Co-Training algorithm belongs to a semi-supervised learning algorithm grouped. Our goal is to assess its capacity to leverage unlabeled data in practice. First, we compare standard single feature SVM to a semisupervised SVM using graph smoothness assumption. Second, we study the proposed CO-DAS method. Third, we are interested to observe the evolution of performance if multiple Co-Training iterations are performed. Finally, we present a complete set of experiments on the IDOL2 database comparing single feature and multifeature baselines compared to the proposed semi-supervised CO-DAS and CO-TA-DAS methods.

Our primary interest is to show how a standard supervised SVM classifier compares to a state-of-the-art semi-supervised Laplacian SVM classifier. Performance of both classifiers is shown in Figure 8. The results show that semi-supervised counterpart performs better if a sufficiently large initial labeled set of training patterns is given. The low performance at low supervision compared to standard supervised classifier can be explained by an improper parameter setting.

Practical application of this method is limited since the total kernel matrix should be computed and stored in the memory of a computer, which scales as $O(n^2)$ with number of patterns. Computational time scales as $O(n^3)$, which is clearly prohibitive for medium and large sized datasets.

*Co-Training with One Iteration.* The CO-DAS method proposed in this work avoids these issues and scales to much larger datasets due to the use of a linear kernel SVM. In Figure 9, performance of the CO-DAS method is shown where we used only one Co-Training iteration. Left and right panels illustrate the best choice of the amount of selected high confidence patterns for classifier retraining and the DAS fusion parameter selection by a cross-validation procedure, respectively. The results show that performance increase using only one iteration of Co-Training followed by DAS fusion is meaningful if the relatively large amount of top confidence patterns are fed for classifier retraining at low supervision rates. Notice that the cross-validation procedure selected CRFH visual feature at low supervision rate. This may hint for overfitting since the SPH descriptor is a richer visual descriptor.

*Co-Training with More Iterations.* Interesting additional insights on the Co-Training algorithm can be gained if we perform more than one iteration (see Figure 10). The figures show the evolution of the performance of a single feature classifier after it was iteratively retrained from the standard baseline up to 10 iterations where a constant portion of high confidence estimates were added after each iteration. The plots show an interesting increase of performance with every iteration for both classifiers with the same trend. First, this hints that both initial classifiers are possibly enough bootstrapped with initial training data and the two visual cues are possibly conditionally independent as required for the Co-Training algorithm to function properly. Secondly, we notice a certain saturation after more than 6-7 iterations in most cases which may hint that both classifiers achieved complete agreement levels.

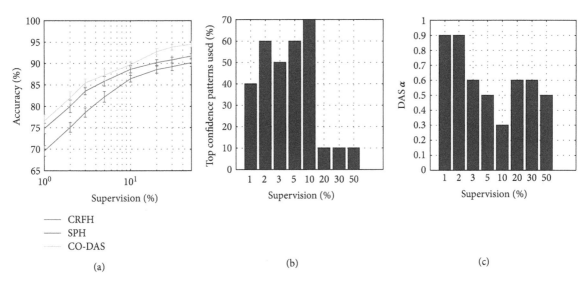

FIGURE 9: Effect of supervision level on the CO-DAS performance and optimal parameters. (a) Accuracy for CO-DAS and single feature approaches. (b) Optimal amount of selected samples for the Co-Training feedback loop. (c) Selected DAS $\alpha$ parameter for late fusion. (IDOL2 dataset, random setup).

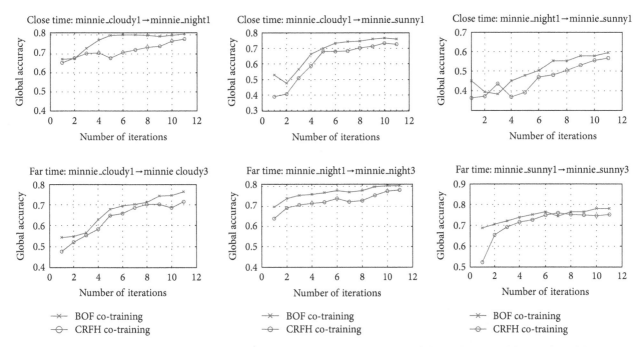

FIGURE 10: Evolution of the accuracy of individual inner classifiers of the Co-Training module as a function of the number of feedback loop iterations. (IDOL2 dataset, video-versus-video setup). The plots are shown for six sequence pairs: (top) same lighting conditions, (bottom) different lighting conditions.

*Conclusion.* Experiments carried out this far show that unlabeled data is indeed useful for image-based place recognition. We demonstrated that a better manifold leveraging unlabeled data can be learned using semi-supervised Laplacian SVM with the assumption of low density class separation. This performance comes at high computational cost, large amounts of required memory, and demands careful parameter tuning. This issue is solved by using more efficient Co-Training algorithm, which will be used in the proposed place recognition system.

### 4.1.5. Random Setup: Comparison of Global Performance

*Motivation.* Random labeling setup represents the conditions with training patterns being scattered across the database. Randomly labeled images may simulate situation when some small portions of video are annotated in a frame by frame manner. In its extreme, few labeled images from every class may be labeled manually.

In this context, we are interested in the performance of the single feature methods, early and late fusion methods,

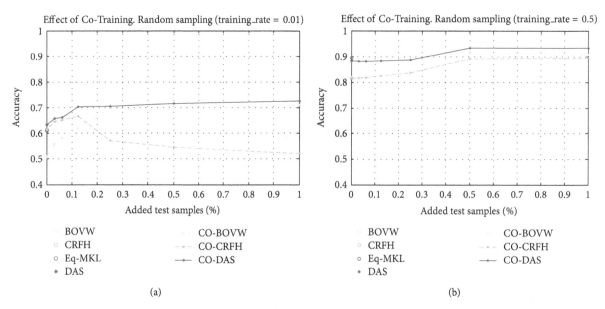

FIGURE 11: Comparison of the performance of single features (BOF, CRFH), early (Eq-MKL) and late fusion (DAS) approaches, with details of Co-Training: performances of the individual inner classifiers (CO-BOF, CO-CRFH) and the final fusion (CO-DAS). Plot of the average accuracy as a function of the amount of Co-Training feedback. The performances are plotted for 1% (a) and 50% (b) of labeled data (IDOL2 dataset, random labeling). See text for more detailed explanation.

and the proposed semi-supervised CO-DAS and CO-TA-DAS methods. In order to simulate various supervision levels, the amount of labeled samples varies from a low (1%) to relatively high (50%) proportion of the database. The results depicting these two setups are presented in Figures 11(a) and 11(b), respectively. The early fusion is performed using the MKL by attributing equal weights for both visual features.

*Low Supervision Case.* The low supervision configuration (Figure 11(a)) is clearly disadvantageous for the single feature methods achieving approximately 50% and 60% of the correct classification for BOVW and CRFH based SVM classifiers. An interesting performance increase can be observed for the Co-Training algorithm leveraging 10% of the top confidence estimates in one re-training iteration, achieving, respectively, 10% and 8% increase for the BOVW and CRFH classifiers. This indicates that the top confidence estimates are not only correct but are also useful for each classifier by improving its discriminatory power on less confident test patterns. Curiously, the performance of the CRFH classifier degrades if more than 10% of high confidence estimates are provided by the BOVW classifier, which may be a sign of increasing the amount of misclassifications being injected. The CO-DAS method successfully performs the fusion of both classifiers and addresses the performance drop in the BOVW classifier, which is achieved by a weighting in favor of the more powerful CRFH classifier.

*High Supervision Case.* At higher supervision levels (Figure 11(b)), the performance of single feature supervised classifiers is already relatively high reaching around 80% of accuracy for both classifiers, which indicates that a significant amount of visual variability present in the scenes has been

captured. This comes as no surprise since at 50% of video annotation in random setup. Nevertheless, the Co-Training algorithm improves the classification by additional 8-9%. An interesting observation for the CO-DAS method shows clearly the complementarity of the visual features even when no Co-Training learning iterations are performed. The high supervision setup permits as much as 50% of the remaining test data annotation for the next re-training rounds before reaching saturation at approximately 94% of accuracy.

*Conclusion.* These experiments show an interest of using the Co-Training algorithm in low supervision conditions. The initial supervised single feature classifiers need to be provided with sufficient number of training data to bootstrap the iterative re-training procedure. Curiously the initial diversity of initial classifiers determines what performance gain can be obtained using the Co-Training algorithm. This explains why at higher supervision levels the performance increase of a re-trained classifier pair may not be significant. Finally, both early and late fusion methods succeed to leverage the visual feature complementarity but failed to go beyond the Co-Training based methods, which confirms the utility of the unlabeled data in this context.

### 4.1.6. Video versus Video: Comparison of Global Performance

*Motivation.* Global performance of the methods may be overly optimistic if annotation is performed only in a random labeling setup. In practical applications a small bootstrap video or a short portion of a video can be annotated instead. We study in a more realistic setup the case with one video being used as training and the place recognition method evaluated on a different video.

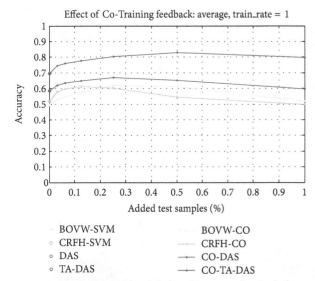

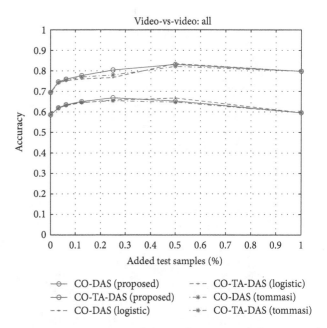

FIGURE 12: Comparison of the global performances for single feature (BOVW-SVM, CRFH-SVM), multiple feature late fusion (DAS), and the proposed extensions using temporal accumulation (TA-DAS) and Co-Training (CO-DAS, CO-TA-DAS). The evolution of the performances of the individual inner classifiers of the Co-Training module (BOVW-CO, CRFH-CO) is also shown. Plot of the average accuracy as a function of the amount of Co-Training feedback. The approaches without Co-Training appear as the limiting case with 0% of feedback (IDOL2 dataset, video-versus-video setup, ALL pairs).

FIGURE 13: Comparison of the performances of the types of confidence measures for the Co-Training feedback loop. Plot of the average accuracy as a function of the amount of Co-Training feedback (video-versus-video setup, ALL pairs).

*Discussion on the Results.* The comparison of the methods in video-versus-video setup is showed in Figure 12. The performances are compared showing the influence of the amount of samples used for the Co-Training algorithm feedback loop. The baseline single feature methods perform around equally by delivering approximately 50% of correct classification. The standard DAS fusion boosts the performance by additional 10%. This confirms the complementarity of the selected visual features in this test setup.

The individual classifiers trained in one Co-Training iteration exceed the baseline and are comparable to performance delivered by standard DAS fusion method. The improvement is due to the feedback of unlabeled patterns in the iterative learning procedure. The CO-DAS method successfully leverages both improvements while the CO-TA-DAS additionally takes advantage of the temporal continuity of the video (a temporal window of size $\tau = 50$ was used).

*Confidence Measure.* On this dataset, a good illustration concerning the amount of high confidence is showed in Figure 12. It is clear that only a portion of the test set data can be useful for classifier re-training. This is governed by two major factors—quality of the data and robustness of the confidence measure. For this dataset, the best portion of high confidence estimates is around 20–50% depending on the method. The best performing TA-CO-TA-DAS method can afford to annotate up to 50% of testing data for the next learning iteration.

*Conclusion.* The results show as well that all single feature baselines are outperformed by standard fusion and simple

Co-Training methods. The proposed methods CO-DAS and CO-TA-DAS perform the best by successfully leveraging two visual features, temporal continuity of the video, and working in semi-supervised framework.

*4.1.7. Effect of the Type of Confidence Measures.* Figure 13 represents the effect of the type of confidence measure used in Co-Training on the performances, for different amounts of feedback in the Co-Training phase. The performances for the Ruping approach is not reported, as it was much lower than the other approaches. A video-versus-video setup was used, with the results averaged over all sequence pairs. The three approaches produce a similar behavior with respect to the amount of feedback: first an increase of the performances, when mostly correct estimates are added to the training set, then a decrease when more incorrect estimates are also considered. When coupled with temporal accumulation, the proposed confidence measure has a slightly better accuracy for moderate feedback. It was therefore used for the rest of experiments.

*4.2. Results on IMMED.* Compared to the IDOL2 database, the IMMED database poses novel challenges. The difficulties arise from increased visual variability changing from location to location, class imbalance due to room visit irregularities, poor lighting conditions, missing or low quality training data, and the large amount of data to be processed.

*4.2.1. Description of Dataset.* The IMMED database consists of 27 video sequences recorded in 14 different locations in real-world conditions. The total amount of recordings

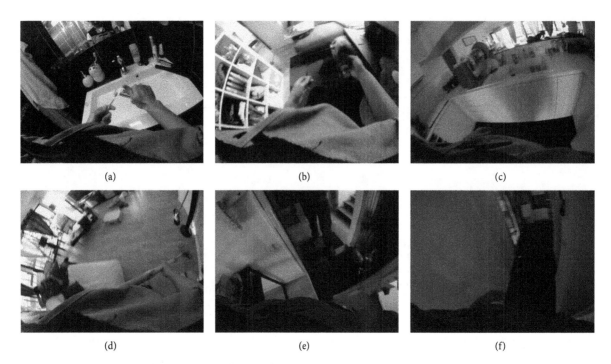

FIGURE 14: IMMED sample images: (a) bathroom, (b) bedroom, (c) kitchen, (d) living room, (e) outside, and (f) other.

exceeds 10 hours. All recordings were performed using a portable GoPro video camera at a frame rate of 30 frames per second with the frame of the resolution of 1280 × 960 pixels. For practical reasons, we downsampled the frame rate to 5 frames per second. Sample images depicting the 6 topological locations are depicted in Figure 14.

Most locations are represented with one short bootstrap sequence depicting briefly the available topological locations for which manual annotation is provided. One or two longer videos for the same location depict displacements and activities of a person in its ecological and unconstrained environment.

Across the whole corpus, the bootstrap video is typically 3.5 minutes long (6400 images) while the unlabeled evaluation videos are 20 minutes long (36000 images) in average. A few locations are not given a labeled bootstrap video; therefore, a small randomly annotated portion of the evaluation videos covering every topological location is provided instead.

The topological location names in all the video have been equalized such that every frame could carry one of the following labels: "bathroom," "bedroom," "kitchen," "living room," "outside," and "other".

### 4.2.2. Comparison of Global Performances

*Setup.* We performed automatic image-based place recognition in realistic video-versus-video setup for each of the 14 locations. To learn optimal parameter values for employed methods, we used the standard cross-validation procedure in all experiments.

Due to a large number of locations, we report here the global performances averaged for all locations. The summary

TABLE 1: IMMED dataset: average accuracy of the single feature approaches.

| Feature/approach | SVM | SVM-TA |
|---|---|---|
| BOVW | 0.49 | 0.52 |
| CRFH | 0.48 | **0.53** |
| SPH | 0.47 | 0.49 |

of the results for single and multiple feature methods is provided in Tables 1 and 2, respectively.

*Baseline-Single Feature Classifier Performance.* As show in Table 1, single feature methods provide relatively low place recognition performance. Surprisingly potentially the more discriminant descriptor SPH is less performant than its more simple BOVW variant. A possible explanation to this phenomena may be that due to the low amount of supervision and a classifier trained on high dimensional SPH features simply overfits.

*Temporal Constraints.* An interesting gain in performance is obtained if temporal information is enforced. On the whole corpus, this performance increase ranges from 2 to 4% in global classification accuracy for all single feature methods. We observe the same order of improvement in multiple feature methods as MKL-TA, for early feature fusion, and DAS-TA, for late classifier fusion. This performance increase over the single feature baselines is constant for the whole corpus and all methods.

*Multiple Feature Exploitation.* Comparing MKL and DAS methods for multiple feature fusion shows interest in favor

TABLE 2: IMMED dataset: average accuracy of the multiple feature approaches.

| Feature/approach | MKL | MKL-TA | DAS | DAS-TA | CO-DAS | CO-TA-DAS |
|---|---|---|---|---|---|---|
| BOVW-SPH | 0.48 | 0.50 | 0.51 | **0.56** | 0.50 | 0.53 |
| BOVW-CRFH | 0.50 | 0.54 | 0.51 | 0.56 | 0.54 | **0.58** |
| SPH-CRFH | 0.48 | 0.51 | 0.50 | 0.54 | 0.54 | **0.57** |
| BOVW-SPH-CRFH | 0.48 | 0.51 | 0.51 | **0.56** | — | — |

of the late fusion method when compared to single feature methods. We observe little performance improvement when using MKL, which can be explained by increased dimensionality space and thus more risk of overfitting. Late fusion strategy is more advantageous compared to respective single feature methods in this low supervision setup by bringing up to 4% with no temporal accumulation and up to 5% with temporal accumulation. Therefore multiple feature information is best leveraged in this context by selecting late classifier fusion.

*Leveraging the Unlabeled Data.* Exploitation of unlabeled data in the learning process is important when it comes to low amounts of supervision and great visual variability encountered in challenging video sequences. The first proposed method termed CO-DAS aims to leverage two visual features while operating in semi-supervised setup. It clearly outperforms all single feature methods and improves on all but BOVW-SPH feature pair compared to DAS by up to 4%. We explain this performance increase by successfully leveraged visual feature complementarity and improved single feature classifiers via Co-Training procedure. The second method CO-TA-DAS incorporates temporal continuity a priori and boosts performances by another 3-4% in global accuracy. This method effectively combines all benefits brought by individual features, temporal video continuity, and taking advantage of unlabeled data.

## 5. Conclusion

In this work we have addressed the challenging problem of indoor place recognition from wearable video recordings. Our proposition was designed by combining several approaches, in order to deal with issues such as low supervision and large visual variability encountered in videos from a mobile camera. Their usefulness and complementarity were verified initially on a public video sequence database IDOL2 then applied to the more complex and larger scale corpus of videos collected for the IMMED project which contains real-world video lifelogs depicting actual activities of patients at home.

The study revealed several elements that were useful for successful recognition in such video corpuses. First, the usage of multiple visual features was shown to improve the discrimination power in this context. Second, the temporal continuity of a video is a strong additional cue, which improved the overall quality of indexing process in most cases. Third, real-world video recordings are rarely annotated manually to an extent where most visual variability present within a location is captured. Usage of semi-supervised

learning algorithms exploiting labeled as well as unlabeled data helped to address this problem. The proposed system integrates all acquired knowledge in a framework which is computationally tractable, yet takes into account the various sources of information.

We have addressed the fusion of multiple heterogeneous sources of information for place recognition from complex videos and demonstrated its utility on the challenging IMMED dataset recorded in real-world conditions. The main focus of this work was to leverage the unlabeled data thanks to a semi-supervised strategy. Additional work could be done in selecting more discriminant visual features for specific applications and more tight integration of the temporal information in the learning process. Nevertheless, the obtained results confirm the applicability of the proposed place classification system on challenging visual data from wearable videos.

## Acknowledgments

This research has received funding from Agence Nationale de la Recherche under Reference ANR-09-BLAN-0165-02 (IMMED project) and the European Community's Seventh Framework Programme (FP7/2007–2013) under Grant Agreement 288199 (Dem@Care project).

## References

[1] A. Doherty and A. F. Smeaton, "Automatically segmenting lifelog data into events," in *Proceedings of the 9th International Workshop on Image Analysis for Multimedia Interactive Services (WIAMIS '08)*, pp. 20–23, May 2008.

[2] E. Berry, N. Kapur, L. Williams et al., "The use of a wearable camera, SenseCam, as a pictorial diary to improve autobiographical memory in a patient with limbic encephalitis: a preliminary report," *Neuropsychological Rehabilitation*, vol. 17, no. 4-5, pp. 582–601, 2007.

[3] S. Hodges, L. Williams, E. Berry et al., "SenseCam: a retrospective memory aid," in *Proceedings of the 8th International Conference on Ubiquitous Computing (Ubicomp '06)*, pp. 177–193, 2006.

[4] R. Mégret, D. Szolgay, J. Benois-Pineau et al., "Indexing of wearable video: IMMED and SenseCAM projects," in *Workshop on Semantic Multimodal Analysis of Digital Media*, November 2008.

[5] A. Torralba, K. P. Murphy, W. T. Freeman, and M. A. Rubin, "Context-based vision system for place and object recognition," in *Proceedings of the 9th IEEE International Conference on Computer Vision*, vol. 1, pp. 273–280, October 2003.

[6] A. Quattoni and A. Torralba, "Recognizing indoor scenes," in *Proceedings of IEEE Conference on Computer Vision and Pattern Recognition (CVPR '09)*, pp. 413–420, June 2009.

[7] R. Mégret, V. Dovgalecs, H. Wannous et al., "The IMMED project: wearable video monitoring of people with age dementia," in *Proceedings of the International Conference on Multimedia (MM '10)*, pp. 1299–1302, ACM Request Permissionss, October 2010.

[8] S. Karaman, J. Benois-Pineau, R. Mégret, V. Dovgalecs, J.-F. Dartigues, and Y. Gaëstel, "Human daily activities indexing in videos from wearable cameras for monitoring of patients with dementia diseases," in *Proceedings of the 20th International Conference on Pattern Recognition (ICPR '10)*, pp. 4113–4116, August 2010.

[9] C. Schüldt, I. Laptev, and B. Caputo, "Recognizing human actions: a local SVM approach," in *Proceedings of the 17th International Conference on Pattern Recognition (ICPR '04)*, pp. 32–36, August 2004.

[10] P. Dollár, V. Rabaud, G. Cottrell, and S. Belongie, "Behavior recognition via sparse spatio-temporal features," in *Proceedings of the 2nd Joint IEEE International Workshop on Visual Surveillance and Performance Evaluation of Tracking and Surveillance*, pp. 65–72, October 2005.

[11] L. Ballan, M. Bertini, A. del Bimbo, and G. Serra, "Video event classification using bag of words and string kernels," in *Proceedings of the 15th International Conference on Image Analysis and Processing (ICIAP '09)*, pp. 170–178, 2009.

[12] D. I. Kosmopoulos, N. D. Doulamis, and A. S. Voulodimos, "Bayesian filter based behavior recognition in workflows allowing for user feedback," *Computer Vision and Image Understanding*, vol. 116, no. 3, pp. 422–434, 2012.

[13] M. Stikic, D. Larlus, S. Ebert, and B. Schiele, "Weakly supervised recognition of daily life activities with wearable sensors," *IEEE Transactions on Pattern Analysis and Machine Intelligence*, vol. 33, no. 12, pp. 2521–2537, 2011.

[14] D. H. Nguyen, G. Marcu, G. R. Hayes et al., "Encountering SenseCam: personal recording technologies in everyday life," in *Proceedings of the 11th International Conference on Ubiquitous Computing (Ubicomp '09)*, pp. 165–174, ACM Request Permissions, September 2009.

[15] M. A. Perez-QuiNones, S. Yang, B. Congleton, G. Luc, and E. A. Fox, "Demonstrating the use of a SenseCam in two domains," in *Proceedings of the 6th ACM/IEEE-CS Joint Conference on Digital Libraries (JCDL '06)*, p. 376, June 2006.

[16] S. Karaman, J. Benois-Pineau, V. Dovgalecs et al., Hierarchical Hidden Markov Model in Detecting Activities of Daily Living in Wearable Videos for Studies of Dementia, 2011.

[17] J. Pinquier, S. Karaman, L. Letoupin et al., "Strategies for multiple feature fusion with Hierarchical HMM: application to activity recognition from wearable audiovisual sensors," in *Proceedings of the 21 International Conference on Pattern Recognition*, pp. 1–4, July 2012.

[18] N. Sebe, M. S. Lew, X. Zhou, T. S. Huang, and E. M. Bakker, "The state of the art in image and video retrieval," in *Proceedings of the 2nd International Conference on Image and Video Retrieval*, pp. 1–7, May 2003.

[19] S.-F. Chang, D. Ellis, W. Jiang et al., "Large-scale multimodal semantic concept detection for consumer video," in *Proceedings of the International Workshop on Multimedia Information Retrieva (MIR '07)*, pp. 255–264, ACM Request Permissions, September 2007.

[20] J. Košecká, F. Li, and X. Yang, "Global localization and relative positioning based on scale-invariant keypoints," *Robotics and Autonomous Systems*, vol. 52, no. 1, pp. 27–38, 2005.

[21] C. O. Conaire, M. Blighe, and N. O'Connor, "Sensecam image localisation using hierarchical surf trees," in *Proceedings of the 15th International Multimedia Modeling Conference (MMM '09)*, p. 15, Sophia-Antipolis, France, January 2009.

[22] J. Košecká, L. Zhou, P. Barber, and Z. Duric, "Qualitative image based localization in indoors environments," in *Proceedings of IEEE Computer Society Conference on Computer Vision and Pattern Recognition*, vol. 2, pp. II-3–II-8, June 2003.

[23] Z. Zovkovic, O. Booij, and B. Krose, "From images to rooms," *Robotics and Autonomous Systems*, vol. 55, no. 5, pp. 411–418, 2007.

[24] L. Fei-Fei and P. Perona, "A bayesian hierarchical model for learning natural scene categories," in *Proceedings of IEEE Computer Society Conference on Computer Vision and Pattern Recognition (CVPR '05)*, pp. 524–531, June 2005.

[25] D. Nister and H. Stewenius, "Scalable recognition with a vocabulary tree," in *Proceedings of IEEE Computer Society Conference on Computer Vision and Pattern Recognition (CVPR '06)*, vol. 2, pp. 2161–2168, 2006.

[26] O. Linde and T. Lindeberg, "Object recognition using composed receptive field histograms of higher dimensionality," in *Proceedings of the 17th International Conference on Pattern Recognition (ICPR '04)*, vol. 2, pp. 1–6, August 2004.

[27] S. Lazebnik, C. Schmid, and J. Ponce, "Beyond bags of features: spatial pyramid matching for recognizing natural scene categories," in *Proceedings of IEEE Computer Society Conference on Computer Vision and Pattern Recognition (CVPR '06)*, vol. 2, pp. 2169–2178, 2006.

[28] A. Bosch and A. Zisserman, "Scene classification via pLSA," in *Proceedings of the 9th European Conference on Computer Vision (ECCV '06)*, May 2006.

[29] J. Sivic and A. Zisserman, "Video google: a text retrieval approach to object matching in videos," in *Proceedings of the 9th IEEE International Conference On Computer Vision*, pp. 1470–1477, October 2003.

[30] J. Knopp, *Image Based Localization [Ph.D. thesis]*, Chech Technical University in Prague, Faculty of Electrical Engineering, Prague, Czech Republic, 2009.

[31] M. W. M. G. Dissanayake, P. Newman, S. Clark, H. F. Durrant-Whyte, and M. Csorba, "A solution to the simultaneous localization and map building (SLAM) problem," *IEEE Transactions on Robotics and Automation*, vol. 17, no. 3, pp. 229–241, 2001.

[32] L. M. Paz, P. Jensfelt, J. D. Tardós, and J. Neira, "EKF SLAM updates in O(n) with divide and conquer SLAM," in *Proceedings of IEEE International Conference on Robotics and Automation (ICRA '07)*, pp. 1657–1663, April 2007.

[33] J. Wu and J. M. Rehg, "CENTRIST: a visual descriptor for scene categorization," *IEEE Transactions on Pattern Analysis and Machine Intelligence*, vol. 33, no. 8, pp. 1489–1501, 2011.

[34] H. Bulthoff and A. Yuille, "Bayesian models for seeing shapes and depth," Tech. Rep. 90-11, Harvard Robotics Laboratory, 1990.

[35] P. K. Atrey, M. Anwar Hossain, A. El Saddik, and M. S. Kankanhalli, "Multimodal fusion for multimedia analysis: a survey," *Multimedia Systems*, vol. 16, no. 6, pp. 345–379, 2010.

[36] A. Rakotomamonjy, F. R. Bach, S. Canu, and Y. Grandvalet, "SimpleMKL," *The Journal of Machine Learning Research*, vol. 9, pp. 2491–2521, 2008.

[37] S. Nakajima, A. Binder, C. Müller et al., "Multiple kernel learning for object classification," in *Workshop on Information-based Induction Sciences*, 2009.

[38] A. Vedaldi, V. Gulshan, M. Varma, and A. Zisserman, "Multiple kernels for object detection," in *Proceedings of the 12th International Conference on Computer Vision (ICCV '09)*, pp. 606–613, October 2009.

[39] J. Yang, Y. Li, Y. Tian, L. Duan, and W. Gao, "Group-sensitive multiple kernel learning for object categorization," in *Proceedings of the 12th International Conference on Computer Vision (ICCV '09)*, pp. 436–443, October 2009.

[40] M. Guillaumin, J. Verbeek, and C. Schmid, "Multimodal semi-supervised learning for image classification," in *Proceedings of IEEE Conference on Computer Vision and Pattern Recognition (CVPR '10)*, pp. 902–909, Laboratoire Jean Kuntzmann, LEAR, INRIA Grenoble, June 2010.

[41] J. Yang, Y. Li, Y. Tian, L. Duan, and W. Gao, "Multiple kernel active learning for image classification," in *Proceedings of IEEE International Conference on Multimedia and Expo (ICME '09)*, pp. 550–553, July 2009.

[42] A. Abdullah, R. C. Veltkamp, and M. A. Wiering, "Spatial pyramids and two-layer stacking SVM classifiers for image categorization: a comparative study," in *Proceedings of the International Joint Conference on Neural Networks (IJCNN '09)*, pp. 5–12, June 2009.

[43] J. Kittler, M. Hatef, R. P. W. Duin, and J. Matas, "On combining classifiers," *IEEE Transactions on Pattern Analysis and Machine Intelligence*, vol. 20, no. 3, pp. 226–239, 1998.

[44] L. Ilieva Kuncheva, *Combining Pattern Classifiers. Methods and Algorithms*, Wiley-Interscience, 2004.

[45] A. Uhl and P. Wild, "Parallel versus serial classifier combination for multibiometric hand-based identification," in *Proceedings of the 3rd International Conference on Advances in Biometrics (ICB '09)*, vol. 5558, pp. 950–959, 2009.

[46] W. Nayer, *Feature based architecture for decision fusion [Ph.D. thesis]*, 2003.

[47] M.-E. Nilsback and B. Caputo, "Cue integration through discriminative accumulation," in *Proceedings of IEEE Computer Society Conference on Computer Vision and Pattern Recognition (CVPR '04)*, vol. 2, pp. II578–II585, July 2004.

[48] A. Pronobis and B. Caputo, "Confidence-based cue integration for visual place recognition," in *Proceedings of IEEE/RSJ International Conference on Intelligent Robots and Systems (IROS '07)*, pp. 2394–2401, October-November 2007.

[49] A. Pronobis, O. Martinez Mozos, and B. Caputo, "SVM-based discriminative accumulation scheme for place recognition," in *Proceedings of IEEE International Conference on Robotics and Automation (ICRA '08)*, pp. 522–529, May 2008.

[50] F. Lu, X. Yang, W. Lin, R. Zhang, R. Zhang, and S. Yu, "Image classification with multiple feature channels," *Optical Engineering*, vol. 50, no. 5, Article ID 057210, 2011.

[51] P. Gehler and S. Nowozin, "On feature combination for multiclass object classification," in *Proceedings of the 12th International Conference on Computer Vision*, pp. 221–228, October 2009.

[52] X. Zhu, "Semi-supervised learning literature survey," Tech. Rep. 1530, Department of Computer Sciences, University of Winsconsin, Madison, Wis, USA, 2008.

[53] X. Zhu and A. B. Goldberg, *Introduction to Semi-Supervised Learning*, Morgan and Claypool Publishers, 2009.

[54] O. Chapelle, B. Scholkopf, and A. Zien, *Semi-Supervised Learning*, MIT Press, Cambridge, Mass, USA, 2006.

[55] M. Belkin, P. Niyogi, and V. Sindhwani, "Manifold regularization: a geometric framework for learning from labeled and unlabeled examples," *The Journal of Machine Learning Research*, vol. 7, pp. 2399–2434, 2006.

[56] U. Von Luxburg, "A tutorial on spectral clustering," *Statistics and Computing*, vol. 17, no. 4, pp. 395–416, 2007.

[57] D. Zhou, O. Bousquet, T. Navin Lal, J. Weston, and B. Scholkopf, "Learning with local and global consistency," *Advances in Neural Information Processing Systems*, vol. 16, pp. 321–328, 2004.

[58] S. Melacci and M. Belkin, "Laplacian support vector machines trained in the primal," *The Journal of Machine Learning Research*, vol. 12, pp. 1149–1184, 2011.

[59] B. Nadler and N. Srebro, "Semi-supervised learning with the graph laplacian: the limit of infinite unlabelled data," in *Proceedings of the 23rd Annual Conference on Neural Information Processing Systems (NIPS '09)*, 2009.

[60] A. Blum and T. Mitchell, "Combining labeled and unlabeled data with co-training," in *Proceedings of the 11th Annual Conference on Computational Learning Theory (COLT' 98)*, pp. 92–100, October 1998.

[61] D. Zhang and W. Sun Lee, "Validating co-training models for web image classification," in *Proceedings of SMA Annual Symposium*, National University of Singapore, 2005.

[62] W. Tong, T. Yang, and R. Jin, "Co-training For Large Scale Image Classification: An Online Approach," *Analysis and Evaluation of Large-Scale Multimedia Collections*, pp. 1–4, 2010.

[63] M. Wang, X.-S. Hua, L.-R. Dai, and Y. Song, "Enhanced semi-supervised learning for automatic video annotation," in *Proceedings of IEEE International Conference on Multimedia and Expo (ICME '06)*, pp. 1485–1488, July 2006.

[64] V. E. van Beusekom, I. G. Sprinkuizen-Kuyper, and L. G. Vuurpul, "Empirically evaluating co-training," Student Report, 2009.

[65] W. Wang and Z.-H. Zhou, "Analyzing co-training style algorithms," in *Proceedings of the 18th European Conference on Machine Learning (ECML '07)*, pp. 454–465, 2007.

[66] C. Dong, Y. Yin, X. Guo, G. Yang, and G. Zhou, "On co-training style algorithms," in *Proceedings of the 4th International Conference on Natural Computation (ICNC '08)*, vol. 7, pp. 196–201, October 2008.

[67] S. Abney, *Semisupervised Learning for Computational Linguistics*, Computer Science and Data Analysis Series, Chapman & Hall, University of Michigan, Ann Arbor, Mich, USA, 2008.

[68] D. Yarowsky, "Unsupervised word sense disambiguation rivaling supervised methods," in *Proceedings of the 33rd Annual Meeting on Association for Computational Linguistics (ACL '95)*, pp. 189–196, University of Pennsylvania, 1995.

[69] W. Wang and Z.-H. Zhou, "A new analysis of co-training," in *Proceedings of the 27th International Conference on Machine Learning*, pp. 1135–1142, May 2010.

[70] C. M. Bishop, *Pattern Recognition and Machine Learning. Information Science and Statistics*, Springer, Secaucus, NJ, USA, 2006.

[71] B. Scholkopf and A. J. Smola, *Learning with Kernels*, MIT Press, Cambridge, Mass, USA, 2002.

[72] R.-E. Fan, K.-W. Chang, C.-J. Hsieh, X.-R. Wang, and C.-J. Lin, "LIBLINEAR: a library for large linear classification," *The Journal of Machine Learning Research*, vol. 9, pp. 1871–1874, 2008.

[73] A. J. Smola, B. Schölkopf, and K.-R. Müller, "Nonlinear component analysis as a kernel eigenvalue problem," *Neural Computation*, vol. 10, no. 5, pp. 1299–1319, 1998.

[74] A. Pronobis, O. Martínez Mozos, B. Caputo, and P. Jensfelt, "Multi-modal semantic place classification," *The International Journal of Robotics Research*, vol. 29, no. 2-3, pp. 298–320, 2010.

[75] T. Hastie, R. Tibshirani, J. Friedman, and J. Franklin, "The elements of statistical learning: data mining, inference and predictionvolume," *The Mathematical Intelligencer*, vol. 27, no. 2, pp. 83–85, 2005.

[76] S. Rüping, A Simple Method For Estimating Conditional Probabilities For SVMs. *American Society of Agricultural Engineers*, 2004.

[77] T. Tommasi, F. Orabona, and B. Caputo, "An SVM confidence-based approach to medical image annotation," in *Proceedings of the 9th Cross-Language Evaluation Forum Conference on Evaluating Systems for Multilingual and Multimodal Information Access (CLEF '08)*, pp. 696–703, 2009.

[78] K. Grauman and T. Darrell, "The pyramid match kernel: discriminative classification with sets of image features," in *Proceedings of the 10th IEEE International Conference on Computer Vision (ICCV '05)*, vol. 2, pp. 1458–1465, October 2005.

[79] J. Luo, A. Pronobis, B. Caputo, and P. Jensfelt, "The KTH-IDOL2 database," Tech. Rep., Kungliga Tekniska Hoegskolan, CVAP/CAS, 2006.

# 5

# Objective No-Reference Stereoscopic Image Quality Prediction Based on 2D Image Features and Relative Disparity

### Z. M. Parvez Sazzad,[1] Roushain Akhter,[2] J. Baltes,[2] and Y. Horita[1]

[1] *Graduate School of Science and Engineering, University of Toyama, Toyama 930-8555, Japan*
[2] *Department of Computer Science, University of Manitoba, Winnipeg, MB, Canada R3T 2N2*

Correspondence should be addressed to Z. M. Parvez Sazzad, sazzad@univdhaka.edu

Academic Editor: Feng Wu

Stereoscopic images are widely used to enhance the viewing experience of three-dimensional (3D) imaging and communication system. In this paper, we propose an image feature and disparity dependent quality evaluation metric, which incorporates human visible system characteristics. We believe perceived distortions and disparity of any stereoscopic image are strongly dependent on local features, such as edge (i.e., nonplane areas of an image) and nonedge (i.e., plane areas of an image) areas within the image. Therefore, a no-reference perceptual quality assessment method is developed for JPEG coded stereoscopic images based on segmented local features of distortions and disparity. Local feature information such as edge and non-edge area based relative disparity estimation, as well as the blockiness and the edge distortion within the block of images are evaluated in this method. Subjective stereo image database is used for evaluation of the metric. The subjective experiment results indicate that our metric has sufficient prediction performance.

## 1. Introduction

Nowadays, three-dimensional (3D) stereo media is becoming immersive media to increase visual experience as natural in various applications ranging from entertainment [1] to more specialized applications such as remote education [2], robot navigation [3], medical applications like body exploration [4], and therapeutic purposes [5]. There are many alternative technologies for 3D image/video display and communication, including holographic, volumetric, and stereoscopic; stereoscopic image/video seems to be the most developed technology at the present [6]. Stereoscopic image consists of two images (left and right views) captured by closely located (approximately the distance between two eyes) two cameras. These views constitute a stereo pair and can be perceived as a virtual view in 3D by human observers with the rendering of corresponding view points. Although the technologies required for 3D image are emerging rapidly, the effect of these technologies as well as image compression on the perceptual quality of 3D viewing has not been thoroughly studied. Therefore, perceptual 3D image quality is an important issue to assess the performance of all 3D imaging

applications. There are several signal processing operations that have been designed for stereoscopic images [7] and some researchers are still working to develop a new standard for efficient multiview image/video coding [8]. They believe the image compression technique that used in 2D image material can also be applied independently on the left and right images of a stereo image pair to save valuable bandwidth and storage capacity. Although subjective assessment is the most accurate method for perceived image quality, it is time consuming, and expensive. Therefore, objective quality evaluation method is required that can automatically predict perceptual image quality.

In the last two decades, a lot of work have been concentrated to develop conventional 2D image/video quality assessment methods. Whereas, still now no comparable effort has been devoted to the quality assessment for 3D/stereoscopic images. A full-reference (FR) quality metric for the assessment of stereoscopic image pairs using the fusion of 2D quality metrics and of the depth information is proposed in [9]. The study evaluated that the FR metric of 2D quality assessment can be used for an extension to 3D with the incorporation of depth information. In [10], the selection of the rate allocation strategy between views is addressed for scalable multiview video codec to obtain the best rate-distortion performance. In [11], a FR quality metric is proposed for stereoscopic color images. The metric is proposed based on the use of binocular energy contained in the left and right retinal images calculated by complex wavelet transform and bandelet transform. In [12], a FR overall stereoscopic image quality metric has been suggested by combining conventional 2D image quality metric with disparity information. In [13], the quality of 3D videos stored as monoscopic color videos that augmented by pixel depth map and finally this pixel information used for color coding and depth data. In [14], the effect of low pass filtering one channel of a stereo sequence is explored in terms of perceived quality, depth, and sharpness. The result found that the correlation between image quality and perceived depth is low for low pass filtering. A comprehensive analysis of the perceptual requirements for 3D TV is made in [15] along with a description of the main artifacts of stereo TV. In [16], the concept of visual fatigue and its subjective counterpart, visual discomfort in relation to stereoscopic display technology, and image generation is reviewed. To guarantee the visual comfort in consumer applications, such as stereoscopic television, it is recommended to adhere to a limit of "one degree of disparity," which still allows sufficient depth rendering for most applications. In [17], the effects of camera base distance and JPEG coding on overall image quality, perceived depth, perceived sharpness, and perceived eye strain are discussed. The relationship between the perceived overall image quality and the perceived depth are discussed in [18]. In [19], an FR quality assessment model is proposed for stereoscopic color images based on texture features of left image as well as disparity information between left and right images. In [20], a positive relationship between depth and perceived image quality for uncompressed stereoscopic images is described. Subjective ratings of video quality for MPEG-2 coded stereo and nonstereo sequences with different bit rates are investigated in [21]. In [22], a crosstalk prediction metric is proposed for stereoscopic images. The method try to predict level of crosstalk perception based on crosstalk levels, camera baseline, and scene content.

Although perceptual quality of stereoscopic images depends mainly on the factors such as the depth perception, level of crosstalk, and visual discomfort, overall perceptual quality reflects the combined effect of the multidimensional factors [16]. We believe that human visual perception is very sensitive to edge information and perceived image distortions are strongly dependent on the local features such as edge, and nonedge areas and also depth/disparity perception is dependent on the local features of images. Therefore, in this work we propose a no-reference (NR) quality assessment method for stereoscopic images based on segmented local features of distortions and disparity. In many practical applications, the reference image is not available, therefore an NR quality assessment approach is desirable. Here, we limit our work to JPEG coded stereoscopic images only. A similar approach based on three local features such as edge, flat, and texture was made in [23]. The metric used many parameters (thirteen) and local features

(three). Consequently, computational cost of the model was high. Therefore, we consider two local features (edge and nonedge) and less parameters with low computational cost in this paper. A previous instantiation of this approach was made in [24] and promising results on simple tests were achieved. In this paper, we generalize this algorithm, and provide a more extensive set of validation results on a stereo image databases. The rest of the paper is organized as follows: Section 2 describes briefly the subjective database that is used to evaluate our method. The details of our approach is given in Section 3. Results are discussed in Section 4 and finally, the paper is concluded in Section 6.

## 2. The Subjective Databases

We conducted subjective experiment on 24 bit/pixel RGB color stereoscopic images in the Media Information and Communication Technology (MICT) laboratory, University of Toyama [23]. The database contained JPEG coded symmetric and asymmetric 490 stereoscopic image pairs (70 symmetric, and 420 asymmetric pairs) of size 640 × 480. Out of all, ten were reference stereo pairs. The seven quality scales (QS: 10, 15, 27, 37, 55, 79, and reference) were selected for the JPEG coder. A double stimulus impairment scale (DSIS) method was used in the subjective experiment. The impairment scale contained five categories marked with adjectives and numbers as follows: "Imperceptible = 5", "Perceptible but not annoying = 4", "Slightly annoying = 3", "Annoying = 2," and "Very annoying = 1". A 10-inch auto stereoscopic, LCD (SANYO) display (resolution: 640 × 480) was used in this experiment. Twenty-four nonexpert subjects were shown the database; most of them were college/university student. Mean opinion scores (MOSs) were then computed for each stereo image after the screening of postexperiment results according to ITU-R Rec. 500-10 [25]. The details of the experiment were discussed in [24].

## 3. Proposed Objective Method

The primary function of the human visual system (HVS) is to extract structural or edge information from the viewing field [26]. Therefore, Human visual perception is very sensitive to edge detection, and consequently, perceive distortions should be strongly dependent on local features such as edge, and nonedge. For example, in theory, the visual distortions of an image increase with an increased rate of compression. However, the relationship between the distortions and the level of compressions is not always straight forward. It strongly depends on the texture contents of an image as well. In order to verify the relationship, we analyse the degradation of images which causes visual difficulty, that is, appearance of image distortions at different compression levels for various textures of images. Here, we consider an image (see Figure 1(a)) that contains a variety of textures such as edge and nonedge areas. Out of all edge (nonuniform) and nonedge (uniform) areas in Figure 1(a), we analyse a small portion of uniform and nonuniform areas which are represented by the top-right rectangular box and the

(a) Reference image; Image taken from [27]

(b) Compressed image; QS = 10

(i) QS = 50

(ii) QS = 25

(i) QS = 50

(ii) QS = 25

(iii) QS = 15

(iv) QS = 10

(iii) QS = 15

(iv) QS = 10

(c) A small portion of an uniform area

(d) A small portion of a nonuniform area

FIGURE 1: Variation of perceived distortion (uniform and nonuniform areas).

bottom-right rectangular box (dotted line), respectively. A high level of JPEG compression is applied to the image which is shown in Figure 1(b). The result shows the blocking distortions are more visible to uniform areas compared to that the nonuniform areas (see the corresponding areas in the compressed image) even though the level of compression is equal. In order to study the relationship more extensively we apply four levels of compression (QS: 50, 25, 15, and 10) to the image and consider expanded views of the portions of uniform and nonuniform areas (see the rectangular box areas) for each level of compression which are shown in Figures 1(c) and 1(d), respectively. These two figures indicate that perceived distortions for these areas are not similar even though the compression levels are equal. In details, blocking distortions are more visible in uniform areas compared to nonuniform areas (see Figures 1(c)(iii) and 1(d)(iii), and also Figures 1(c)(iv) and 1(d)(iv)). Similarly, the blur distortions are more visible in the nonuniform areas compared to uniform areas (see Figures 1(c)(iii) and 1(d)(iii), and also Figures 1(c)(iv) and 1(d)(iv)). The results indicate that visibility of image distortions are strongly depended on local features such as edge and nonedge areas.

Thus, we also believe that 3D depth perception is strongly dependent on objects, structures, or textures edges of stereo image content. Therefore, an NR perceptual stereoscopic image quality assessment method is proposed based on

segmented local features of distortions and disparity in this research. An efficient 2D compression technique, JPEG codec is applied independently on the left and right views of the stereo image pairs. Since JPEG is a block based discrete cosine transform (DCT) coding technique, both blocking and edge distortions may be created during quantization of DCT coefficients in the coded images. Blocking effect occurs due to the discontinuity at block boundaries, which is generated because the quantization in JPEG is block based and the blocks are quantized independently. Here, blockiness of a block is calculated as the average absolute difference around the block boundary. The edge distortion, which makes blurring effect, is mainly due to the loss of high-frequency DCT coefficients, which smooths the image signal within each block. Thus, higher blurring represents a smoother image signal which causes the reduction of signal edge points. Consequently, average edge point detection measures of blocks give more insight into the relative edge distortion in the image. Here, zero-crossing technique is used as an edge detector. Although, the impact of coding distortions on the perceived stereoscopic image quality of an asymmetric image pair depends on the visual appearance of the artifact, where blockiness appears to be much more disturbing than blur [28], we take into account the maximum blockiness and edge distortion measures between the left and right views. Therefore, we consider higher blockiness

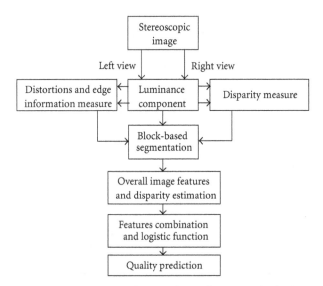

FIGURE 2: Proposed NR quality evaluation method.

and lower zero-crossing values between the two views. For simplicity, only the luminance component is considered to make overall quality prediction of color stereo images. As image distortions as well as disparity are estimated based on segmented local features, a block based segmentation algorithm is applied to identify edge and nonedge areas of an image which is discussed in details in [24]. Subsequently, the distortions and disparity measures are described in the next Sections. The block diagram of the proposed method is shown in Figure 2.

### 3.1. Image Distortions Measure.
We estimate blockiness and zero-crossing to measure JPEG coded image distortions in spatial domain based on segmented local features. Firstly, we calculate blockiness and zero-crossing of each $8 \times 8$ block of the stereo image pair separately (left and right images). Secondly, we apply the block ($8 \times 8$) based segmentation algorithm to the left and right images individually to classify edge, and nonedge blocks in the images [24]. Thirdly, we average each value of blockiness and zero-crossing separately for edge, and nonedge blocks of each image of the stereo pair. Fourthly, the total blockiness and zero-crossing of the stereo image pair is estimated respectively based on the higher blockiness value and lower zero-crossing value between the left and right images distinctly for edge, and nonedge blocks. And finally, we update these blockiness and zero-crossing values by some weighting factors that are optimized by an optimization algorithm. The mathematical features, blockiness and zero-crossing measures within each block of the images are calculated horizontally and then vertically.

For horizontal direction: let the test image signal be $x(m, n)$ for $m \in [1, M]$ and $n \in [1, N]$, a differencing signal along each horizontal line is calculated by

$$d_h(m, n)$$
$$= x(m, n + 1) - x(m, n), \quad n \in [1, N-1], \ m \in [1, M]. \tag{1}$$

Blockiness of a block ($8 \times 8$) in horizontal direction is estimated by

$$B_{bh} = \frac{1}{8} \sum_{i=1}^{8} |d_h(i, 8j)|, \tag{2}$$

where "$i$" and "$8j$" are, respectively, number of row and column position, and $j = 1, 2, 3, \ldots (N/8)$.

For horizontal zero-crossing (ZC) we have

$$d_{h\text{-sign}}(m, n) = \begin{cases} 1 & \text{if } d_h(m, n) > 0, \\ -1 & \text{if } d_h(m, n) < 0, \\ 0 & \text{otherwise,} \end{cases} \tag{3}$$

$$d_{h\text{-mul}}(m, n) = d_{h\text{-sign}}(m, n) \times d_{h\text{-sign}}(m, n + 1).$$

We define for $n \in [1, N - 2]$:

$$z_h(m, n) = \begin{cases} 1 & \text{if } d_{h\text{-mul}}(m, n) < 0, \\ 0 & \text{otherwise,} \end{cases} \tag{4}$$

where the size of $z_h(m, n)$ is $M \times (N-2)$. The horizontal zero-crossing of a block ($8 \times 8$), $ZC_{bh}$, is calculated as follows:

$$ZC_{bh} = \sum_{i=1}^{8} \sum_{j=1}^{8} z_h(i, j), \tag{5}$$

Thus, we can calculate blockiness and zero-crossing of each available block of the left and right images.

For vertical direction: we can also calculate the differences of signal along each vertical line as follows:

$$d_v(m, n)$$
$$= x(m + 1, n) - x(m, n), \quad n \in [1, N], \ m \in [1, M - 1]. \tag{6}$$

Similarly, the vertical features of blockiness ($B_{bv}$) and zero-crossing ($ZC_{bv}$) of the block are calculated. Therefore, the overall features $B_b$ and $ZC_b$ per block are given by

$$B_b = \frac{B_{bh} + B_{bv}}{2}, \quad ZC_b = \frac{ZC_{bh} + ZC_{bv}}{2}. \tag{7}$$

Consequently, the average blockiness value of edge, and nonedge areas of the left image are calculated by:

$$Bl_e = \frac{1}{N_e} \sum_{b=1}^{N_e} B_{be},$$
$$Bl_n = \frac{1}{N_n} \sum_{b=1}^{N_n} B_{bn}, \tag{8}$$

where $N_e$ and $N_n$ are, respectively, the number of edge, and nonedge blocks of the image. Similarly, the average blockiness values of $Br_e$, and $Br_n$ for the right image are calculated.

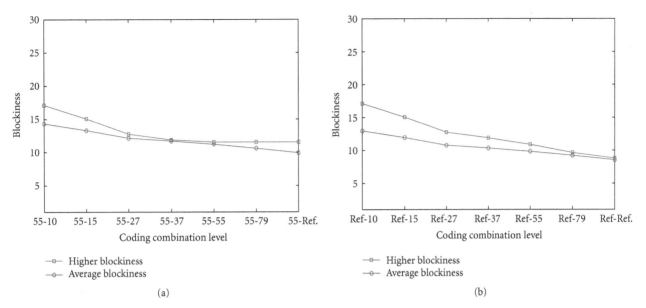

FIGURE 3: Blockiness versus different coding levels for Cattle image pairs (a) L, R: QS55-Seven different coding levels. (b) L, R: Ref-Seven different coding levels.

Accordingly, the average zero-crossing values of $ZCl_e$, and $ZCl_n$ for the left image are estimated by

$$ZCl_e = \frac{1}{N_e} \sum_{b=1}^{N_e} ZC_{be},$$

$$ZCl_n = \frac{1}{N_n} \sum_{b=1}^{N_n} ZC_{bn}. \qquad (9)$$

Similarly, the average zero-crossing values of $ZCr_e$, and $ZCr_n$ for the right image are calculated. We then calculate the total blockiness and zero-crossing features of edge, and nonedge areas of the stereo image. For the total blockiness features ($B_e$ and $B_n$) of the stereo image, we consider only the higher values between the left and right images by the following algorithm:

$$B_{e/n}(\text{Bl}, \text{Br}) = \max(\text{Bl}, \text{Br}). \qquad (10)$$

However for zero-crossing features ($ZC_e$, and $ZC_n$), we estimate lower values between the left and right images by the following algorithm:

$$ZC_{e/n}(\text{ZCl}, \text{ZCr}) = \min(\text{ZCl}, \text{ZCr}). \qquad (11)$$

Finally, the overall blockiness, and zero-crossing of each stereo image pair are calculated by

$$B = B_e^{w_1} \cdot B_n^{w_2}$$

$$Z = ZC_e^{w_3} \cdot ZC_n^{w_4}, \qquad (12)$$

where $w_1$ and $w_2$ are the weighting factors for the blockiness of edge, and nonedge areas and also $w_3$ and $w_4$ are the weighting factors for zero-crossing.

*3.1.1. Significance of Considering the Maximum Blockiness of a Stereo Pair.* In this section, we discuss the reason for choosing the maximum blockiness of a stereo pair for our model. The goal is to measure the maximum possible blockiness within a stereo pair so that of the metric can correlate well with human viewers' perception without actual human. Because, blockiness is one of the most annoying artifacts for human eyes. Moreover, the model is developed both for symmetric and asymmetric images. In order to take into count the highest degradation, we consider the maximum blockiness between the left and the right views. To explain the consideration of the maximum blockiness, we took a stereo image "Cattle" (the image from the MICT database [26]). The coding levels versus blockiness of the stereo image are shown in Figure 3. We examine both the highest and average blockiness between the two views. Figure 3 shows variations of blockiness with the increasing of bit rate. The results indicate that the blockiness variation is higher in case of highest of blockiness compared to the average blockiness for increasing of bit rate. The normalized MOS (NMOS) versus blockiness ($N$-blockiness) with increasing bit rate for two types of stereo images is shown in Figure 4. The coding levels (L, R: Ref-10, Ref-15, Ref-27, Ref-37, Ref-55, Ref-79, and Ref-Ref), and (L, R: 79-10, 79-15, 79-27, 79-37, 79-55, 79-79, and 79-Ref) in the Figure 4 indicate increasing bit rate. Although NMOS scores show an increasing trend with decreasing $N$-blockiness, the consideration of maximum blockiness (Higher-$B$) correlates inversely better with NMOS compared to average blockiness (Average-$B$). Here, NMOS versus the maximum $N$-blockiness features for edge (i.e, non-plane) and nonedge (i.e., plane) areas along with a wide variety of quality pairs for Car and Cattle images are also shown in Figure 5. The two blockiness features ($B_e$ and $B_n$) support the similar trend of inverse nature with respect to NMOS. Therefore, the above results suggest that the consideration of the maximum blockiness with the two blockiness features is

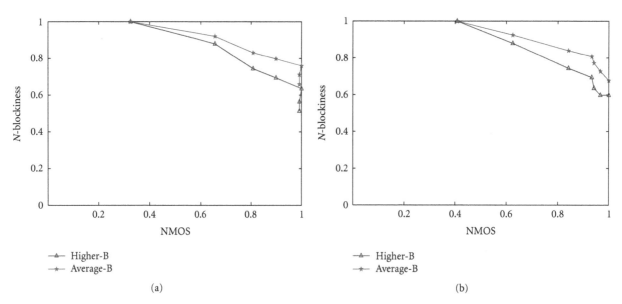

FIGURE 4: Normalized MOS versus blockiness for different Cattle image pairs. (a) L, R: Ref-QS10, Ref-QS15, Ref-QS27, Ref-QS37, Ref-QS55, Ref-QS79, and Ref-Ref, (b) L, R: QS79-QS10, QS79-QS15, QS79-QS27, QS79-QS37, QS79- QS55, QS79-QS79, and QS79-Ref.

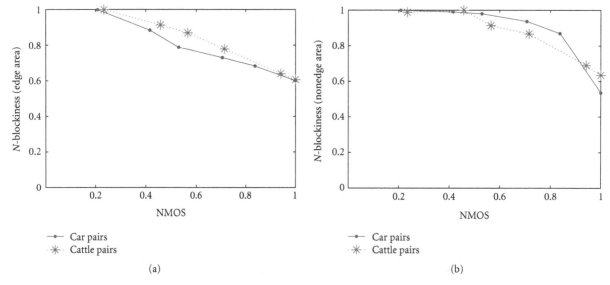

FIGURE 5: Normalized MOS versus blockiness for edge and nonedge areas of different Car and Cattle image pairs. (a) NMOS versus $N$-blockiness (edge areas, $B_e$), (b) NMOS versus $N$-blockiness (nonedge areas, $B_n$).

more justified than the average blockiness for developing of an objective model.

*3.1.2. Significance of Considering the Minimum Zero-Crossing of a Stereo Pair.* An analysis of choosing the minimum zero-crossing value between the left and the right views of a stereo pair is given in this section. In [29], it has been discussed that the average edge point detection within image blocks gives better insight of edge distortion measurement within an image. Consequently, the zero-crossing values show a decreasing (i.e., increasing edge distortion) trend with the increasing compression level. Therefore, there is a relationship with the transition of zero-crossing and the overall edge distortion within an image. In order to study the

relationship, we take a stereo image pair, Cattle. Normalized MOS (NMOS) versus zero-crossing ($N$-zero crossing) of the stereo image is shown in Figure 6. We consider both the minimum (Lower-ZC) and the average zero-crossing (Average-ZC) value of the stereo pair. The Figure 6 shows that the minimum zero-crossing measure is correlated better to the NMOS score compared to that of the average zero-crossing. In addition, the $N$-zero crossing values show an increasing trend for increasing bit rate. Subsequently, the NMOS versus the minimum $N$-Zero crossing features for edge and nonedge areas over a variety of quality pairs for Car and Cattle images are shown in Figure 7. The two zero crossing features follow the similar trend of correlation with respect to NMOS. Therefore, the results indicate that

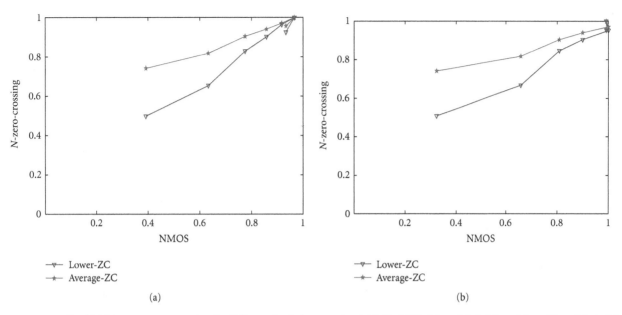

FIGURE 6: Normalized MOS versus zero-crossing for different Cattle image pairs. (a) L, R: QS55-QS10, QS55-QS15, QS55-QS27, QS55-QS37, QS55-QS55, QS55-QS79, and QS55-Ref, (b) L, R: Ref-QS10, Ref-QS15, Ref-QS27, Ref-QS37, Ref-QS55, Ref-QS79, and Ref-Ref.

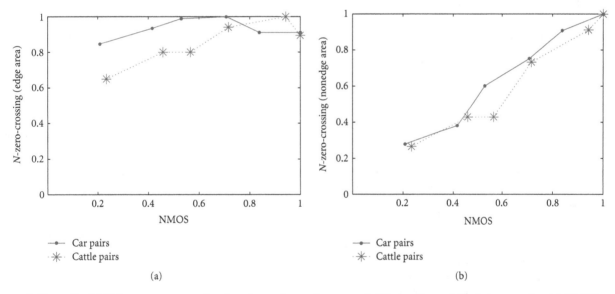

FIGURE 7: Normalized MOS versus zero-crossing for edge and nonedge areas of different Car and Cattle image pairs. (a) NMOS versus $N$-Zero crossing (edge areas, $ZC_e$), (b) NMOS versus $N$-Zero crossing (nonedge areas, $ZC_n$).

the two zero crossing features ($ZC_e$ and $ZC_n$) measures along with the minimum zero-crossing are more justified than the average zero-crossing to develop the quality prediction metric.

3.2. Relative Disparity Measure. To measure disparity, we use a simple feature-based block matching approach. Many feature-based approaches are applied for stereo matching/disparity estimation which are discussed in [30]. Here, a fixed block based difference zero-crossing (DZC) approach is employed in this work. The principal of the disparity estimation is to divide the left image into nonoverlapping $8 \times 8$ blocks with classification of edge and nonedge blocks.

For each $8 \times 8$ block of the left image, stereo correspondence searching is conducted based on minimum difference zero-crossing (MDZC) rate between the corresponding block and up to $\pm 128$ pixels of the right image. The disparity estimation approach is shown in Figure 8. Here, zero-crossing (horizontal and vertical) of a block is estimated according to Section 3.1. "1," and "0" indicate zero-crossing (edge) and nonzero-crossing (nonedge) points, respectively. In order to reduce computational cost, we restricted the correspondence search to 1D only (i.e., horizontally) and within $\pm 128$ pixels. Moreover, the stereoscopic images database that we consider in this research are epipolar rectified images. Therefore, the displacement between the left and right view of a stereo

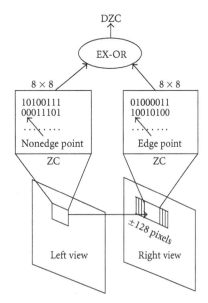

FIGURE 8: Disparity estimation approach.

searching block of right image in horizontal direction, respectively. The $DZC_h$ of the block are estimated by the following equation:

$$DZC_h = ZCl_h \oplus ZCr_h, \tag{15}$$

Thus, we can calculate $DZC_h$ rate ($DZCR_h$) of the 8×8 block by

$$DZCR_h = \frac{1}{8 \times 8} \sum DZC_h. \tag{16}$$

Therefore, the average $DZCR_h$ ($AZC_h$) for edge, and nonedge blocks of the left image are calculated by

$$AZC_{h_e} = \frac{1}{N_e} \sum_{e=1}^{N_e} DZCR_{h_e}, \tag{17}$$

$$AZC_{h_n} = \frac{1}{N_n} \sum_{e=1}^{N_n} DZCR_{h_n}, \tag{18}$$

where $N_e$ and $N_n$ are, respectively, the number of edge, and nonedge blocks of the left image.

For vertical direction: similarly, we can calculate $AZC_{v_e}$ and $AZC_{v_n}$. Subsequently, the total relative disparity features for edge, $AZC_e$ and nonedge, $AZC_n$ areas are estimated by the following equation:

$$AZC_e = \frac{AZC_{h_e} + AZC_{v_e}}{2}, \qquad AZC_n = \frac{AZC_{h_n} + AZC_{v_n}}{2}. \tag{19}$$

Finally, the overall relative disparity feature is estimated by

$$DZ = AZC_e^{w_5} \cdot AZC_n^{w_6} \tag{20}$$

where $w_5$ and $w_6$ are, respectively, the weighting factors of the disparity features for edge, and nonedge areas. In order to verify the estimation of the two disparity features ($AZC_e$ and $AZC_n$) the normalized MOS versus the disparity features for edge and nonedge areas over the different quality pairs for Car and Cattle images are shown in Figure 11. The two disparity features also maintained the similar increasing trend of correlation nature with respect to NMOS. Therefore, it is indicated that the two disparity features measures are also justified to develop the prediction metric. Although 3D depth perception is a complex process, we believe it has a strong correlation with objects/structural information of a scene content that is near to the viewers. In order to verify this statement, we compare three stereoscopic images of similar scene contents and noticed that the distance of the near objects/structures to the viewers in second and third images is decreasing in comparison with the first image that is shown in Figure 12. Consequently, the depth perceptions are increasing from the images one to third according to the viewer's perception. Eventually, the proposed disparity feature (DZ) measure is shown in Figure 13 for edge and nonedge areas within the images. The figure shows the normalized DZ features for the two different areas of

pair is restricted in horizontal direction only. The depth maps of the two sample stereo image pairs for block size $4 \times 4$, $8 \times 8$, and $16 \times 16$ with searching area $\pm 128$ pixels are shown in Figure 9. Colors in the depth maps that are indicated by vertical color bars in right are estimated depths of the image pairs. Subsequently, depth maps of different symmetric and asymmetric Cattle images are shown in Figure 10. Figures 9 and 10 show that the performance of the disparity algorithm is adequate for the block size $8 \times 8$ with searching areas of $\pm 128$ pixels. The effect of different block size and searching areas on this disparity estimation are discussed in details in [29]. Although disparity is a measure of position displacement between the left and right images, an intensity based DZC rate is determined between the block of a left image and the corresponding searching block in the right image as relative disparity in this work.

In order to measure the relative disparity, firstly, the segmentation algorithm is applied to left image only to classify edge and nonedge blocks. Secondly, block-based DZC is estimated in the two corresponding blocks between the left and right images. Thirdly, we average the DZC rate values separately for edge and nonedge blocks. Finally, the values are updated with some weighting factors. If $ZCl$, and $ZCr$ be the zero-crossing of a block of left image and the corresponding searching block of right image, respectively. The DZC of the block can be estimated by the following equation:

$$DZC = ZCl \oplus ZCr, \tag{13}$$

where the symbol, "$\oplus$" indicates a logical Exclusive-OR operation. Subsequently, DZC rate (DZCR) is calculated by

$$DZCR = \frac{1}{8 \times 8} \sum DZC. \tag{14}$$

For horizontal direction: let $ZCl_h$, and $ZCr_h$ be the zero-crossing of a block of left image and the corresponding

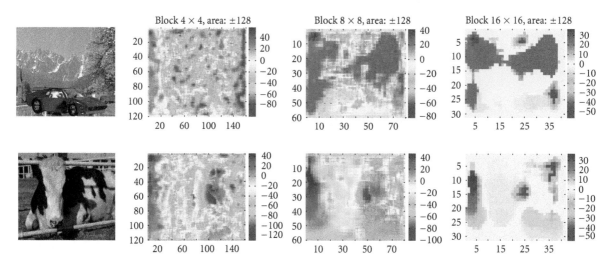

FIGURE 9: Car and Cattle images and its depth maps with different block sizes and searching area $\pm 128$.

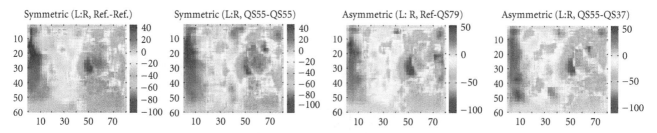

FIGURE 10: Depth maps of distinct symmetric and asymmetric pairs for Cattle images.

the images. The DZ values for edge areas in Figure 13(a) indicate that the first image's depth is lower than the second and similarly, the DZ value of second image is lower than the third image. Therefore, the increasing trend of DZ features for edge areas on similar scene contents confirms the human visual depth perception of the images. Although the DZ features for edge areas support the depth perception, we also consider the DZ features for nonedge areas to measure the relative depth perception of other objects/structures of scene contents in this algorithm.

*3.3. Features Combination.* We can combine the artifacts and disparity features to develop a stereo quality assessment metric in different way. In order to investigate the best suitable features combination equation, we studied the following equations:

*Case 1.*

$$S = \alpha(\text{DZ}) \cdot B \cdot Z \tag{21}$$

*Case 2.*

$$S = \alpha + \beta(\text{DZ}) \cdot B \cdot Z \tag{22}$$

*Case 3.*

$$S = \alpha(\text{DZ}) + \beta(B) + \gamma(Z) \tag{23}$$

*Case 4.*

$$S = \alpha(\text{DZ}) + \beta B \cdot Z, \tag{24}$$

where $\alpha$, $\beta$, and $\gamma$ are the method parameters. The method parameters and weighting factors ($w_1$ to $w_6$) are must be estimated by an optimization algorithm with the subjective test data. The proposed method performance is also studied without disparity by the following equation:

$$S = \alpha + \beta B \cdot Z. \tag{25}$$

We consider a logistic function as the nonlinearity property between the human perception and the physical features. Finally, the obtained MOS prediction, $\text{MOS}_p$, is derived by the following equation [31]:

$$\text{MOS}_p = \frac{4}{1 + \exp[-1.0217(S - 3)]} + 1. \tag{26}$$

Here, Particle Swarm Optimization (PSO) algorithm is used for optimization [32].

## 4. Results

In order to verify the performance of our method we consider the MICT stereo image database (see Section 2). To use the database, we divide the database into two parts for training and testing. The training database consists of five randomly selected reference stereo pairs (from the total ten) and all of their different combinations of symmetric/asymmetric coded stereo images (245 stereo pairs). The testing database consists of the other five reference stereo pairs and their symmetric/asymmetric coded versions (245 stereo pairs), and also there is no overlapping

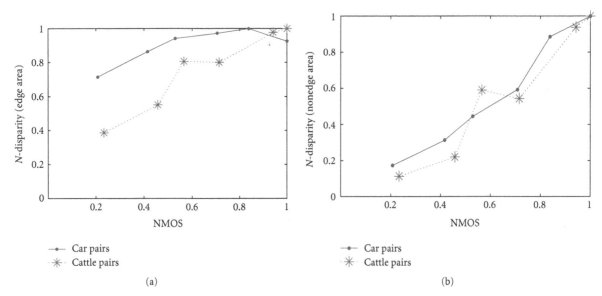

FIGURE 11: Normalized MOS versus Disparity for edge and nonedge areas of different Car and Cattle image pairs: (a) NMOS versus $N$-Disparity (edge areas, $AZC_e$) (b) NMOS versus $N$-Disparity (nonedge areas, $AZC_n$).

FIGURE 12: Images with different depth perception based on variation of near objects' distance: Decreasing distance of near objects (from images I to III) creates a significant increase of depth perception.

between training and testing. In order to provide quantitative measures on the performance of the proposed method, we follow the standard performance evaluation procedures employed in the video quality experts group (VQEG) FR-TV Phase II test [33], where mainly pearson linear correlation coefficient (CC), average absolute prediction error (AAE), root mean square prediction error (RMSE), and outlier ratio (OR) between objective (predicted), and subjective scores were used for evaluation. The evaluation result along with all above mentioned features combination equations are shown in Table 1. The table indicates that out of all the combined equations, (24) (Case 4) provides the highest prediction performance among others. Consequently, the proposed method considers (24). The method's parameters and weighting factors are obtained by the PSO optimization algorithm with all of the training images are shown in Table 2. To measure the performance as well as justification of the estimated image features of our proposed method we also consider the following prediction performances:

(1) Methods with disparity:

    (i) proposed model (i.e., considering blockiness, zero-crossing, and disparity) using the features combining Equation (24);

TABLE 1: Evaluation results on different features combined equations with disparity.

| Methods | Training | | | |
| --- | --- | --- | --- | --- |
| | CC | AAE | RMSE | OR |
| Case 1 | 0.916 | 0.907 | 1.044 | 0.298 |
| Case 2 | 0.953 | 0.332 | 0.401 | 0.086 |
| Case 3 | 0.961 | 0.286 | 0.348 | 0.065 |
| Case 4 (considered) | 0.964 | 0.276 | 0.336 | 0.061 |
| | Testing | | | |
| Case 1 | 0.865 | 0.918 | 1.064 | 0.314 |
| Case 2 | 0.942 | 0.339 | 0.406 | 0.053 |
| Case 3 | 0.931 | 0.348 | 0.431 | 0.037 |
| Case 4 (considered) | 0.940 | 0.339 | 0.413 | 0.040 |

TABLE 2: Method parameters and weighting factors (MOS scale, 1 to 5).

| | | |
| --- | --- | --- |
| $\alpha = 58.064452$ | $\beta = -51.026118$ | |
| $w_1 = 0.036062$ | $w_2 = 0.00513$ | $w_3 = 0.010634$ |
| $w_4 = -0.026979$ | $w_5 = -0.017522$ | $w_6 = 0.013169$ |

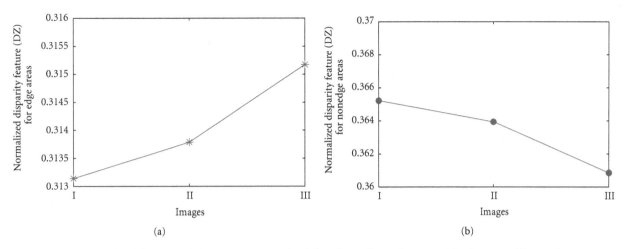

FIGURE 13: Normalized disparity of the images (I, II, and III) for edge and nonedge areas. (a) Edge areas, (b) nonedge areas.

(ii) method considering only blockiness and disparity using the following features combined equation:

$$S = \alpha(\text{DZ}) + \beta B. \tag{27}$$

(iii) method considering only zero-crossing and disparity using the following features combined equation:

$$S = \alpha(\text{DZ}) + \beta Z. \tag{28}$$

(iv) conventional method with disparity (i.e., consider blockiness, zero-crossing, and disparity without segmentation) using the features combining Equation (24).

(2) Methods without disparity:

(i) method considering blockiness, and zero-crossing using the features combine Equation (25).

(ii) method considering only blockiness by using the following equation:

$$S = \alpha + \beta B. \tag{29}$$

(iii) method considering only zero-crossing using the following equation:

$$S = \alpha + \beta Z. \tag{30}$$

(iv) conventional method considering blockiness, and zero-crossing using (25) without segmentation.

(3) Another method:

(i) method considering the blockiness and zero-crossing distinctly for the two views of a stereo pair and measure the quality score of the left

and the right views independently using the features combining Equation (25), and average them without disparity, "2D quality mean" [18].

The evaluation results of all the above mentioned methods are summarized in Tables 3, 4, and 5. Table 3 shows that the proposed method's performances for every one of the evaluation metrics are quite sufficient both for the training and the testing datasets. It has also been observed from the Table 3 that the proposed method provides sufficient prediction accuracy (higher CC), and sufficient prediction consistency (lower OR). The result in Table 3 also prove that the proposed method (i.e., incorporation of the perceptual difference of image distortions and disparity) demonstrates superior quality prediction performance compare to the conventional method with disparity. Tables 3 and 4 also show that the method performances are superior compared to the without disparity. Whereas, 2D quality mean performance is not sufficient even compared to without disparity approach (i.e., considering only blockiness and zero-crossing) (see Tables 4 and 5). Although, the incorporation of disparities measure to the FR stereo image quality assessment method [9] indicates poor results, our proposed method (with relative disparity) indicates better result compared to without disparity (i.e., considering only blockiness and zero-crossing). It is clear from Tables 3 and 4 that all methods performances with disparity are superior compared to without disparity. Therefore, the relative disparity measure which is considered in our proposed method can be a significant measure for 3D quality prediction. In order to understand the significance of estimated image features (i.e., blockiness and zero-crossing), we consider the above mentioned methods which used both features, blockiness and zero-crossing individually with and without disparity. It is clear from Tables 3 and 4 that the performance of the method considering only zero-crossing is better compared to the method considering only blockiness both for with and without disparity. Therefore, zero-crossing feature is more significant compared to blockiness feature for quality prediction. Proposed method's weighting factors also show

TABLE 3: Methods' evaluation results for training and testing with disparity.

| Methods | Training | | | | 
|---|---|---|---|---|
| | CC | AAE | RMSE | OR |
| Proposed method | 0.964 | 0.276 | 0.336 | 0.061 |
| Only blockiness with disp. | 0.867 | 0.529 | 0.664 | 0.086 |
| Only zero-crossing with disp. | 0.897 | 0.484 | 0.578 | 0.110 |
| Conventional method with disp. | 0.903 | 0.479 | 0.597 | 0.114 |
| | Testing | | | |
| Proposed method | 0.940 | 0.339 | 0.413 | 0.040 |
| Only blockiness with disp. | 0.833 | 0.537 | 0.724 | 0.106 |
| Only zero-crossing with disp. | 0.804 | 0.578 | 0.707 | 0.102 |
| Conventional method with disp. | 0.881 | 0.473 | 0.577 | 0.127 |

TABLE 4: Methods' evaluation results for training and testing without (wo) disparity.

| Methods | Training | | | |
|---|---|---|---|---|
| | CC | AAE | RMSE | OR |
| Blockiness and zero-crossing wo disp. | 0.953 | 0.322 | 0.401 | 0.074 |
| Only blockiness wo disp. | 0.705 | 1.037 | 1.199 | 0.367 |
| Only zero-crossing wo disp. | 0.883 | 0.515 | 0.610 | 0.110 |
| Conventional method wo disp. | 0.904 | 0.530 | 0.646 | 0.131 |
| | Testing | | | |
| Blockiness and zero-crossing wo disp. | 0.932 | 0.349 | 0.432 | 0.053 |
| Only blockiness wo disp. | 0.705 | 1.041 | 1.196 | 0.359 |
| Only zero-crossing wo disp. | 0.814 | 0.595 | 0.719 | 0.114 |
| Conventional method wo disp. | 0.854 | 0.548 | 0.649 | 0.159 |

TABLE 5: Another method's evaluation results for training and testing.

| Method | Training | | | |
|---|---|---|---|---|
| | CC | AAE | RMSE | OR |
| 2D quality mean | 0.912 | 0.432 | 0.55 | 0.078 |
| | Testing | | | |
| 2D quality mean | 0.89 | 0.40 | 0.534 | 0.057 |

TABLE 6: Evaluation results comparison on MICT database.

| Method | Training | | | |
|---|---|---|---|---|
| | CC | AAE | RMSE | OR |
| Proposed, NR | 0.964 | 0.276 | 0.336 | 0.061 |
| Method, NR [23] | 0.966 | 0.292 | 0.367 | 0.069 |
| Method, FR [9] | 0.945 | 0.310 | 0.381 | 0.065 |
| 2D quality mean, FR [34] | 0.779 | 0.715 | 0.846 | 0.261 |
| | Testing | | | |
| Proposed, NR | 0.940 | 0.339 | 0.393 | 0.037 |
| Method, NR [23] | 0.935 | 0.350 | 0.421 | 0.065 |
| Method, FR [9] | 0.929 | 0.370 | 0.441 | 0.082 |
| 2D quality mean, FR [34] | 0.758 | 0.722 | 0.844 | 0.208 |

the deviance. Weighting factors ($w_3$ and $w_4$) of zero-crossing are higher compared to weighting factors ($w_1$ and $w_2$) of blockiness (see Table 2).

The MOS versus $MOS_p$ of our proposed method for training and testing images are respectively shown in Figures 14(a), and 14(b). The symbols "*" and "+," respectively, indicate $MOS_p$ points for the databases of training and testing. Figure 14 confirms that the proposed method's overall quality prediction performance is sufficient not only on known dataset but also on unknown dataset. The MOS versus $MOS_p$ performance of the proposed method is also shown in Figure 15 distinctly for symmetric and asymmetric images. Figure 15 shows that the overall prediction performance is almost equally well for both symmetric and asymmetric coded pairs. However, the performance

trend is slightly inferior for symmetric pairs compared to asymmetric pairs. Because, the proposed method takes into account the highest visual artifacts between the two views. Subsequently, the highest visual artifacts measures are not significant in those symmetric pairs who are very low levels of compression or close to reference pairs. The $MOS_p$ points "*" and the error bars of ±2 standard deviation intervals of four different stereo images are shown in Figure 16. Error bars show the ±2 standard deviation interval of the MOS. The figure indicates the predictions consistently performed well in almost similar nature on variety of image contents. Although, the incorporation of disparities measure to the FR stereo image quality metrics [9] indicate poor results, our method with the relative disparity indicates better results compared to without disparity. Therefore, the local features-based relative disparity and distortions can be a significant measure for overall stereoscopic image quality prediction. In order to estimate computational cost of the proposed algorithm, we calculate the computing time of the algorithm on an Intel (R) Core (TM) i3 processor with 2.53 GHz clock speed and 2 GB RAM accompanied with Windows 32-bit operating system. Figure 17 shows the average computing time of stereo images with different resolutions. The average computational cost, specifically for 640 × 480 pixels stereo image, of our proposed algorithm is approximately 52 sec which is sufficient to perform the computation on the machine configuration.

## 5. Performance Comparison

In this section, we compare the performance of my proposed method against our recently published NR model [23]. The method uses three local features (edge, flat, and texture) and the MICT database. Our proposed method's evaluation results on the same database are shown in Table 6. The table shows that the performance of our proposed method is superior compared to the published method both for the training and testing databases. As a comparison, we can also compare the performance of my proposed method against the currently published FR method presented in [9]. We evaluate the performance of the method on the same database (MICT database). Table 6 shows that the performance of our proposed model is better even compared

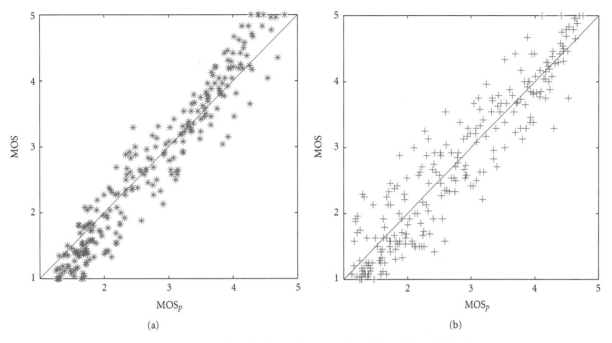

FIGURE 14: Proposed method's MOS versus MOS$_p$. (a) Training, (b) Testing.

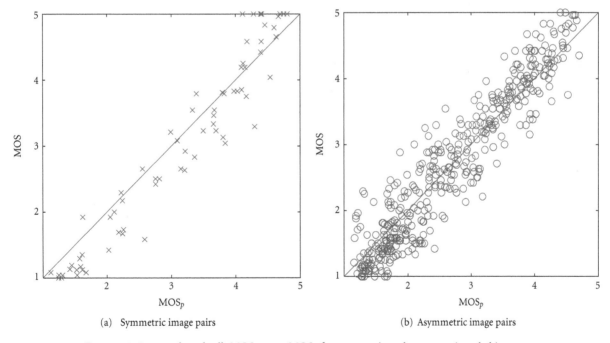

(a) Symmetric image pairs

(b) Asymmetric image pairs

FIGURE 15: Proposed method's MOS versus MOS$_p$ for symmetric and asymmetric coded images.

to the FR method [9]. We want to make another comparison according to the idea of some researches. Some researchers claim 2D image quality metric can be used for 3D or stereoscopic image quality prediction by averaging the 2D quality metric for the left and the right views without the disparity features estimation [18]. We want to point out simple 2D averaging technique is not suitable for stereoscopic image quality prediction even if a good quality 2D FR quality metric is used for quality prediction. According to this idea, we compare the performance of our proposed method against

the popular FR objective method for 2D quality assessment [34]. We also evaluate the performance of the method on the same database. Table 6 shows that the performance of our proposed model is more better compared to the averaging method of 2D quality. It is apparent from this result that the 2D quality mean approach is not enough for 3D quality prediction. The proposed method's performance can also be compared with another recently published FR stereo image quality assessment [11]. The method is also used the same MICT database. The FR method's reported CC on the MICT

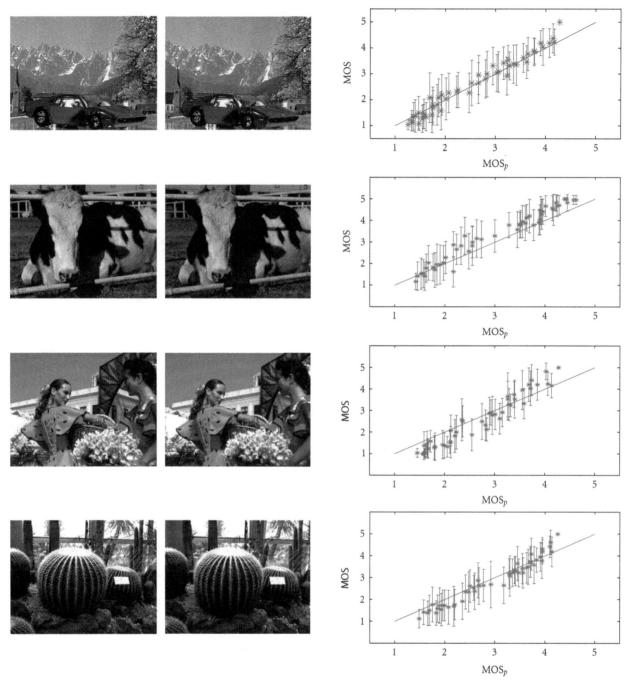

FIGURE 16: The $MOS_p$ performances on texture variety of stereo pairs over the quality range. The predictions points $*$ and $\pm 2$ standard deviation intervals are shown for each stereo pair.

database is 0.97, whereas our proposed NR method CC on the same database is 0.96. It indicates that even though our method is NR the prediction performance is very close to the FR method [11]. Moreover, the FR method converted the MOS scale 1–5 linearly to the MOS scale 0-1, which is not truly mapped the subjective scores between the two scales [35].

In order to extensively verify the performance of the proposed method, we consider another stereo image database. The database was created by IVC and IRCCyN laboratory, University of Nantes, France. As the proposed method is designed for JPEG coded stereo images, we use only the JPEG coded images from the database. In the database, there are thirty JPEG coded stereo images for six different reference images. The images were coded at a wide range of bit rates ranging from 0.24 bpp to 1.3 bpp. The details of the database are discussed in [9]. As the database used difference mean opinion score (DMOS) with different scale (DMOS scale, 0 to 100), it is very difficult to develop a mathematical relationship between the two different scales (MOS scale: 1 to 5, and DMOS scale: 0 to 100). Although Pinson and Walf presented a mapping method to convert one subjective

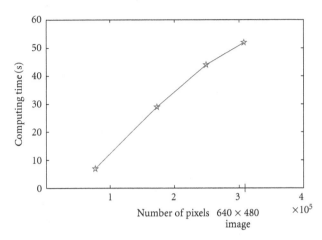

FIGURE 17: Computation time of the proposed algorithm.

TABLE 7: Method parameters and weighting factors (continuous DMOS scale, 0 to 100).

| | | |
|---|---|---|
| $\alpha = 140.62388$ | $\beta = -85.924017$ | |
| $w_1 = -0.017834$ | $w_2 = -0.000617$ | $w_3 = 0.019968$ |
| $w_4 = 0.017483$ | $w_5 = 0.000042$ | $w_6 = 0.00717$ |

scale to another, the performance was not sufficient for all subjective data sets [35]. Consequently, we estimate the suitable optimized model parameters and weighting factors for DMOS scale, 0 to 100 by using the same equations with different logistic function as follows:

$$\text{DMOS}_{p(100)} = \frac{99}{1 + \exp[-1.0217(S - 50)]} + 1. \quad (31)$$

Therefore, in order to use the database we randomly divide the database into two parts for training and testing and also there is no overlapping between training and testing. The method's parameters and weighting factors with the training images are shown in Table 7 for DMOS scale, 0 to 100. The proposed method's CCs for the training and testing images are, respectively, 0.93 and 0.91. Subsequently, the proposed method's performance can again be compared with the FR method (e.g., C4 d2: considering better performance disparity algorithm, "bp Vision") [9]. The prediction performance for all JPEG coded stereo images is shown in Table 8. The table shows that proposed NR method's performance is almost better for the evaluation metrics even compared to the FR method. It is clear from the table that our proposed NR method performance is sufficient and better compared to the published FR method. Therefore, the Tables 6 and 8 confirm that our proposed method performance is sufficient and better compared to the others recently published method.

## 6. Conclusion

In this paper, we propose an NR stereoscopic image quality assessment method for JPEG coded symmetric/asymmetric images which used the perceptual differences of local

TABLE 8: Evaluation results of the comparison on IVC-IRCCYN laboratory's database.

| Method | JPEG stereo images | | | |
|---|---|---|---|---|
| | CC | AAE | RMSE | OR |
| Proposed, NR | 0.925 | 7.689 | 9.612 | 0.033 |
| Method (C4 $d_2$), FR [9] | 0.927 | 8.610 | 10.141 | 0.033 |

features such as edge and nonedge. Local features based distortions and relative disparity measures are estimated in this approach. A popular subjective database is used to verify the performance of the method. The result shows that the method performs quite well over wide range of stereo image content and distortion levels. Although the approach is used only for JPEG coded stereo images, future research can be extended to generalize the approach irrespective of any coded stereoscopic images.

## References

[1] A. Kubota, A. Smolic, M. Magnor, M. Tanimoto, T. Chen, and C. Zhang, "Multiview imaging and 3DTV," *IEEE Signal Processing Magazine*, vol. 24, no. 6, pp. 10–21, 2007.

[2] A. M. William and D. L. Bailey, "Stereoscopic visualization of scientific and medical content," in *Proceedings of the ACM SIGGRAPH 2006 Educators Program–International Conference on Computer Graphics and Interactive Techniques (SIGGRAPH '06)*, Boston, Mass, USA, August 2006.

[3] J. Baltes, S. McCann, and J. Anderson, "Humanoid Robots: Abarenbou and DaoDan," RoboCup 2006—Humanoid League Team Description Paper.

[4] C. F. Westin, "Extracting brain connectivity from diffusion MRI," *IEEE Signal Processing Magazine*, vol. 24, no. 6, pp. 124–152, 2007.

[5] Y. A. W. De Kort and W. A. Ijsselsteijn, "Reality check: the role of realism in stress reduction using media technology," *Cyberpsychology and Behavior*, vol. 9, no. 2, pp. 230–233, 2006.

[6] N. A. Dodgson, "Autostereoscopic 3D displays," *Computer*, vol. 38, no. 8, pp. 31–36, 2005.

[7] M. Z. Brown, D. Burschka, and G. D. Hager, "Advances in computational stereo," *IEEE Transactions on Pattern Analysis and Machine Intelligence*, vol. 25, no. 8, pp. 993–1008, 2003.

[8] A. Smolic and P. Kauff, "Interactive 3-D video representation and coding technology," *IEEE, Special Issue on Advances in Video Coding and Delivery*, vol. 93, no. 1, pp. 98–110, 2005.

[9] A. Benoit, P. Le Callet, P. Campisi, and R. Cousseau, "Quality assessment of stereoscopic images," *EURASIP Journal on Image and Video Processing*, vol. 2008, Article ID 659024, 2008.

[10] N. Qzbek, A. M. Tekalp, and E. T. Tunali, "Rate allocation between views in scalable stereo video coding using an objective stereo video quality measure," in *Proceedings of the IEEE International Conference on Acoustics, Speech and Signal Processing (ICASSP '07)*, pp. I1045–I1048, Honolulu, Hawaii, USA, April 2007.

[11] R. Bensalma and M. C. Larabi, "Towards a perceptual quality metric for color stereo images," in *Proceedings of the 17th IEEE International Conference on Image Processing (ICIP '10)*, pp. 4037–4040, Hong Kong, September 2010.

[12] J. You, L. Xing, A. Perkis, and X. Wang, "Perceptual quality assessment for stereoscopic images based on 2D image quality metrics and disparity analysis," in *Proceedings of the International Workshop on Video Processing and Quality Metrics*

*for Consumer Electronics (VPQM '01)*, Scottsdale, Ariz, USA, 2010.

[13] A. Tikanmaki and A. Gotchev, "Quality assessment of 3D video in rate allocation experiments," in *Proceedings of the IEEE International Symposium on Consumer Electronics (ISCE '08)*, Algarve, Portugal, April 2008.

[14] L. Stelmach, W. J. Tam, D. Meegan, and A. Vincent, "Stereo image quality: effects of mixed spatio-temporal resolution," *IEEE Transactions on Circuits and Systems for Video Technology*, vol. 10, no. 2, pp. 188–193, 2000.

[15] L. M. J. Meesters, W. A. Ijsselsteijn, and P. J. H. Seuntiëns, "A survey of perceptual evaluations and requirements of three-dimensional TV," *IEEE Transactions on Circuits and Systems for Video Technology*, vol. 14, no. 3, pp. 381–391, 2004.

[16] M. T. M. Lambooij, W. A. Ijsselsteijn, and I. Heynderickx, "Visual discomfort in stereoscopic displays: a review," in *Stereoscopic Displays and Virtual Reality Systems XIV*, vol. 6490 of *Proceedings of the SPIE*, January 2007.

[17] P. Seuntiens, L. Meesters, and W. Ijsselsteijn, "Perceived quality of compressed stereoscopic images: effects of symmetric and asymmetric JPEG coding and camera separation," *IEEE ACM Transactions on Applied Perception*, vol. 3, no. 2, pp. 95–109, 2009.

[18] C. T. E. R. Hewage, S. T. Worrall, S. Dogan, and A. M. Kondoz, "Prediction of stereoscopic video quality using objective quality models of 2-D video," *Electronics Letters*, vol. 44, no. 16, pp. 963–965, 2008.

[19] Y. Horita, Y. Kawai, Y. Minami, and T. Murai, "Quality evaluation model of coded stereoscopic color image," in *Visual Communications and Image Processing*, vol. 4067 of *Proceedings of the SPIE*, pp. 389–398, June 2000.

[20] W. A. Ijsselsteijn, H. de Ridder, and J. Vliegen, "Subjective evaluation of stereoscopic images: effects of camera parameters and display duration," *IEEE Transactions on Circuits and Systems for Video Technology*, vol. 10, no. 2, pp. 225–233, 2000.

[21] W. J. Tam and L. B. Stelmach, "Perceived image quality of MPEG-2 stereoscopic sequences," in *Human Vision and Electronic Imaging II*, vol. 3016 of *Proceedings of the SPIE*, pp. 296–301, San Jose, Calif, USA, February 1997.

[22] L. Xing, J. You, T. Ebrahimi, and A. Perkis, "A perceptual quality metric for stereoscopic crosstalk perception," in *Proceedings of the 17th IEEE International Conference on Image Processing (ICIP '10)*, pp. 4033–4036, Hong Kong, September 2010.

[23] Z. M. P. Sazzad, S. Yamanaka, Y. Kawayoke, and Y. Horita, "Stereoscopic image quality prediction," in *Proceedings of the International Workshop on Quality of Multimedia Experience (QoMEx '09)*, pp. 180–185, San Diego, CA, USA, July 2009.

[24] R. Akhter, Z. M. Parvez Sazzad, Y. Horita, and J. Baltes, "No-reference stereoscopic image quality assessment," in *Stereoscopic Displays and Applications XXI*, vol. 7524 of *Proceedings of the SPIE*, San Jose, CA, USA, January 2010.

[25] ITU-R, "Methodology for the subjective assessment of the quality of television pictures," Tech. Rep. BT.500-10, Geneva, Switzerland, 2000.

[26] Z. Wang, *Rate scalable foveated image and video communications [Ph.D. thesis]*, Department of ECE, The University of Texas at Austin, 2003.

[27] University of Manitoba, http://umanitoba.ca/.

[28] D. V. Meegan, L. B. Stelmach, and W. J. Tam, "Unequal weighting of monocular inputs in binocular combination: implications for the compression of stereoscopic imagery," *Journal of Experimental Psychology: Applied*, vol. 7, no. 2, pp. 143–153, 2001.

[29] R. Akhter, *Perceptual image quality for stereoscopic vision [M.S. thesis]*, Department of Computer Science, University of Manitoba, 2011.

[30] B. P. McKinnon, *Point, line segment, and region-based stereo matching for mobile robotics [M.S. thesis]*, Department of Computer Science, University of Manitoba, 2009.

[31] Z. M. Parvez Sazzad, Y. Kawayoke, and Y. Horita, "No reference image quality assessment for JPEG2000 based on spatial features," *Signal Processing: Image Communication*, vol. 23, no. 4, pp. 257–268, 2008.

[32] J. Kennedy and R. Eberhart, "Particle swarm optimization," in *Proceedings of the IEEE International Conference on Neural Networks*, pp. 1942–1948, Perth, Australia, December 1995.

[33] VQEG, "Final Report from the video quality experts group on the validation of objective models of video quality assessment, FR-TV Phase II (August 2003)," http://www.vqeg.org/.

[34] Z. Wang, A. C. Bovik, H. R. Sheikh, and E. P. Simoncelli, "Image quality assessment: from error visibility to structural similarity," *IEEE Transactions on Image Processing*, vol. 13, no. 4, pp. 600–612, 2004.

[35] M. Pinson and S. Wolf, "An objective method for combining multiple subjective data sets," in *Proceedings of the SPIE Video Communications and Image Processing*, Lugano, Switzerland, July 2003.

# 6

# Optimal H.264 Scalable Video Scheduling Policies for 3G/4G Wireless Cellular and Video Sensor Networks

**Vamseedhar R. Reddyvari and Aditya K. Jagannatham**

*Department of Electrical Engineering, Indian Institute of Technology Kanpur, Kanpur 208016, India*

Correspondence should be addressed to Aditya K. Jagannatham, adityaj@iitk.ac.in

Academic Editor: Mei-Ling Shyu

We consider the problem of optimal H.264 scalable video scheduling, with an objective of maximizing the end-user video quality while ensuring fairness in 3G/4G broadband wireless networks and video sensor networks. We propose a novel framework to characterize the video quality-based utility of the H.264 temporal and quality scalable video layers. Subsequently, we formulate the scalable video scheduling framework as a Markov decision process (MDP) for long-term average video utility maximization and derive the optimal index based-scalable video scheduling policies ISVP and ISVPF towards video quality maximization. Further, we extend this framework to multiuser and multisubchannel scenario of 4G wireless networks. In this context, we propose two novel schemes for long-term streaming video quality performance optimization based on maximum weight bipartite and greedy matching paradigms. Simulation results demonstrate that the proposed algorithms achieve superior end-user video experience compared to competing scheduling policies such as Proportional Fairness (PF), Linear Index Policy (LIP), Rate Starvation Age policy (RSA), and Quality Proportional Fair Policy (QPF).

## 1. Introduction

The advent of portable smart devices and broadband enabling wireless technologies such as LTE and WiMAX have led to the availability of a plethora of video applications and services such as video conferencing, multimedia streaming, interactive gaming, and real-time video monitoring in 3G/4G wireless networks. A typical scenario in a 4G network is shown in the Figure 1. Video sensor networks are another paradigm which is gaining popularity due to its application in digital security and online surveillance. This demand for such wireless broadband services is expected to continue to increase in the future with progressive innovations in wireless technologies and devices leading to universal appeal of such services combined with ubiquitous availability of smart phones. Further, video content, which is the key to such popular 3G/4G services, is expected to progressively comprise a dominating fraction of the wireless traffic. However, the erratic wireless environment coupled with the tremendous heterogeneity in the display and decoding capabilities of wireless devices such as smart phones, tablets, and notebooks renders conventional fixed profile video transmission unsuitable in such scenarios.

H.264 based scalable video coding (SVC) has gained significant popularity in the context of video transmission over wireless links owing to its several advantages over conventional video coding. SVC avoids the problem of simulcasting fixed profile video streams at different spatial and temporal profiles by embedding a base low resolution stream in a hierarchical stream consisting of several differential enhancement layers. Another significant advantage of SVC over conventional video coding is graceful degradation of video quality in the event of packet drops due to network congestion. As a result of these advantages, SVC is rapidly increasing in popularity as a de facto scheme for video coding in wireless networks. Reliable video transmission over bandwidth constrained wireless packet networks is further challenging compared to conventional broadband applications such as FTP and internet access due to the high delay sensitivity of video. Hence efficient video scheduling algorithms are critical towards QoS enforcement and end-user video quality maximization in broadband 4G networks.

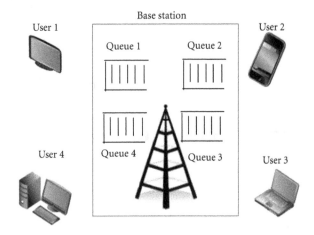

FIGURE 1: Typical 4G cellular network with heterogeneous users.

Considerable research has been carried out towards optimal resource allocation and scheduling with Quality of Service (QoS) constraints in wireless networks. The authors in [1] proposed an index-based Highest Urgency First (HUF) scheme towards multiuser scheduling which assigns an urgency parameter to each scheduling request and schedules the packets with the highest urgency factor. The authors in [2] employ distinct service classes to differentiate flows and schedule them according to priority. However, such generic data scheduling schemes are video agnostic. They do not utilize the unique structure of coded digital video and thus result in suboptimal schemes for video quality maximization. On the other front, some work has been carried out in terms of scheduling video data with maximum quality. The authors in [3] proposed a scheduling policy to maximize video quality rendered at the receiver by taking into account the temporal error concealment of the video frames at the receiver. The authors in [4] considered the problem of adaptive scheduling policy for real-time video transmission and derived optimal policies by employing a Markov decision process framework. However, both these works do not take the fairness of users into consideration while deriving the scheduling policies. Hence, in this paper, we consider the problem of optimal scheduler design for scalable video data transmission in downlink 3G/4G wireless networks with a constraint on user fairness. In this context, we present a novel framework to characterize the utility of the different scalable video layers in an H.264 SVC video stream. Further, we set up the video scheduling problem in 3G systems such as HSDPA where a single channel such as the high speed downlink shared channel (HS-DSCH) is scheduled amongst multiple users as an MDP and derive a novel video utility index based scalable video scheduling policy for scheduling of scalable video data in infinite queue length (ISVP) and fixed queue length (ISVPF) scenarios. Simulation results demonstrate that these schemes outperform the proportional fair resource allocation and linear index policy (LIP) based schedulers in terms of net video quality. A preliminary work on the ISVP policy has been published by us in a conference article in [5]. In this work, we have enhanced the results significantly by including multichannel multiuser scenarios and performing extensive simulations with more number of users and comparing with additional policies.

Further, OFDM/OFDMA [6, 7] has emerged as a ubiquitous technology for broadband wireless networks because of its significant advantages. In OFDM, a wideband channel can be decomposed into several parallel narrowband frequency flat wireless fading channels thus avoiding the problem of intersymbol interference in frequency selective channels. In such scenarios, efficient multiuser multi-sub-carrier channel allocation algorithms are critical towards QoS enforcement and video quality maximization in next generation networks. However as mentioned earlier, the existing scheduling algorithms [1, 2, 8–10] are generic and do not take into account the structure of coded video transmission which results in suboptimal enduser video quality in broadband wireless access. Hence in this paper, we consider the problem of optimal multiuser 4G OFDMA channel allocation to maximize the video quality while maintaining QoS fairness amongst users.

The rest of the paper is organized as follows. In Section 2 we develop the utility framework for scalable coded videos. In Sections 3 and 4, we derive the optimal 3G video scheduling policies for infinite and finite queue sizes, respectively. In Section 6, we derive the optimality criteria for 4G OFDM channel allocation in multiuser streaming scenarios. In Section 7 we describe optimal channel allocation algorithms to achieve the above optimality criteria. In Section 8, we present the simulation results, and in Section 9, we conclude.

## 2. Scalable Video Utility Framework

H.264 supports three modes of video scalability—temporal, quality, and spatial. In our work, we consider video scheduling for temporal and quality scalable H.264 video and the extension to spatially scalable video sequences is relatively straight forward. Coded digital video streams such as H.264 employ a *group of pictures* (GOP) structure for differential pulse-code modulation (DPCM) based video coding. In a scalable video sequence, temporal scalability is achieved through dynamic GOP size scaling by insertion or deletion of additional temporal layers. An example of the temporally scalable GOP structure with dyadic temporal enhancement video layers is shown in Figure 2. The $T_0$ frames are the base layer *intracoded* video frames while $T_1$ frames are *intercoded* and those of subsequent layers such as $T_2$ are *bidirectional predictively* coded from frames in lower layers. Quality scalability is achieved by using different quantization parameters for the quality video layers. The base quality layer $X_0$ as shown in Figure 3 is coded with a coarse quantization parameter $q_0$. The subsequent higher layer $X_1$ is differentially coded with a lower quantization parameter $q_1$ and so on for each higher layer. The highest quality corresponds to the lowest quantization parameter $q_{min}$. Thus, the net video rate can be scaled dynamically by appropriately choosing the temporal and quality video layers. It can be readily seen from the above GOP description that different component frames of the H.264 salable video GOP have differing

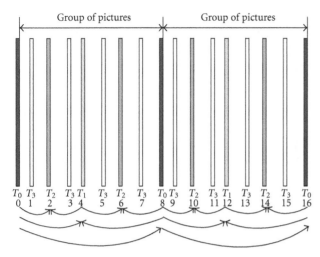

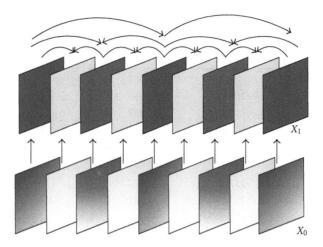

FIGURE 3: Temporal and quantization scalability.

FIGURE 2: H.264 group of pictures (GOP) structure for temporal scalability.

impacts on the net video quality and hence have different utilities. For example considering temporal scalability, it can be observed that the base layer $T_0$ has a significant impact on video quality compared to the enhancement layers $T_1, T_2$, since frames in $T_0$ can be decoded independently as they are intracoded. However, failing reception of $T_0$ frames, one cannot decode the enhancement layer frames of $T_1, T_2$. Hence, a realistic video scheduling framework is needed which ascribes differentiated video utilities accurately characterizing the impact of a particular GOP component on the net video quality. Further, we define the per bit normalized utility $\mathcal{U}_{(i,j)}$ associated with temporal layer $i$ and quality layer $j$ as the ratio of the impact on video quality $\tilde{Q}_{(i,j)}$ to frame size $B_{(i,j)}$ as

$$\mathcal{U}_{(i,j)} = \frac{\tilde{Q}_{(i,j)}}{B_{(i,j)}}. \quad (1)$$

The above quantity $\mathcal{U}_{(i,j)}$ can be interpreted as the utility of scheduling each bit of the video layer, thus associating a higher utility with video sequences of smaller frame sizes compared to larger ones. Below, we propose a framework to compute the quality and size parameters $\tilde{Q}_{(i,j)}, B_{(i,j)}$ in H.264 scalable video scenarios.

*2.1. Video Layer Frame Size Model.* The JSVM reference H.264 codec [11] developed jointly by the ITU-T H.264 and the ISO/IEC MPEG-4 AVC groups can be conveniently employed to characterize the frame sizes of the respective scalable video coded streams. Let $\mathcal{V}_{(m,n)}$ denote the scalable video stream comprising of $m+1$, that is, $0, 1, \ldots, m$ temporal layers and $n + 1$ quality video layers, while $\tilde{\mathcal{V}}_{(m,n)}$ denotes the exclusive $m$th temporal and $n$th quality layer. We consider 4 temporal layers at the standard frame rates of 3.75, 7.5, 15, and 30 frames per second and 3 quantization layers in JSVM corresponding to quantization parameters (QP) 40, 36, and 32. The quantization step-size $q$ corresponding to the quantization parameter QP is given as $q = 2^{((QP-4)/6)}$ [12].

Hence, the quantization step-sizes corresponding to QP = 40, 36, 32 are $q = 64, 40.32, 25.40$, respectively. We employ the notation $R_{(m,n)}$ to denote the bit-rate of the stream $\mathcal{V}_{(m,n)}$. Table 1 illustrates the computed layer rates and frame sizes for the standard *Crew* video [13]. For instance, the rate $R_{(0,0)}$ comprising of the spatial and quality base layers exclusively is given as $R_{(0,0)} = 79.2$ Kbps. Hence, the average base layer frame size can be derived by normalizing with respect to the base-layer frame rate of $f_{(0,0)} = 3.75$ frames per second as

$$B_{(0,0)} = \frac{R_{(0,0)}}{f_{(0,0)}} = 21.12 \text{ Kb}. \quad (2)$$

The JSVM codec yields the cumulative bit-rate corresponding to the combination of base and enhancement layers of the video stream. Hence the rate $R_{(0,1)}$ corresponds to the cumulative bit-rate of the scalable video stream consisting of video layers $\tilde{\mathcal{V}}_{(0,0)}$ and $\tilde{\mathcal{V}}_{(0,1)}$. The differential rate $\tilde{R}_{(0,1)}$ comprising exclusively of the differential video rate arising from the quality layer enhancement frames is given as

$$\tilde{R}_{(0,1)} = R_{(0,1)} - R_{(0,0)}$$
$$= 165.80 - 79.2 = 86.6 \text{ Kbps}. \quad (3)$$

Further, employing the dyadic video scalability model, the exclusive rate of the $\tilde{\mathcal{V}}_{(0,1)}$ layer frames is 3.75 fps, as one such differential frame is added for each $\tilde{\mathcal{V}}_{(0,0)}$ base layer frame. Therefore, the size of each frame belonging to layer $\tilde{\mathcal{V}}_{(0,1)}$ is given as $B_{(0,1)} = 86.6/3.75 = 23.09$ Kb. Similarly one can derive the differential rate and frame sizes associated with the temporal layer $\tilde{\mathcal{V}}_{(1,0)}$. Further, as the cumulative rate $R_{(1,1)}$ incorporates the layers $\tilde{\mathcal{V}}_{(1,1)}$, $\tilde{\mathcal{V}}_{(0,1)}$, $\tilde{\mathcal{V}}_{(1,0)}$, and $\tilde{\mathcal{V}}_{(0,0)}$, the differential rate $\tilde{R}_{(1,1)}$ is given as

$$\tilde{R}_{(1,1)} = (R_{(1,1)} - R_{(0,1)}) - (R_{(1,0)} - R_{(0,0)}) = 32.4 \text{ Kbps}. \quad (4)$$

The differential bit-rates and frame sizes of the higher enhancement layers can be derived similarly. It can be noted that because of the dyadic nature of the scalability, the differential frame rates progressively double for every higher

TABLE 1: Calculation bit rate for SVC video with 4 temporal and 3 quantization layers for *Crew* video.

| Video stream | Cumulative rate $R_{(m,n)}$ | Cumulative quality $Q_{(m,n)}$ | Differential relation $Y_{(m,n)} = R_{(m,n)}$ or $Q_{(m,n)}$ | Differential rate $\widetilde{R}_{(m,n)}$ | Differential quality $\widetilde{Q}_{(m,n)}$ | $N$ (Kb) | Utility $\mathcal{U}_{(m,n)}$ |
|---|---|---|---|---|---|---|---|
| $\mathcal{V}_{(0,0)}$ | 79.2 | 41.301 | $Y_{(0,0)}$ | 79.2000 | 41.3012 | 21.120 | 1.9556 |
| $\mathcal{V}_{(0,1)}$ | 165.80 | 48.395 | $Y_{(0,1)} - Y_{(0,0)}$ | 86.6000 | 7.0943 | 23.093 | 0.3072 |
| $\mathcal{V}_{(0,2)}$ | 315.80 | 53.477 | $Y_{(0,2)} - Y_{(0,1)}$ | 150.0000 | 5.0822 | 40.000 | 0.1271 |
| $\mathcal{V}_{(1,0)}$ | 107.40 | 57.801 | $Y_{(1,0)} - Y_{(0,0)}$ | 28.2000 | 16.5005 | 7.520 | 2.1942 |
| $\mathcal{V}_{(1,1)}$ | 226.40 | 67.730 | $(Y_{(1,1)} - Y_{(0,1)}) - (Y_{(1,0)} - Y_{(0,0)})$ | 32.4000 | 2.8343 | 8.640 | 0.3280 |
| $\mathcal{V}_{(1,2)}$ | 441.60 | 74.843 | $(Y_{(1,2)} - Y_{(0,2)}) - (Y_{(1,1)} - Y_{(0,1)})$ | 65.2000 | 2.0304 | 17.386 | 0.1168 |
| $\mathcal{V}_{(2,0)}$ | 137.50 | 67.027 | $(Y_{(2,0)} - Y_{(1,0)})/2$ | 15.0500 | 4.6130 | 4.013 | 1.1494 |
| $\mathcal{V}_{(2,1)}$ | 292.80 | 78.541 | $((Y_{(2,1)} - Y_{(1,1)}) - (Y_{(2,0)} - Y_{(1,0)}))/2$ | 18.1500 | 0.7924 | 4.840 | 0.1637 |
| $\mathcal{V}_{(2,2)}$ | 575.90 | 86.788 | $((Y_{(2,2)} - Y_{(1,2)}) - (Y_{(2,1)} - Y_{(1,1)}))/2$ | 33.9500 | 0.5676 | 9.053 | 0.0627 |
| $\mathcal{V}_{(3,0)}$ | 171.40 | 68.735 | $(Y_{(3,0)} - Y_{(2,0)})/4$ | 8.4750 | 0.4269 | 2.260 | 0.1889 |
| $\mathcal{V}_{(3,1)}$ | 369.70 | 80.542 | $((Y_{(3,1)} - Y_{(2,1)}) - (Y_{(3,0)} - Y_{(2,0)}))/4$ | 10.7500 | 0.0733 | 2.866 | 0.0256 |
| $\mathcal{V}_{(3,2)}$ | 727.30 | 89.000 | $((Y_{(3,2)} - Y_{(2,2)}) - (Y_{(3,1)} - Y_{(2,1)}))/4$ | 18.6250 | 0.0525 | 4.966 | 0.0106 |

TABLE 2: Quality parameter values $c, d$ for standard videos.

| Video | Akiyo | City | Crew | Football |
|---|---|---|---|---|
| $c$ | 0.11 | 0.13 | 0.17 | 0.08 |
| $d$ | 8.03 | 7.35 | 7.34 | 5.38 |

enhancement layer. Hence, the frame rates associated exclusively with enhancement layers $\widetilde{\mathcal{V}}_{(2,0)}$ and so forth are 7.5 and so on. Following the described procedure one can successively compute the corresponding bit-rates and associated frame sizes of the differential video layers. The bit-rates of several enhancement layers of the video sequence *Crew* are shown in Table 1. It can be seen that the frame sizes progressively decrease with increasing enhancement layer identifier due to the progressively increasing coding gain arising from the DPCM coding.

*2.2. Video Layer Quality Model.* We employ the standard video quality model proposed in [12, 14], which gives the quality of the scalable video stream coded at frame rate $t$ and quantization step-size $q$ as

$$Q = Q_{max}\left(\frac{e^{-c(q/q_{min})}}{e^{-c}}\right)\left(\frac{1 - e^{-d(t/t_{max})}}{1 - e^{-d}}\right), \quad (5)$$

where $q_{min} = 25.40$ is the minimum quantization-step size corresponding to QP = 32, $t$ is frame rate or temporal resolution, $t_{max}$ is the maximum frame rate, $Q_{max}$ is the maximum video quality at $t = t_{max}, q = q_{min}$, set as $Q_{max} = 89$, and $c, d$ are the characteristic video quality parameters. The procedure for deriving the parameters $c, d$ specific to a video sequence is given in [12]. These are indicated in Table 2 for the standard video sequences *Akiyo*, *City*, *Crew*, and *Football*. The screen shots of these four standard videos are shown in Figure 4. The procedure to compute the differential video layer quality can be described as follows. Consider the standard video sequence *Crew*. Let the cumulative impact of the scalable video stream comprising of $m$ temporal and $n$ quality layers be denoted by $Q_{(m,n)}$. This $Q_{(m,n)}$ is calculated

by substituting $m$th layer frame rate and $n$th layer quantization parameter in (5). Hence, the quality associated with the video stream $\widetilde{\mathcal{V}}_{(0,0)} = \mathcal{V}_{(0,0)}$ consisting of the base temporal and quality layers coded at $t = 3.75$ fps and $q = 64$ corresponding to quantization parameter QP = 40 is given as

$$Q_{(0,0)} = Q_{max}\left(\frac{e^{-0.17(64/25.398)}}{e^{-0.17}}\right)\left(\frac{1 - e^{-7.34(3.75/30)}}{1 - e^{-7.34}}\right) = 41.30. \quad (6)$$

Similarly the quality for video stream $\mathcal{V}_{(1,0)}$ with frame rate $t = 7.5$ and $q = 64$ is given by

$$Q_{(1,0)} = Q_{max}\left(\frac{e^{-0.17(64/25.398)}}{e^{-0.17}}\right)\left(\frac{1 - e^{-7.34(7.5/30)}}{1 - e^{-7.34}}\right) = 57.80. \quad (7)$$

Employing the frame size as computed in the section above, the per-bit normalized video utility can be computed utilizing the relation in (1) as

$$U_{(0,0)} = \frac{Q_{(0,0)}}{B_{(0,0)}} = \frac{41.30}{21.12} = 1.95. \quad (8)$$

Thus, the above utility can be employed as a convenient handle to characterize the scheduler reward towards scheduling a particular video stream. Further, similar to the rate derivation in the above section, the quantity $Q_{(m,n)}$ denotes the cumulative quality. Hence, the differential quality $\widetilde{Q}_{(1,0)}$ associated with layer $\widetilde{\mathcal{V}}_{(1,0)}$ for instance is derived as $\widetilde{Q}_{(1,0)} = Q_{(1,0)} - Q_{(0,0)} = 16.50$ for *Crew*. The differential per-bit utility associated with layer $\widetilde{\mathcal{V}}_{(1,0)}$ can be computed as, $U_{(1,0)} = 2.19$ and so on. The differential layer qualities and per-bit utilities of the scalable GOP frames for the standard video sequence *Crew* are shown in the Table 1. The utilities of the four standard video sequences mentioned above are shown in Table 3. It can be seen from the table that the utility exhibits a decreasing trend across the enhancement layers, thus clearly demonstrating the different priorities associated with the GOP

TABLE 3: Utility for different standard videos.

| Video layer | Akiyo | City | Crew | Football |
|---|---|---|---|---|
| $\tilde{\mathcal{V}}_{(0,0)}$ | 12.6906 | 3.2618 | 1.9556 | 1.2266 |
| $\tilde{\mathcal{V}}_{(0,1)}$ | 1.1172 | 0.3178 | 0.3072 | 0.1185 |
| $\tilde{\mathcal{V}}_{(0,2)}$ | 0.4269 | 0.1223 | 0.1271 | 0.0466 |
| $\tilde{\mathcal{V}}_{(1,0)}$ | 24.2893 | 6.0859 | 2.1942 | 1.1310 |
| $\tilde{\mathcal{V}}_{(1,1)}$ | 2.0239 | 0.6943 | 0.3280 | 0.1049 |
| $\tilde{\mathcal{V}}_{(1,2)}$ | 0.8982 | 0.3289 | 0.1168 | 0.0389 |
| $\tilde{\mathcal{V}}_{(2,0)}$ | 9.3842 | 2.7179 | 1.1494 | 0.7410 |
| $\tilde{\mathcal{V}}_{(2,1)}$ | 0.8447 | 0.2993 | 0.1637 | 0.0639 |
| $\tilde{\mathcal{V}}_{(2,2)}$ | 0.3737 | 0.1405 | 0.0627 | 0.0223 |
| $\tilde{\mathcal{V}}_{(3,0)}$ | 1.2832 | 0.4206 | 0.1889 | 0.2299 |
| $\tilde{\mathcal{V}}_{(3,1)}$ | 0.1351 | 0.0424 | 0.0256 | 0.0170 |
| $\tilde{\mathcal{V}}_{(3,2)}$ | 0.0638 | 0.0198 | 0.0106 | 0.0063 |

components. In the next section we derive an optimal policy towards video quality maximization while ensuring fairness in QoS.

## 3. Index-Based Scalable Video Policy (ISVP)

Employing the framework illustrated in [15], we model the scalable video scheduling scenario as a Markov decision process (MDP). The state of user $u$ at time $n$ is modeled as a combination of the channel state $s_u^n$ and the video state $v_u^n$ of the head of the queue frame of user $u$. Further, we also incorporate the user starvation age $a_u^n$ in the system state to ensure fairness in video scheduling. We assume that $s_u^n \in \{1, 2, \ldots L+1\}$, where each state represents a maximum bitrate $\mathcal{R}(s_u^n)$ supported by the fading channel between user $u$ and base station at time instant $n$. The vector $\mathbf{s}^n$ at time instant $n$ defined as $\mathbf{s}^n = [s_1^n, s_2^n, \ldots, s_U^n]^T$ characterizes the joint channel state of all users. We assume that $\{\mathbf{s}^n, n \geq 0\}$ is an irreducible discrete time Markov Chain [16] with the $L+1$ dimensional probability transition matrix $\mathbf{P}^u = [p_{i,j}^u]$. The objective of the scheduler is to allocate the shared wireless channel by scheduling the users in each time slot in such a way that maximizes the quality of scalable video without leading to starvation of users as shown in Figure 5. From the GOP structure illustrated previously in the context of scalable video, the video data state for each user $v_u^n \in \{1, 2, \ldots, G\}$, where $G$ is the number of frames in a GOP. Similar to above, the joint video state of the $U$ users can be denoted as $\mathbf{v}^n = [v_1^n, v_2^n, \ldots, v_U^n]^T$. The starvation age $a_u^n$ corresponds to the number of slots for which a particular user has not been served. This quantity is initialized as 0 to begin with and incremented by one for every slot for each user who is not served in that slot. If a particular user is served in the current slot, his starvation age is reset to 0. Let $\omega(n)$ denote the user scheduled at time slot $n$. The starvation age transition for a particular user is given as

$$a_u^n = \begin{cases} a_u^n + 1, & \text{if } \omega(n) \neq u \\ 0, & \text{if } \omega(n) = u. \end{cases} \tag{9}$$

The total user starvation age is similarly denoted by vector $\mathbf{a}^n$ obtained by stacking the starvation ages of all the users. The starvation age is important parameter as it can be used to characterize the fairness. If the starvation age of all users is almost same then we can say that fairness is achieved. If the starvation age of users is low then we can say that the users are not starved. Ideally the starvation of all users should be equal and close to zero. The system state vector $\mathbf{g} = [(\mathbf{v}^n)^T, (\mathbf{s}^n)^T, (\mathbf{a}^n)^T]^T$ characterizes the complete state of the system. The action $\omega(n)$ at any time instant $n$ corresponds to choosing one of the $U$ users. Employing the video utility framework developed above, the reward corresponding to serving user $u$ in slot $n$ is given as

$$r_n(u) = \mathcal{U}(v_u^n)\mathcal{R}(s_u^n) - \sum_{l \neq u} K_l a_l^n, \tag{10}$$

where $\mathcal{U}(v_u^n)$ gives the utility of the video packet of user $u$ in state $v_u^n$ and $K_l$ is a constant which can control the trade-off between quality and fairness. The transition probability from state $\mathbf{g} = [(\mathbf{v})^T, (\mathbf{s})^T, (\mathbf{a})^T]^T$ to $\tilde{\mathbf{g}} = [(\tilde{\mathbf{v}})^T, (\tilde{\mathbf{s}})^T, (\tilde{\mathbf{a}})^T]^T$ contingent on scheduling user $u$ is given as

$$p(\tilde{\mathbf{g}} \mid \mathbf{g}, u) = p_{s_1, \tilde{s}_1}^1 p_{s_2, \tilde{s}_2}^2 \cdots p_{s_U, \tilde{s}_U}^U \tag{11}$$

if $\tilde{v}_u = v_u + 1 \bmod G$, $\tilde{a}_u = 0$ and $\tilde{a}_z = a_z + 1$, $\tilde{v}_z = v_z$ for all $z \neq u$. Our objective is to derive the optimal policy which maximizes the long-term average reward $\lim_{T \to \infty} (1/T) E_T(\mathbf{g})$, where $E_T(\mathbf{g})$ denotes the maximum reward over $T$ time periods with initial state $\mathbf{g}$. As this is an infinite horizon problem [17] with a very large state space, conventional schemes for policy derivation are impractical. We therefore employ the novel procedure proposed in [15] to derive the optimal scalable video scheduling policy termed ISVP.

**Corollary 1.** *An index policy $I_u(\mathbf{g})$ close to the optimal policy for long-term expected average reward maximization in the context of the video scheduling paradigm defined above is given as*

$$I_u(\mathbf{g}) = \mathcal{U}(v_u)\mathcal{R}(s_u) + K_u a_u(U+1) + K_u U. \tag{12}$$

*Proof.* As described in (10), the proposed reward structure is $\mathcal{U}(v_u)\mathcal{R}(s_u) - \sum_{z \neq u} K_z a_z$. Replacing the channel state with the joint video and channel state vector $[\mathbf{v}^T, \mathbf{s}^T]^T$, reward with the proposed reward in (10) and applying Theorem 2 in [15] yields the desired result. □

The above result guarantees that ISVP, which schedules the video user with the highest index $I_u(\mathbf{g})$, is close to the optimal policy and maximizes the video utility while minimizing the starvation age of all users.

## 4. Finite Queue Video System Model

The above proposed optimal ISVP policy maximizes the scalable video quality at the received users when the queue size is assumed to be infinity. In this section, we derive the optimal

| (a) | (b) | (c) | (d) |

FIGURE 4: Screen shots of standard videos *Akiyo*, *City*, *Football*, and *Crew*.

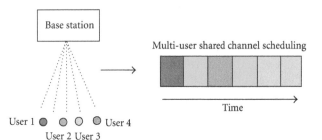

FIGURE 5: Scheduling in shared wireless channel.

policy which maximizes scalable video quality when the buffer size in the base station is finite. The system model is identical to the one developed previously for video streaming except that the scalable video coded packets are buffered in a finite length queue at the base station. The state of user $u$ at time $n$ is modified to include the queue state $\mathbf{q}_u^n$ with the state space $\Omega_{q_u}$ along with the channel state $s_u^n$. The quantity $\mathbf{q}_u^n$ is a vector of utilities of the packets in the queue of user $u$ at time instant $n$. The vector $\mathbf{q}^n$ at time instant $n$ defined as $\mathbf{q}^n = [\mathbf{q}_1^n, \mathbf{q}_2^n, \ldots, \mathbf{q}_U^n]$ characterizes the queue state of all the $U$ mobile video users. Hence, the system state vector $\mathbf{g} = [(\mathbf{q}^n)^T, (\mathbf{s}^n)^T, (\mathbf{a}^n)^T]^T$ characterizes the complete state of the system. The action $\omega(n)$ at any time instant $n$ corresponds to choosing one of the $U$ users. We define the reward of scheduling a user $u$ in slot $n$ as

$$R_u^n = \mathbf{q}_u^n[1] \cdot \mathcal{R}(s_u^n) - \sum_{v \neq u} K_v \left( \sum_{i=1}^{i=\min\{a_v, L_v\}} \mathbf{q}_v^n[i] \right). \quad (13)$$

Observe that the reward is proportional to the rate of the channel and also utility of the scheduled video to maximize the quality of the video. Second the penalty for not scheduling a user in a time slot is proportional to the starvation age of that user. We choose this penalty function as sum of utilities of frames in the queue with number of frames as minimum of starvation age and number of frames in the queue. Hence this penalty term is implicitly proportional to the starvation age and utility of the frames of unscheduled users. The term $K_v$ controls the weight of penalty function compared to the positive reward. Third mathematical tractability is also considered in defining the reward. For

example the chosen reward is a regenerative process which simplifies the derivation of the optimum policy in future sections.

## 5. Optimal Finite Queue Length Video Scheduling Policy (ISVPF)

Similar to the previously derived policy for infinite queue lengths, let the initial policy be a random policy meaning allocate user $u$ with probability $\alpha_u$. The policy iteration step is to choose the user $u$ which maximizes the index

$$I_u(\mathbf{i}^n, \mathbf{a}^n) = \mathbf{q}_u^n[1] \cdot \mathcal{R}(s_u^n)$$
$$- \sum_{v \neq u} K_v \left( \sum_{k=1}^{\min\{a_v^n, L_v^n\}} \mathbf{q}_v^n[k] \right) \quad (14)$$
$$+ \sum_{\mathbf{i}} P_{\mathbf{i}^n \mathbf{i}^{(n+1)}} h_r \left( \mathbf{i}^{(n+1)}, \mathbf{a}^{(n+1)} \right),$$

where, $\mathbf{i}^n = [\mathbf{q}^n, \mathbf{s}^n] \in \Omega_{q_1} \times \cdots \times \Omega_{q_u} \times \Omega_c$, $\mathbf{a}^{(n+1)} = [a_1^n + 1, \ldots, a_{u-1}^n + 1, 0, a_{u+1}^n + 1, \ldots, a_U^n + 1]$ and $h_r(\mathbf{i}^{(n+1)}, \mathbf{a}^{(n+1)})$ is the bias term of randomized policy starting in state $(\mathbf{i}^{(n+1)}, \mathbf{a}^u)$. To derive the bias term, add the expression below

$$\sum_v K_v \left( \sum_{k=1}^{\min\{a_v^n, L_v^n\}} \mathbf{q}_v[k] \right) - \sum_{\mathbf{i}} P_{\mathbf{i}^n \mathbf{i}^{(n+1)}} h_r \left( \mathbf{i}^{(n+1)}, \mathbf{a}^n + \mathbf{e} \right) \quad (15)$$

to (14), where $\mathbf{e} = [1, 1, \ldots, 1]$. As this expression is independent of $u$ adding, this will not affect the outcome. The resulting equation is

$$I_u(\mathbf{i}^n, \mathbf{a}^n) = \mathbf{q}_u^n[1] \cdot \mathcal{R}(s_u^n) + K_u \left( \sum_{k=1}^{\min\{a_u^n, L_u^n\}} \mathbf{q}_v^n[k] \right)$$
$$+ \sum_{\mathbf{i}} P_{\mathbf{i}^n \mathbf{i}^{(n+1)}} \left( h_r \left( \mathbf{i}^{(n+1)}, \mathbf{a}^u \right) \quad (16)$$
$$- h_r \left( \mathbf{i}^{(n+1)}, \mathbf{a}^n + \mathbf{e} \right) \right).$$

To compute the index, we need to find the difference in biases. Consider two different sample paths of the stochastic process $(\mathbf{i}^{(n,m)}, \mathbf{a}^{(n,m)})$, $m \in \{1, 2\}$ such that, $w^1(n) = w^2(n)$, $\mathbf{i}^{(n,1)} = \mathbf{i}^{(n,2)}$, $n \geq 0$, and $\mathbf{a}^{(0,1)} = \mathbf{a}^u$, $\mathbf{a}^{(0,2)} = \mathbf{a}^n + \mathbf{e}$.

Let $\acute{n}$ be the first time instant at which user $u$ is scheduled, then

$$a_v^{(n,1)} = a_v^{(n,2)}, \quad v \neq u, \forall n$$

$$a_u^{(n,1)} = a_u^{(n,2)}, \quad \text{if } n > \acute{n} \tag{17}$$

$$a_u^{(n,1)} = n, \quad a_u^{(n,2)} = a_u^n + 1 + n, \quad \text{if } n \leq \acute{n}.$$

The difference in biases is equal to the average difference in the reward acquired in these two sample paths. However in this scenario, the reward differs only in cost term for user $u$ till time slot $\acute{n} = n_0$. Therefore,

$$h_r\left(\mathbf{i}^{(n+1)}, \mathbf{a}^u\right) - h_r\left(\mathbf{i}^{(n+1)}, \mathbf{a}^n + \mathbf{e}\right)$$

$$= \sum_{n=1}^{n_0} G_u\left(a_u^n + n + 1\right) - G_u(n), \tag{18}$$

where $G_u^n(n) = K_u(\sum_{k=1}^{\min\{n, L_u^n\}} \mathbf{q}_u^n[k])$.

Since $\acute{n}$ follows a geometrical distribution with parameter $\alpha_u$ the average value of the difference in biases considered above is

$$r \sum_{n_0=1}^{\infty} \alpha_u (1 - \alpha_u)^{n_0 - 1} \left( \sum_{n=1}^{n_0} G_u(a_u^n + n + 1) - G_u(n) \right)$$

$$= \alpha_u \left( G_u(a_u^n + 2) - G_u(1) \right)$$

$$+ \alpha_u (1 - \alpha_u) \left( G_u(a_u^n + 2) - G_u(1) + G_u(a_u^n + 3) - G_u(2) \right)$$

$$+ \alpha_u (1 - \alpha_u)^2 \left( G_u(a_u^n + 2) - G_u(1) + G_u(a_u^n + 3) \right.$$

$$\left. - G_u(2) + G_u(a_u^n + 4) - G_u(3) \right) \cdots$$

$$= G_u(a_u^n + 2)\left( \alpha_u + \alpha_u(1 - \alpha_u) + \alpha_u(1 - \alpha_u)^2 + \cdots \right)$$

$$- G_u(1)\left( \alpha_u + \alpha_u(1 - \alpha_u) + \alpha_u(1 - \alpha_u)^2 + \cdots \right)$$

$$+ G_u(a_u^n + 3)\left( \alpha_u(1 - \alpha_u) + \alpha_u(1 - \alpha_u)^2 + \cdots \right)$$

$$- G_u(2)\left( \alpha_u(1 - \alpha_u) + \alpha_u(1 - \alpha_u)^2 + \cdots \right) \cdots$$

$$= \sum_{n_0=1}^{\infty} (1 - \alpha_u)^{n_0 - 1} \left( G_u(a_u^n + n_0 + 1) - G_u(n_0) \right)$$

$$= \sum_{n_0=1}^{\infty} (1 - \alpha_u)^{n_0 - 1}$$

$$\times \underbrace{\left[ K_u\left( \sum_{k=1}^{\min\{a_u^n + n_0 + 1, L_u^n\}} \mathbf{q}_u^n[k] \right) - K_u\left( \sum_{k=1}^{\min\{n_0, L_u^n\}} \mathbf{q}_u^n[k] \right) \right]}_{= \Phi(\mathbf{q}_u^n)}$$

$$= \sum_{n_0=1}^{L_u^n} (1 - \alpha_u)^{n_0 - 1} K_u\left( \sum_{k=n_0+1}^{\min\{a_u^n + n_0 + 1, L_u^n\}} \mathbf{q}_u^n[k] \right), \tag{19}$$

where the last equality follows from the fact that for $n_0 > L_u^n$, the term $\Phi(\mathbf{q}_u^n)$ is equal to 0. Hence the final index $I_u(\mathbf{i}^n, \mathbf{a}^n)$ for finite queue video scheduling is given by

$$I_u(\mathbf{i}^n, \mathbf{a}^n) = \mathbf{q}_u^n[1] \cdot \mathcal{R}(s_u^n) + K_u\left( \sum_{k=1}^{\min\{a_u^n, L_u^n\}} \mathbf{q}_v^n[k] \right)$$

$$+ \sum_{n_0=1}^{L_u^n} (1 - \alpha_u)^{n_0 - 1} K_u\left( \sum_{k=n_0+1}^{\min\{a_u^n + n_0 + 1, L_u^n\}} \mathbf{q}_u^n[k] \right). \tag{20}$$

## 6. Multiuser OFDMA Video Streaming Model

In the previous section, we have derived the optimal policy for a single shared channel scenario. In this section, we extend this to a multiple channel scenario by deriving an optimal channel allocation policy for 4G wireless systems. Consider a 4G OFDMA cellular base station BS streaming videos to a set of $U$ cellular users. Let the users be indexed by $u, 1 \leq u \leq U$. The H.264 scalable coded video packets of these users are buffered at the Base station in their respective individual queues of infinite queue lengths. Consider $N$ different OFDMA sub-channels to be allocated by the BS to the users for video transmission refer to Figure 6. Similar to the standard scheduling models established in literature we consider slotted time and channel allocation at every time slot. In this wireless video streaming scenario we wish to design a scheduler for multiuser sub-channel allocation towards video quality maximization while maintaining fairness amongst users. As already described above, the scalable coded video stream can be adapted to comprise varying combinations of temporal, quality, and spatial scalable layers. As described in Section 2, each video layer is naturally of varying utility with respect to its graded impact on the net video quality. These utility parameters for different frame components of the scalable GOP structure had been derived therein and are key towards resource allocation for video quality maximization. The normalized utility representing the per bit impact on net video quality can be computed efficiently employing the framework described in this work. Below we model this wireless video streaming scenario as a multidimensional Markov decision process (MDP) to derive the optimal multiuser multichannel OFDMA video streaming policy. Let the user state be modelled as a combination of the $N$ dimensional channel state vector, $\mathbf{s}_u^n = [s^n(u, 1), s^n(u, 2), \ldots, s^n(u, N)]^T$, where $s^n(u, c)$ represents a maximum supported bit-rate of $\mathcal{R}(s^n(u, c))$ between the BS and user $u$ over channel $c$ at time slot $n$, video state of the head of the line packet $v_u^n$. This video state corresponds to the identity of the frame in the scalable GOP. Hence the joint multiuser multichannel state $\mathbf{S}^n \in \mathbb{R}^{N \times U}$ can be obtained from the individual channel state vectors as $\mathbf{S}^n = [\mathbf{s}_1^n, \mathbf{s}_2^n, \ldots, \mathbf{s}_U^n]$. Similarly the joint video state vector $\mathbf{v}^n \in \mathbb{R}^U$ of the $U$ users can be defined as $\mathbf{v}^n = [v_1^n, v_2^n, \ldots, v_U^n]^T$. Let the starvation age of user be denoted by $a_u^n$. This starvation age is initialised to 0 to begin with and is incremented by one in every time slot if the user is not scheduled, while being reinitialised to 0 once the user is scheduled. Hence the update relation for this starvation age parameter $a_u^n$ can be described as

$$a_u^n = \begin{cases} a_u^n + 1, & \text{if } u \notin \omega(n), \\ 0, & \text{if } u \in \omega(n), \end{cases} \qquad (21)$$

where $\omega(n) \subset \{1, 2, \ldots, U\}$ is the set of users scheduled to transmit in time slot $n$. The action is choosing any $N$ users among $U$ users at every time slot. The net video quality reward of assigning users $u_1, u_2, \ldots, u_N$ in time slot $n$ to channels 1 through $N$, respectively, is given as

$$r_n(u_1, \ldots, u_N) = \sum_{i=1}^{N} \mathcal{U}\left(v_{u_i}^n\right) \mathcal{R}(s^n(u_i, i)) - \sum_{v \notin \{u_1, \ldots, u_N\}} K_v a_v^n, \qquad (22)$$

where, $\mathcal{U}(v_{u_i}^n)$ denotes the video utility achieved by scheduling user $u_i$ over the $i$th channel and $K_v$ is the penalty factor corresponding to the starvation age. Deriving the optimal policy to maximize the above long-term reward for this multidimensional MDP yields the optimal scheduler policy for video quality maximization. However it is significantly challenging to obtain the optimal policy solution of this MDP. This arises due to the fact that the above MDP has an extremely large state space which grows exponentially with the number of users and channels. Thus it is inefficient to employ conventional policy and value iteration techniques to derive the optimal policy as they require a significantly large time for convergence. Hence in such scenarios, one can initialize with a random policy and employ a one step policy iteration to derive a policy that is sufficiently close to the optimal policy [18]. Now consider an initial random policy for individual user selection towards sub-channel allocation. The policy improvement step towards deriving the optimal policy for allocation of $N$ sub-channels towards video quality maximization is to choose the set of $N$ different users which maximizes the index $I_{\mathbf{u}}(\mathbf{i}^n, \mathbf{a}^n)$ given as

$$I_{\mathbf{u}}(\mathbf{i}^n, \mathbf{a}^n) = \sum_{i=1}^{N} \mathcal{U}\left(v_{u_i}^n\right) \mathcal{R}(s^n(u_i, i))$$
$$- \sum_{v \notin \{u_1, \ldots u_N\}} K_v a_v^n + \sum_{\mathbf{i}} P_{\mathbf{i}^n \mathbf{i}^{(n+1)}} h_r\left(\mathbf{i}^{(n+1)}, \mathbf{a}^{(\mathbf{n+1})}\right), \qquad (23)$$

where $\mathbf{i}^n = (\mathbf{S}^n, \mathbf{v}^n)$ is the joint multiuser multichannel and video queue state at time slot $n$ and $h_r(\mathbf{j}^{(n+1)}, \mathbf{a}^{\mathbf{u}})$ is the bias term of the randomized policy starting in state $(\mathbf{i}^{(n+1)}, \mathbf{a}^{(n+1)})$. The starvation age of each user in $n + 1$ time slot $\mathbf{a}^{(n+1)}$ is obtained by incrementing the previous starvation age by one if the user is not scheduled and assigning 0 if user is scheduled. This is represented by

$$\mathbf{a}_{u_i}^{(n+1)} = \begin{cases} a_{u_i}^n + 1, & \text{if } u_i \notin \{u_1, \ldots, u_N\} \\ 0, & \text{otherwise.} \end{cases} \qquad (24)$$

Hence the optimal video policy depends on the bias term which is derived employing the procedure below. Let $\mathbf{u} = \{u_1, u_1 \ldots, u_N\}$ be the set of users scheduled in time slot $n$.

To simplify the above equation, we add the following $\mathbf{u}$ independent term given as

$$\sum_{v=1}^{U} K_v a_v^n - \sum_{\mathbf{i}^{(n+1)}} P_{\mathbf{i}^n \mathbf{i}^{(n+1)}} h_r\left(\mathbf{i}^{(n+1)}, \mathbf{a}^n + \mathbf{e}\right), \qquad (25)$$

where $\mathbf{e} = [1, 1, \ldots, 1]^T$. Adding the above term to the (23), the resulting expression for the index $I_{\mathbf{u}}(\mathbf{i}^n, \mathbf{a}^n)$ can be simplified as

$$I_{\mathbf{u}}(\mathbf{i}^n, \mathbf{a}^n) = \sum_{i=1}^{N} \mathcal{U}\left(v_{u_i}^n\right) \mathcal{R}(s^n(u_i, i)) + \sum_{i=1}^{N} K_{v_i} a_{v_i}^n$$
$$+ \sum_{\mathbf{i}^{(n+1)}} P_{\mathbf{i}^n \mathbf{i}^{(n+1)}} \left(h_r\left(\mathbf{i}^{n+1}, \mathbf{a}^{(n+1)}\right) - h_r\left(\mathbf{i}^{n+1}, \mathbf{a}^n + \mathbf{e}\right)\right). \qquad (26)$$

From the above equation, it is clear that the optimal index depends only on the difference in the bias terms $(h_r(\mathbf{i}^{n+1}, \mathbf{a}^{(n+1)}) - h_r(\mathbf{i}^{n+1}, \mathbf{a}^n + \mathbf{e}))$. To compute this consider two different sample paths of the stochastic process of the randomized policy $(\mathbf{i}^{(n,m)}, \mathbf{a}^{(n,m)})$, $m \in \{1, 2\}$ such that $\omega^1(n) = \omega^2(n)$, $\mathbf{i}^{(n,1)} = \mathbf{i}^{(n,2)}$, $n \geq 0$ and $\mathbf{a}^{(0,1)} = \mathbf{a}^{(n+1)}$, $\mathbf{a}^{(0,2)} = \mathbf{a}^n + \mathbf{e}$. Let $n_i$ be the first time instant at which user $u_i$ is scheduled. It can be readily observed that the difference in biases is equal to the average difference in the reward acquired in these two sample paths. However in this scenario, the rewards differ only in cost term for users $u_i$ till time slot $n_i$. Therefore,

$$a_v^{(n,1)} = a_v^{(n,2)}, \quad v \notin \mathbf{u}, \ \forall n$$
$$a_{u_i}^{(n,1)} = a_{u_i}^{(n,2)}, \quad u_i \in \mathbf{u}, \text{ if } n > n_i, \qquad (27)$$
$$a_{u_i}^{(n,1)} = n, \quad a_{u_i}^{(n,2)} = a_{u_i}^n + 1 + n, \quad u_i \in \mathbf{u}, \text{ if } n \leq n_i.$$

Hence, employing the above relations for the starvation age vector, the expression for the bias difference $h_r(\mathbf{i}^{(n+1)}, \mathbf{a}^{(n+1)}) - h_r(\mathbf{i}^{(n+1)}, \mathbf{a}^n + \mathbf{e})$ can be derived as

$$h_r\left(\mathbf{i}^{(n+1)}, \mathbf{a}^{(n+1)}\right) - h_r\left(\mathbf{i}^{(n+1)}, \mathbf{a}^n + \mathbf{e}\right)$$
$$= \sum_{i=1}^{N} \sum_{n=1}^{n_i} K_{u_i}\left(a_{u_i}^n + n + 1\right) - K_{u_i}(n). \qquad (28)$$

Since the policy is random, $n_i$ is a random variable which follows geometric distribution with $p = N/U$. Therefore the expected value of the difference in bias term can be further simplified as

$$h_r\left(\mathbf{i}^{(n+1)}, \mathbf{a}^{(n+1)}\right) - h_r\left(\mathbf{i}^{(n+1)}, \mathbf{a}^n + \mathbf{e}\right)$$

$$= \sum_{i=1}^{N}\sum_{n_i=1}^{\infty} p(1-p)^{(n_i-1)} \sum_{i=1}^{n_i} K_{u_i}\left(a_{u_i}^n + n + 1\right) - K_{u_i}(n)$$

$$= \sum_{i=1}^{N}\sum_{n_i=1}^{\infty} (1-p)^{(n_i-1)} K_{u_i}\left(a_{u_i}^n + n_i + 1\right) - K_{u_i}(n_i) \quad (29)$$

$$= \sum_{i=1}^{N} K_{u_i}\left(a_{u_i}^n + 1\right)\left(\sum_{n_i=1}^{\infty}(1-p)^{(n_i-1)}\right)$$

$$= \frac{1}{p}\sum_{i=1}^{N} K_{u_i}\left(a_{u_i}^n + 1\right) = \frac{U}{N}\sum_{i=1}^{N} K_{u_i}\left(a_{u_i}^n + 1\right).$$

Substituting the above expression in (23), the resulting expression for the user video scheduler index $I_{\mathbf{u}}(\mathbf{i}^n, \mathbf{a}^n)$ can be simplified as

$$I_{\mathbf{u}}(\mathbf{i}^n, \mathbf{a}^n) = \sum_{i=1}^{N} \mathcal{U}\left(v_{u_i}^n\right)\mathcal{R}(s^n(u_i, i))$$

$$+ \sum_{i=1}^{N} K_{u_i}a_{u_i}^n$$

$$+ \frac{U}{N}\sum_{\mathbf{i}^{(n+1)}} P_{\mathbf{i}^n\mathbf{i}^{n+1}}\sum_{i=1}^{N} K_{u_i}\left(a_{u_i}^n + 1\right) \quad (30)$$

$$= \sum_{i=1}^{N} \mathcal{U}\left(v_{u_i}^n\right)\mathcal{R}(s^n(u_i, i))$$

$$+ K_{u_i}a_{u_i}^n + K_{u_i}\left(a_{u_i}^n + 1\right)\left(\frac{U}{N}\right).$$

Let $w(u,c)$ be defined as $w(u,c) = \mathcal{U}(v_u^n)\mathcal{R}(s^n(u,c)) + K_u a_u^n + K_u(a_u^n + 1)(U/N)$. Then the index $I_{\mathbf{u}}(\mathbf{i}^n, \mathbf{a}^n)$ can be simplified as

$$I_{\mathbf{u}}(\mathbf{i}^n, \mathbf{a}^n) = \sum_{i=1}^{N} w(u_i, i). \quad (31)$$

Therefore the optimal video scheduler policy chooses $N$ users such that it maximises the sum component index $\sum_{i=1}^{N} w(u_i, i)$. Next we describe a fast algorithm to compute the multiuser multi-sub-channel allocation towards video quality maximization based on the above index optimization.

## 7. Bipartite User Subchannel Index Maximization

The above multiuser index maximization can be readily viewed as a maximum weight bipartite matching computation. Consider a bipartite graph $(U, C, E)$ such that the partitions contain the $U$ users and the $N$ channels as the nodes

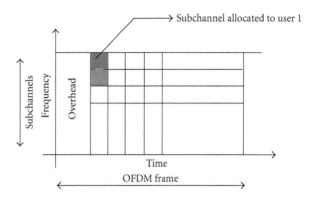

FIGURE 6: OFDM subchannel allocation with respect to time.

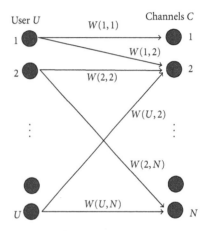

FIGURE 7: Bipartite graph with users and channels as nodes of the graph.

and the $U \times N$ edges between each user $u$ to each channel $c$ are associated with the weight $w(u,c)$ as shown in Figure 7. The optimal index computation for video scheduling thus reduces to computing the maximally wighted bipartite user sub-channel matching. This can be achieved through the Hungarian algorithm-based sub channel allocation given below. The input to the algorithm is a matrix $W$ whose $(i,j)$th element represents weight of the edge between user $i$ and channel $j$ which is equal to $w(i, j)$. The algorithm is described below.

The Hungarian method given in Algorithm 1 thus yields the optimal index based user sub-channel allocation for long term video quality maximization. However, it has a complexity of $O((U + N)^3)$. Hence to reduce the computational complexity we present a suboptimal greedy algorithm of complexity $O(U^2)$ in Algorithm 2.

## 8. Simulation Results

We compare the performance of the proposed video optimal policies with LIP proposed in [15], proportional fair (PF) scheduling policy, and two heuristic policies. The LIP is an index policy with index $I_u^l(\mathbf{s}^n, \mathbf{a}^n)$ defined exclusively in terms of the channel state vector $\mathbf{s}^n$ and multiuser starvation vector $\mathbf{a}^n$ as $I_u^l(\mathbf{s}^n, \mathbf{a}^n) = \mathcal{R}(s_u^n) + K_u a_u(U + 1) + K_u U$. The LIP is

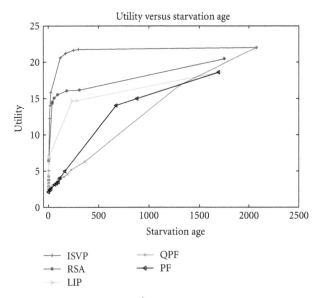

FIGURE 8: Utility ($\hat{\Psi}$) versus starvation age ($\hat{\chi}$).

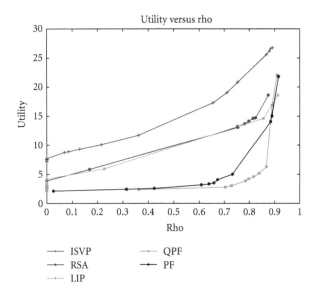

FIGURE 9: Utility ($\hat{\Psi}$) versus Rho ($\widehat{\rho_d}$).

an optimal policy for maximizing bit rate with a constraint on fairness. It is generic in sense it does not depend on the type of data transmitted. Whereas the policies ISVP, ISVPF we have proposed are suited for transmission of video data through wireless channel. These policies take advantage of the scalability of video and hence they are dynamically scalable with the state of the changing wireless environment.

The PF scheduling policy is equivalent to an index policy $I_u^p(\mathbf{s}^n) = \mathcal{R}(s_u^n)/Q_u(n)$ where $Q_u(n)$ is given as

$$Q_u(n+1) = \begin{cases} (1-\tau)Q_u(n) + \tau\mathcal{R}(s_u^n), & \text{if } u = \omega(n) \\ (1-\tau)Q_u(n), & \text{if } u \neq \omega(n), \end{cases} \quad (32)$$

where $\omega(n)$ is the scheduled user in slot $n$ and $\tau$ is the damping coefficient. As the above two policies are generic, we also compare our results with two other heuristic policies.

The first heuristic policy is the Quality Proportional Fair (QPF) policy. It is similar to PF policy except that the rate is replace by product of utility and rate. The QPF scheduling policy is equivalent to an index policy $I_u^{\text{QPF}}(\mathbf{s}^n) = \mathcal{U}(s_u^n)\mathcal{R}(s_u^n)/Q_u(n)$ where $Q_u(n)$ is given as

$$Q_u(n+1) = \begin{cases} (1-\tau)Q_u(n) + \tau\mathcal{U}(s_u^n)\mathcal{R}(s_u^n), & \text{if } u = \omega(n) \\ (1-\tau)Q_u(n), & \text{if } u \neq \omega(n). \end{cases} \quad (33)$$

The second heuristic policy is Rate Starvation Age policy (RSA). It is an Index policy with index directly proportional to rate and starvation age. The index $I_u^{\text{RSA}}$ is defined as $I_u^{\text{RSA}}(\mathbf{s}^n, \mathbf{a}^n) = \mathcal{R}(s_u^n) + K_u a_u$. These policies are extended appropriately for comparison in multichannel scenarios. For multi channel scenario, we applied Greedy matching and Hungarian matching algorithms with the weights of the edges equal to above indexes $I^{\text{LIP}}$ and $I^{\text{PF}}$. For finite queue case whenever the buffer is full, the incoming packets are dropped.

We consider the performance measures $\Psi$, the expected per-slot long-term utility, $\chi$, the expected starvation age and $\rho_d$, the probability that a user is not served for longer than $d$ time slots, for evaluation of the policies. We consider an $L + 1 = 5$ channel state model with supported rate states $\mathcal{R}(s_u^n) \in \{38.4, 76.8, 102.6, 153.6, 204.8\}$ Kbps. We considered $U = 12$ users transmitting the standard videos *Akiyo*, *City*, *Crew*, and *Football*. We use $T = 10^5$ slots and $P = 100$ sample paths of the Markov chain. The state transition matrix is similar to the one considered in [15], with $\beta = 0.999$. The $K_u$ value is varied for the ISVP and LIP schemes while $\tau$ is varied for the PF scheme. The starvation age and utility are calculated for different values of parameter $K_u$ in the range $[0, 500]$. In case of the PF policy, the parameter $\tau$ is varied appropriately in the range $[0, 1]$.

Figure 8 shows a comparison of the video utility of the proposed ISVP policy with LIP, PF, RSA, and QPF policies. It can be observed that the proposed ISVP policy yields the maximum video utility amongst the five competing policies. Further, as $K_u \to \infty$ and $\tau \to 1$, the LIP and PF policies effectively converge to the round-robin policy. Hence, the utility and starvation age coincide at this point. Further when $K_u = 0$ the index remains same for ISVP and QPF policies so they also coincide. Figure 9 shows the plot between utility and the probability $\rho_d$ that a user is starved for more than $d$ slots. This is also plotted by varying the parameters as mentioned above. We observe that the utility is maximum for a particular probability for the proposed ISVP scheme compared to other policies. Thus, the proposed ISVP scheduler maximizes the net video quality while not compromising on fairness. Further the ISVP policy we proposed is an index policy and index calculation is of order $O(1)$ similar to PF and LIP policy so the cost of computation remains same which is $O(U)$.

Figures 10 and 11 show a comparison of the video utility of the proposed ISVPF policy with that LIP, RSA, QPF, and PF policies when each user queue sizes are equal to $L_u = 500$. It can be observed that the proposed ISVPF policy yields the maximum video utility amongst the five competing policies.

(1) Identify the largest element $\alpha$ of the matrix $W$ and replace each element $w(u,c)$ with $\alpha - w(u,c)$.
(2) From every row of the resultant matrix subtract the row minimum that is, $w(i,j) = w(i,j) - \min_j(w(i,j))$, $\forall i$.
(3) From every column of the matrix subtract the column minimum that is, $w(i,j) = w(i,j) - \min_i(w(i,j))$; $\forall j$.
(4) **while** True **do**
(5)    In every row match a row and column if there is only one 0 in a row and strike off the other 0's in the
       matched column that is, $i \leftrightarrow j$, if $w(i,j) = 0$, and $w(i',j) \neq 0$, $\forall i' \neq i$, $\forall i \in \{1, 2, \ldots, U\}$
(6)    In every column match a row and column if there is only one 0 in the column and strike off the other 0's
       in the matched row that is, $i \leftrightarrow j$, if $w(i,j) = 0$, and $w(i,j') \neq 0$, $\forall j' \neq j$, $\forall j \in \{1, 2, \ldots, N\}$
(7)    **if** Allocation is not complete **then**
(8)       Draw minimum number of lines passing through all zeroes.
(9)       Identify the smallest number $\theta$ amongst all elements through which no line is passing.
(10)      For each element subtract $\theta$ if no line is passing through and add $\theta$ if two lines are passing through.
(11)   **else**
(12)      break
(13)   **end if**
(14) **end while**

ALGORITHM 1: Hungarian matching.

(1) **for** $i = 0$ to $N$ **do**
(2)    Match the $i$th channel with user $u$ having the highest
       weight $w(u,i)$.
(3)    Set $w(u,j) = -\infty$, $j \neq i$.
(4) **end for**

ALGORITHM 2: Greedy matching.

Figure 9 shows the plot between utility and the probability $\rho_d$ that a user is starved for more than $d$ slots. We observe that the utility is maximum for a particular probability for the proposed ISVPF scheme compared to other policies. Thus, the proposed ISVPF scheduler maximizes the net video quality for finite buffers at the base station while not compromising on fairness.

In this section, we compare through simulations the performance of the proposed optimal multichannel allocation policies, Hungarian MultiChannel Optimal Allocation (HMOA), and Greedy MultiChannel Sub-Optimal Allocation (GMOA) with that of the LIP policy proposed in [15] and the standard Proportional Fair (PF) scheduler. Since these are designed for single shared channel scheduling we extend them to multichannel scheduling, by employing the Hungarian (HMLIP, HMPF) and Greedy matching (GMLIP, GMPF) paradigms described above. It can be observed from Figures 12 and 13 that the proposed HMOA policy yields the maximum video quality amongst the competing multiuser multichannel video scheduling policies. Although the GMOA is not optimal but it performs better than PF policy. Further, as $K_u \to \infty$ and $\tau \to 1$, the LIP and PF policies effectively converge to the round-robin policy. Hence, the utility and starvation age coincide at this point.

## 9. Conclusions

In this paper, we developed a novel framework to characterize the differential utility of the H.264 scalable video

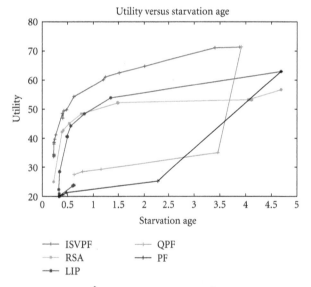

FIGURE 10: Utility ($\hat{\Psi}$) versus Starvation Age ($\hat{\chi}$) when queue length = 500.

stream layers. Based on the proposed framework, a utility-starvation based reward paradigm has been proposed to characterize the scheduling decisions. The end-user video quality maximization has been formulated as an appropriate Markov decision process, and an optimal index based ISVP and ISVPF have been derived towards scheduling the scalable video frames for net video quality maximization in next generation wireless networks. We demonstrated through simulations that the derived ISVP and ISVPF policies achieve better utility compared to PF, LIP, RSA, and QPF policies. Further, we extended this to multiuser multichannel scenarios. The multichannel allocation problem was formulated as an MDP, and the optimal index based channel allocation policy was derived towards video quality maximization which also ensured fairness of video QoS. Two novel index based video scheduling schemes, namely, the Hungarian and

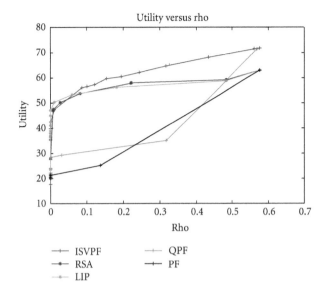

FIGURE 11: Utility ($\widehat{\Psi}$) versus Rho ($\widehat{\rho}_d$) when queue length = 500.

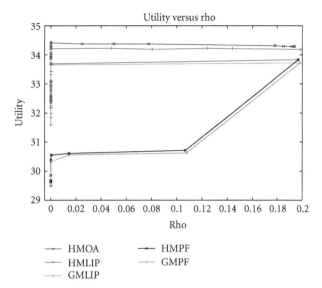

FIGURE 13: Utility ($\widehat{\Psi}$) versus Rho ($\widehat{\chi}$).

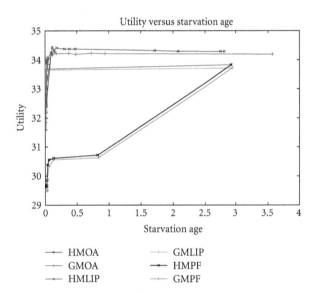

FIGURE 12: Utility ($\widehat{\Psi}$) versus Starvation Age ($\widehat{\chi}$).

Greedy MultiChannel Allocation were derived for multiuser multichannel video scheduling. Simulation results demonstrate that the proposed HMOA and GMOA schemes achieve a significantly higher video quality for a given starvation age compared to standard LIP and PF policies.

## Notation

| | |
|---|---|
| $U$: | Number of users |
| $\mathcal{V}(m,n)$: | Video stream with $m$ temporal layers and $n$ quantization layers |
| $\mathcal{R}(m,n)$: | Bit rate of $\mathcal{V}(m,n)$ |
| $\mathcal{Q}(m,n)$: | Quality of $\mathcal{V}(m,n)$ |
| $\mathcal{U}(m,n)$: | Utility of video stream |
| $n$: | Time slot index |
| $s^n$: | State of the channel at slot $n$ |
| $L$: | Number of channel states |
| $v^n$: | Video state of a HOL frame at slot $n$ |
| $a^n$: | Starvation age at slot $n$ |
| $\mathcal{R}(s)$: | Maximum bit rate of channel at state $s$ |
| $\mathbf{q}_u^n$: | Vector of utilities of packets of user $u$ at time slot $n$ |
| $L_u$: | Maximum queue size of user $u$ |
| $\tau$: | Damping coefficient of PF policy |
| $\chi$: | Expected starvation age |
| $\beta$: | Probability that a channel state remains in same state |
| $N$: | Number of channels |
| $\widetilde{\mathcal{V}}(m,n)$: | Video stream of $m$th temporal layer and $n$th quantization layer |
| $\widetilde{\mathcal{R}}(m,n)$: | Bit rate of $\widetilde{\mathcal{V}}(m,n)$ |
| $\widetilde{\mathcal{Q}}(m,n)$: | Quality of $\widetilde{\mathcal{V}}(m,n)$ |
| $\omega(n)$: | Set of users scheduled at time slot $n$ |
| $u$: | User index |
| $\mathbf{s}^n$: | Joint channel state of all users at slot $n$ |
| $\mathbf{P}^u$: | Probability transition matrix of user $u$ |
| $\mathbf{v}^n$: | Joint video state of all users at slot $n$ |
| $\mathbf{a}^n$: | Joint starvation age of all users at slot $n$ |
| $K$: | Weight factor for starvation age |
| $\mathbf{q}^n$: | Joint vector of utilitiesvector of all users at time slot $n$ |
| $h_r$: | Bias term of random policy $r$ |
| $\Psi$: | Expected per slot long-term utility |
| $\rho_d$: | Probability that user is not served for morethan $d$ slots |
| $P$: | Number of sample paths |
| PF: | Proportional Fair |
| ISVPF: | Index based scalable video scheduling Policy for finite queue size |
| QoS: | Quality of service |
| GOP: | Group of pictures |
| JSVM: | Joint Scalable Video Model |

QPF:    Quality Proportional Fair policy
HMOA:   Hungarian Multi-Channel Optimal
        Allocation
HMPF:   Hungarian Matching Proportional Fair
        policy
GMPF:   Greedy Matching Proportional Fair policy
MDP:    Markov decision process
ISVP:   Index based scalable video scheduling policy
SVC:    Scalable video coding
HUF:    Highest urgency first
QP:     Quantization parameter
LIP:    Linear Index Policy
RSA:    Rate Starvation Age policy
HMLIP:  Hungarian matching LIP
GMLIP:  Greedy matching LIP
GMOA:   Greedy Multichannel sub-Optimal
        Allocation.

# References

[1] Y. N. Lin, Y. D. Lin, Y. C. Lai, and C. W. Wu, "Highest Urgency First (HUF): a latency and modulation aware bandwidth allocation algorithm for WiMAX base stations," *Computer Communications*, vol. 32, no. 2, pp. 332–342, 2009.

[2] K. Wongthavarawat and A. Ganz, "IEEE 802.16 based last mile broadband wireless military networks with quality of service support," in *Proceedings of IEEE Military Communications Conference (MILCOM '03)*, vol. 2, pp. 779–784, October 2003.

[3] P. De Cuetos and K. W. Ross, "Optimal streaming of layered video: joint scheduling and error concealment," in *Proceedings of the 11th ACM International Conference on Multimedia (MM '03)*, pp. 55–64, New York, NY, USA, November 2003.

[4] C. Chen, R. W. Heath Jr., A. C. Bovik, and G. De Veciana, "Adaptive policies for real-time video transmission: a Markov decision process framework," in *Proceedings of the 18th IEEE International Conference on Image Processing (ICIP '11)*, pp. 2249–2252, Brussels, Belgium, September 2011.

[5] V. R. Reddyvari and A. K. Jagannatham, "Quality optimal policy for H.264 scalable video scheduling in broadband multimedia wireless networks," in *Proceedings of the International Conference on Signal Processing and Communications (SPCOM '12)*, Indian Institute of Science, Bangalore, India, July 2012.

[6] D. Tse and P. Viswanath, *Fundamentals of Wireless Communication*, Cambridge University Press, New York, NY, USA, 2005.

[7] A. Goldsmith, *Wireless Communications*, Cambridge University Press, New York, NY, USA, 2005.

[8] X. Liu, E. K. P. Chong, and N. B. Shroff, "A framework for opportunistic scheduling in wireless networks," *Computer Networks*, vol. 41, no. 4, pp. 451–474, 2003.

[9] R. Agrawal, A. Bedekar, R. J. La, R. Pazhyannur, and V. Subramanian, "Class and channel condition based scheduler for EDGE/GPRS," in *Modelling and Design of Wireless Networks*, Proceeding of SPIE, pp. 59–69, August 2001.

[10] J. Kim, J. Cho, and H. Shin, "Resource allocation for scalable video broadcast in wireless cellular networks," in *Proceedings of IEEE International Conference on Wireless and Mobile Computing, Networking and Communications (WiMob '05)*, pp. 174–180, August 2005.

[11] "JSVM 9.19.14 (joint scalable video model) software for the scalable video coding (SVC) project of the joint video team (JVT) of the ISO/IEC moving pictures experts group (MPEG)".

[12] Y. Wang, Z. Ma, and Y. F. Ou, "Modeling rate and perceptual quality of scalable video as functions of quantization and frame rate and its application in scalable video adaptation," in *Proceedings of the 17th International Packet Video Workshop (PV '09)*, pp. 1–9, May 2009.

[13] http://media.xiph.org/video/derf/.

[14] Y. F. Ou, T. Liu, Z. Zhao, Z. Ma, and Y. Wang, "Modeling the impact of frame rate on perceptual quality of video," in *Proceedings of the IEEE International Conference on Image Processing (ICIP '08)*, pp. 689–692, October 2008.

[15] N. Bolia and V. Kulkarni, "Index policies for resource allocation in wireless networks," *IEEE Transactions on Vehicular Technology*, vol. 58, no. 4, pp. 1823–1835, 2009.

[16] V. Kulakarni, *Modeling and Analysis of Stochastic Systems*, Chapman and Hall, New York, NY, USA, 1995.

[17] M. Puterman, *Markov Decision Processes: Discrete Stochastic Dynamic Programming*, John Wiley & Sons, New York, NY, USA, 1994.

[18] P. Bender, P. Black, M. Grob, R. Padovani, N. Sindhushayana, and A. Viterbi, "CDMA/HDR: a bandwidth-efficient high-speed wireless data service for nomadic users," *IEEE Communications Magazine*, vol. 38, no. 7, pp. 70–77, 2000.

# 7

# Multimodal Semantics Extraction from User-Generated Videos

**Francesco Cricri,**[1] **Kostadin Dabov,**[1] **Mikko J. Roininen,**[1] **Sujeet Mate,**[2]
**Igor D. D. Curcio,**[2] **and Moncef Gabbouj**[1]

[1] *Department of Signal Processing, Tampere University of Technology, P.O. Box 553, 33101 Tampere, Finland*
[2] *Nokia Research Center, P.O. Box 1000, 33721 Tampere, Finland*

Correspondence should be addressed to Francesco Cricri, francesco.cricri@tut.fi

Academic Editor: Wei-Ta Chu

User-generated video content has grown tremendously fast to the point of outpacing professional content creation. In this work we develop methods that analyze contextual information of multiple user-generated videos in order to obtain semantic information about public happenings (e.g., sport and live music events) being recorded in these videos. One of the key contributions of this work is a joint utilization of different data modalities, including such captured by auxiliary sensors during the video recording performed by each user. In particular, we analyze GPS data, magnetometer data, accelerometer data, video- and audio-content data. We use these data modalities to infer information about the event being recorded, in terms of layout (e.g., stadium), genre, indoor versus outdoor scene, and the main area of interest of the event. Furthermore we propose a method that automatically identifies the optimal set of cameras to be used in a multicamera video production. Finally, we detect the camera users which fall within the field of view of other cameras recording at the same public happening. We show that the proposed multimodal analysis methods perform well on various recordings obtained in real sport events and live music performances.

## 1. Introduction

The widespread use of camera-enabled mobile devices has allowed people to record anything that they find interesting in their daily life. In particular, one of the most popular means for recording videos is represented by mobile phones which, thanks to their easy portability, are available at any time of the day. Interesting things that people consider worth capturing are very diverse; examples may include funny moments with friends or with the family, music shows, celebrations such as weddings. In particular, there are some situations in which a multitude of people happen to be recording the same scene at the same time. These situations are usually public happenings such as sport events or live music performances. In this paper, we target such kind of scenarios, in which videos of the same event are recorded by multiple people for their own personal archives using their handheld devices (we use the terms *happening* and *event* interchangeably).

As also stated in [1, 2], user-generated videos are then seldom watched either by the people who have shot them or by others. One of the main reasons is the lack of effective tools for automatically organizing the video archives in such a way that it would be easy for a user to retrieve a particular video. For example, it would be beneficial to automatically *classify* videos according to genre (i.e., sport, music, travels, etc.), scene (i.e., indoors versus outdoors, cityscape versus landscape), type of venue where the event is held (e.g., stadium-like venues).

Applications targeting video browsing or automatic creation of video summaries would benefit from the availability of salient information about the videos, such as salient events (e.g., a goal that was scored during a football match), and salient regions (e.g., the goal area).

Video recordings captured by multiple cameras at the same event can be utilized for automatically generating a *multicamera video mash-up* (i.e., a temporal sequence of video segments recorded by different cameras and stitched together one after the other) or a *multicamera summary*. These kinds of applications would benefit from the availability of several types of information, such as which cameras provide the best views in terms of some specified quality measures, or where other cameras are positioned with respect to one specific recording camera.

In this work, we perform multimodal analysis of videos recorded by multiple users at a public happening in order to extract information for indexing the recorded content. The obtained indexing can then be utilized for automatically organizing video archives into classes or for automatically generating multicamera video mash-ups and summaries.

We propose methods for classifying the type of recorded event according to the following criteria:

(i) *indoor versus outdoor event*, by utilizing the GPS lock status information from all the recording devices;

(ii) *event genre* (sport versus live music): we propose novel multimodal features (i.e., features derived from auxiliary sensor data) which are used, in combination with content-based features, to classify the event genre by means of machine learning techniques;

(iii) *event layout* (stadium versus nonstadium): for this we analyze the way by which cameras are spatially distributed and oriented (i.e., the structure of the camera network).

Furthermore we developed methods which identify the following aspects in a multicamera recording scenario:

(i) the *area of interest* within the event area, by exploiting the locations of the recording devices and the way by which they are pointed by their users;

(ii) the *optimal cameras* to be used for automatically producing a multicamera video mash-up;

(iii) the *cameras in the field of view* of other recording cameras.

The novelties which are common to all the methods proposed in this paper are mainly two.

(1) We analyze *contextual data* solely or in combination with video and audio content data. Such contextual data is captured by *auxiliary sensors* (which are embedded within the recording devices) during the video recording activity. In particular we consider data captured by accelerometers, electronic compasses, and GPS receivers.

(2) We exploit the availability of *multiple devices recording the same event* for increasing the robustness of the analysis (thanks to higher redundancy) and for inferring semantic information which would otherwise be hard to extract by analyzing only a single video.

The paper is organized as follows: Section 1.1 introduces the auxiliary sensors used in this work, Section 2 presents the prior works for each of the proposed algorithms, Section 3 describes our proposed methods, Section 4 presents the experimental evaluation, Section 5 is a discussion on the achieved results, and Section 6 concludes the paper.

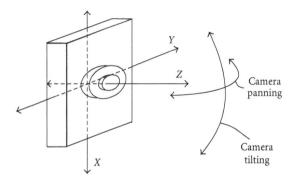

FIGURE 1: Camera movements and data axes used by the accelerometer and compass; the $X$-axis is perpendicular to the horizontal plane.

*1.1. Auxiliary Sensors in Mobile Devices.* Since one of the main contributions of this work is the exploitation of auxiliary sensor modality for analyzing user-generated video content, it is important to introduce the sensors we use:

(i) GPS receiver,

(ii) accelerometer,

(iii) compass (triaxial magnetometer).

Nowadays GPS receivers are present in many electronic devices. For example they are embedded in most modern smartphones, as they are used by those mobile applications which require the location information, such as maps, weather widgets, and image geo-tagging functionality.

A triaxial accelerometer records acceleration across three mutually perpendicular axes. One very important characteristic of this sensor is that when there is lack of other acceleration it senses static acceleration of 1 g (approximately 9.8 m/s$^2$ at sea level) in the direction of Earth's center of mass. This relatively strong static acceleration allows identifying the tilt of the camera with respect to the horizontal plane, that is, the plane that is perpendicular to the gravitation force. We fix the camera orientation with respect to the three perpendicular accelerometer measurements axes as shown in Figure 1.

We consider electronic compasses realized from triaxial magnetometers. These sensors output the instantaneous horizontal orientation towards which they are pointed with respect to the magnetic north. That is, the output of the compass is given in degrees from the magnetic north. By using a triaxial magnetometer, the sensed orientation of the camera is correct even in the presence of tilt (with respect to the horizontal plane). In case of a camera embedding these sensors, a compass can provide information about panning movements.

We assume that the sensor readings are sampled at a fixed (but possibly different for the individual sensors) sampling rate. Also, we assume that the sampling timestamps for the sensor data are available and they are aligned with the start of video recording. The recorded sensor data can be regarded as a separate data stream. In Section 4, we show that these assumptions are reasonable and can be readily satisfied without specialized hardware setup.

## 2. Prior Art

In this section we report on prior works addressing problems which are similar to those considered by our proposed methods. For each of these works we describe the approach, the type of data which is analyzed, the main differences with respect to our methods, and what are the advantages and drawbacks of our approaches with respect to the prior art. In particular, we focus on works addressing the classification of videos (based on indoor/outdoor scene, on the genre, and on the layout of the recorded event), the identification of the area of interest, the selection of optimal cameras, and the detection of cameras which fall within the field of view of other cameras.

*2.1. Classification of Videos according to Indoor versus Outdoor Scene.* Many authors have previously worked on analyzing video content for the purpose of classification. A survey on this topic is given in [3]. Regarding the classification of video into indoor/outdoor scene, Serrano et al. [4] proposed an efficient method in which a two-stage classification approach using Support Vector Machines is applied on low-level color and texture features. The authors report accuracy results which are comparable to other more computationally expensive methods. Recently, Lipowezky and Vol developed an indoor/outdoor detector which is suitable for mobile phone cameras [5]. The proposed method works on the Bayer domain image and uses photometrical and colorimetrical features which are normally computed in mobile phones for white balance gains evaluation. The classification step is based on gentle boosting. In [6] the authors propose to use the following features for indoor/outdoor scene classification of images: histograms of Ohta color space, multiresolution simultaneous autoregressive model parameters, and coefficients of a shift-invariant DCT. The method results in 90.3% of correct classification. Payne and Singh [7] propose a method for indoor/outdoor image classification by analyzing the straightness of edge contours in an image. They assume that indoor images in general have larger proportion of straight edges compared to outdoor images. The method recognizes outdoor scenes with strong natural elements and indoor images with structural edges clearly visible, but has problems with urban outdoor scenes and cluttered indoor images. Thus this work would have some limitations when applied on videos of outdoor public happenings, which are often held in urban areas.

All these works address the problem of scene classification by analyzing content data, which is a computationally expensive approach, even though attempts to decrease the complexity have been done, as it is shown for example in [5]. In our method we do not analyze video or audio content at all and instead we only rely on the GPS receiver data provided by multiple recording devices which are present at the event.

*2.2. Classification of Videos according to the Genre.* Various approaches to the classification of video based on genre have been proposed in the past—using mostly video content analysis. In [8] the authors propose to use domain-knowledge independent features (in particular Scale Invariant Feature Transform) and a bag-of-visual-words-(BoVW-) based model with an innovative codebook generation. For the final classification a k-nearest neighbor classifier is adopted. The method was tested on videos of 23 different sports; therefore it aimed mainly at categorizing subgenres of the sport video genre. The work presented in [9] deals with the use of a hierarchical ontology of video genres. Visual spatio-temporal features are extracted from videos and they are classified using hierarchical Support Vector Machines. In particular the authors propose to construct two optimal SVM binary trees, local and global, in order to find the best tree structure of the genre ontology. The extracted temporal features are average shot length, cut percentage, average color difference, and camera motion, whereas the spatial features are face frames ratio, average brightness and average color entropy. We want to point out that some of these features, namely, average shot length and cut percentage, could not be applied for analyzing user-generated video which is usually unstructured and unedited. It is worth noting that the authors mention that music videos are characterized by larger frame difference (in terms of color histograms), which is a feature that we take into account in our event genre classifier. The proposed method is tested on TV recordings. In [10] the authors discriminate among five video genres—cartoon, commercial, music, news, and sport—by exploiting a combined model of extracted features which are categorized into editing (shot boundary changes), color (color histogram, average brightness, and average saturation), texture (statistics extracted from the gray level cooccurrence matrix, contrast, homogeneity energy, entropy, and correlation), and motion (brightness change, peacefulness of the video, dynamic feature in RGB space). The classifier used is the modified Directed Acyclic Graph Support Vector Machine model. In [11] multimodal features are extracted from TV programs and classified by a parallel neural network into seven genres (commercials, news, weather forecasts, cartoons, music, talk show, and football). The extracted features are color, texture, motion, average shot length, shot cluster duration and saturation, shot length distribution, shot temporal activity, face position distribution, covering percentage of faces, face number distribution, audio segmentation analysis, background audio analysis, and average speech rate. The authors report a classification accuracy rate of 96%. In [2] a genre classification for home videos is proposed, which is of particular interest to us as we target nonprofessionally produced video content too. The authors extract low-level features from MPEG compressed domain claiming that these features are robust to low production quality, which is a common case for home videos. The authors target only those video genres which are specific to home videos, that is, travel, sports, family and pets, event, and entertainment. The extracted features are camera motion (by analyzing motion vectors), subject motion, audio class, audio volume, luminance, color, and flashlight. The authors report that by using ensemble learning they achieve *F*-measure values of about 0.7 to 0.8.

As we have already mentioned, the discussed genre classification methods analyze video or audio content by extracting usually complex features. Also, for most of these works the authors consider professionally recorded video content, which is very different from user-generated content. Apart from content data, in our genre classification method we analyze also data captured by the electronic compass and the accelerometer for extracting camera motion features. In this way we avoid performing content-based motion estimation which is computationally expensive and its performance is limited by the presence of moving objects in the recorded scene.

*2.3. Classification of the Event Layout.* As for our knowledge, no previous works have addressed the specific issue of classifying the type of venue in which a public event is taking place. However, there are some works that address similar issues and they are all based on content analysis, like the previously discussed prior art on indoor/outdoor scene classification and on genre classification. A recent paper ([12]) presents an interesting approach for location recognition. The authors use Speeded-Up Robust Feature (SURF) descriptors to detect objects in images. Location recognition is done by matching the detected objects and their spatial relations between query and database images. However, their approach is aimed for matching images of same exact location rather than classifying between different location types. Schroth et al. [13] give a detailed description of a close-real-time mobile server-based visual location recognition system. They use Maximally Stable Extremal Regions (MSER) as feature detector, Speeded-Up Robust Feature (SURF), and Compressed Histograms of Gradients (CHoG) as key-point descriptors, and the Bag-of-Features (BoF) model for forming the overall descriptor. Also in this case, their visual content-based approach considers matching exact locations rather than location types. Apart from these approaches for location recognition based on image matching, other authors have dealt with the problem of determining the structure of a network of visual sensors, which is what we perform for achieving the type of venue classification. In [14] the authors proposed to measure the statistical dependence between observations in different cameras. In one of the tests they performed, two cameras are positioned at two nonoverlapping portions of a road. In another test five cameras belonging to a real traffic network were used. As also the authors state, the obtained results are approximate but promising. The authors also propose a method for learning the absolute locations of cameras by exploiting the information given by a GPS-enabled device which moves through the recorded area.

As opposed to these content-based approaches, we propose to infer the type of venue by only analyzing the location and the orientation of the cameras. We achieve this by utilizing the data provided by the GPS receiver, the accelerometer, and the compass. These sensors directly provide, respectively, the location, vertical orientation, and horizontal orientation, which would be hard to estimate by means of content analysis only.

*2.4. Area of Interest.* Analysis of the area or region of interest for multiple temporally aligned video recordings of a common scene has been addressed in several previous works, such as in [15, 16]. In [15] Thummanuntawat et al. use a codebook of local visual features extracted from group of pictures (GOP) formed from the frames of the different views. The resulting features are used with spatial and appearance models as well as motion and depth estimation to track the regions of interest in the scene. Hayet et al. use local image features extracted from video content of multiple cameras to track players in a soccer match [16]. They use modular system architecture and distributed computing to compensate for the high computational cost of local feature extraction and multitarget tracking. Carlier et al. [17] propose a crowd-sourced approach for determining regions of interest (ROI) in a video. They collect usage patterns from a zoomable web video player and consider the regions on which the viewers zoom in as the ROIs. They use Gaussian Mixture Models (GMM) to model the ROIs from the pool of user patterns. Cinematographic rules are applied to retarget a high-definition video for small-screen devices based on the ROIs. According to their user studies the approach produces results comparable to handmade retargeting by experts. However, their approach generalizes poorly to new videos with no user zoom preference data.

As opposed to these works, our method for area of interest identification exploits the interest implicitly shown by the camera users on a particular area. We achieve this by analyzing the location of the cameras and how they are pointed.

*2.5. Selection of Optimal Cameras.* In [18] the authors propose a system for automatic selection of viewpoint from a set of cameras recording a scene. Their aim is to create one real-time video stream edited according to a set of cinematographic rules based on person tracking (body, head, and hands). Different criteria are used for estimating view suitability such as the tracked person position within the view, relative orientation to the camera based on the estimated direction of movement of the person, detection of skin blobs within the view, and positional relations of the cameras to approximate the action axis rule (also known as 180-degree rule). They also describe methods for video retargeting and viewpoint interpolation by extracting 3D information with a plane-sweeping algorithm. The approach assumes fixed camera positions. In [19] the authors present a method for autonomous viewpoint switching according to perceptual pleasantness, game semantics, viewing device constraints, and user preferences in the context of basketball game multicamera recordings. Context-dependent trade-offs between the introduced concepts of "completeness" (i.e., displaying all relevant information), "closeness" (i.e., displaying details), and "smoothness" (i.e., perceptual and semantic continuity) are used as the basis of a two-way hierarchical view switching approach. A fixed camera setup is used in the work.

*2.6. Discussion about Prior Art.* Most of the discussed methods for analysis of video are based on content analysis; thus they are computationally expensive. Moreover, exploiting only one or few data modalities may not be sufficient for

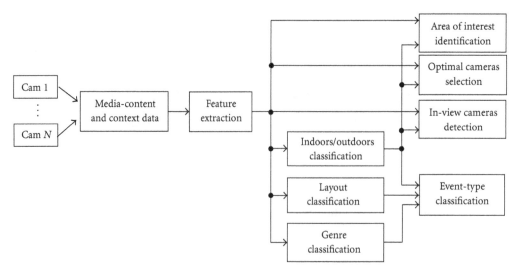

FIGURE 2: Processing steps for extracting semantics from content data and context data (i.e., auxiliary sensor data captured by the electronic compass, the accelerometer, and the GPS receiver) captured by multiple cameras (denoted in the figure as "Cam") in a public event.

describing the recorded scene in a complete way. Some prior works have jointly analyzed video content, audio content, and text, but the joint use of other types of sensors, such as motion sensors (which nowadays are embedded in most smartphones), together with the more traditional content analysis is still not very popular in the research community. Furthermore, apart from few exceptions, previous works do not consider the availability of media captured by different cameras at the same event.

In contrast to the above works, in this paper we propose to jointly analyze auxiliary sensor data and media content data from multiple capturing devices. Utilizing such auxiliary sensor data allow us to perform operations of low computational cost and to obtain information which would otherwise be hard to extract by means of content analysis only (such as the orientation of a camera).

## 3. Multimodal Semantics Extraction

In this section we describe the proposed methods for multimodal analysis of user-generated videos. We extract semantic information from the camera locations, from the camera attitude (i.e., the orientation of the camera), and from the recorded media content (video and audio). In particular, we perform the following types of analysis:

  (i) classification of the event type;

 (ii) identification of the main area of interest;

(iii) detection of the optimal set of cameras to be used in a multicamera video production;

(iv) detection of devices which fall within the field of view of cameras.

In all these analysis methods we assume that the user-generated videos have been captured at the same public event and that they are available, together with the associated

auxiliary sensor data (to which we also refer as "context" data), to a computing device performing the actual analysis (e.g., a network server). Figure 2 illustrates the processing steps for the proposed semantics extraction methods. It is important to notice that the data (content and context) captured by different cameras at the same event must be aligned to a common timeline, in order to allow for joint analysis. However, the data alignment is not the focus of this work and therefore we do not elaborate on it here. In the following we first introduce the features which are used by our proposed methods.

*3.1. Feature Extraction.* We extract several features from different data modalities and we introduce them in the following subsections. We provide reasons for extracting these specific features in the description of the proposed analysis methods.

*3.1.1. Video Segmentation and Visual Features.* We analyze visual features in combination with audio, compass, and accelerometer features for the task of event genre classification. Obviously, as visual features are extracted from video frames, analyzing all the frames of all videos recorded by multiple cameras at each public event is expensive in terms of computational complexity, other than not necessary. In fact, video content usually contains a lot of temporal redundancy, that is, frames which are temporally close to each other are very similar. This is especially true for user-generated videos, which are usually unedited, that is, they do not contain shot boundaries as each video is usually recorded continuously without pauses. Thus, it is reasonable to consider one frame as representative of a certain number of other nearby frames, and to extract visual features only from such representative frames. In order to overcome the aforementioned issues of computational cost, selection of a subset of the original frames should be performed for each video, where the obtained subset represents the whole video.

There exist different strategies for obtaining such a subset of frames. One of the most common strategies consists of temporally segmenting a video by means of *shot boundary detection* techniques. However, some of the visual features that we extract are derived from the changes in subsequent representative frames, which need to be separated by the same number of frames for all videos. Thus, we have considered another strategy that consists of uniformly sampling the video frames, for example, by selecting one frame every ten seconds of video.

In this work we propose to extract the following *global* visual features for each representative frame: *average brightness, dominant color, Local Binary Patterns* (LBP) [20], and *color layout* [21]. By considering subsequent representative frames we extract also the following features: *difference of average brightness* and *difference of dominant color*.

Furthermore, we extract local visual features detected by means of Dense Scale-Invariant Feature Transform (DSIFT) in order to compare their performance with respect to the global visual features previously described, in terms of genre classification accuracy. DSIFT is an extension of SIFT [22]. In particular, instead of extracting key points in a sparse way, they are densely extracted from the whole image surface, that is, each frame is divided into blocks and SIFT key points are then extracted from each of such blocks.

*3.1.2. Audio Features.* By analyzing the audio track of each video recorded at a public event we extract a set of features which are then classified by a Bayesian network. For the audio feature extraction and classification we use the work described in [23].

*3.1.3. Compass and Accelerometer Data Features.* We extract features by analyzing the data captured by the compass and the accelerometer sensors. From the raw electronic compass data (which represent the horizontal orientations of the camera with respect to magnetic North) captured while recording each video, we extract the following features.

(i) *Average horizontal camera orientation* ($\varphi$)—for each video we compute the average of all orientations (given by the compass heading) towards which the camera has been pointed during the video recording activity. The average is computed as the *circular mean*. In particular, $\varphi$ is expressed as degrees with respect to magnetic North.

(ii) *Camera panning rate*—as the horizontal camera orientation is sampled at a relatively high rate (i.e., 10 Hz), it is possible to automatically detect camera panning movements by analyzing raw compass data (as described in [24]). For each video we compute the panning rate as the ratio between the total number of panning movements and the duration of the recorded video.

From the data captured by the accelerometer during the recording of each video we extract the following features.

(i) *Average vertical camera orientation* ($\alpha$)—by analyzing the static acceleration on each of the three orthogonal axes of the accelerometer it is possible to determine for each instant the angle by which the device is tilted with respect to the horizontal plane. For each video we compute the average $\alpha$ of such instantaneous vertical orientations.

(ii) *Camera tilting rate*—by analyzing the dynamic distribution of the gravity of Earth $g$ ($\sim 9.81$ m/s$^2$) on the three accelerometer axes it is possible to automatically detect camera tilting movements, as also described in [24]. From the detected tilting movements in each video we derive the camera tilting rate.

*3.1.4. GPS Data Features.* GPS receivers output different types of data. In this work, we consider only the location information, the measurement time, and the lock status. We analyze these data for obtaining the following features.

(i) *Average GPS location*—we use the GPS receiver embedded in most modern mobile phones for obtaining the instantaneous GPS location of the cameras in terms of coordinate pairs (latitude and longitude). In order to cope with errors in estimating the location, we compute the average of all GPS locations obtained for each camera. In doing this we assume that, while recording videos of the event, the person holding the camera has stayed approximately at the same location. Thus, we obtain the average GPS location of each camera.

(ii) *GPS lock status*—GPS receivers need to be able to communicate with a sufficient number of GPS satellites in order to estimate their location. If this requirement is fulfilled then the GPS receiver is "locked," otherwise its status is "not locked." We check the GPS lock status of all the recording devices and we assign the label "locked" or "not locked" to the feature *GPS lock status* if the majority of the devices are, respectively, locked or not locked.

*3.2. Event-Type Classification.* For event-type classification we consider the following three aspects of public events: the environment where the event is taking place (we also refer to this as scene classification), the layout of the event, and the event genre. First we classify each of these aspects. The event type is then inferred by simply combining the class labels of these aspects, that is, *indoors* versus *outdoors* for the environment, *stadium* versus *nonstadium* for the layout, and *live music* versus *sport* for the genre. Any combination of these class labels is possible and it represents the final classification of the event type.

In the following we discuss how the extracted multimodal features are used to classify each of these three aspects of public events.

*3.2.1. Indoor versus Outdoor Scene.* The first analysis step that we perform for inferring the type of an event consists of determining whether the event was held indoors or outdoors. We achieve this in a robust yet simple way, by exploiting sensor-data (instead of the more traditional video content data, as described in Section 2) captured by multiple cameras recording the event. In particular, we use the data provided by the GPS receivers embedded in camera-enabled mobile phones. It is worth noting that for this analysis any portable device which embeds a GPS receiver can be used and not only camera-enabled devices, as our method does not analyze video content data. In particular we exploit only the information regarding the lock status of the GPS receiver. If the device is in an indoor environment (e.g., inside a building) then it would not be able to "see" a sufficient number of satellites (if not at all) and therefore it will not be locked. Therefore we exploit the GPS lock status for understanding whether the devices are indoors or outdoors. However, there are some situations in which, even if the device is outdoors, due to the presence of surrounding buildings or other tall structures the GPS receiver is not able to receive the signal from a sufficient number of satellites; therefore it will not be locked. In such situations, which is common in practice, an indoors/outdoors classification method which relies solely on one GPS receiver would fail. To overcome this, we exploit the multiuser data availability, that is, we consider the GPS lock status of all the GPS-enabled devices present at the public event. In this way, outlier devices that in an outdoor environment are not able to have GPS-receiver locked (e.g., due to tall structures in their vicinities) are isolated and not taken into account. Thus, if most of the devices are locked, we conclude that the event is held outdoors, otherwise indoors.

The classification between indoor and outdoor scene is used not only by the event-type classifier, but also for other analysis steps that we propose in this work. In fact the identification of an outdoor event enables the following methods which use GPS data: detection of the area of interest, selection of optimal cameras, and detection of in-view cameras.

### 3.2.2. Layout of the Event.
Public happenings are usually held in venues which are specifically designed for allowing people attending the event to enjoy it in an optimal and comfortable way. We refer to the particular structure of such venues as the *layout* of the event. Regarding sport events, the most typical layouts are stadiums (consisting of a central field or stage, which is partly or completely surrounded by the area designated for the people attending the event—for example, for football, rugby, volleyball, and tennis matches), circuit tracks (e.g., for Formula 1 races, motorbike races), and more spatially distributed layouts (e.g., for golf, rally races, bike races, and marathons). For live music events, most often the audience is on one or more sides of the performance stage. In a "proscenium stage," which is the most typical type of stage for music performances, the audience stands or sits only on one side (see Figure 3). However, for big music events, stadiums are the preferred venues as they are usually large enough to contain thousands of spectators.

We propose a method which discriminates two categories of layouts.

(i) *Stadium* layout—those layouts that can be regarded as stadium-like (i.e., where the audience/spectators area has elliptical shape—see Figure 4),

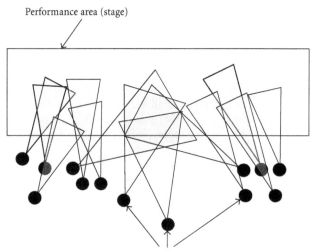

Performance area (stage)

People in the audience recording the performance

Figure 3: View from the top of a public event (live musical performance) with Nonelliptical layout (nonstadium).

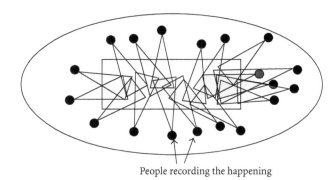

People recording the happening

Figure 4: View from the top of a public happening (sport) with elliptical layout (stadium).

(ii) *Nonstadium* layout—those layouts in which the audience/spectators area does not have elliptical shape (e.g., proscenium stages in the case of live music or theater, etc.).

The main idea of the proposed method is to estimate the camera network structure (i.e., how the cameras are spatially distributed and oriented) in order to infer the layout of the event. For this we analyze the locations of the camera users and how they are pointing their camera (i.e., the horizontal camera orientations). Furthermore, we analyze also the tilt angles of the cameras. Location, horizontal orientation, and tilt angle contribute with a different weight to the final classification of the layout. Our method does not perform any video-content analysis to infer the layout of the event which usually requires high computational costs. Figure 5 shows the processing steps required for classifying the layout of an event.

We analyze the GPS position of the cameras to understand whether they are distributed in an elliptical pattern or not. In particular, for each camera we consider its average location throughout the duration of the whole event. If the

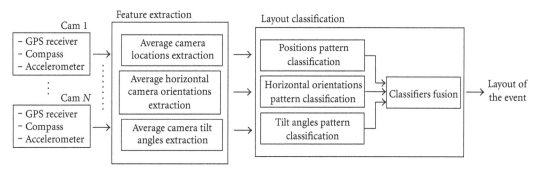

FIGURE 5: Processing steps for classifying the layout of an event.

camera locations pattern is of elliptical shape, then we assign the nominal value "Elliptical" (numerical value *1*) to it, otherwise "Nonelliptical" (numerical value *0*). In order to classify the camera location pattern, we use an optimization approach that consists of fitting the camera locations to an ellipse and then evaluating the error (i.e., the distance of each camera location from the best-fit ellipse). This can be summarized as shown in Algorithm 1.

Regarding the horizontal orientation information, we consider the average orientation $\varphi$ that each camera had during the video recording. If the cameras are oriented towards similar orientations, that is, their orientations fall within a predefined and narrow angular range (e.g., 90 degrees), then we assign the nominal value "Directional" (which corresponds to numerical value *0*) to the camera orientations pattern of the event. Otherwise we assign the nominal value "Nondirectional" (numerical value *1*).

Finally, regarding the vertical camera orientation, we consider the average tilt angle $\alpha$ of all the cameras, which represents the most common vertical orientation throughout the recorded event. If the cameras were mostly tilted downwards during the event, we assign a nominal value "stadium" (numerical value *1*) to the tilt angles pattern, otherwise "nonstadium" (numerical value *0*).

For the final classification of the layout, we assign a different weight to the locations pattern loc, the horizontal orientations pattern $\text{orient}_h$ and the vertical orientations pattern $\text{orient}_v$. Then we use the numerical values of the patterns for computing a weighted average:

$$\text{layout} = \frac{w_l \cdot \text{loc} + w_h \cdot \text{orient}_h + w_v \cdot \text{orient}_v}{w_l + w_h + w_v}, \quad (1)$$

where $w_l$, $w_h$, and $w_v$ are nonnegative weights. Each weight represents the confidence on the discriminative power that each pattern has in the considered layout classification problem. These weights can be obtained through a supervised learning step. However in our case we have assigned the weights empirically after performing extensive experimentations. The final decision on the layout is taken by comparing the weighted average layout with a predefined threshold $\text{Thr}_{\text{layout}}$. If layout is more than $\text{Thr}_{\text{layout}}$ then we classify the event as being held in a *stadium*-like layout, otherwise in a *nonstadium*-like layout.

GPS location information of the cameras is available only for those events held in an outdoor environment.

However, if our system detects that the event is held indoors (this information is provided by the indoor versus outdoor scene classification described in Section 3.2.1), the layout classification method will simply not consider location data and it will instead analyze only compass data and accelerometer data.

*3.2.3. Event Genre.* In video genre classification the most commonly considered genres are *movie, news, sport, music, commercials,* and *documentary,* as can be seen also in [2, 8–11]. In this work we consider user-generated videos which have been recorded at a public event. This means that we target specific use cases in which it is likely that a relatively high number of people gather together for attending something of common interest. Thus, we focus on discriminating only between those event genres which comply with this scenario: *sport events* and *live music events.*

We approach the problem of event genre classification by analyzing multiple data modalities collected by multiple cameras present at the event (see Figure 6). In particular we analyze video content data, audio content data, and data from auxiliary sensors (electronic compass, accelerometer). In this way we aim at achieving a robust classification thanks to a more complete description of the scene. As an example, merely applying a simple music occurrence detector to the audio tracks of the recordings and classifying the videos into music or sport genre based on whether the videos contain more music or nonmusic sections, would fail in the following situations: first, in music events people might record things which happened before or after the music show for even longer time than the actual musical performance. Second, many sport events have distinct background music played during breaks and some even during the actual sport activities. Finally, the classification performance easily deteriorates with user-generated real world data—particularly with audio recorded from the audience area using mobile phones, because of the nonprofessional quality of the microphones and because of the background noise originating from the crowd (we have confirmed this experimentally and we give further details on our experiments in the Section 4). Nevertheless, the audio modality contributes significantly to the genre classification task, and its setbacks can be compensated with information from the additional modalities.

(1) *Compute the average location of each camera over the whole time during which that camera has been recording.*

(2) *Apply optimization for fitting the average camera locations to an ellipse, and find the optimal parameters that define the best-fit ellipse.*

(3) *Evaluate the Euclidean distance between each average camera location and the best-fit ellipse. If the average distance is less than a predefined threshold, then we assign the nominal value "Elliptical" to the camera locations pattern of the considered event.*

ALGORITHM 1: Layout classification based on camera locations.

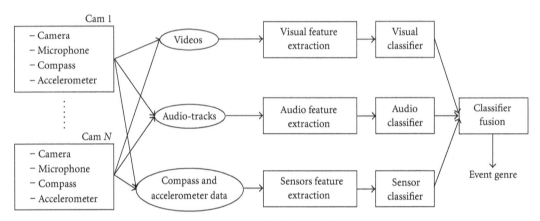

FIGURE 6: Processing steps for classifying the event genre.

Among the features that we discussed in Section 3.1, for classifying the event genre we use the following ones: *brightness, brightness difference, dominant color, dominant color difference, LBP, color layout, audio features* (described in [23]), *camera panning rate,* and *camera tilting rate.* In Section 4 we compare the classification performances achieved by using these features in different combinations and also when combined with SIFT-based features.

The reasons for choosing this particular set of features are given in what follows. Based on visual and aural inspection of videos belonging to sport and music genres we have noticed big differences in the brightness feature. In fact, live music events are usually held in relatively dark places, whereas sport happenings are characterized by good illumination conditions. Dominant colors are also discriminative for these two event genres, as soccer videos are characterized by green hue, ice-hockey matches by white hue, and so on for other sports, whereas live music events are characterized by many different hues thanks to the frequently changing stage lights, especially by hues such as red, purple, blue; also, in concerts held indoors or at night time another dominant color is usually represented by the black of the scene around the main stage, especially for those cameras which record from longer distances with respect to the stage. Changes in the brightness value and in colors are usually much higher and frequent for live music performances than for sports, due to the stage lights. The texture present in sport videos is usually much more uniform than in live music videos, because of the field (in case of football, ice-hockey, etc.) or tracks (e.g., skiing). Also the color layout was found to be a discriminating feature between the considered genres, as they have different patterns

of spatial distributions of colors. For example in football games the green field usually occupies a big portion in the central and bottom parts of the images. Finally, we chose to analyze the camera motion (panning and tilting rate) as it is usually higher when recording sport events (as also stated in [2, 25]).

The actual classification is performed by employing a *late fusion* strategy [26]. As can be seen in Figure 6, each recording device captures data of different modalities, namely, video, audio, compass, and accelerometer data. Feature extraction is performed separately thus obtaining visual, audio, and sensors (compass and accelerometer) feature vectors. The following set of three classifiers is then utilized (one classifier for each data modality).

(i) A Support Vector Machine (SVM) [27] represents the visual classifier, which is used to classify the visual feature vectors.

(ii) A Bayesian network represents the audio classifier, which classifies the audio feature vectors. For this we use the work described in [23]. In particular, we obtain a class label for each temporal segment of predefined length. We then classify the event as the audio class label which occurs most often throughout all videos.

(iii) Another SVM is used to classify the sensors feature vectors.

In Section 4 we give details on how we trained the classifiers. The results of these three classifiers are fused by computing a weighted average where the weights are derived

(1) *Obtain the location and horizontal orientation of each camera which is recording during the considered instant (or temporal segment)—we define such a camera as a recording camera.*

(2) *We derive a linear equation for each recording camera, which represents the direction towards which the camera is pointed. We express the equation in the point-slope form:*

$$y - y_1 = m_1(x - x_1),$$

*where the point coordinates $(x_1, y_1)$ are the camera location coordinates, and the slope $m_1$ is derived from the horizontal orientation.*

(3) *For each pair $i$ of recording cameras we solve a system of two such linear equations representing the pointing directions of the considered cameras. By solving each system we find the intersecting point $P_i^{int}$ between the two pointing directions. As a result we obtain a set $S_t^{int}$ of intersections between all the pairs of recording cameras, for the considered instant $t$.*

(4) *We apply a clustering on all intersecting points, so as to discover the main cluster. In this way we are able to isolate outlier intersections which do not belong to the area of interest. The obtained main cluster represents the instantaneous area of interest $A_t$ of the event.*

(5) *For each instantaneous area of interest we determine its representative point of interest $C_t$ as the centroid of the main cluster. In particular we compute $C_t$ as the average of the intersecting points belonging to the main cluster.*

ALGORITHM 2: Area of interest identification.

from the classification performance of each single classifier on a test set, that is, each weight represents the confidence of the respective classifier. In the results section we also provide a comparison on the genre classification accuracy achieved by using different combinations of features.

*3.3. Area of Interest Identification.* In some application scenarios, such as in video content retrieval, it is important to identify the area that attracts the attention of people attending a public event for which videos have been recorded. We propose a novel method for automatically identifying this *area of interest* (we refer to it also as the *AOI*) by analyzing only auxiliary sensor data. Our method is based on the fair assumption that the interest of those people recording videos at the event represents a good indicator of the general interest of all the other attendees, especially when the number of recording cameras is statistically significant. We propose to analyze the way the camera persons are recording at a given time instant $t$, in order to identify the instantaneous area of interest $A_t$ of the event (see Figure 7). By combining all the instantaneous areas of interest identified throughout the whole duration of the event, we then obtain the main area of interest of the event $A_{main}$.

In particular our method exploits the availability of camera location and camera horizontal orientation information. Therefore we do not analyze video or audio content, which would require high computational costs.

For each instant $t$ (or temporal segment of predefined length), we perform the steps in Algorithm 2.

The result of applying these steps for every instant (or temporal segment) is a set of instantaneous areas of interest. The main area of interest $A_{main}$ of the event is then derived simply by averaging the coordinates of the intersections forming all instantaneous areas of interest (we use a trimmed mean so as to isolate outlier instantaneous AOIs). We determine the main point of interest $C_{main}$ by computing a trimmed mean of the coordinates of all the instantaneous points of interest.

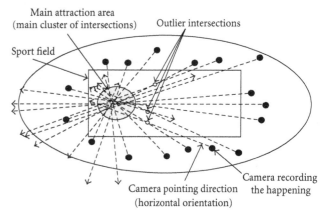

FIGURE 7: Identification of the area of interest of a public event held in a stadium (view from the top).

*3.4. Selection of Optimal Set of Cameras.* In multicamera video production (i.e., generation of a mash-up of videos capturing the same scene from multiple cameras) it is important to respect one of the most widely used techniques in filmmaking: the *180-degree rule* [28]. Such a rule is necessary in order not to confuse the viewer of the final video mash-up with regard to the direction of movement of objects within the scene. For example, in the particular case of a football match, the direction of movement of the ball should be consistent when there happens to be a view-switch (i.e., a switch between different cameras) in the video mash-up. In professional video broadcast of football matches this is achieved by placing the cameras only on one side of the football field. This same rule applies for any other type of scene which is recorded by multiple cameras, such as for interviews or live music shows.

Unfortunately, when handling user-generated videos captured by multiple cameras it is not possible to assume that the cameras lied only on one side of the main scene, since users recording the videos can be located anywhere

---

(1) *Determine the main point of interest P, by applying the method described in Section 3.3.*

(2) *Consider all the lines which intersect the main point of interest, each line having a different slope m and representing a candidate separating line. For each line, count the number of cameras that lie on each of the two sides of the line.*

(3) *Select the candidate separating line which yields the maximum number of cameras on one of its two sides. The selected line represents the optimal separating line, and the optimal set of cameras to be used for generating video mash-ups is made of those cameras on the most populated side of the optimal separating line.*

---

ALGORITHM 3: Selection of optimal cameras.

in the stadium or audience area. Therefore there is a need to determine how such cameras were positioned during the event, in order to be able to utilize only those ones which are compatible with the 180-degree rule in the production of a video mash-up. These cameras constitute the *optimal set of cameras*, which is a subset of all cameras recording the event.

We propose a method for automatically determining the optimal set by selecting those cameras which lie on only one of the two sides of the *optimal separating line*. A separating line is an imaginary line which divides the recorded scene into two parts. For example, in Figure 8 a football field and one possible separating line are illustrated. In our method a separating line is determined by two parameters: the point $P(x_P, y_P)$ which is intersected by the line and the slope $m$ of the line. In particular, the intersection point must lie within the recorded scene (i.e., within the area of interest, such as the football field in a football match or the performance stage in a live music show). The optimal separating line is characterized by the optimal slope $m_{opt}$ which yields the maximum number of cameras on one of the two sides of the separating line:

$$y - y_P = m_{opt}(x - x_P). \qquad (2)$$

Our method relies exclusively on the locations of the recording cameras and on a representative point of the main scene. In particular, the GPS locations of all the cameras present at the event are analyzed. We consider as the representative point $P$ of the main scene the *main point of interest* (determined with the method described in Section 3.3). The method can be summarized in the steps shown in Algorithm 3.

*3.5. Detection of In-View Cameras.* We propose a method for automatically detecting the presence of cameras within the field of view (FOV) of a recording camera, during a public event (see Figure 9). The method is not restricted to detect only camera devices, but it can be used for detecting the presence of any other device for which location information is available, such as GPS-enabled devices. Potential uses of the proposed method are mainly in the field of automatic video mash-up generation and, more in general, in video content retrieval. For example, it would be beneficial to know which specific persons (who hold a GPS-enabled device) are likely to be in the view of the recording camera, or to know whether a camera is recording approximately the same scene as other cameras present at an event.

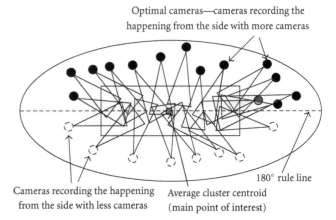

FIGURE 8: Identification of the 180-degree rule line (the *separating line*) and selection of optimal cameras (view from the top).

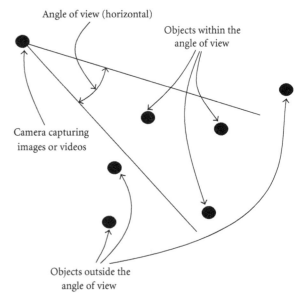

FIGURE 9: Detection of in-view cameras (view from the top).

For each camera which is recording an event, our method exploits the availability of the location, the pointing orientation, and the field of view of the camera. Furthermore the location of any other GPS-enabled device present at the event is considered. The method consists of the steps described in Algorithm 4.

---

(1) *Determine the slopes $m_1^{FOV}$ and $m_2^{FOV}$ of the two lines $l_1^{FOV}$ and $l_2^{FOV}$ which delimit the field of view of the recording camera, by using the camera pointing angle (horizontal orientation) and the angle of view.*

(2) *Determine the slope $m_i$ of each line $l_i$ connecting the position $P_c$ of the recording camera to the position $P_i$ of each other device i present at the event.*

(3) *Determine whether each device lies within the determined field of view, by evaluating the slope $m_i$ of each line $l_i$ with respect to the slopes of the two lines $l_1^{FOV}$ and $l_2^{FOV}$. If $m_i$ is within the range $[m_1^{FOV}, m_2^{FOV}]$, then the device i is considered to be within the field of view of the recording camera.*

---

ALGORITHM 4: Detection of in-view cameras.

## 4. Results

In this section we evaluate the performance of the proposed methods. As we analyze streams of sensor measurements recorded simultaneously with the video recording, there are no publicly available datasets that already contain such sensor data. In addition, we analyze data captured by multiple devices at the same time and at the same event. Therefore, for our experiments we use test datasets obtained as described in Section 4.1.

*4.1. Test Datasets.* We used publicly available smart phones and simple dedicated software to enable collection of the sensor data synchronously with video recording. The default sampling rate for each sensor was used, that is, 40 samples/second for the accelerometer, 10 samples/second for the compass, and 1 sample every 5 seconds for the GPS. Each sample is further labeled with its timestamp. The time alignment between a recorded video and the recorded sensor data was straightforward to obtain, as the video start- and stop-recording times were obtained from the creation time of the media file and were then matched to the timestamps of the sensor measurements. The software application that we used stored the sensor measurements (and associated timestamps) as data streams associated with the recorded video.

We used two datasets for our experiments. Dataset 1 contains data (user-generated videos and associated context data) collected at public events of both sport genre and live music genre, held either indoors or outdoors and in stadium or nonstadium layouts. In particular the recorded events were the followings: three football matches held in outdoor stadiums (the number of videos is 54, the total length of all videos is about 720 minutes), two ice hockey matches held in indoor stadiums (71 videos with total length of about 684 minutes), four live music performances held in proscenium stages, from which two were outdoors and two indoors (156 videos for all four events, spanning an overall duration of 890 minutes). The data was collected by multiple users that were attending the events and were sparsely located in the audience (or among the spectators in the case of sport events). Dataset 1 has been used for testing the event-type classification. Dataset 2 contains a subset of the events included in Dataset 1. This second dataset has been used for testing the identification of the area of interest of the event, the selection of optimal cameras, and the detection of in-view cameras. Dataset 2 includes only outdoor events.

TABLE 1: Event genre classification results by analyzing only audio content.

| Event | Ground truth audio class | Automatically extracted audio class |
|---|---|---|
| Football match 1 | No music | Music |
| Football match 2 | No music | No music |
| Football match 3 | No music | Music |
| Ice-hockey match 1 | No music | Music |
| Ice-hockey match 2 | No Music | Music |
| Concert 1 | Music | Music |
| Concert 2 | Music | Music |
| Concert 3 | Music | No music |
| Concert 4 | Music | Music |

In particular, the events belonging to this dataset are three football matches and two live music shows. It is worth noting that the people recording the various public events were not given any specific instructions on the way of recording. On the contrary, they were only asked to record the event as they would normally do when they want to obtain videos for their personal use.

*4.2. Classifying the Type of Event.* In order to evaluate the event-type classifier, we present our experimental results obtained by classifying each of the events in Dataset 1 according to the following aspects: indoor/outdoor scene, layout, and event genre. These aspects define the final event type.

In particular, regarding the event genre classification, before analyzing multiple data modalities we made some evaluations on using only audio classification for achieving discrimination between *sport* and *live music* event genres. For this, the audio classifier described in [23] has been applied on audio content extracted from the video recordings belonging to Dataset 1. Classification results are given in Table 1. As can be seen, the performance of the audio classifier on user-generated data is not very high even though in our experiments we used high-end phones embedding microphones of higher quality than the most common devices that people use. As an outcome of this preliminary test, we decided to analyze additional data modalities apart from audio content data to achieve event genre classification, as already described in Section 3.2.3.

As we use a supervised classification approach, the three classifiers used for genre classification were firstly trained.

TABLE 2: Classification of events according to scene, genre, and layout.

| Event | Indoor/outdoor scene classification | | Event genre classification | | Layout classification | |
| --- | --- | --- | --- | --- | --- | --- |
| | Ground truth | Proposed method | Ground truth | Proposed method | Ground truth | Proposed method |
| Football match 1 | Outdoor | Outdoor | Sport | Sport | Stadium | Stadium |
| Football match 2 | Outdoor | Outdoor | Sport | Sport | Stadium | Stadium |
| Football match 3 | Outdoor | Outdoor | Sport | Sport | Stadium | Stadium |
| Ice-hockey match 1 | Indoor | Outdoor | Sport | Sport | Stadium | Stadium |
| Ice-hockey match 2 | Indoor | Indoor | Sport | Sport | Stadium | Stadium |
| Concert 1 | Outdoor | Outdoor | Live music | Live music | Nonstadium | Nonstadium |
| Concert 2 | Outdoor | Outdoor | Live music | Live music | Nonstadium | Stadium |
| Concert 3 | Indoor | Indoor | Live music | Live music | Nonstadium | Nonstadium |
| Concert 4 | Indoor | Indoor | Live music | Live music | Nonstadium | Nonstadium |
| Classification accuracy (%) | — | 88.9 | — | 100 | — | 88.9 |

Regarding the *visual classifier*, the training was performed by using the Columbia Consumer Video (CCV) database [29] as the training data, which is a dataset of YouTube videos of different topics, such as several types of sport (soccer, skiing, and ice skating), music performances, and wedding ceremonies. In particular, we selected only those videos which are labeled as sport or music performances.

Regarding the *audio classifier*, as we already mentioned, the work described in [23] was used to classify the audio track of each video as either "music" or "No-music." The Bayesian network has been trained with data captured by mobile phones.

Regarding the *sensor classifier*, there are no publicly available datasets of compass and accelerometer data captured during video recording. Therefore the training dataset is made of sensor data captured by our phones during public happenings. In particular, we considered a different set of phones with respect to those used for testing the classification performance, in order to obtain a training set and a testing set which are as much independent as possible.

The experimental results on classifying scene, layout, and genre by analyzing multiple data modalities are presented in Table 2. Regarding the layout classification for *Concert 2*, we obtained a misclassification (*stadium* instead of *nonstadium*) because the event was held in a big venue in which the camera users happened to be distributed almost in an elliptical way.

Based on the classification accuracies reported in Table 2, the proposed event-type classification method performs well in real-world usage scenarios.

We also performed a comparison on the use of different sets of features for event genre classification. In particular, we analyzed the classification performance for each of the following feature-sets:

(i) *feature-set* $S_1$: audio features only;

(ii) *feature-set* $S_2$: sensors features only;

(iii) *feature-set* $S_3$: only DSIFT (Bag-of-Visual-Words approach);

(iv) *feature-set* $S_4$: only global visual features;

(v) *feature-set* $S_5$: combination of audio and sensors features;

(vi) *feature-set* $S_6$: combination of DSIFT and sensors features;

(vii) *feature-set* $S_7$: combination of global visual features and sensors features;

(viii) *feature-set* $S_8$: combination of audio features, DSIFT and sensors features;

(ix) *feature-set* $S_9$: combination of audio features, global visual features and sensors features. This is the set that we propose to use.

The Bag-of-Visual-Words approach is one of the state-of-the-art methods for classifying images and videos, apart from being used also for detecting objects and salient events. One work in which the video genre is classified using BoVW is the one presented in [8]. The BoVW approach works in two phases:

(1) codebook generation and classifier training phase;

(2) classification phase.

For both phases we densely extract a set of SIFT points from each frame of each video. In the first phase (codebook generation) the points extracted from training videos are clustered into a set of code words using the $k$-means clustering algorithm. For each representative frame we derive a histogram of code words occurrences and this is achieved by mapping the extracted SIFT points to the obtained code words. The obtained histograms are then used to train a SVM classifier. In the second phase (classification), we consider each representative frame of each video and, by mapping the extracted set of SIFT points to the previously generated code-words, we obtain a histogram of code-words occurrences. Such a histogram represents the feature vector which will be classified by the SVM trained in the first phase.

The results of this comparison are reported in Tables 3 and 4. In particular, in Table 4 we report on the classification results obtained by combining features from different modalities of data. Our proposed approach (feature-set $S_9$) which uses a combination of audio features, global visual features, and sensors features performs the best in terms of classification accuracy.

TABLE 3: Performance comparison for the event genre classification task using different feature-sets.

| Event | Ground truth event genre | Automatic event genre classification | | | |
|---|---|---|---|---|---|
| | | Feature-set $S_1$ (audio) | Feature-set $S_2$ (sensors) | Feature-set $S_3$ (DSIFT) | Feature-set $S_4$ (global visual features) |
| Football match 1 | Sport | Live music | Sport | Sport | Sport |
| Football match 2 | Sport | Sport | Sport | Sport | Sport |
| Football match 3 | Sport | Live music | Sport | Sport | Sport |
| Ice-hockey match 1 | Sport | Live music | Sport | Live music | Sport |
| Ice-hockey match 2 | Sport | Live music | Sport | Live music | Live music |
| Concert 1 | Live music | Live music | Live music | Live music | Live music |
| Concert 2 | Live music | Live music | Live music | Live music | Sport |
| Concert 3 | Live music | Sport | Live music | Live music | Live music |
| Concert 4 | Live music | Live music | Sport | Live music | Live music |
| Total accuracy (%) | — | 44.4 | 88.9 | 77.8 | 77.8 |

TABLE 4: Performance comparison for the event genre classification task using different feature-sets.

| Event | Ground truth event genre | Automatic event genre classification | | | | |
|---|---|---|---|---|---|---|
| | | Feature-set $S_5$ (audio, sensors) | Feature-set $S_6$ (DSIFT, sensors) | Feature-set $S_7$ (global visual, sensors) | Feature-set $S_8$ (audio, DSIFT, sensors) | Feature-set $S_9$ (audio, global visual, sensors)—Proposed set |
| Football match 1 | Sport | Sport | Sport | Sport | Sport | Sport |
| Football match 2 | Sport | Sport | Sport | Sport | Sport | Sport |
| Football match 3 | Sport | Sport | Sport | Sport | Sport | Sport |
| Ice-hockey match 1 | Sport | Sport | Sport | Sport | Live music | Sport |
| Ice-hockey match 2 | Sport | Sport | Sport | Sport | Live music | Sport |
| Concert 1 | Live music | Sport | Sport | Sport | Live music | Live music |
| Concert 2 | Live music | Live music | Live music | Live music | Live music | Live music |
| Concert 3 | Live music | Live music | Live music | Live music | Live music | Live music |
| Concert 4 | Live music | Live music | Live music | Live music | Live music | Live music |
| Total accuracy (%) | — | 88.9 | 88.9 | 88.9 | 77.8 | 100 |

TABLE 5: Experimental results on area of interest identification (AOI) applied on Dataset 2. MSE stands for Mean Square Error.

| Event | Number of instantaneous AOIs | Main AOI (identified versus not identified) | MSE of distances from the identified main AOI (meters) |
|---|---|---|---|
| Football match 1 | 930 | Identified | 6.8 |
| Football match 2 | 756 | Identified | 5.7 |
| Football match 3 | 549 | Identified | 31.1 |
| Concert 1 | 555 | Identified | 13.2 |
| Concert 2 | 345 | Identified | 44.0 |

4.3. *Identifying the Area of Interest.* Videos belonging to Dataset 2 have been used for testing the identification of the area of interest. We performed an evaluation by visually estimating where the main area of interest of the whole event is. We plotted the obtained locations of the main area of interest and then visually evaluated whether it has been identified correctly or not. In particular, for sport events we mark the estimated main area of interest as "Identified" if it

was located within the football field. For live music events we mark it as "Identified" if it was on the stage (or slightly behind the stage). Table 5 summarizes our experiments on the area of interest identification. In the table, for each recorded event, we report the total number of instantaneous areas of interest (i.e., the number of analyzed temporal segments), the identification of the main AOI, and the *Mean Square Error* (MSE) of the distances from each camera to the identified main AOI. We are able to identify the main AOI in all the events of Dataset 2. Furthermore we obtain different accuracies for the estimated distances between cameras and area of interest. In particular, for *Concert 2* we obtained the highest MSE value, which is due to an identification of the main AOI behind the performance stage (which represents the ground truth main AOI) and due to inaccuracies in the GPS measurements.

4.4. *Selecting the Optimal Set of Cameras.* Tests on the selection of the optimal cameras according to the 180-degree rule have been carried out on Dataset 2. The method that we proposed for determining the optimal cameras relies on the correct identification of the main area of interest of the event; in particular it uses the center of the main AOI and considers

TABLE 6: Experimental results on identifying the optimal cameras. *P* stands for *Precision*, *R* for *Recall*, and *F* for *F-measure*.

| Event | All cameras (index) | Ground truth sets of optimal cameras | Automatically identified optimal set of cameras | $P$ | $R$ | $F$ |
|---|---|---|---|---|---|---|
| Football match 1 | $[1,2,3,4,5,6]$ | $[1,2,3], [2,3,4,5], [5,6]$ | $[2,3,4,5,6]$ | 0.8 | 1.0 | 0.89 |
| Football match 2 | $[1,2,3,4,5,6]$ | $[1,2,3,4], [4,5,6]$ | $[1,2,3,4]$ | 1.0 | 1.0 | 1.0 |
| Football match 3 | $[1,2,3,4,5]$ | $[1,2], [2,3], [4,5]$ | $[1,2,3]$ | 0.75 | 1.0 | 0.86 |
| Concert 1 | $[1,2,3,4,5,6,7,8,9]$ | $[1,2,3,4,5,6,7,8,9]$ | $[1,2,3,4,5,6,7,8,9]$ | 1.0 | 1.0 | 1.0 |
| Concert 2 | $[1,2,3,4,5,6,7,8,]$ | $[1,2,3,4,5,6,7,8]$ | $[1,2,3,4,5,6,7,8]$ | 1.0 | 1.0 | 1.0 |
| Average over all events | — | — | — | 0.91 | 1.0 | 0.95 |

TABLE 7: Experimental results for detecting in-view cameras. *P* stands for *Precision*, *R* for *Recall*, and *F* for *F-measure*.

| Event | $P$ | $R$ | $F$ |
|---|---|---|---|
| Football match 1 | 0.86 | 0.71 | 0.77 |
| Football match 2 | 0.78 | 0.58 | 0.67 |
| Football match 3 | 1.0 | 0.78 | 0.88 |
| Concert 1 | 0.74 | 0.69 | 0.71 |
| Concert 2 | 0.76 | 0.81 | 0.78 |
| Average over all events | 0.83 | 0.71 | 0.77 |

this as the point intersected by the separating line. Regarding the ground truth, there could be more than one optimal set of cameras, and this was taken into account in our experiments. The experimental results are reported in Table 6.

We use the following measures for evaluating the performance of the selection method:

(i) precision (*P*)—fraction of the automatically selected cameras which belong to one of the ground truth sets of optimal cameras;

(ii) recall (*R*)—fraction of the optimal cameras belonging to one of the ground truth optimal sets which are correctly selected by our method;

(iii) balanced *F*-measure (*F*)—it is computed as the harmonic mean of the precision and recall.

As can be seen in Table 6, for *Football match 1* and *Football match 3* our method has introduced one additional camera with respect to one of the ground truth optimal sets. This error was caused by the inaccuracies in the GPS data measurements. Regarding *Concert 1* and *Concert 2*, as the shows were held in proscenium stages and all the recording cameras were located in front of the stage, the ground truth optimal sets include all the cameras. The proposed method correctly identified these optimal sets.

*4.5. Detecting In-View Cameras.* We have tested the detection of cameras which are within the field of view of other cameras by using Dataset 2. Table 7 summarizes the experimental results. For evaluating the performance of the detection method we use similar measures as for the selection of optimal cameras.

In particular, (i) precision (*P*)—fraction of the detected cameras which are indeed in the field of view of other

cameras; (ii) recall (*R*)—fraction of the true in-view cameras which are detected correctly; (iii) balanced *F*-measure (*F*)—it is computed as the harmonic mean of the precision and recall.

## 5. Discussion

User-generated content has seen a tremendous growth during the latest years [30] and the analysis of such content is becoming an important research problem. In this work we show that context data from multiple user-generated videos can provide important information about the environment in which they were recorded. This information can subsequently be exploited by various other applications (such as video retrieval, summarization, and mash-up creation).

One of the main contributions of this work is the exploitation of multiple modalities of data for analyzing user-generated content. The auxiliary sensor modalities not only allow for precise information about the location and the orientation of the recording device but also their processing involves much less computations than traditional content analysis methods. For example, all the auxiliary sensors that we use in this work produce less than 200 samples per second, whereas one second of HD video content at 25 frames per second contains 23 million pixels.

In this work we used GPS data for indoor/outdoor scene classification, for identification of event layout and area of interest, for selection of optimal cameras, and for detection of in-view cameras. The GPS is usually available only for public events held outdoors. However, if an indoor positioning system is available then our methods can be easily extended to indoor events. As GPS location information is affected by errors originated from several sources, it is worth discussing the effects of such errors on the methods that we proposed in this paper. In a recent paper [31] the authors claim that the average location error experienced on modern mobile phones vary between 8 and 12 meters. In the work described in [32] (from 2011) mobile phones are considered and GPS errors are reported to be between 0 and 5 meters. In particular, different models of modern smartphones are tested for estimating the GPS inaccuracies. For one of such models, 97% of the measurements were found to be affected by errors within 5 meters. As we already mentioned, in order to cope with GPS inaccuracies and especially with outlier location measurements, we capture the location information multiple times for each camera and then we compute a trimmed mean of such measurements.

Regarding the method that we proposed for indoor/outdoor scene classification, inaccuracies in the GPS location information do not affect the performance of our algorithm. However, if the recorded event is held outdoors and most of the GPS receivers are not locked then our method would provide wrong information. This situation might happen when the event area is small and it is surrounded by tall buildings or other structures. In stadium-like venues there are usually no buildings which are too close to the event area, and we have experimentally verified that the structures which constitute the spectator sections do not represent major problems in terms of direct line of sight.

Regarding the identification of the event layout, as typical positioning errors in mobile phones are within 5 or 10 meters and stadiums have much larger dimensions, such errors do not have big effects on the estimation of the layout, that is, it is still possible to determine if the cameras are distributed in an elliptical way by using our approach based on curve fitting. We have proven this experimentally in our tests in which all the stadium-like venues were correctly identified.

The proposed method for identifying the area of interest is more sensitive to GPS positioning inaccuracies. However, we do not aim at precisely determining the exact position where the interest point (or focus point) is located; instead we are interested in identifying a wider area that can give indicative information about where the show (sport match or music performance) is located within the whole event area. Therefore, slightly inaccurate location measurements (as those previously discussed) do not interfere with this goal.

The selection of optimal cameras relies on the identification of the area of interest and on the position of each camera with respect to such area. The performance of this method could be impaired by inaccuracies in the location information. In fact, because of such errors, a camera which is in reality on one side with respect to the 180 degree line can be erroneously detected as being on the other side. We have experienced this in our tests (Table 6), in which the automatically selected optimal cameras not always completely corresponded to the ground truth optimal cameras. Finally, regarding the proposed method for detecting cameras which fall within the field of view of other cameras, location inaccuracies in both the recording camera and the target cameras could affect the results. In fact, if a target camera is close to the border of the field of view of the recording camera, even small location errors in either the target or the recording camera can affect the detection accuracy. Another case in which small GPS inaccuracies would produce incorrect detection results is when the recording camera and the target camera are close to each other.

## 6. Conclusions

In this work we propose a set of methods for automatically extracting semantic information about public happenings such as sport and live music events. The methods rely on the analysis of user-generated videos recorded at those events by multiple recording devices. In particular, we extract information about the recorded scene by taking into account the locations of the cameras and other contextual information of the recording activity. Auxiliary sensor data, together with video and audio content data, is analyzed for determining the type of event being recorded. In particular, we are able to identify the layout of the event, the event genre, and whether the event is held indoors or outdoors. Furthermore, we have proposed algorithms for identifying the area of interest of an event and for automatically selecting the optimal set of cameras to be used for a multicamera video production, according to the 180-degree rule which is a widely used technique in filmmaking. Finally a method for detecting devices which are within the field of view of cameras was described. We performed experiments for evaluating the proposed algorithms on real test data. In particular we obtained the following classification accuracies for, respectively, scene, genre, and layout: 88.9%, 100%, and 88.9%. The main area of interest has been identified in all the test cases. By using the identified main areas of interest, we were able to select the optimal cameras with an average $F$-measure of 0.95. Finally, for the detection of in-view cameras we obtained an average $F$-measure of 0.77. Thus, our experimental results show that the proposed methods perform well in several real public events.

## References

[1] R. Oami, A. B. Benitez, S. F. Chang, and N. Dimitrova, "Understanding and Modeling User Interests in Consumer Videos," in *IEEE International Conference on Multimedia and Expo*, pp. 1475–1478, Taipei, Taiwan, 2004.

[2] M. Sugano, T. Yamada, S. Sakazawa, and S. Hangai, "Genre Classification Method for Home Videos," in *IEEE International Workshop on Signal Processing*, pp. 1–5, Rio de Janeiro, Brazil, 2009.

[3] D. Brezeale and D. J. Cook, "Automatic video classification: a survey of the literature," *IEEE Transactions on Systems, Man and Cybernetics C*, vol. 38, no. 3, pp. 416–430, 2008.

[4] N. Serrano, A. Savakis, and J. Luo, "A computationally efficient approach to indoor/outdoor scene classification," in *16th IEEE International Conference on Pattern Recognition*, pp. 146–149, Quebec City, Canada, 2002.

[5] U. Lipowezky and I. Vol, "Indoor-outdoor detector for mobile phone cameras using gentle boosting," in *IEEE Conference on Computer Vision and Pattern Recognition Workshops*, pp. 31–38, San Francisco, Calif, USA, 2010.

[6] M. Szummer and R. W. Picard, "Indoor-outdoor image classification," in *IEEE International Workshop on Content-Based Access of Image and Video Database*, pp. 42–51, Bombay, India, 1998.

[7] A. Payne and S. Singh, "Indoor vs. outdoor scene classification in digital photographs," *Pattern Recognition*, vol. 38, no. 10, pp. 1533–1545, 2005.

[8] N. Zhang and L. Guan, "An efficient framework on large-scale video genre classification," in *IEEE International Workshop on Multimedia Signal Processing*, pp. 481–486, Saint-Malo, France, 2010.

[9] X. Yuan, W. Lai, T. Mei, X. S. Hua, X. Q. Wu, and S. Li, "Automatic video genre categorization using hierarchical SVM," in *IEEE International Conference on Image Processing*, pp. 2905–2908, Atlanta, Ga, USA, 2006.

[10] J. Xinghao, S. Tanfeng, and C. Bin, "A novel video content classification algorithm based on combined visual features model," in *2nd International Congress on Image and Signal Processing (CISP '09)*, October 2009.

[11] M. Montagnuolo and A. Messina, "Multimodal genre analysis applied to digital television archives," in *19th International Conference on Database and Expert Systems Applications (DEXA '08)*, pp. 130–134, Turin, Italy, September 2008.

[12] A. Feryanto and I. Supriana, "Location recognition using detected objects in an image," in *International Conference on Electrical Engineering and Informatics*, pp. 1–4, Ban-dung, Indonesia, 2011.

[13] G. Schroth, R. Huitl, D. Chen, M. Abu-Alqumsan, A. Al-Nuaimi, and E. Steinbach, "Mobile visual location recognition," *IEEE Signal Processing Magazine*, vol. 28, no. 4, pp. 77–89, 2011.

[14] K. Tieu, G. Dalley, and W. E. L. Grimson, "Inference of non-overlapping camera network topology by measuring statistical dependence," in *10th IEEE International Conference on Computer Vision*, vol. 2, pp. 1842–1849, Beijing, China, 2005.

[15] T. Thummanuntawat, W. Kumwilaisak, and J. Chinrungrueng, "Automatic region of interest detection in multi-view video," in *International Conference on Electrical Engineering/ Electronics Computer Telecommunications and Information Technology (ECTI-CON '10)*, pp. 889–893, Chiang Mai, Thailand, May 2010.

[16] J. B. Hayet, T. Mathes, J. Czyz, J. Piater, J. Verly, and B. Macq, "A modular multi-camera framework for team sports tracking," in *IEEE Conference on Advanced Video and Signal Based Surveillance (AVSS '05)*, pp. 493–498, Como, Italy, September 2005.

[17] A. Carlier, V. Charvillat, W. T. Ooi, R. Grigoras, and G. Morin, "Crowdsourced automatic zoom and scroll for video retargeting," in *18th ACM International Conference on Multimedia ACM Multimedia (MM '10)*, pp. 201–210, Firenze, Italy, October 2010.

[18] P. Doubek, I. Geys, T. Svoboda, and L. Van Gool, "Cinematographic rules applied to a camera network," in *5th Workshop on Omnidirectional Vision, Camera Networks and Non-Classical Cameras*, pp. 17–29, Prague, Czech Republic, 2004.

[19] F. Chen and C. DeVleeschouwer, "Personalized production of basketball videos from multi-sensored data under limited display resolution," *Elsevier Journal of Computer Vision and Image Understanding*, vol. 114, no. 6, pp. 667–680, 2010.

[20] T. Ojala, M. Pietikainen, and D. Harwood, "Performance evaluation of texture measures with classification based on Kullback discrimination of distributions," in *12th IAPR International Conference on Pattern Recognition*, vol. 1, pp. 582–585, Jerusalem, Palestine, 1994.

[21] MPEG-7, "ISO/IEC 15938, Multimedia Content Description Interface," http://www.iso.org/iso/iso_catalogue/catalogue_tc/catalogue_detail.htm?csnumber=34228.

[22] D. G. Lowe, "Object recognition from local scale-invariant features," in *IEEE International Conference on Computer Vision*, vol. 2, pp. 1150–1157, Corfu, Greece, 1999.

[23] T. Lahti, *On low complexity techniques for automatic speech recognition and automatic audio content analysis*, Doctoral thesis, Tampere University of Technology, 2008.

[24] F. Cricri, K. Dabov, I. D. D. Curcio, S. Mate, and M. Gabbouj, "Multimodal Event Detection in User Generated Videos," in *IEEE International Symposium on Multimedia*, pp. 263–270, Dana Point, Calif, USA, December 2011.

[25] V. Kobla, D. DeMenthon, and D. Doermann, "Identification of sports videos using replays, text, and camera motion features," in *Storage and Retrieval for Media Databases*, vol. 3972 of *Proceedings of SPIE*, pp. 332–343, 2000.

[26] C. G. M. Snoek, M. Worring, and A. W. M. Smeulders, "Early versus late fusion in semantic video analysis," in *ACM International Conference on Multimedia*, pp. 399–402, Singapore, 2005.

[27] V. N. Vapnik, *The Nature of Statistical Learning Theory*, Springer, New York, NY, USA, 1995.

[28] B. Foss, *Filmmaking: Narrative and Structural Techniques*, Silman James Press, Los Angeles, Calif, USA.

[29] Y. G. Jiang, G. Ye, S. F. Chang, D. Ellis, and A. C. Loui, "Consumer video understanding: A benchmark database and an evaluation of human and machine performance," in *1st ACM International Conference on Multimedia Retrieval (ICMR '11)*, Trento, Italy, April 2011.

[30] M. Cha, H. Kwak, P. Rodriguez, Y. Y. Ahn, and S. Moon, "Analyzing the video popularity characteristics of large-scale user generated content systems," *IEEE/ACM Transactions on Networking*, vol. 17, no. 5, pp. 1357–1370, 2009.

[31] Y. Odaka, S. Takano, Y. In, M. Higuchi, and H. Murakami, "The evaluation of the error characteristics of multiple GPS terminals," in *Recent Researches in Circuits, Systems, Control and Signals*, pp. 13–21, 2011.

[32] T. Menard, J. Miller, M. Nowak, and D. Norris, "Comparing the GPS capabilities of the Samsung Galaxy S, Motorola Droid X, and the Apple iPhone for Vehicle Tracking Using FreeSim_Mobile," in *14th IEEE International Conference on Intelligent Transportation Systems*, pp. 985–990, Washington, DC, USA, 2011.

# 8

# Color Image Quality Assessment Based on CIEDE2000

**Yang Yang,[1, 2] Jun Ming,[1] and Nenghai Yu[2]**

[1] *Key IC&SP Laboratory of Ministry of Education, Anhui University, Hefei 230039, China*
[2] *MOE-Microsoft Key Laboratory of Multimedia Computing & Communication, University of Science and Technology of China, Hefei 230027, China*

Correspondence should be addressed to Yang Yang, skyyang@mail.ustc.edu.cn

Academic Editor: Qi Tian

Combining the color difference formula of CIEDE2000 and the printing industry standard for visual verification, we present an objective color image quality assessment method correlated with subjective vision perception. An objective score conformed to subjective perception (OSCSP) $Q$ was proposed to directly reflect the subjective visual perception. In addition, we present a general method to calibrate correction factors of color difference formula under real experimental conditions. Our experiment results show that the present DE2000-based metric can be consistent with human visual system in general application environment.

## 1. Introduction

Image quality assessment is one of the basic technologies for image information engineering. Many researchers are seeking an objective quality assessment metric which can be calculated simply but can accurately reflect subjective quality of human perception [1–3]. Most of these studies aim at the reduction of deviation between the subjective and objective quality assessment results. Due to the wide application of color image, color image quality assessment becomes more and more important. To represent the color image visual perception, the three attributes (brightness, hue, and saturation) must be exploited [4]. At present, most of color image quality assessment methods convert a color image to the brightness, hue, and saturation corresponding space (including XYZ, YUV, HSL, and opponent color space) and then adopt the gray scale image quality assessment for each channel [5–8]. However, this kind of conversion cannot completely describe the nonlinear perception of brightness, hue, and saturation in a color image. It is well known that color image quality assessment results depend on the coincidence degree of color space and visual perception. Thus, it is highly desirable to convert color image to a color space which can reflect the subjective visual characteristics more properly. In the present color image assessment method, we propose to convert color image into the uniform color-difference color space.

Based on the JND (just noticeable difference) idea of XYZ system in the colorimetric, uniform color-difference space was proposed to establish a linear relationship between the changes of brightness, hue, and saturation and visual perception through the subjective visual perception experiment. It has been experimentally shown that uniform color-difference space assessment results are much better than opponent color space and YUV color space [9]. Presently, CIEDE2000 is regarded as the best uniform color-difference model coinciding with subjective visual perception. It normalizes brightness, hue, and saturation of the visual perception to the same unit [10–12]. With this model, we can directly get a numerical result, named color-difference parameter $\Delta E$, which can reflect the color difference between two images. Many researchers have exploited this color-difference parameter $\Delta E$ from CIEDE2000 formula into the image quality assessment [13, 14]. However, this objective parameter, color-difference parameter $\Delta E$, cannot directly correspond to the subjective visual perception, such as subjective five-level assessment metric. It is noted that in the printing industry, a visual perception metric, based on National Bureau of Standards (NBS) unit (or modified Judd), relates the value of $\Delta E$ to visual perception [15].

In the present color image quality assessment method, we adopted the NBS unit idea to convert the value color-difference parameter $\Delta E$ from CIEDE2000 to a precise objective score conformed to subjective perception (OSCSP) $Q$ to directly reflect the subjective visual perception. Different from the well-known subjective five-level metrics, our OSCSP $Q$ converted from $\Delta E$ can be a real number $Q \in [0, 5]$ consistent with subjective perception. Our experiments in various distorted images show the present color image quality assessment metric can give an objective assessment result nicely coinciding with subjective visual perception.

## 2. CIEDE2000 Color Difference Formula and Its Environmental Parameters Calibration

CIEDE2000 color difference formula presents the relationship of color difference value $\Delta E$ and lightness difference $\Delta L'$, hue difference $\Delta H'$, and chroma difference $\Delta C'$. It is defined as

$$\Delta E$$
$$= \sqrt{\left(\frac{\Delta L'}{K_L S_L}\right)^2 + \left(\frac{\Delta C'}{K_C S_C}\right)^2 + \left(\frac{\Delta H'}{K_H S_H}\right)^2 + R_T \left(\frac{\Delta C'}{K_C S_C}\right)\left(\frac{\Delta H'}{K_H S_H}\right)}.$$
(1)

Here the parameter factors, $K_L, K_C, K_H$, are correction factors related with observation environment. Lightness, chroma, and hue weighting factors, $S_L, S_C, S_H$, respectively describe visual perception action on three attributes. Rotation factor $R_T$ is used to correct deflection in the blue region of the ellipse axis direction for visual perception. Figure 1 indicates the basic steps to calculate the color-difference value $\Delta E$ based on CIEDE2000 formula.

Under the condition of CIE standard observe environment, the parameter factor $K_L = K_C = K_H = 1$. As it is impossible to fully meet the standard observation conditions in the real experiment, we have to calibrate these three correction factors $K_L, K_C, K_H$ based on the idea of JND (just noticeable difference). The so-called visual JND means that the human eye can just feel the difference of the lightness, hue, and chroma between two objects. We change one of these three attributes (lightness or hue or chroma) of one object and keep the other two parameters unchanged to get just noticeable difference between this object and the reference one. This JND case corresponds to the condition of color-difference parameter $\Delta E = 0.5$ according to Table 1. For example, we can determine the lightness correction factor $K_L$ as follows. Firstly, choose two test images which have only lightness distortion $\Delta L'$ without hue distortion $\Delta H'$ and chroma distortion $\Delta C'$. Secondly, change the lightness of one image so that we can percept the just noticeable difference at certain $\Delta L'$. Lastly, we can determine the proper $K_L$ factor through (1) as JND condition means $\Delta E = 0.5$. In this way, we can fit out all the values of $K_L, K_C, K_H$ satisfying $\Delta E = 0.5$ under real experimental conditions.

## 3. Subjective Measurement Standard Establishment and Related Notes

In order to directly relate the color-difference parameter $\Delta E$ from the CIEDE2000 to the subjective visual perception, we adopt the idea of NBS unit to convert $\Delta E$ to an

objective score conformed to subjective perception (OSCSP) $Q$ to reflect the subjective visual perception through a nonlinear transformation as (2). To get this transformation, we need firstly extend the five-level metric by including two extreme states: the minimum color difference and the maximum color difference to get a subjective assessment metric as shown in Table 1 through the experiment. Then, we can define the OSCSP Q for the present subjective assessment metric as

$$Q = \begin{cases} 5, & \Delta \overline{E} < 0.5, \ k = 1, \\ 7 - k, \\ \quad -\dfrac{\Delta \overline{E} - \Delta E_{\min}(k)}{\Delta E_{\max}(k) - \Delta E_{\min}(k)}, & 0.5 \le \Delta \overline{E} \le 24, \ k \in 2,3,4,5,6, \\ 0, & \Delta \overline{E} > 24, \ k = 7. \end{cases}$$
(2)

Table 1 presents the detailed relationship of the OSCSP $Q$, perception of color difference, and NBS units.

For any distorted image, we can get the OSCSP $Q$ through the following processing.

(1) Firstly, we get the primary display of original image $R_1[i, j], G_1[i, j], B_1[i, j]$ and distorted image $R_2[i, j], G_2[i, j], B_2[i, j]$. Here, $i \in [1, M], j \in [1, N]$.

(2) Secondly, we calculate color difference value $\Delta E[i, j]$ of each pixel according to (1) and get color difference average value $\Delta \overline{E} = (1/MN) \sum_{1 \le i \le M} \sum_{1 \le j \le N} \Delta E[i, j]$.

(3) Finally, $Q$ is calculated according to (2) for each image. Compared with the previous methods, the present color image quality assessment method proposes an objective score conformed to subjective perception (OSCSP) $Q$, which cannot only be directly gotten by objective numerical calculation but also reflect the subjective visual perception more accurately. When compared with the traditional subjective five-level metrics based on human scoring, the present objective metrics is more convenient and can be operated in real time for online color image assessment.

## 4. Experimental Systems and Assessment Results

To prove that the present OSCSP $Q$ can accurately reflect the subjective visual perception, we have performed experiments on various distorted images from image database provided by image and video image quality engineering laboratory (LIVE) from University of Texas at Austin [16]. Our experimental environment is set according to the basic conditions for observation room. The experimental monitor is Founder FN980-WT, which has a resolution of $1440 \times 900$ 32-bit true color. To get repeatable experimental results, we calibrate the color temperature as 6500 K, brightness 80, contrast 70, and observable color grade 61.

TABLE 1: Subjective assessment metric based on CIEDE2000 Color difference.

| $k$ | $\Delta E_{\min}(k)$ | $\Delta E_{\max}(k)$ | Perception of color difference | $Q$ |
|---|---|---|---|---|
| 1 | 0.0 | 0.5 | Hardly | 5 |
| 2 | 0.5 | 1.5 | Slight | $5 - (\Delta\overline{E} - 0.5)$ |
| 3 | 1.5 | 3.0 | Noticeable | $4 - (\Delta\overline{E} - 1.5)/1.5$ |
| 4 | 3.0 | 6.0 | Appreciable | $3 - (\Delta\overline{E} - 3)/3$ |
| 5 | 6.0 | 12.0 | Much | $2 - (\Delta\overline{E} - 6)/6$ |
| 6 | 12.0 | 24.0 | Very much | $1 - (\Delta\overline{E} - 12)/12$ |
| 7 | 24.0 | $\infty$ | Strongly | 0 |

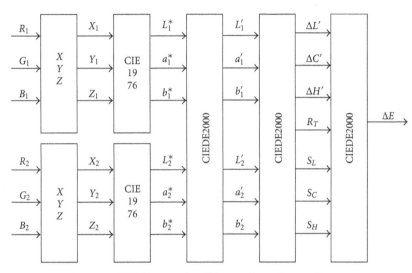

FIGURE 1: CIEDE2000 color difference formula step diagram.

    "womanhat"      "sailing2"      "woman"      "lighthouse"      "statue"

FIGURE 2: The five reference images.

TABLE 2: CC between algorithm and DMOS.

| | Model | WN | Blur | FF | JPEG | JP2K |
|---|---|---|---|---|---|---|
| | "womanhat" | 0.9760 | 0.9800 | 0.9210 | 0.9130 | 0.9460 |
| | "sailing2" | 0.9670 | 0.9570 | 0.8530 | 0.9100 | 0.8760 |
| CIEDE2000 | "woman" | 0.9640 | 0.9920 | 0.9630 | 0.9730 | 0.9920 |
| | "lighthouse" | 0.9860 | 0.9680 | 0.9970 | 0.9430 | 0.9670 |
| | "statue" | 0.9730 | 0.9940 | 0.9640 | 0.9680 | 0.9640 |
| | Average | 0.9732 | 0.9782 | 0.9396 | 0.9414 | 0.9490 |
| PSNR (average) | | 0.9066 | 0.8358 | 0.9034 | 0.8526 | 0.8534 |
| SSIM (average) | | 0.8386 | 0.9192 | 0.8720 | 0.8128 | 0.8264 |

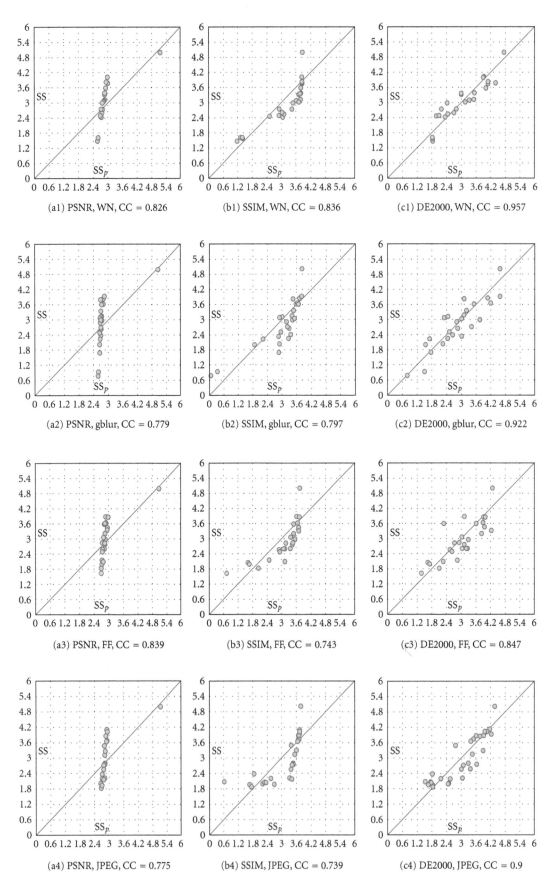

(a1) PSNR, WN, CC = 0.826

(b1) SSIM, WN, CC = 0.836

(c1) DE2000, WN, CC = 0.957

(a2) PSNR, gblur, CC = 0.779

(b2) SSIM, gblur, CC = 0.797

(c2) DE2000, gblur, CC = 0.922

(a3) PSNR, FF, CC = 0.839

(b3) SSIM, FF, CC = 0.743

(c3) DE2000, FF, CC = 0.847

(a4) PSNR, JPEG, CC = 0.775

(b4) SSIM, JPEG, CC = 0.739

(c4) DE2000, JPEG, CC = 0.9

FIGURE 3: Continued.

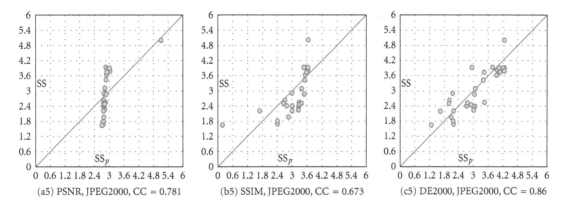

(a5) PSNR, JPEG2000, CC = 0.781    (b5) SSIM, JPEG2000, CC = 0.673    (c5) DE2000, JPEG2000, CC = 0.86

FIGURE 3: The linear correlation graphs from PSNR, SSIM, and DE2000-based method. (a1) to (a5), (b1) to (b5), and (c1) to (c5), respectively show the results for PSNR, SSIM, and DE2000 with five types of distortions.

TABLE 3: MAE between algorithm and DMOS.

| Model | | WN | Blur | FF | JPEG | JP2K |
|---|---|---|---|---|---|---|
| CIEDE2000 | "womanhat" | 0.041 | 0.029 | 0.049 | 0.074 | 0.066 |
| | "sailing2" | 0.040 | 0.063 | 0.068 | 0.072 | 0.062 |
| | "woman" | 0.047 | 0.025 | 0.049 | 0.042 | 0.021 |
| | "lighthouse" | 0.030 | 0.047 | 0.013 | 0.060 | 0.045 |
| | "statue" | 0.042 | 0.020 | 0.039 | 0.050 | 0.049 |
| | Average | 0.0400 | 0.0368 | 0.0436 | 0.0596 | 0.0486 |
| PSNR (average) | | 0.0764 | 0.0994 | 0.0700 | 0.0992 | 0.0880 |
| SSIM (average) | | 0.0938 | 0.0762 | 0.0780 | 0.0928 | 0.0552 |

After setting the experimental environment, we need to firstly determine the correction parameter $K_L, K_C, K_H$ values under this real experimental condition based on the idea of JND as mentioned above. To get a better calibration, we get a set of $K_L, K_C, K_H$ values, respectively using $R, G, B$ three primary colors signals and multiple random signals and then average them to reach the final calibrated correction parameters: $K_L = 0.65, K_C = 1.0,$ and $K_H = 4.0$. Following experimental results used these correction parameters.

The LIVE database contains nearly 1000 images with five types of distortions: JPEG2000 and JPEG compression with various compression ratios, images contaminated by white Gaussian noise (WN), Gaussian blurred images (gblur), and JPEG2000 compressed images transmitted over simulated fast fading Rayleigh channel with bit errors typical for the wireless transmission (FF). For these images, the Differential Mean Opinion Score (DMOS) values range between 0 and 100. Smaller is DMOS, better is the image quality. We normalized the DMOS to a subject scores (SS) ranged between 0 and 5 by the expressions SS = 5 ∗ (100 − DMOS)/ 100 so that it can be compared with the subjective assessment metric. Higher is SS, better is the image quality.

The popular LIVE database contains 29 different images and a total of 982 images (reference and distorted). As an example, we choose five different images named "woman-hat", "sailing2," "woman," "lighthouse," "statue," and a total of 170 images (including reference and distorted) in our experiment. The references of these five images are shown

in Figure 2. We can compare our DE2000-based method with the well-known metric PSNR and structural similarity (SSIM). We firstly calculate objective results of PSNR, SSIM and our objective score conformed to subjective perception (OSCSP) $Q$ for all the images. Through the least-square method between the subjective scores (SS) of these images and those objective results from PSNR, SSIM, and our method, we can obtain a set of value named prediction subjective scores ($SS_p$) to reflect the conformity between objective scores and subjective perception.

In Figure 3, we present linear correlation graphs from PSNR, SSIM, and our DE2000-based method for five typical types distorted images. For all these five typical types of distorted images, the present DE2000-based algorithm can give correlation results much closer to the diagonal than the PSNR and SSIM. Correspondingly, CC values of our DE2000-based method are found to be the highest.

The linear correlation coefficient (CC) and the mean absolute error (MAE) are used to quantitatively compare the image quality assessment (IQA) results of the present DE2000-based method with the PSNR and SSIM. Tables 2 and 3, respectively, show CC and MAE of PSNR, SSIM and CIEDE2000. Parameters CC and MAE present the correlation of objective and subjective scores (SS). CC is higher, objective assessment results are more coincide with the subjective visual perception. MAE is lower, objective assessment results are also more coincide with the subjective visual perception. Compared with PSNR and SSIM, our

DE2000-based method gives larger CC and smaller MAE for all these images.

## 5. Conclusion

By exploiting the idea of NBS, we have established a color image quality assessment metric based on color difference formula of CIEDE2000. We propose to use an objective score conformed to subjective perception (OSCSP) $Q$ directly gotten by objective numerical calculation to reflect the subjective visual perception of any color image. In addition, we present a general method to calibrate correction factors of this CIEDE2000 color difference formula under the real experimental conditions so that we can experimentally compare the present metric with other objective IQA method such as PSNR and SSIM in general application environment. The experiment results prove that the present DE2000-based metric can assess color image quality finely.

## Acknowledgments

This work was supported by Fundamental Research Funds for the Central Universities (no. WK2100230002), National Science and Technology Major Project (no. 2010ZX03004-003), National Natural Science Foundation of China (no. 60872162), and Young Research Foundation of Anhui University (no. KJQN1012).

## References

[1] A. C. Bovik, "Perceptual video processing: seeing the future," *Proceedings of the IEEE*, vol. 98, no. 11, pp. 1799–1803, 2010.

[2] A. C. Bovik, "What you see is what you learn," *IEEE Signal Processing Magazine*, vol. 27, no. 5, pp. 117–123, 2010.

[3] S. O. Lee and D. G. Sim, "Objectification of perceptual image quality for mobile video," *Optical Engineering*, vol. 50, no. 6, Article ID 067404, 2011.

[4] C. F. Hall, *Digital color image compression in a perceptual space [Ph.D. thesis]*, University of Southern California, 1978.

[5] N. Thakur and S. Devi, "A new method for color image quality assessment," *International Journal of Computer Applications*, vol. 15, no. 2, pp. 10–17, 2011.

[6] A. Toet and M. P. Lucassen, "A new universal colour image fidelity metric," *Displays*, vol. 24, no. 4-5, pp. 197–207, 2003.

[7] P. Le Callet and D. Barba, "A robust quality metric for color image quality assessment," in *Proceedings of the International Conference on Image Processing (ICIP'03)*, pp. 437–440, September 2003.

[8] C. J. van den Branden Lambrecht, "Color moving pictures quality metric," in *Proceedings of the IEEE International Conference on Image Processing (ICIP'96)*, pp. 885–888, September 1996.

[9] V. Monga, W. S. Geisler, and B. L. Evans, "Linear color-separable human visual system models for vector error diffusion halftoning," *IEEE Signal Processing Letters*, vol. 10, no. 4, pp. 93–97, 2003.

[10] M. R. Luo, G. Cui, and B. Rigg, "The development of the CIE 2000 colour-difference formula: CIEDE2000," *Color Research and Application*, vol. 26, no. 5, pp. 340–350, 2001.

[11] R. G. Kuehni, "CIEDE2000, milestone or final answer?" *Color Research and Application*, vol. 27, no. 2, pp. 126–127, 2002.

[12] M. R. Luo, G. Cui, and B. Rigg, "Further comments on CIEDE2000," *Color Research and Application*, vol. 27, no. 2, pp. 127–128, 2002.

[13] G. M. Johnson and M. D. Fairchild, "A top down description of S-CIELAB and CIEDE2000," *Color Research and Application*, vol. 28, no. 6, pp. 425–435, 2003.

[14] S. Chen, A. Beghdadi, and A. Chetouani, "Color image assessment using spatial extension to CIE DE2000," in *Proceedings of the International Conference on Consumer Electronics (ICCE'08), Digest of Technical Papers*, pp. 1–2, Las Vegas, Nev, USA, January 2008.

[15] C. Hu, *Printing Color and Chromaticity*, Printing Industry Press, 1993.

[16] H. R. Sheikh, Z. Wang, L. Cormack, and A. C. Bovik, "LIVE image quality assessment database release 2," http://live.ece.utexas.edu/research/quality.

# 9

# Parlay X Web Services for Policy and Charging Control in Multimedia Networks

**Ivaylo Atanasov, Evelina Pencheva, and Dora Marinska**

*Department of Telecommunications, Technical University of Sofia, 1000 Sofia, Bulgaria*

Correspondence should be addressed to Evelina Pencheva, enp@tu-sofia.bg

Academic Editor: Mohamed Hamdi

The paper investigates the capabilities of Parlay X Web Services for Policy and Charging Control (PCC) in managing all Internet-protocol-based multimedia networks (IMSs). PCC is one of the core features of evolved packet networks. It comprises flow-based charging including charging control and online credit control, gating control, and Quality of Service (QoS) control. Based on the analysis of requirements for PCC, the functionality for open access to QoS management and advanced charging is identified. Parlay X Web Services are evaluated for the support of PCC, and some enhancements are suggested. Implementation aspects are discussed, and Parlay X interfaces are mapped onto IMS control protocols. Use cases of Parlay X Web Services for PCC are presented.

## 1. Introduction

IMS stands for internet protocol multimedia subsystem which is an architectural framework for service delivery in evolved packet networks. IMS enables various types of multimedia services based on access independency and IP connectivity [1]. The main requirement for IMS in conjunction with IP connectivity access network (IP-CAN) is to provide quality of service. Quality of service (QoS) is used to differentiate multimedia offering from traditional Internet services, which in most cases do not provide QoS. In order to provide a mechanism for service-aware QoS control and coherent charging, the Policy and Charging Control architecture is standardized. The Policy and Charging Control (PCC) is a key concept in IMS architecture and it is designed to enable flow-based charging, including, for example, online credit control, as well as policy control, which includes support for service authorization and QoS management [2].

In IMS, the user equipment negotiates with the network the session parameters by means of Session Initiation Protocol (SIP) signaling [3]. The service-related information is delivered to PCC functional entities and is used to form authorized IP QoS data (e.g., maximum bandwidth and QoS class) and charging rules as well as user plane event reporting (e.g., bearer loss recovery, access network change, and out of credit) for any access network [4].

To stimulate service provisioning and to allow applications outside of the network operator domain to invoke communication functions, an approach to opening the network interfaces is developed [5]. The open access to network functions allows 3rd party applications to make use of network functionality and to receive information from the network through application programming interfaces (APIs). Parlay X Web Services are highly abstracted means for access to network functionality [6]. Parlay X provides APIs for a palette of network functions such as call control, data session control, mobility, messaging, QoS control, and charging.

In this paper, we assess the support of existing Parlay X Web Services for access to PCC functions in multimedia networks.

The paper is structured as follows. Some related works are discussed in Section 2. The PCC architecture with User Data Convergence is discussed in Section 3. Based on the PCC architectural framework, the requirements for open access to flow-based charging and policy control are summarized in Section 4. The standardized capabilities of Parlay X Web Services for open access to PCC are evaluated in Section 5. In Section 6, some enhancements to Parlay X Web Services are suggested having in mind the identified requirements. The Parlay X interfaces implementation requires mapping of interfaces methods onto network control protocols messages. Such mapping does not exist as the PCC specifications are defined after the specification of Parlay X Web Services. The suggested mapping is sketched in Section 7. The Parlay X interfaces applicability is illustrated by typical use cases. Finally, Section 8 concludes by highlighting the benefits of third party QoS management in IP-based multimedia networks.

## 2. Related Work

PCC allows flexible QoS management of ongoing multimedia sessions in case of changing both the access networks and user devices with different capabilities. The PCC can also contribute to seamless service continuity in case of handover between two wireless networks without user intervention and with minimal service disruptions.

Good and Ventura [7] propose a multilayered policy control architecture that extends the general resource management function being standardized; this extended architecture gives application developers greater control over the way the services are treated in the transport layer. Good et al. [8] suggest enhancements to the PCC framework that extend the end-to-end inter-domain mechanisms to discover the signaling routes at the service control layer and use this to determine the paths traversed by the media at the resource control layer. Because the approach operates at these layers, it is compatible with existing transport networks and exploits already existing QoS control mechanisms. In [9], it is presented an architecture with policy-based network management focusing on access network optimization while taking service level agreements (SLAs), business objectives, routing rules, service information, user profiles, and platform conditions into account. Zhao et al. [10] present a policy-based radio resources allocation scheme. Different channel allocation algorithms and channel allocation strategies form a series of policies, thus constituting a policy-based channel allocation scheme. A policy-based service provisioning system is proposed [11] in order to provide different classes of services.

The necessity of open access to QoS control is substantiated in [12]. Stojanovic et al. [13] address an open issue of end-to-end service specification and mapping in next-generation networks. A centralized approach has been considered via the third party agent that manages the negotiation process in a group of domains. The authors suggest a general structure of the service specification form, which contains technical parameters related to a particular service request. Bormann et al. [14] extend the mediation layer between the operators core network and the charging system by adding capabilities for online charging control. The authors present a prototype that implements and

extends parts of the standardized PCC architecture by the use of the open source JAIN SLEE-based framework Mobicents. Akhatar [15] develops a system and method for providing QoS enablers for 3rd party applications. In one embodiment, the method comprises user equipment establishing a session with a third party application server hosting a selected third party application and receiving from the third party application server QoS information comprising at least one of the pluralities of QoS attributes and configuring a QoS of a radio access network in accordance with the obtained QoS information. The method further comprises activating the radio access network QoS for the selected application and establishing an application session with the third party application server via the radio access network. Koutsopoulou et al. [16] present a platform that extends the existing charging collection information mechanisms and billing systems to provide for advanced and flexible charging mechanisms and pricing policies. An approach to per-flow charging with increased scalability of QoS support charging is suggested in [17].

The Parlay X "Application-Driven Quality of Service" (ADQ) [18], defined in 3GPP TS 29.199-17, allows applications to control the QoS available on user connection. It may be used for dynamic management of QoS parameters available on multimedia sessions.

The Parlay X "Payment" Web Service [19], defined in 3GPP TS 29.199-6, supports payment reservation, prepaid payments, and postpaid payments. It may be used for charging of both volume and currency amounts, a conversion function and a settlement function in case of a financially resolved dispute.

The Parlay X interfaces are defined before the standardization of IMS PCC. The analysis of PCC functions shows that these interfaces do not cover all QoS management functions that network operator can expose.

## 3. Architecture for Open Access to Policy and Charging Control

A possible deployment of Parlay X Web Services in PCC architecture is shown in Figure 1.

Policy and Charging Control architecture is defined in 3GPP TS 23.203 specifications [20]. The Policy and Charging Rule Function (PCRF) encompasses policy control decision and flow-based charging control functionalities. The Policy and Charging Enforcement Function (PCEF) includes service data flow detection, policy enforcement, and flow-based charging functions. It is located at the media gateway. The Online Charging System (OCS) performs online credit control functions. It is responsible for interacting in real time with the user's account and for controlling or monitoring the charges related to service usage. Offline Charging System (OFCS) is responsible for charging process where charging information is mainly collected after the end of the session and it does not affect in real time the service being used.

The Home Subscriber Server (HSS) contains all subscription-related information needed for PCC rules. If the PCC architecture supports User Data Convergence

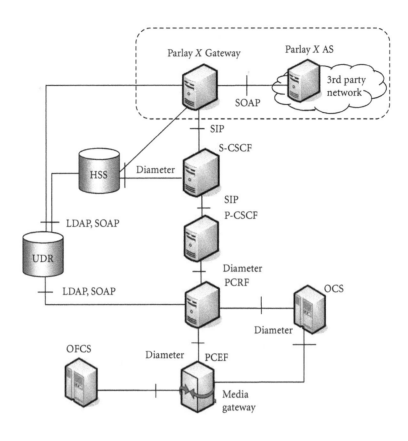

FIGURE 1: Deployment of Parlay X Web Services in PCC.

(UDC) defined in 3GPP TS 23.335 [21], then the User Data Repository (UDR) acts as a single logical repository for user data. The user data may, for example, contain information about default QoS parameters that have to be applied each time the user creates a session. Functional entities such as HSS and Application Servers keep their application logic, but they do not locally store user data permanently.

Call Session Control Functions (CSCFs) include functions that are common for all services. The Proxy CSCF (P-CSCF) is the first point of contact for user equipment. It deals with SIP compression, secured routing of SIP messages, and SIP sessions monitoring. Serving CSCF (S-CSCF) is responsible for user registration and session management.

Application Servers (ASs) run 3rd party applications that are outside the network operator domain. Parlay X Gateway is a special type of AS that provides Web Services interfaces for 3rd party applications and supports IMS protocols toward the network.

Diameter [22] is the control protocol in interfaces where authentication, authorization, and accounting functions are required. The control protocol in interfaces where session management is performed is Session Initiation Protocol (SIP) [23]. Lightweight Data Access Protocol (LDAP) and Simple Object Access Protocol (SOAP) are the control protocols used to create, read, modify, and delete user data in the UDR and to subscribe for and receive notifications about user data changes [24].

Note that not all charging-related interfaces and policy control functions are shown in Figure 1 for the sake of simplicity.

In Section 4, we study the functionalities of PCC and UDC in order to determine the requirements for open access to QoS management.

## 4. Requirements for Open Access to Policy and Charging Control

The PCC includes mechanisms for controlling the bearer traffic by using IP policies.

*4.1. Gating and QoS Control.* During the multimedia session establishment and modification, the user equipment negotiates a set of media characteristics. If the network operator applies policy control, then the P-CSCF sends the relevant session description information to the PCRF in order to form IP QoS authorization data. The 3rd party application can be involved in the process of QoS authorization by requesting specific QoS parameters to be applied, modified, or removed. Figure 2 illustrates the application control on QoS resource authorization for given SIP session.

*Functional Requirement 1.* During the SIP session establishment, 3rd party application may require to apply or to modify temporary specific QoS features on user session(s).

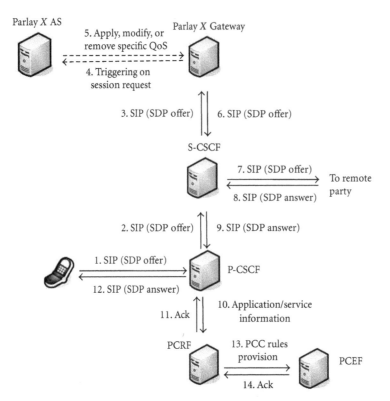

FIGURE 2: Application control on QoS during session establishment.

The required functions include applying temporary QoS parameters, modifying temporary QoS parameters, and removing QoS parameters for a predefined duration (e.g., for session duration). The application logic is activated in case of session initiation, modification, or termination.

In IMS, it is primary the network that decides what kind of bearer the user equipment needs during communication. Having application/service information and based on subscription information and policies, PCRF provides its decision in a form of PCC rules, which are used by the PCEF for gating control.

Any QoS events, such as indication of bearer release or bearer loss/recovery, are reported by the PCEF to the PCRF and P-CSCF. Using the policy control capabilities, the P-CSCF is able to track status of the IMS signaling and user plane bearers that the user equipment currently uses and to receive notifications when some or all service data flows are deactivated. To receive notifications about QoS events the 3rd party application needs to manage its subscriptions for notifications. By using information about bearers and signaling path status, the 3rd party application can improve service execution.

For example, the application can initiate session release on behalf of the user after indication that all service flows assigned to the ongoing session are released, but the P-CSCF has not received session termination request from the user itself. The scenario is shown in Figure 3.

*Functional Requirement 2.* The required functions for 3rd party application to manage the QoS event subscription include the following: creating notifications and setting the criteria for QoS; changing notifications by modification of the QoS event criteria; enabling/disabling notifications, and querying for the event criteria set; reporting notifications upon QoS event occurrences.

*Functional Requirement 3.* The 3rd party application should be able to request QoS resource release. Using this function, the application can prevent unauthorized bearer resources after SIP session termination.

*4.2. Usage Monitoring.* The 3rd party application may be interested in the accumulated usage of network resources on per-IP-CAN-session and user basis. This capability may be required for applying QoS control based on the total network usage in real time. For example, the 3rd party application may change the charging rate based on the resource usage (e.g., applying discounts after a specified volume have been reached). Another example is the assignment of a common quota for both fixed and mobile accesses for a limited time period for a defined set of subscriptions. During each session the network elements monitor the common quota, which may be consumed by one or more devices over either the wireless or fixed networks. When a defined percentage of the common quota and/or all common quota has been consumed, the 3rd party application may be notified of the event. When the common quota has been consumed the 3rd party application may block the access to the services.

*Functional Requirement 4.* The 3rd party application should be able to set the applicable thresholds for monitoring. Usage monitoring, if activated, will be performed for a

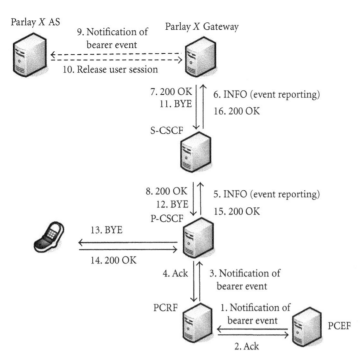

FIGURE 3: Notification of QoS resource release and application-initiated session release.

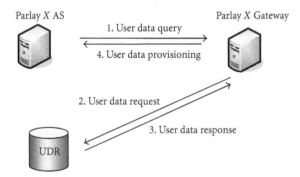

FIGURE 4: Open access to QoS-related user data.

particular application, a group of applications, or all detected traffic within a specific multimedia session. The 3rd party application should be notified when the provided usage monitoring thresholds have been reached.

*4.3. User Data Access.* The 3rd party application may need to retrieve QoS-related user data that are stored in the UDR. For example, the 3rd party application may query the UDR to obtain the QoS-related data from the user profile or its specific components, or it may browse the existing QoS-related data in user profiles in the various UDRs. The 3rd party application may add new QoS-related data in the user profile, remove, or/and modify specific QoS-related data from the repository. It is the responsibility of the Service Provider to define which QoS-related data may be modified or deleted by application providers.

The application access to QoS-related data, stored in the user profile, is depicted in Figure 4.

*Functional Requirement 5.* The required functions for access to QoS-related user data include the following: querying QoS data in order to retrieve the QoS parameters applied to user sessions by default; creating QoS data in order to add new QoS parameters in user profile; modifying QoS data in order to set new default QoS parameters; deleting QoS in order to erase the QoS parameters from the user profile.

Subscription/notification procedures allow the Parlay X Gateway to get notified when particular QoS data for specific user are updated in the UDR. Using functions for access to QoS-related user data, the 3rd party application can receive up-to-date information. For example, the 3rd application may request notifications about changes in QoS-related data in the user profile as shown in Figure 5. In a similar way, the 3rd party application may cancel one or several existing subscriptions.

When the data identified in subscription are changed or when the invoked subscription requests retrieval of all initial values of the referenced data, the 3rd party application is notified as shown in Figure 6.

*Functional Requirement 6.* To be aware of user's data changes, the 3rd party application needs functions for subscription management and means for notifications when such QoS-related events occur.

*4.4. Charging Control.* The charging function in PCC supports the following charging models: volume-based charging, time-based charging, time- and -volume-based charging, event-based charging, and no charging. It is possible to apply different rates and charging models (e.g., depending on the user location). The charging system selects the applicable rate based on QoS provided for the service, time of day, and

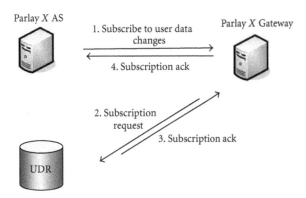

FIGURE 5: Subscription to QoS-related user data change.

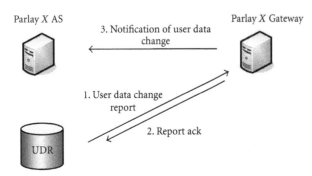

FIGURE 6: Notifications upon changes of user data.

so forth. In case of online charging, the charging actions are taken upon PCEF events (e.g., reauthorization upon QoS change).

*Functional Requirement 7.* In addition to functions for online and offline charging control, notification function is also required. To provide QoS-based charging and flow-based charging, the 3rd party application needs to be notified when some service data flows (e.g., video stream) or all service data flows (i.e., media streams of particular SIP session) have been deactivated, when the session has been terminated, or when access network has been changed.

The event types that should be reported to the 3rd party application involved in QoS management are summarized in Table 1. These event types can affect the QoS resource authorization and charging.

## 5. Evaluation of Parlay X Web Services Compared to Policy and Charging Control

*5.1. Parlay X Application-Driven Quality of Service.* The "Application-Driven Quality of Service" (ADQ) is a Parlay X Web Service that allows applications to control the QoS available on user connection. Configurable service attributes are upstream rate, downstream rate, and other QoS parameters specified by the service provider. Changes in QoS may be applied either for defined time interval or each time the user connects to the network.

TABLE 1: QoS-related event types.

| Event type | Description |
| --- | --- |
| Loss/release of bearer | Loss of bearer that can result in QoS degradation (e.g., the service data flows are deactivated as a consequence). If all the bearers are lost, the application can request QoS resource release |
| Recovery/establishment of bearer | Recovery or establishment of a new bearer |
| IP-CAN change | The access network providing IP connectivity is changed, which can result in applying specific charging |
| Out of credit | The user credit limit is reached |
| Session termination | The session terminates normally |
| Usage report | Reports that the usage threshold provided by the 3rd party application have been reached |

The ADQ ApplicationQoS interface defines operations for applying a new QoS feature to an end user connection. The ApplyQoSFeature operation is used by 3rd party application to request a default QoS feature to be set up on the end user connection, which results in a permanent change in the class of service provided over the end user connection. A default QoS feature governs the traffic flow on the end user connection whenever there are no temporary QoS features active on the connection. The ApplyQoSFeature operation is used by 3rd party application to request also a temporary QoS feature to be set up on the end user connection for a specified period of time. The ModifyQoSFeature operation is used by 3rd party application to alter the configurable service attributes (e.g., duration) of an active temporary QoS feature instance. The RemoveQoSFeature operation is used by 3rd party application to release a temporary QoS feature, which is currently active on the end user connection. Therefore, these operations provide functions required to apply, modify, and remove temporary QoS parameters (e.g., for session duration).

The ADQ Web Service enables applications to register with the service for notifications about network events that affect QoS, temporary configured on the user's connection.

The ADQ ApplicationQoSNotificationManager is used by 3rd party application to manage their registration for notifications. The startQoSNotification operation is used by 3rd party application to register their interest in receiving notifications of a specific event type(s) in context of specific end users. The stopQoSNotification operation is used by 3rd party application to stop receiving notifications by canceling an existing registration. Therefore, these operations provide functions required to manage the QoS event subscription.

The ADQ ApplicationQoSNotification interface provides the operations for notifying the Application about the impact of certain events on QoS features that were active on the end user connection when these events occurred. The notifyQoS operation reports a network event that has occurred against end user(s) active QoS features. Therefore, this operation provides functions required to report notifications upon QoS event occurrence.

As to 3GPP TS 29.214 [25] there are indications reported over the Rx reference point by the PCRF to the P-CSCF such as recovery of bearer, establishment of bearer, IP-CAN change, out of credit, and usage report. These indications can not be forwarded to the 3rd party application by the existing definition of the enumerated type QoSEvent.

Currently, not supported by ADQ Web Service functions required for policy control include usage monitoring and resources release.

The Parlay X "Application-Driven QoS" Web service defines operations that allow retrieval of the current status of user sessions, including history list of all QoS transactions previously requested against a user session. As far as the getQoSStatus operation of the ApplicationQoS interface is used by the 3rd party application to access the currently available QoS features on a user session, it is impossible for the 3rd party application to retrieve the configured QoS features stored in the user profile. Further, if the QoS-related data in the user profile have been changed by administrative means, the 3rd party application cannot be notified.

*5.2. Parlay X Payment.* The Parlay X "Payment" Web Service supports payment reservations, prepaid payments, and postpaid payments. It supports payments for any content in an open, Web-like environment. When combined with ADQ Web Service, the "Payment" may be used for charging based on the negotiated QoS. The features for QoS-based charging are restricted to temporary configured QoS parameters but cannot reflect the dynamic QoS change during the session. Flow-based charging is also impossible, as far as the Parlay X "Call notification" Web Service, defined in 3GPP TS 29.199-3 [26], does not provide notifications about media addition or deletion for a particular session. Location-based charging can be applied by combination of Parlay X "Terminal Location," defined in 3GPP TS 29.199-9 [27], and "Payment" Web Services.

Table 2 shows the Parlay X Web Services support for advanced charging.

# 6. Enhancement to Parlay X Web Services for PCC Support

We suggest the following interfaces to be added to the definition of "Application-Driven QoS" Web Service in order to support the PCC functionality.

*6.1. New Interfaces for Usage Monitoring.* The UsageMonitoringManager interface may be used by the 3rd party application to manage the usage monitoring for the accumulated usage of network resources on a per-session and user basis. The startUsageMonitoring operation may be used by the 3rd party application to set the applicable thresholds and to activate the usage monitoring. The operation parameters

TABLE 2: Advanced charging functions.

| Functions | Parlay X Interface | Operations |
| --- | --- | --- |
| QoS-based charging | Application-Driven QoS and Payment | Notify QoS event and charge amount, refund amount |
| Time-of-day-based charging | Call Notification and Payment | Notify called number and charge amount, refund amount |
| Location-based charging | Terminal Location and Payment | Get location and charge amount, refund amount |
| Service flow-based charging | Audio Call and Payment | Get media for participant and charge amount, refund amount |

specify the threshold volume and whether the usage monitoring will be performed for a particular application, a group of applications, or all detected traffic belonging to a specific end user session. The stopUsageMonitoring operation may be used by the 3rd party application to cancel the usage monitoring.

The UsageMonitoringNotification interface may be used to report to the 3rd party application when threshold levels are reached. The usageMonitoringReport operation may be used to report the accumulated usage.

*6.2. Enhancement to ADQ ApplicationQoS Interface.* A new operation that may be defined for the ADQ ApplicationQoS interface is releaseQoSResources. The operation releases the QoS resources reserved for the user session. It may be used by the 3rd party application to release the authorized QoS resources (e.g., on receiving notification that all bearers assigned to user session are lost).

*6.3. New Interfaces for Access to QoS-Related User Data.* The UserDataChangeManager interface may be used by the 3rd party application to manage subscriptions for changes of user's data. The startUserDataChangeNotifications operation may be used by the 3rd party application to subscribe to receive notifications about changes in QoS-related data in user profile, made by network operator or another application. The stopUserDataChangeNotifications operation may be used by the 3rd party application to cancel the subscription for user data changes.

The UserDataChangeNotification interface may be used to report to the 3rd party application any changes in QoS-related data in the user profile. For this purpose the notifyUserDataChange operation is used.

The QoSUserData interface may be used by the 3rd party application to access to QoS-related data stored in the user profile. The interface provides operations to submit, modify, and delete QoS related data. It also provides operations to query for QoS-related data including data identifier, metadata, control data, and QoS data upload date (matching-specific criteria). The application invokes the submitQoSData operation to submit QoS-related data into the user profile. The ADQ Web Service uploads the metadata of the QoS data to the network and the UDR stores the data. The modifyQoSData operation allows a 3rd party application to update previously submitted QoS-related and metadata. The UDR restricts modification to the submitted owner and puts the data into an invisible state until it completes the modification approval. The deleteQoSData operation allows a 3rd party application to delete QoS-related data. The readQoSData operation allows a 3rd party application to fetch the metadata of previously submitted QoS-related data. Request may include multiple data identifiers. The queryQoSData operation allows a 3rd party application to query for QoS-related data that match with specified identifiers.

*6.4. Enhancement to Call Notification Functionality.* We also suggest a new operation notifyMediaChange of the Call-Notification interface of the Parlay X "Call Notification" Web Service. The notifyMediaChange operation informs the 3rd party application that a media component is added to ongoing session or removed from ongoing session.

## 7. Mapping of Parlay X Interfaces onto Network Protocols

In order to make an adequate implementation of Parlay X "Application-Driven QoS" and "Payment" Web Services in the network, the interfaces operations have to be mapped onto messages of network control protocol.

*7.1. SIP-Based Interface.* The interfaces between the application server (Parlay X Gateway) and S-CSCF and between S-CSCF and P-CSCF are SIP based. SIP session information (including QoS parameters) is described by means of Session Description Protocol (SDP) and is transferred within the SIP message body. The initial request is sent as SIP INVITE message. The SIP re-INVITE message is used for modification of established session. QoS-related information about SIP session is transferred by INFO message. The management of the subscription to QoS-related events and notifications about QoS-related events are provided by means of SIP SUBSCRIBE/NOTIFY mechanism. The initial filter criteria for application triggering are stored as a part of user data stored and are downloaded to the S-CSCF on user registration.

Table 3 shows the mapping of ADQ interfaces onto SIP signaling.

The getQoSHistory operation does not require any signaling in the network and only some actions in the Parlay X Gateway.

*7.2. LAPD- and SOAP-Based Interfaces.* All procedures related to querying or to deleting data from the UDR and to creating or updating data within the UDR are controlled by LDAP as specified in 3GPP TS 29.335 [24]. The subscription/notification operations related to changes in user data stored within the UDR are transferred by HTTP in

Table 3: Mapping overview of ADQ interfaces onto SIP.

| ADQ interface operation | SIP message |
| --- | --- |
| startQoSNotification | SUBSCRIBE/200[SUBSCRIBE] |
| startQoSNotification | SUBSCRIBE/200[SUBSCRIBE] |
| notifyQoSEvent | NOTIFY/200[NOTIFY] |
| startUsageMonitoring | SUBSCRIBE/200[SUBSCRIBE] |
| stopUsageMonitoring | SUBSCRIBE/200[SUBSCRIBE] |
| usageMonitoringReport | NOTIFY/200[NOTIFY] |
| applyQoSFeature (temporary) | re-INVITE |
| modifyQoSFeature | re-INVITE |
| removeQoSFeature | re-INVITE |
| getQoSStatus | INFO |
| releaseQoSResources | BYE, 200[BYE] |

SOAP envelopes. Any changes in user profile create an LAPD session. To initiate an LDAP session, the Parlay X Gateway first establishes a transport connection with the UDR and then initiates an LDAP session by sending a BindRequest message. Termination of the LDAP session is initiated by the Parlay X Gateway by sending an UnbindRequest message or by the UDR by sending a Notice of Disconnection message.

In order to allow the application to relate a number of operations such as Create, Delete, and Update and to have them performed in one unit of interaction a transaction is used.

The Parlay X Gateway makes subscription for notifications about user data changes on behalf of 3rd party application by Subscribe messages. Subscribe request messages use the HTTP Post method and contain a SOAP message envelope. Subscribe response messages are coded as HTTP response message and contain a SOAP envelope. The Parlay X Gateway is notified about changes in QoS related data in user profile by Notify messages. Notify request messages use the HTTP Post method and contain a SOAP message envelope. Notify response messages are coded as HTTP response message, and contain a SOAP message envelope.

Table 4 shows the mapping of ADQ interfaces onto LAPD signaling.

*7.3. Diameter-Based Interfaces.* When User Data Convergence is not supported, the Parlay X Gateway is connected to the HSS. The protocol between the Parlay X Gateway and HSS is Diameter, and the 3rd party application access to user data is through Diameter commands.

To perform any changes in user data the Parlay X Gateway opens a Diameter dialogue. All 3rd party application initiated updates in user data are reflected in the HSS through the Diameter commands Profile-Update-Request/Answer (PUR/PUA). The access to user data is provided by the Diameter commands User-Data-Request/Answer (UDR/UDA).

The Parlay X Gateway subscribes to receive notifications on behalf of the 3rd party application using Diameter commands Subscribe-Notifications-Request/Answer (SNR/

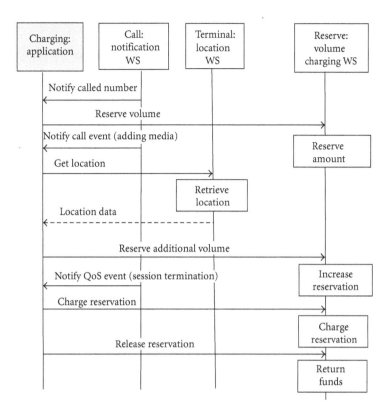

FIGURE 7: Use case of location-based charging.

TABLE 4: Mapping overview of the suggested ADQ interfaces onto UDC protocols.

| ADQ interface operation | UDC protocol message |
| --- | --- |
| submitQoSData | LDAP AddRequest/LDAP AddResponse |
| modifyQoSData | LDAP ModifyRequest/LDAP ModifyResponse |
| deleteQoSData | LDAP DelRequest/LDAP DelResponse |
| readQoSData | LDAP SearchRequest |
| queryQoSData | LDAP SearchRequest/LDAP SearchResultEntry, SearchResultReference, and SearchResultDone |
| notifyUserDataChange | HTTP Post/HTTP Response |
| startUserDataChangeNotifications | HTTP Post/HTTP Response |
| stopUserDataChangeNotifications | HTTP Post/HTTP Response |

SNA). Push-Notification-Request/Answer (PNR/PNA) commands are used to notify the Parlay X Gateway about events of interest.

The Rx reference point is defined between the P-CSCF and the PCRF. It is used for policy and charging control. In the context of PCC, the Diameter Authentication-Authorization-Request/Answer (AAR/AAA) commands are used to deliver SIP session information. The Re-Authorization-Request/Answer (RAR/RAA) commands report events related to QoS. The Session-Termination-Request/Answer (STR/STA) commands are used to release the resources, authorized earlier for a SIP session. The Abort-Session-Request/Answer (ASR/ASA) commands are used to provide information that all bearer resources, allocated to SIP session, are released.

## 8. Use Cases for Advanced Charging

To illustrate the usage of Parlay X interfaces for advanced charging we provide two use cases for service flow location-based charging and QoS-based charging.

Ann has a prepaid subscription. Shopping at a mall she decides to call Peter to invite him to a party. While discussing the details, Ann is hesitating which dress to choose and adds a video component to let Peter help her. Because of the high level of traffic load, the video stream is more expensive than usual at premises of the mall. The charging application knows that Ann is a prepaid user and, therefore, it needs to obtain permission from the online charging system (OCS). The OCS processes the credit control request and uses internal rating function to determine the rate of the

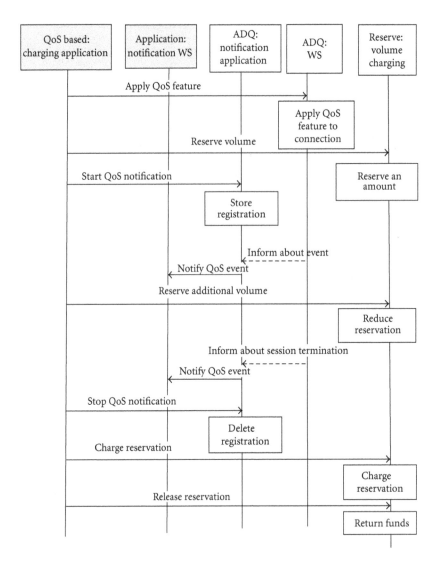

FIGURE 8: Use case of QoS-based charging.

desired service according to the service-specific information provided by the IMS entity if the cost was not given in the request. Then, OCS reserves an initial amount of money from Ann's account and returns the corresponding number of minutes Ann is allowed to talk. The charging application requests Ann's location when she decides to modify the media session including the video component. As Ann is in an area with scarce resources, the application determines that different charging rate has to be applied. The credit control request with charging rate information is sent to the OCS, which reserves the additional amount of money and returns the corresponding number of resources. When the minutes granted to Ann have been consumed or the service has been terminated, the OCS is informed and deducts Ann's amount from the account. The sequence diagram is shown in Figure 7.

Figure 8 shows a use case of ADQ interfaces for charging, based on the provided QoS on user session. The 3rd party application uses also the "Payment" interface and "Call Notification" interface.

In the scenario, Peter is at the stadium enjoying a football match. Peter decides to share the emotion with his friend who is away. Peter wants to send to him a video of the football match. However, the current service offering does not support the requested rate and hence it is required a temporary bit rate upgrade for the duration of the video. The QoS management application invokes the applyQoSFeature to apply new QoS parameters to the user session, specifying the higher bit rate and the duration the temporary QoS parameters should be applied. Assuming that the network allows the requested bit rate, the user's rate will be increased to the rate requested by the application for the specified duration. The application subscribes to notifications of events related to QoS available on user session. During the multimedia session the QoS goes down, so the application is notified and generates charging information based on the delivered QoS, thus correcting the requested one.

## 9. Conclusion

The open access to QoS management functions allows for the 3rd party applications dynamic control on QoS available on user sessions. The required functionality for open access to QoS management might be derived from the functional architecture of policy and charging control in the IP Multimedia Subsystem. The access to QoS control, gating control, flow-based charging, and user data management provides 3rd party applications with flexibility in QoS management.

So far standardized application programming interfaces do not support the entire policy and charging control functionality that network operator can expose. The evaluation of the interfaces for QoS management accessed by the 3rd party applications substantiates the need of further extension of management functions in order to provide greater flexibility in expressing communication details.

If the Parlay X approach is adopted in interface definition, besides the access to dynamic QoS control, 3rd party applications can benefit from other APIs that expose a variety of network functions. Implementation issues of the Parlay X APIs provisioning impact on the interfaces toward the network, which are left unconstrained. So, any extension of the functionality of QoS management interfaces has to be mapped onto IMS control protocols like SIP, Diameter, LDAP, and SOAP. The Parlay X Gateway has to incorporate state machines representing the 3rd party application view of interface objects that are extended with respect to the added functionality and the control protocol state machines.

The extension of the open access to QoS control adds more flexibility in resource management as far as the QoS provisioning is one of the main requirements to the IMS. Possible stakeholders that may benefit from Application-managed Quality of Service include Value Added Service providers for QoS management and 3rd party provided services that run on application servers on behalf of particular user groups.

## Acknowledgment

The research is in the frame of Project DDBY02/13/ 17.02.2010 funded by the Bulgarian Ministry of Youth, Education and Science.

## References

[1] F. Gouveia, S. Wahle, N. Blum, and T. Megedanz, "Cloud computing and EPC/IMS integration: new value-added services on demand," in *Proceedings of the 5th International ICST Mobile Multimedia Communications Conference*, 2009.

[2] S. Ouellette, L. Marchand, and S. Pierre, "A potential evolution of the policy and charging control/QoS architecture for the 3GPP IETF-based evolved packet core," *IEEE Communications Magazine*, vol. 49, no. 5, pp. 231–239, 2011.

[3] U. Iqbal, Y. Javed, S. Rehman, and A. Khanum, "SIP-based QoS management framework for IMS multimedia services," *International Journal of Computer Science and Network Security*, vol. 10, no. 5, pp. 181–188, 2010.

[4] Y. Wang, W. Liu, and W. Guo, "Architecture of IMS over WiMAX PCC and the QoS mechanism," in *Proceedings of the IET 3rd International Conference on Wireless, Mobile and Multimedia Networks (ICWMNN '10)*, pp. 159–162, 2010.

[5] M. Jain and M. Prokopi, "The IMS 2.0 service architecture," in *Proceedings of the 2nd International Conference on Next Generation Mobile Applications, Services, and Technologies (NGMAST '08)*, pp. 3–9, September 2008.

[6] J. Yang and H. Park, "A design of open service access gateway for converged Web service," in *Proceedings of the10th International Conference on Advanced Communication Technology*, pp. 1807–1810, February 2008.

[7] R. Good and N. Ventura, "Application driven policy based resource management for IP multimedia subsystems," in *Proceedings of the 5th International Conference on Testbeds and Research Infrastructures for the Development of Networks and Communities and Workshops (TridentCom '09)*, April 2009.

[8] R. Good, F. C. De Gouveia, N. Ventura, and T. Magedanz, "Session-based end-to-end policy control in 3GPP evolved packet system," *International Journal of Communication Systems*, vol. 23, no. 6-7, pp. 861–883, 2010.

[9] S. Musthaq, O. Salem, C. Lohr, and A. Gravey, "Policy-based QoS management for multimedia communication," 2008, http://cs.anu.edu.au/iojs/index.php/ifip/article/viewFile/13518/446.

[10] F. Zhao, L. Jiang, and C. He, "Policy-based radio resource allocation for wireless mobile networks," in *Proceedings of the IEEE International Conference Neural Networks and Signal Processing (ICNNSP '08)*, pp. 476–481, June 2008.

[11] S. G. Selvakumar, S. Paul Antony Xavier, and V. Balamurugan, "Policy based service provisioning system for WiMAX network: an approach," in *Proceedings of the International Conference on Signal Processing Communications and Networking (ICSCN '08)*, pp. 177–181, January 2008.

[12] M. Elkotob, *Autonomic resource management in IEEE 802.11 open access networks*, Dissertation, Lules University of Technology, Luleå, Sweden, 2008, http://epubl.ltu.se/1402-1757/2008/38/LTU-LIC-0838-SE.pdf.

[13] M. D. Stojanovic, S. V. B. Rakas, and V. S. Acimovic-Raspopovic, "End-to-end quality of service specification and mapping: he third party approach," *Computer Communications*, vol. 33, no. 11, pp. 1354–1368, 2010.

[14] F. Bormann, A. Braun, S. Flake, and J. Tacken, "Towards a policy and charging control architecture for online charging," in *Proceedings of the International Conference on Advanced Information Networking and Applications Workshops (WAINA '09)*, pp. 524–530, May 2009.

[15] H. Akhatar, "System and method for providing quality of service enablers for third party applications," Patent application number: 20090154397, 2009, http://www.faqs.org/patents/app/20090154397.

[16] M. Koutsopoulou, A. Kaloxylos, A. Alonistioti, and L. Merakos, "A platform for charging, billing, and accounting in future mobile networks," *Computer Communications*, vol. 30, no. 3, pp. 516–526, 2007.

[17] X. Duan, "Method for establishing Diameter session for packet flow based charging," 2007, http://www.freshpatents.com/%20Method-for-establishing-diameter-session-for-packet-flow-based-charging-dt20070816ptan20070189297.php.

[18] 3GPP TS 29.199-17 v9.0.0, "Open Service Access (OSA); Parlay X Web Services; Part 17: Application-driven Quality of Service (QoS), (Release 9)," 2009.

[19] 3GPP TS 29.199-6 v8.1.0, "Open Service Access (OSA); Parlay X Web Services; Part 6: Payment, (Release 9)," 2009.

[20] 3GPP TS 23.203 v11.2.0, "Policy and charging control architecture, (Release 9)," 2011.

[21] 3GPP TS 23.335 User Data Convergence (UDC), "Technical realization and information flows, (Release 9), v9.3.0," 2010.

[22] P. Calhoun, E. Guttman, G. Zorn, and J. Arkko, "RFC 3588 Diameter Base Protocol," 2003.

[23] 3GPP TS 24.229 v9.2.0, "IP Multimedia Call Control Protocol based on Session Initiation Protocol (SIP) and Session Description Protocol (SDP), (Release 9)," 2009.

[24] 3GPP TS 29.335 User Data Convergence (UDC), "User Data repository Access Protocol over the Ud interfaces, Release 9, v9.2.0," 2010.

[25] 3GPP TS 29.214 v11.1.0, "Policy and Charging Control over Rx reference point, (Release 9)," 2011.

[26] 3GPP TS 29.199-2 v9.0.0, "Open Service Access (OSA); Parlay X Web Services; Part 3: Call Notification, (Relase 9)," 2009.

[27] 3GPP TS 29.199-9 v9.0.0, "Open Service Access (OSA); Parlay X Web Services; Part 9: Terminal Location, (Relase 9)," 2009.

# 10

# Distortion-Based Slice Level Prioritization for Real-Time Video over QoS-Enabled Wireless Networks

**Ismail A. Ali, Martin Fleury, and Mohammed Ghanbari**

*School of Computer Science and Electronic Engineering, University of Essex, Colchester CO4 3SQ, UK*

Correspondence should be addressed to Martin Fleury, fleum@essex.ac.uk

Academic Editor: Martin Reisslein

This paper presents a prioritization scheme based on an analysis of the impact on objective video quality when dropping individual slices from coded video streams. It is shown that giving higher-priority classified packets preference in accessing the wireless media results in considerable quality gain (up to 3 dB in tests) over the case when no prioritization is applied. The proposed scheme is demonstrated for an IEEE 802.11e quality-of-service- (QoS-) enabled wireless LAN. Though more complex prioritization systems are possible, the proposed scheme is crafted for mobile interactive or user-to-user video services and is simply implemented within the Main or the Baseline profiles of an H.264 codec.

## 1. Introduction

There have recently emerged two forms of video streaming to mobile devices. The first, HTTP adaptive streaming [1], employing reliable TCP transport, has no need to protect the video stream against channel errors but is subject to delays. These delays mainly arise from the repeated transmissions that TCP imposes whenever packets are lost. Additionally, delay may occur due to the pull-based nature of the service. Therefore, though suitable for some forms of one-way commercial streaming, HTTP adaptive streaming is unsuitable for interactive services such as video conferencing. It is also unsuitable for mobile user-to-user streaming, because of the need to create multiple copies of the same video at different resolutions and set up a complex management structure to allow client access to an appropriate stream. Therefore, a second native form of streaming is necessary for delay- or storage-intolerant video streaming, and it is this form of streaming that is the subject of this paper. In this form of streaming [2], video is pushed from the server without the need for a feedback channel to make continual client requests. The Real-time Transport Protocol (RTP) with underlying Internet Protocol (IP)/User Datagram Protocol (UDP) for network routing and transport updates the client-side decoder with synchronization information. If MPEG-2

Transport Stream (TS) packets are multiplexed within each RTP packet, then audio can accompany video in a single packet stream. Adaptive bitrate adjustments (through scalable coding or transcoding) can occur, based on performance metrics carried by Real-time Transport Control Protocol (RTCP) packets, and pseudo-VCR functionality, if needed, is available through the Real-time Streaming Protocol (RTSP).

When mobile video streaming in native mode with IP/UDP/RTP packetization, there is a need to avoid periodic increased delay due to less efficient intracoded I-pictures [3] at the start of each Group of Pictures (GoP). One of the advantages of native streaming, is that an IPPP... picture structure can be adopted on wireless networks. This means that there is just one I-picture at the start of a stream, followed by a continuous stream of predictively coded P-pictures. In contrast, in HTTP adaptive streaming each video chunk (i.e., a GoP) must have a point of random access at the start of each chunk [1], for example, an I-picture. However, using a continuous sequence of predominantly intercoded P-pictures runs the risk upon packet loss of spatiotemporal propagation of errors. To counteract this problem, an H.264/AVC codec permits the inclusion of intracoded macroblocks (MBs) within the P-slices making up a compressed video frame. These MBs can be placed naturally by the encoder, if, for example, no suitable predictive reference exists from an occluded region. However, they can also be forcibly inserted as a form of nonperiodic intrarefresh. Notice that nonperiodic intrarefresh still allows random access to take place (if needed), as discussed further in Section 2. There are various forms of nonperiodic intrarefresh including: random placement of intracoded MBs up to a given number within each picture [4]; as part of an evolving isolated region [5]; as a line of intracoded MBs that cycles in position over a sequence of pictures [6]. The issue of which of these to choose is an interesting debate but as insertion of a cyclic intracoded line certainly does result in a complete refresh despite corrupted data [6], this paper assumes that this simply implemented mechanism is used.

The introduction of a cyclic intracoded line results in unequal error sensitivity within individual slices of video pictures, as a result of the additional intracoded MBs. To exploit this, individual slice-bearing packets within each video frame can be dropped and the effect on the objective video quality (PSNR) of the whole frame measured. Packets resulting in the highest video quality penalty (when dropped) can then be given the highest priority, while the ones introducing the least penalty are given the lowest priority level. In this work, we apply this proposed prioritization scheme to quality-of-service (QoS) enabled wireless LAN delivery. Specifically, we employ IEEE 802.11e [7], a QoS amendment that adds four queuing prioritization levels to the access of standard IEEE 802.11 (WiFi) networks. As compared to our preliminary work in [8], the proposed scheme does not require any modification to the standard H.264/Advanced Video Coding (AVC) slicing. Instead, the scheme can be applied to any preencoded video stream provided there are a reasonable number of slices per frame. Like the work in [8], this paper's scheme also involves just one video frame delay, as the packets of the video frame to be analyzed should be available to perform the distortion analysis. It ought to be mentioned that the original raw video is not required for this analysis, as the decoded frame without drops can act as a reference for the PSNR calculations. Other work by the authors explored alternative ways to prioritize data in the presence of a cyclic intracoded line or examined the impact of a cyclic intracoded line. In [9], the line split the frame into three unequal regions and a scheme was presented that ensured the regions' areas were properly assigned to slices. Then in [10], regions were allowed to wrap around a frame's boundaries so that region sizes could be equalized. The latter scheme was found to be preferable to a simple geometrical division. Finally, in [11], it was shown that compared to employing periodic intrafresh with an intracoded I-frame, insertion of a cyclic intracoded line was especially favourable for less active video sequences. However, the work in [11] made no contribution to the issue of prioritization. In fact, both the other two schemes [9, 10] differed from the present proposal because prioritization of slices was determined by the position of the cyclic intracoded line within each video frame rather than through distortion analysis.

The remainder of this paper is organized as follows. Section 2 considers the context to the experiments in this paper. Section 3 details our prioritization scheme. The scheme is then evaluated in Section 4, which contains generic and network-specific results. Finally, Section 5 makes some concluding remarks.

## 2. Context

This Section explains the context to this work, in the sense that it explains what forms of intracoded intrarefresh are possible and why a popular feature or tool of H.264/AVC, Flexible Macroblock Ordering (FMO) [3] was not used in conjunction with prioritization. Furthermore, it reviews research on how best to prioritize video data, when mapping the priority classes to a wireless LAN QoS structure.

For mobile applications with limited processing power and constrained bandwidths, the omission of both bi-predictively coded B and periodic I-pictures is advantageous. Due to the risk of burst errors within wireless channels through entry of the mobile receiver into a deep fade, there is a risk of the loss of many of the I-picture packets. This can render useless the remainder of a GoP as, due to predictive coding, all subsequent pictures in the GoP employ the I-picture as a predictive coding reference anchor. As remarked in Section 1, it is still possible to provide random access to a video stream by what is known as gradual decoding (or decoder) refresh (GDR) [5], without the need for periodic I-pictures. Thus, prioritizing video packets according to their picture type (I, B, or P) is not convenient for mobile applications. Currently a prioritization scheme based on the three data partitions available under H.264/AVC [12] is also not convenient in practice. Data partitioning is only available in the H.264/AVC the Extended profile whereas mobile devices tend to rely on hardware implementations of the codec in the Baseline profile. In fact, data partitioning is not implemented in many software implementations of the codec such as QT, Nero, and LEAD, to name a few at random.

Though forced random insertion of intracoded MBs within a video stream is possible [4], this arrangement does not necessarily permit GDR, as it does not account for the direction of motion within a sequence. However, it should be noticed that in [13] the problem of duplication of MBs in random insertion was avoided and MBs to be intracoded were selected according to whether they could be error concealed or not. In GDR, in the presence of packet loss, the stream is reset gradually to a clean state, from which future predictions can be made. However, forced intrarefresh with an MB line can permit GDR. If there are $N$ lines per picture then the worst-case GDR should take place within $2N-1$ pictures [6]. Periodic intracoded pictures do permit more flexible random access, as might be used to support pseudo-VCR functionality. However, for wireless viewing of typically short clips VCR functionality is not uppermost in the mind of the viewer. Besides, the end-to-end packet delay is also reduced by the dispersed insertion of intrarefresh MBs, as periodic intracoded frames result in an influx of packets into transmission buffers, causing the waiting time to increase. All the same, one should note that I-pictures or GDR allow viewers to join a live stream at a point other than at the start of a broadcast, as might well occur during a video conference. Additional I-pictures might also be used (if scene cut detection is in place) to reset a stream after a change of scene.

We have utilized distortion analysis at the slice level. It is also possible [14] to undertake distortion analysis at the MB level. However, analysis at an individual MB level significantly increases the computational complexity arising from the required video content analysis. Moreover, methods exploiting "explicit" FMO also increase the bitrate and the degree of interpacket dependency due to the need to include additional packets with the updated MB maps for every picture. Other adaptive schemes such as in [15] have relied on feedback from the receiver. Once the decoder detects an error, it informs the encoder, which transmits intracoded MBs to halt any error propagation. However, this procedure is unsuitable for conversational video services such as videophone or mobile teleconferencing. In fact, though an interesting case for evolving isolated regions as a form of GDR is made in [5], the irregular nature of the regions formed in which all predictive reference is internal means that explicit FMO must be used.

Because the position of a cyclic intracoded line of MBs is easily predicted from one picture to the next, it does not require the overhead of an MB map. Consequently, the work in this paper does not use FMO explicit mode. In fact, as previously remarked, it does not use FMO at all and, hence, avoids the overhead associated with FMO [16]. This is also convenient, as many content creation tools such as QuickTime Pro do not allow the use of FMO and the H.264/AVC Constrained Baseline and Main profiles do not support FMO.

Previous experiments by the authors of [17] have involved prioritization through layered coding with the Scalable Video Coding (SVC) extension of H.264. Again in practice, this scheme currently runs into an implementation problem, as apparently hardware implementations of H.264/SVC do not exist, restricting the type of mobile device that can be used. However, cross-layer signalling is available in the H.264/SVC Network Abstraction Layer Unit (NALU) header as a 6-bit priority id field. Others have also experimented with mapping SVC layers to IEEE 802.11e priority classes. For example, the authors of [18] present a packet significance level algorithm for placing packets in an appropriate priority queue. The authors show that their algorithm is preferable to a static allocation of base layer and enhancement layers across the priority queues.

The possibility of mapping priority classes to the wireless QoS structure of IEEE 802.11e [7] has been explored by a good number of research papers over the years since IEEE 802.11e's development from late 2005. IEEE 802.11e itself is further considered in Section 3.2. In [19], prioritization was managed at a frame level, rather than the subframe scheme in this paper. Prioritization was dynamic in the sense that it depended both on the frame type (I-, B-, or P-frame) and the queue occupation of the normal video queue. A problem with this approach is that B-frames are not present in the Baseline profile of H.264/AVC, which is intended to limit energy consumption on mobile devices. In fact, the intracoded line technique also makes it possible to dispense

with all but the first I-frame. The cross-layer signalling between frame type and IEEE 802.11e priority queue is achieved through marking the Type of Service (TOS) field in the IP header (now replaced by the 6-bit Differentiated Services Code Point (DSCP) field). As the video queue fills up a Random Early Detection (RED) algorithm allocates packets to alternative priority queues according to their frame type priority. However, if header compression is employed then packets may not be queued with their IP headers intact, impeding cross-layer signalling in a wireless network. It must also be remarked that IP headers are not available at the application layer, whereas the codec generated headers described in Section 3.2 are accessible.

In [20], packet classification is performed at the subframe- or slice-level. However, the authors employ the same method of prioritization as in [12] that is through data-partitioned video encoding. A practical problem with that approach is that data-partitioning is only present in the Extended profile of H.264/AVC. The Gilbert-Elliott model for "bursty" channels is employed to govern dynamic allocation of packets to queues. However, it is unclear how a statistical channel model can predict actual channel conditions at any one point in time, though clearly a simulation will confirm the results. For cross-layer signalling the authors use a similar method to the one described in this paper, that is through the H.264/AVC generated header. In contrast, prioritization by packet deadline is an interesting idea of [21], which has apparently not been presented before in this context. A packet scheduler tries to ensure that each packet is transmitted before its display deadline expires. An extension would be to transmit before a packet's decode deadline expires, as this may be a longer deadline. How cross-layer signalling would be used to identify deadlines was not specified but presumably Real-time Transport Protocol (RTP) headers could be inspected.

## 3. Proposed Scheme

This Section outlines the prioritization scheme itself; a sample application to wireless QoS (as might be used at a hotspot or within a home network); some video configuration issues.

*3.1. Prioritization Scheme.* Using a horizontal (or vertical) sliding intrarefresh line, Figure 1, reduces spatiotemporal error propagation arising from packet loss. However, introducing an intracoded MB line within a temporally predicted picture represents a significant percentage of the bits devoted to compressing the whole picture. Nevertheless, a packet containing data from an intra-code MB line represents a small portion of the image area. Therefore, only a small potential quality penalty arises from the loss of a packet containing intracoded MBs due to the small image area affected. Therefore, those packets containing some or all data originating from the intracoded MB line are of lower priority than other packets, as far as the effect on the reconstruction video quality at the decoder is concerned.

In the prioritization assignment algorithm, the compressed data is broken up into fixed-size slices. A slice [18]

(a)                  (b)                  (c)

FIGURE 1: Cyclic intracoded MB line technique for the *Paris* test sequence, showing successive MB lines in lighter shading, with some slice boundaries also shown.

```
pktsBuffered ← 0
loop
    receive a packet
    if (new frame received = true) then
        decode the frame (to be used as a reference for PSNR calculations)
        n = 0
        while n < pktsBuffered do
            move packet n from buffer1 to buffer2
            calculate PSNR for the remaining packets in buffer1, put the n : PSNR result in list1
            move back packet n from buffer2 to buffer1
            n ← n + 1
        end while
        sort list1 in ascending order according to PSNR field
        remove ⌊pktsBuffered/3⌋ elements from list1 and assign Pri2 to corresponding packets in buffer1 (set NRI to "10")
        remove next ⌊pktsBuffered − ⌊pktsBuffered/3⌋/2⌋ elements from list1 and assign Pri2 to corresponding packets in buffer1
        (set NRI to "01")
        assign Pri0 to packets in buffer1 corresponding to the remaining elements in list1 (set NRI to "00")
        flush buffer1
        pktsBuffered ← 0
    else
        add packet to FIFO buffer1
        pktsBuffered ← pktsBuffered + 1
    end if
end loop
```

ALGORITHM 1: Algorithm to assign priorities to slices using slice distortion, ⌊..⌋ denotes the floor operation.

is a self-contained decoding unit with a header containing resynchronization information. In the test implementation, slices are formed by selecting MBs in raster-scan order, as shown in Figure 1. Algorithm 1 describes the algorithms employed. (In the Algorithm, annotation concerning NRI for cross-layer signalling is explained in Section 3.2.) In an implementation, a maximum slice size can be fixed, as occurs in our evaluation (refer to Section 3.3). All slices are at the maximum except possibly for the last one to be formed. However, treatment of MBs to slice assignment is implementation dependant. For each slice-bearing packet, the impact on the reconstruction PSNR is tested by removing that packet's data from that frame's compressed bitstream and then finding the PSNR relative to the decoded frame (refer back to Section 1). This process is repeated for each slice within the frame. The resulting PSNRs are then sorted into rank order so that priority classification classes can be formed. In the test implementation, there are just three priority classes to match suitable classes within IEEE 802.11e. Thus, once the slices are in rank order the top third of the slices are assigned to the highest priority, the middle third to the intermediate priority, and the lowest third to the lowest priority. If the number of slices was not an exact multiple of three then additional slices are assigned to the lower priorities in turn. For example, if there are two extra slices they can be individually assigned to the two lower priority classes. Other possibilities exist but these are not critical to evaluation of the scheme. The mapping to IEEE 802.11e priority classes is now described.

*3.2. IEEE 802.11e EDCA and Cross-Layer Signalling.* We have employed IEEE 802.11e [7] to exploit the proposed prioritization scheme. IEEE 802.11e Enhanced Distributed Channel Access (EDCA) adds QoS support to legacy IEEE 802.11 wireless networks by introducing four Access Categories

(ACs): AC0, AC1, AC2, and AC3 for Background (BK), Best-Effort (BE), Video (Vi), and Voice (Vo), respectively, in order of increasing priority. Each AC has its associated queue (set to 40 variable-sized packets in tests) with entry to the queue defined by a mapping function. Should several packets emerge simultaneously from the queues then contention is resolved by the virtual collision handler before a transmission attempt.

To better deliver priority-classified packets and exploit the unequal error sensitivity, this paper proposes mapping different priority packets across the IEEE 802.11e EDCA ACs as an effective alternative to assigning the complete stream to AC2. Priority 2 packets are mapped to AC2, the default access category for video. The least important priority 0 packets are mapped to AC0 while priority 1 packets are mapped to AC1. Each AC has different Distributed Coordination Function (DCF) parameters for the Carrier Sense Multiple Access/Collision Avoidance (CSMA/CA) back-off mechanism. In tests (Section 4), the default IEEE 802.11e Medium Access Control (MAC) parameter values for the IEEE 802.11b radio were employed but an extension is to tune these parameters to set a desired quality/delay tradeoff.

Figure 2 shows the cross-layer signalling architecture adopted in this article to signal the priorities to the MAC layer. Briefly, H.264/AVC Network Abstraction Layer (NAL) units (virtual packets output by an H.264/AVC encoder) contain the priority information by virtue of the two Nal_Ref_Idc (NRI) bits within a NAL unit header. At the application layer (specifically, the NAL sublayer), the NRI bits of NALUs are changed according to the importance of each NALU as determined by the distortion analysis. At the MAC layer, packets are classified and mapped to the IEEE 802.11e ACs based on the NRI bits in NALU headers.

### 3.3. Video Configuration.
The H.264/AVC Main profile encoded different Common Intermediate Format (CIF) frames ($352 \times 288$ pixels/frame) test sequences at 30 fps with $4:2:0$ chroma subsampling. Notice that the Main profile does not include FMO, which precludes the selection of individual MBs to form priority classes (refer back to Section 2). The same applies to the Constrained Baseline Profile, which is suitable for video conferencing applications. The Baseline Profile does include FMO and is suitable for mobile streaming applications, though no strong relationship exists between profiles and target applications [19]. However, that profile does not support more complex forms of coding such as data partitioning, which, as previously mentioned, otherwise might be employed for the purpose of packet prioritization.

The use of an IPPP... coding structure in this study reduces the decoding complexity on mobile devices that would occur were bipredictive B-frames to be included. Recall that the cyclic intra-code line of MBs was introduced to mitigate the risk of spatiotemporal error propagation across successive P-pictures. Context Adaptive Variable Length Coding (CAVLC) entropy coding (CAVLC is applied to the quantized transform coefficients, while Universal VLC

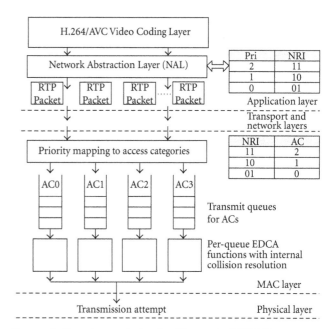

FIGURE 2: Cross-layer priority signalling to the IEEE 802.11e access categories.

(UVLC) is applied to other syntactic elements. The alternative, Context Adaptive Binary Adaptive Coding (CABAC) results in a 10–15% gain in coding efficiency, but cannot be implemented as CAVLC can be through switchable look-up-tables. Consequently, CABAC is omitted from the Baseline profile because of its complexity) [22] and single-frame reference was employed, with both settings selected to reduce computation on mobile devices. Motion-copy error concealment [23] was set at the decoder as an effective means of concealment except for sequences with very rapid motion. Streams were coded with a CBR target of 1 Mbps. Packet size payloads and, hence, slice sizes were limited to a maximum of 500 B to reduce the risk of error from long packets and network fragmentation.

The motion estimation search range was also set to eight to reduce computation. This setting has an effect on potential contamination from an unclean area to an already cleansed area of a picture sequence. Notice that the H.264/AVC Constrained Intraprediction (CIP) flag was also set, as otherwise reference to intercoded MBs is possible, which negates the ability of the insertion of a cyclic MB line to arrest the propagation of spatiotemporal errors. Some loss of coding efficiency arises from setting CIP but this is inevitable, as some form of intrarefresh cannot be avoided. However, if random placement of forced intracoded MBs took place then the need for CIP would result in a greater deterioration in video quality. This is because the MBs of an intracoded MB line are adjacent and consequently well correlated with each other. However, randomly placed MBs may be far apart and, hence, not well correlated. The result is that spatial reference will not be an effective form of prediction, even if the search range could extend far enough.

TABLE 1: Mean Y-PSNR gain (loss) when dropping different priority packets, as compared to dropping randomly over a range of test sequences.

|  |  | ΔPSNR (dB) | | | | |
|---|---|---|---|---|---|---|
| Loss rate (%): | | 2 | 4 | 6 | 8 | 10 |
| Akiyo | Drop Pri 0 | 1.73 | 2.62 | 3.3 | 3.94 | 4.21 |
| | Drop Pri 1 | 0.61 | 0.69 | 0.9 | 1.15 | 1.27 |
| | Drop Pri 2 | −1.52 | −2.33 | −2.52 | −2.37 | −2.41 |
| Mobile | Drop Pri 0 | 1.85 | 2.76 | 3.12 | 3.31 | 3.57 |
| | Drop Pri 1 | 0.53 | 0.94 | 1.16 | 1.42 | 1.43 |
| | Drop Pri 2 | −2.1 | −2.34 | −2.22 | −2.12 | −2 |
| Soccer | Drop Pri 0 | 1.77 | 2.63 | 3.03 | 3.25 | 3.38 |
| | Drop Pri 1 | 0.26 | 0.61 | 0.72 | 0.85 | 0.91 |
| | Drop Pri 2 | −1.69 | −2.17 | −2.24 | −2.17 | −2.19 |
| Foreman | Drop Pri 0 | 1.99 | 3.03 | 3.31 | 3.45 | 3.67 |
| | Drop Pri 1 | 0.61 | 0.88 | 0.93 | 0.87 | 1.09 |
| | Drop Pri 2 | −1.68 | −2.09 | −2.19 | −2.18 | −2.02 |
| Football | Drop Pri 0 | 0.69 | 1.13 | 1.47 | 1.42 | 1.42 |
| | Drop Pri 1 | 0.26 | 0.63 | 0.82 | 0.88 | 0.82 |
| | Drop Pri 2 | −1.07 | −1.43 | −1.27 | −1.27 | −1.38 |
| Highway | Drop Pri 0 | 2.01 | 3.18 | 3.88 | 4.5 | 4.54 |
| | Drop Pri 1 | 0.72 | 1.18 | 1.37 | 1.49 | 1.37 |
| | Drop Pri 2 | −1.95 | −2.44 | −2.71 | −2.67 | −2.78 |

## 4. Evaluation

In this Section, we test the generic behavior of the scheme before considering an example IEEE 802.11e WLAN simulation.

*4.1. Uniform Drop Tests.* The test sequences of *Paris* and *Stefan* were employed. The former is typical of TV studio clips that can be appreciated on a mobile device [24] for the audio as well as the video and the latter has high temporal coding complexity. In Figures 3 and 4, the impact of dropping prioritized packets is compared to random drops. (Error bars represent one standard deviation in the plots herein.)

As is evident, there is a considerable gain from only dropping those packets classified into the low priority (Drop-pri-0) up to the given percentage on the horizontal axis. Dropping packets solely from priority one class (Drop-pri-1) is somewhat better than random drops but if only high-priority packets are dropped (Drop-pri-2) there is a serious deterioration in video quality. The effect of increased coding complexity on *Stefan*, Figure 4, is to decrease the mean video quality level for the given bit-budget without affecting the overall pattern. Table 1 confirms this behavior for a variety of video content type. The gain seems greatest at higher packet loss rates for relatively static sequences.

*4.2. Network Simulations.* To show the advantage of the proposed scheme, the application scenario in Figure 5 was simulated with the well-known ns-2 network simulator. Each plot in the following graphs is the result of around 1000

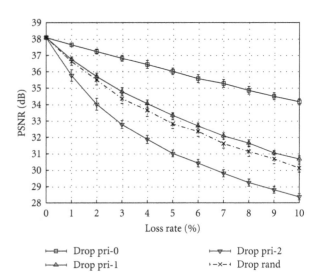

FIGURE 3: Mean Y-PSNR for the *Paris* video sequence when dropping packets from different priorities.

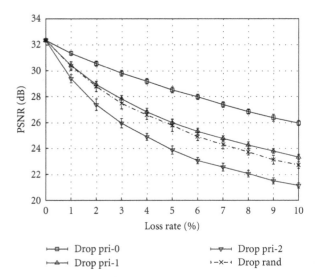

FIGURE 4: Mean Y-PSNR for the *Stefan* video sequence when dropping packets with different priorities.

runs after performing statistical analysis to find the mean and standard deviation at the given loss rate percentages. The scenario consists of a tablet computer receiving video streamed from a streaming server plugged-in at the wireless home router. There is also a smartphone sending Voice-over-IP (VOIP) traffic to the Internet and a laptop computer competing for bandwidth, while performing web browsing. In situations as in Figure 5, IEEE 802.11e was developed to offer prioritized access to delay-sensitive applications by prioritizing traffic over higher priority queues in order to reduce packet drops through buffer overflow. Table 2 details the traffic sources feeding into the home router's output buffer.

In Figures 6 and 7, the impact of the congesting traffic (along with self-congestion from the streaming video) is

TABLE 2: Traffic in the scenario of Figure 6.

| Traffic type | Source | Destination | IEEE 802.11e AC | Protocol | Data rate (kbps) |
|---|---|---|---|---|---|
| Video | Streaming server | TV | 2 (2, 0, 1 when mapping) | UDP | 1000 |
| CBR | Phone | Internet | 3 | UDP | 16–160 |
| CBR | Laptop | Internet | 1 | UDP | 200 |
| CBR | Laptop | Internet | 0 | TCP | 200 |

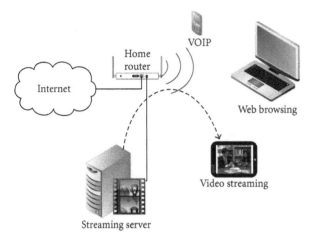

FIGURE 5: Simulated IEEE 802.11b test scenario.

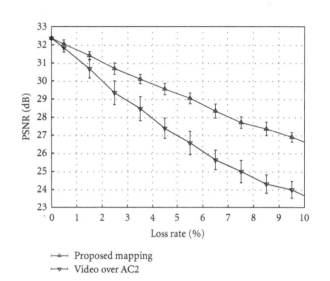

FIGURE 7: Mean Y-PSNR for the *Stefan* video sequence for the simulated network scenario.

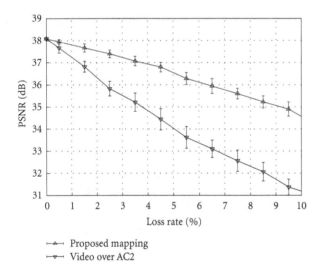

FIGURE 6: Mean Y-PSNR for the *Paris* video sequence for the simulated network scenario.

compared with the effect of mapping the entire video stream to the IEEE 802.11e designated AC2 class. At its worst, for a packet loss rate of 10%, there is over 3 dB gain from the proposed mapping for streaming the *Paris* studio scene. Again, the impact is a little reduced for the more active *Stefan* sequence but still well-worth applying. Table 3 presents the PSNR gain when using the proposed mapping scheme over assigning the video stream's packets to AC2 for a range of test sequences.

*4.3. Discussion.* Others have also presented performance evaluations that have highlighted the advantages of employing prioritization mappings. The work in [25] is a comparison of mapping schemes for IEEE 802.11e. The study [25] employed Standard Definition television frames, rather than the CIF frames employed by other studies more concerned with common mobile device screen resolutions. The standard mapping to AC2 was compared to one that distinguished between I-, P-, and B-frames and another that grouped I- and P-frames into the same priority category. As has already been remarked in Section 2, this type of frame-level slice classification lacks the flexibility of subframe or slice classifications. However, if mobile devices are not used then retaining a traditional slicing structure for broadcast video may be required for compatibility reasons. In fact, if B-frames are available to be dropped then the authors found that a sudden drop in quality after packet losses could be avoided. This was not the case under the default video mapping. The authors also observed that less active sequences suffered less from impairments after packet drops. A related observation was made by the authors of this paper in [11], which, as previously remarked, indicated that a measure of temporal activity such as the number of nonzero motion vectors, could guide whether periodic I-frames were employed or not.

The work in [26] simulated the performance of a priority classification based on H.264 data partitioning in a scenario in which voice-over-IP and data traffic were also present. Up

TABLE 3: Mean Y-PSNR gain when applying the proposed mapping scheme, as compared to assigning the video stream to AC2 for a range of test sequences.

| | PSNR gain (dB) | | | | | | | | | |
|---|---|---|---|---|---|---|---|---|---|---|
| Loss rate | 0.5 | 1.5 | 2.5 | 3.5 | 4.5 | 5.5 | 6.5 | 7.5 | 8.5 | 9.5 |
| Soccer | 0.29 | 0.85 | 1.20 | 1.96 | 1.59 | 2.21 | 2.68 | 2.83 | 3.13 | 3.25 |
| Foreman | 0.38 | 1.02 | 1.58 | 1.99 | 2.24 | 2.39 | 2.54 | 2.89 | 3.01 | 3.11 |
| Highway | 0.21 | 0.73 | 1.04 | 1.38 | 1.84 | 2.02 | 2.46 | 2.67 | 2.71 | 2.86 |
| Football | 0.00 | 0.10 | 0.08 | 0.09 | 0.31 | 0.29 | 0.44 | 0.50 | 0.69 | 0.45 |

to 20 nodes generated traffic within the IEEE 802.11 network. This work, which is contemporary with that reported in [12], confirms the advantage of this type of mapping. The authors of [27] also employed priority classification based on data partitioning but tested the results in an indoor wireless testbed with three laptops as receivers. Best-effort TCP traffic was also present. Again, the study confirmed the advantages of mapping across some of the access categories but this time in a situation with real-world access contention.

## 5. Conclusion

The main intent of this paper is to demonstrate a simple procedure for prioritization of video packets that can be implemented across H.264 profiles without the need for flexible macroblock ordering. Slice-based distortion analysis reduces the implementation overhead compared to individual MB-based optimizations. The paper has demonstrated considerable gain in video quality from the resulting prioritization classification when modelled in a home network. Because delay sensitive applications were targeted, the scheme tolerates a single video frame delay, during which slice-level distortion analysis is performed. It is also possible to extend the scheme to slice distortion analysis across multiple frames but this clearly will incur more delay implications. The emerging High Efficiency Video Coding (HEVC) standard considers ways to improve implementation efficiency, particularly for high-definition (HD) video. Though for testing efficiency our results are presented for CIF video, the findings can be applied to HD video over other high data rate members of the IEEE 802.11 family, such as IEEE 802.11ac. However, in that case larger slice sizes should be selected.

## References

[1] O. Oyman and S. Singh, "Quality of experience for HTTP adaptive streaming services," *IEEE Communications Magazine*, vol. 50, no. 4, pp. 20–27, 2012.

[2] B. Bing, *3D and HD Broadband Video Networking*, Artech-House, Boston, Mass, USA, 2010.

[3] I. E. G. Richardson, *H.264 and MPEG-4 Video Compression*, John Wiley & Sons, Chichester, UK, 2004.

[4] P. Haskell and D. Messerschmitt, "Resynchronization of motion compensated video affected by ATM cell loss," in *Proceedings of the IEEE International Conference on Acoustics, Speech, and Signal Processing (ICASSP '92)*, pp. 545–548, March 1992.

[5] M. M. Hannuksela, Y. K. Wang, and M. Gabbouj, "Isolated regions in video coding," *IEEE Transactions on Multimedia*, vol. 6, no. 2, pp. 259–267, 2004.

[6] R. M. Schreier and A. Rothermel, "Motion adaptive intra refresh for low-delay video coding," in *Proceedings of the International Conference on Consumer Electronics (ICCE '06)*, pp. 453–454, Las Vegas, Nev, USA, January 2006.

[7] "Wireless LAN Medium Access Control (MAC) and Physical Layer (PHY) Specifications Amendment 8: Medium Access Control (MAC) Quality of Service Enhancements," IEEE Std 802. 11e-2005 (Amendment to IEEE Std 802. 11, 1999 Edition (Reaff 2003), 2005.

[8] I. Ali, S. Moiron, M. Fleury, and M. Ghanbari, "Prioritized packetization for video with intra-refresh macroblock line," in *Proceedings of the IEEE International Conference on Multimedia and Expo (ICME '11)*, pp. 1–6, July 2011.

[9] I. Ali, S. Moiron, M. Fleury, and M. Ghanbari, "Enhanced prioritization for video streaming over QoS-enabled wireless networks," in *Proceedings of the IEEE Wireless Advanced (WiAd '11)*, pp. 268–272, June 2011.

[10] I. Ali, S. Moiron, M. Fleury, and M. Ghanbari, "Enhanced prioritization for video streaming over wireless home networks with IEEE 802. 11e," in *Proceedings of the IEEE International Symposium on Broadband Multimedia Systems and Broadcasting (BMSB '11)*, pp. 1–6, June 2011.

[11] I. Ali, M. Fleury, and M. Ghanbari, "Content-aware intra-refresh for video streaming over lossy links," in *Proceedings of the IEEE International Conference on Consumer Electronics (ICCE '12)*, pp. 118–119, January 2012.

[12] A. Ksentini, M. Naimi, and A. Guéroui, "Toward an improvement of H.264 video transmission over IEEE 802.11e through a cross-layer architecture," *IEEE Communications Magazine*, vol. 44, no. 1, pp. 107–114, 2006.

[13] G. Côté and F. Kossentini, "Optimal intra coding of blocks for robust video communication over the Internet," *Signal Processing*, vol. 15, no. 1, pp. 25–34, 1999.

[14] X. Wang, C. Kodikara, A. H. Sadka, and A. M. Kondoz, "Robust GOB intra refresh scheme for H.264/AVC video over UMTS," in *Proceedings of the 6th IEE International Conference on 3G and Beyond*, pp. 1–4, November 2005.

[15] J. T. Wang and P. C. Chang, "Error-propagation prevention technique for real-time video transmission over ATM networks," *IEEE Transactions on Circuits and Systems for Video Technology*, vol. 9, no. 3, pp. 513–523, 1999.

[16] W. T. Tan, E. Setton, and J. Apostolopoulos, "Lossless FMO and slice structure modification for compressed H.264 video," in *Proceedings of the 14th IEEE International Conference on Image Processing (ICIP '07)*, vol. 4, pp. IV285–IV288, September 2007.

[17] I. A. Ali, M. Fleury, and M. Ghanbari, "Congestion-resistant scalable media stream mapping for an IEEE 802.11E sensor

network," in *Proceedings of the 17th IEEE International Conference on Image Processing (ICIP '10)*, pp. 2901–2904, September 2010.

[18] X. Li, T. Ren, and J. Xu, "A cross-layer design for transmission of scalable H.264 video over IEEE 802.11e networks," in *Proceedings of the 1st International Conference on Computational Problem-Solving (ICCP '10)*, pp. 306–309, December 2010.

[19] R. Soni, N. Chilamkurti, G. Giambene, and S. Zeadally, "A cross-layer design for H.264 video stream over wireless local area networks," in *Proceedings of the International Symposium on Computer Science and its Applications (CSA '08)*, pp. 387–392, October 2008.

[20] W. T. Chen, T. C. Lin, Y. C. Chang, and J. C. Chen, "Dynamic packet selection for H.264 video streaming over IEEE 802.11e WLANs," in *Proceedings of the IEEE Wireless Communications and Networking Conference (WCNC '08)*, pp. 3133–3138, March 2008.

[21] Q. Liu, Z. Zou, and C. W. Chen, "A deadline-aware virtual contention free EDCA scheme for H.264 video over IEEE 802.11e wireless networks," in *Proceedings of the IEEE International Symposium of Circuits and Systems (ISCAS '11)*, pp. 625–628, May 2011.

[22] T. Wiegand, G. J. Sullivan, G. Bjøntegaard, and A. Luthra, "Overview of the H.264/AVC video coding standard," *IEEE Transactions on Circuits and Systems for Video Technology*, vol. 13, no. 7, pp. 560–576, 2003.

[23] Y. K. Wang, M. M. Hannuksela, V. Varsa, A. Hourunranta, and M. Gabbouj, "The error concealment feature in the H.26L test model," in *Proceedings of the International Conference on Image Processing (ICIP '02)*, vol. 2, pp. 729–732, September 2002.

[24] F. Agboma and A. Liotta, "Addressing user expectations in mobile content delivery," *Mobile Information Systems.*, vol. 3, no. 3-4, pp. 153–164, 2007.

[25] R. MacKenzie, D. Hands, and T. O'Farrell, "QoS of video delivered over 802.11e WLANs," in *Proceedings of the IEEE International Conference on Communications (ICC '09)*, pp. 1246–1250, June 2009.

[26] C. Casetti, C. F. Chiasserini, L. Merello, and G. Olmo, "Supporting multimedia traffic in 802.11e WLANs," in *Proceedings of the IEEE Vehicular Technology Conference (VTC '05)*, pp. 2340–2344, May 2005.

[27] R. Haywood, S. Mukherjee, and X. H. Peng, "Investigation of H.264 video streaming over an IEEE 802.11e EDCA wireless testbed," in *Proceedings of the IEEE International Conference on Communications (ICC '09)*, pp. 1516–1520, June 2009.

# 11

# Division-Free Multiquantization Scheme for Modern Video Codecs

**Mousumi Das, Atahar Mostafa, and Khan Wahid**

*Department of Electrical and Computer Engineering, University of Saskatchewan Saskatoon, SK, Canada S7N5A9*

Correspondence should be addressed to Khan Wahid, khan.wahid@usask.ca

Academic Editor: Dimitrios Tzovaras

The current trend of digital convergence leads to the need of the video encoder/decoder (codec) that should support multiple video standards on a single platform as it is expensive to use dedicated video codec chip for each standard. The paper presents a high performance circuit shared architecture that can perform the quantization of five popular video codecs such as H.264/AVC, AVS, VC-1, MPEG-2/4, and JPEG. The proposed quantizer architecture is completely division-free as the division operation is replaced by shift and addition operations for all the standards. The design is implemented on FPGA and later synthesized in CMOS $0.18\,\mu$m technology. The results show that the proposed design satisfies the requirement of all five codecs with a maximum decoding capability of 60 fps at 187 MHz on Xilinx FPGA platform for 1080 p HD video.

## 1. Introduction

An evident trend in modern world is the digital convergence in the current electronic consumer products. People want the portable devices to have various functions like Video on Demand (VOD), Digital Multimedia Broadcasting (DMB), Global Positioning System (GPS) or the navigation system, Portable Multimedia Player (PMP), and so on. Due to such demand, it is necessary to support the widely used video compression standards in a single system-on-chip (SoC) platform. So the goal is to find a way so that the multicodec system achieves high performance, as well as low cost.

Most modern multimedia codecs (both encoder and decoder) employ transform-quantization pair as shown in Figure 1. A significant research has been conducted to combine and efficiently implement the transform units for multiple codecs, but little research is focused on the implementation of multiquantizer unit. A unified Inverse Discrete Cosine Transform (IDCT) architecture to support five standards (such as, AVS, H.264, VC-1, MPEG-2/4, and JPEG) is presented in [1]. A design to support the $4 \times 4$ transform and quantization of H.264 has been presented in [2]. The $8 \times 8$ transform and quantization for H.264 is presented in [3] and [4]. Several other designs based on H.264 codec have been reported in [5–10]. The authors

in [11] present a design for the quantization for AVS. The design in [12] describes an MPEG-2 encoder. In [13], another JPEG encoder is implemented for images where the quantization block is designed using multiplication and shift operation instead of division. The design in [14] describes a multistandard video decoder to support four codecs—AVS, H.264, VC-1, and MPEG-2. Silicon Image Inc. currently supplies a Multi-standard High-Definition Video Decoder (MSVD-HD) core that supports H.264, VC-1, and MPEG-1/2 codecs [15]. Their multiplexed decoder chip costs 970 K gates using TSMC 90 nm technology (including complete memory interfacing, stream reader functionality, and extra logic for context switch support).

However, none of the existing designs can compute the quantization of any video codecs. In this paper, we present a new division-free quantization algorithm (DFQA) and its efficient implementation to compute the quantization units for five multimedia codecs: JPEG [16], MPEG-2/4 [17], VC-1 [18], H.264/AVC [19], and AVS [20].

While developing the architecture, we have carefully considered all the quantization ($Q$) coefficients of the $Q$-tables of different standards and established a relationship between them. The quantization in MPEG-2/4 and JPEG is defined as the division of the DCT coefficient by the corresponding $Q$-values specified by the $Q$-matrices. On the other

TABLE 1: Description of different parameters of the proposed DFQA.

| Parameters | AVS | H.264 | VC-1 | MPEG-2/4 | JPEG |
|---|---|---|---|---|---|
| $r$ | 0 | 0 | 4 | 4 | 0 |
| offset | 1 | 0–0.5 | 0 | 0 | 0 |
| qbits | 14 | 16 + (QP mod 6) | 0 | 0 | 0 |
| $n$ | 15 | 16 + (QP mod 6) | 8 | 8 | 8 |
| qs_bit | 0 | 0 | 5 | 5 | 0 |

hand, the two most popular video standards, H.264/AVC and AVS exploit multiplication and shift operation for the purpose of quantization to avoid the division operation for reduced computational complexity. The quantization in VC-1 is user-defined and similar to the process in MPEG-2 [21]. Based on the observation, we propose a new multiquantizer architecture to support these five codecs. The architecture is later synthesized into both FPGA and ASIC level and the cost is compared with existing designs. The design serves as a key unit in a multicodec system in transcoding applications [22] and [23].

## 2. Proposed Division-Free Quantization Algorithm (DFQA)

Quantization ($Q$) is defined as the division of the DCT coefficient by the corresponding $Q$-value. But in H.264 and AVS, it is done by multiplication and right shift operation. Hence these standards define their own Multiplication Factors (MF). These MFs are multiplied with the transform coefficients and finally right shifted. However, the quantization in VC-1, MPEG-2/4, and JPEG is defined as division operation only (using $8 \times 8$ matrices). As a result, it is challenge to establish a relationship that is general enough to merge all these schemes. After careful observation, a novel generalized algorithm is developed that is divided into three steps given as follows.

*Step 1.*

$$p = (w[i, j] \ll r) \cdot \text{MF}[i, j], \quad \text{for } i, j = 0, \dots, 7, \tag{1}$$
where $\ll r = $ left shift by $r$ bits.

*Step 2.*

$$q = p + (offset \ll qbits). \tag{2}$$

*Step 3.*

$$y = q \gg (n + qs_{bit}),$$
where $\gg (n + qs\_bit) = $ right shift by $(n + qs\_bit)$ bits, $(3)$

where $w$ denotes the transform coefficient, MF is the Multiplying factor, and $y$ denotes the corresponding quantized value (level). The description of the rest of the parameters is listed in Table 1.

Moreover, QP is the quantization parameter which specifies MFs. In the next sections, we apply the general DFQA to individual codecs.

*2.1. DFQA Applied to H.264.* In this section, we apply the generalized DFQA to perform the quantization operation in H.264. Firstly, the transform coefficients coming from the transform unit is directly multiplied by MF as the value of $r$ is equal to 0 for this standard and hence no left shift operation is applied to the transform coefficients. In the second stage offset is left shifted by $qbits$ and then added to the result coming from the first stage. This value is finally right shifted by $n = (16 + \text{QP mod } 6)$ bits in the third stage, which is the final stage of the proposed DFQA. In case of H.264 as specified in [19], Multiplication Factor MF depends on $m$ (= QPmod 6) and the position $(i, j)$ of the element as follows:

$$\text{MF}[m; i, j] = \begin{cases} M_{m0} \text{ for } (i, j) \text{ with } & i = [0, 4], \ j = [0, 4], \\ M_{m1} \text{ for } (i, j) \text{ with } & i = [1, 3, 5, 7], \ j = [1, 3, 5, 7], \\ M_{m2} \text{ for } (i, j) \text{ with } & i = [2, 6], \ j = [2, 6], \\ M_{m3} \text{ for } (i, j) \text{ with } & (i = [0, 4], \ j = [1, 3, 5, 7]) \cap (i = [1, 3, 5, 7], \ j = [0, 4]), \\ M_{m4} \text{ for } (i, j) \text{ with } & (i = [0, 4], \ j = [2, 6]) \cap (i = [2, 6], \ j = [0, 4]), \\ M_{m5} \text{ for } (i, j) \text{ with } & (i = [2, 6], \ j = [1, 3, 5, 7]) \cap (i = [1, 3, 5, 7], j = [2, 6]). \end{cases} \tag{4}$$

The matrix MF for H.264 is specified as

$$\text{MF} = \begin{bmatrix} 13107 & 11428 & 20972 & 12222 & 16777 & 15481 \\ 11916 & 10826 & 19174 & 11058 & 14980 & 14290 \\ 10082 & 8943 & 15978 & 9675 & 12710 & 11985 \\ 9362 & 8228 & 14913 & 8931 & 11984 & 11259 \\ 8192 & 7346 & 13159 & 7740 & 10486 & 9777 \\ 7282 & 6428 & 11570 & 6830 & 9118 & 8640 \end{bmatrix} . \tag{5}$$

*2.2. DFQA Applied to AVS.* Next, we apply the DFQA to perform the quantization operation of AVS. In this case only the DFQA parameters are changed according to Table 1. For AVS, based on [25], MF depends on QP. Each QP specifies one particular MF. The value of MF for the particular QP is given by Table 2. Once QP is specified the corresponding MF is multiplied with the transform coefficient in the first step of the DFQA. Again in case of AVS, the transform coefficient is

TABLE 2: Quantization table for AVS encoder.

| QP | 0 | 1 | 2 | 3 | 4 | 5 | 6 | 7 |
|----|---|---|---|---|---|---|---|---|
| MF | 32768 | 29775 | 27554 | 25268 | 23170 | 21247 | 19369 | 17770 |
| QP | 8 | 9 | 10 | 11 | 12 | 13 | 14 | 15 |
| MF | 16302 | 15024 | 13777 | 12634 | 11626 | 10624 | 9742 | 8958 |
| QP | 16 | 17 | 18 | 19 | 20 | 21 | 22 | 23 |
| MF | 8192 | 7512 | 6889 | 6305 | 5793 | 5303 | 4878 | 4467 |
| QP | 24 | 25 | 26 | 27 | 28 | 29 | 30 | 31 |
| MF | 4091 | 3756 | 3444 | 3161 | 2894 | 2654 | 2435 | 2235 |
| QP | 32 | 33 | 34 | 35 | 36 | 37 | 38 | 39 |
| MF | 2048 | 1878 | 1722 | 1579 | 1449 | 1329 | 1218 | 1117 |
| QP | 40 | 41 | 42 | 43 | 44 | 45 | 46 | 47 |
| MF | 1024 | 939 | 861 | 790 | 724 | 664 | 609 | 558 |
| QP | 48 | 49 | 50 | 51 | 52 | 53 | 54 | 55 |
| MF | 512 | 470 | 430 | 395 | 362 | 332 | 304 | 279 |
| QP | 56 | 57 | 58 | 59 | 60 | 61 | 62 | 63 |
| MF | 256 | 235 | 215 | 197 | 181 | 166 | 152 | 140 |

TABLE 3: Comparison with the existing designs (quantization only).

| Arch. | Size | Tech. | No. of LUT | No. of slice | Freq. (MHz) | Supporting standards | | | | |
|-------|------|-------|-----------|--------------|-------------|-------|---------|------|------|-----|
| | | | | | | H.264 | MPEG-2/4 | JPEG | VC-1 | AVS |
| [2] | 4 × 4 | Virtex2(xc2vp7) | 286 | 143 | 135 | Y | o | o | o | o |
| [7] | 4 × 4 | XilinxV2P30FF896 | 956 | — | 108 | Y | o | o | o | o |
| [8] | 4 × 4 | Virtex2(xc2vp7) | 1954 | 977 | 94 | Y | o | o | o | o |
| Proposed | 8 × 8 | Virtex4(LX60) | 553 | 298 | 187 | Y | Y | Y | Y | Y |

Y: Yes; o: No; —: No information.

not left shifted by $r$ bits as the value of $r$ is 0 which is similar to the case of H.264. After that in second step this result is added to the 14 bits left shifted *offset* value, which is eventually right shifted by 15 bits in the final step.

*2.3. DFQA Applied to VC-1 and MPEG-2/4.* VC-1 uses multiple transform sizes but the same quantization rule is applied to all the coefficients. This standard allows both dead-zone and regular uniform quantization. In uniform quantization, the quantization intervals are identical. A dead-zone is an interval on the number line around zero, such that unquantized coefficients lying in the interval are quantized to zero. All the quantization intervals except the dead-zone are of same size—the dead-zone being typically larger. The use of dead-zone leads to substantially bit savings at low bitrates. However, at a high level the quantization process (scalar quantization where each transform coefficient is independently quantized and coded) in VC-1 is similar to the corresponding process in MPEG-2 standard. As the quantization in VC-1 is user defined and according to [21] this process is similar to the corresponding process in MPEG-2 standard in this proposed architecture, the quantization parameters for VC-1 and MPEG-2/4 standards are the same. As specified by [26], the MPEG-2/4 standard uses two quantization matrices, Intra matrix and non-intra-matrix. Here we focus only on the Intramatrix. The intraquantization matrix is shown in Figure 2:

However, we generate MF for each of the coefficient of the quantization matrix specified in Figure 2. This MF is then right shifted by 8 bits. For example, dividing a DCT coefficient coming from transform unit by a quantization value 19 can be expressed as

$$\frac{DCT}{19} = \frac{DCT}{19} * \frac{14}{14} \approx \frac{DCT * 14}{2^8}. \tag{6}$$

Hence for 19, the corresponding MF is 14. Moreover, the quantization in VC-1 and MPEG/2-4 needs the denominator of (6) to be multiplied by quantization step (QS), and in this proposed architecture for simplicity we choose QS $= 32 = 2^5$, where 5 is denoted as $qs\_bit$ in Table 1. So the right-hand side of (6) can be characterized as

$$\frac{DCT * 14}{2^8 * 32} = \frac{DCT * 14}{2^8 * 2^5} = \frac{DCT * 14}{2^{13}}. \tag{7}$$

The following matrix shows the MFs for the corresponding quantization matrix in Figure 2:

$$MF = \begin{bmatrix} 31 & 16 & 14 & 12 & 10 & 9 & 9 & 8 \\ 16 & 16 & 12 & 10 & 9 & 9 & 8 & 7 \\ 14 & 12 & 10 & 9 & 9 & 8 & 8 & 7 \\ 12 & 12 & 10 & 9 & 9 & 8 & 7 & 7 \\ 12 & 10 & 9 & 9 & 8 & 7 & 6 & 5 \\ 10 & 9 & 9 & 8 & 7 & 6 & 5 & 4 \\ 10 & 9 & 9 & 8 & 7 & 5 & 4 & 4 \\ 9 & 9 & 7 & 7 & 5 & 4 & 4 & 3 \end{bmatrix}. \tag{8}$$

TABLE 4: Comparison with existing designs (transform and quantization).

| Arch. | Matrix size | Tech. | No. of LUT | No. of slice | Freq. (MHz) | Supporting standards | | | | |
|---|---|---|---|---|---|---|---|---|---|---|
| | | | | | | H.264 | MPEG-2/4 | JPEG | VC-1 | AVS |
| [3] | $8 \times 8$ | Virtex2(XC2VP30) | 2887 | 1624 | 112 | Y | o | o | o | o |
| [4] | $8 \times 8$ | Virtex2(XC2V4000) | 29018 | 14509 | 69 | Y | o | o | o | o |
| [5] | $8 \times 8$ | Startix II | 7323 | — | 100 | Y | o | o | o | o |
| [6] | $4 \times 4$ | Virtex2(XC2V1500) | 246 | 123 | 115 | Y | o | o | o | o |
| [9] | $4 \times 4$ | Virtex2(2V8000FF1157) | 2498 | 1249 | 81 | Y | o | o | o | o |
| [10] | $4 \times 4$ | Virtex2(XC2V1500) | 1386 | 693 | 99 | Y | o | o | o | o |
| Proposed | $8 \times 8$ | Virtex4(LX60) | 1722 | 972 | 187 | Y | Y | Y | Y | Y |

Y: Yes; o: No; —: No information.

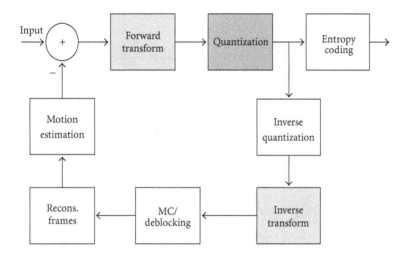

FIGURE 1: Functional block diagram of a modern video encoder.

$$\begin{bmatrix}
8 & 16 & 19 & 22 & 26 & 27 & 29 & 34 \\
16 & 16 & 22 & 24 & 27 & 29 & 34 & 37 \\
19 & 22 & 26 & 27 & 29 & 34 & 34 & 38 \\
22 & 22 & 26 & 27 & 29 & 34 & 37 & 40 \\
22 & 26 & 27 & 29 & 32 & 35 & 40 & 48 \\
26 & 27 & 29 & 32 & 35 & 40 & 48 & 58 \\
26 & 27 & 29 & 34 & 38 & 46 & 56 & 69 \\
27 & 29 & 35 & 38 & 46 & 56 & 69 & 83
\end{bmatrix}$$

FIGURE 2: Intra quantization matrix for VC-1 and MPEG-2/4.

$$\begin{bmatrix}
16 & 11 & 10 & 16 & 24 & 40 & 51 & 61 \\
12 & 12 & 14 & 19 & 26 & 58 & 60 & 55 \\
14 & 13 & 16 & 24 & 40 & 57 & 69 & 56 \\
14 & 17 & 22 & 29 & 51 & 87 & 80 & 62 \\
18 & 22 & 37 & 56 & 68 & 109 & 103 & 77 \\
24 & 35 & 55 & 64 & 81 & 104 & 113 & 92 \\
49 & 64 & 78 & 87 & 103 & 121 & 120 & 101 \\
72 & 92 & 95 & 98 & 112 & 100 & 103 & 99
\end{bmatrix}$$

FIGURE 3: Luminance quantization matrix for JPEG.

TABLE 5: Comparison of multiquantization schemes (VLSI implementation).

| Codecs | No. of gates |
|---|---|
| H.264 [2] | 1.75 K |
| AVS [11] | 7.2 K |
| MPEG-2/4 [12] | 9 K |
| JPEG [24] | 4.1 K |
| VC-1 [21] | 9 K |
| Estimated total cost (5 codecs—standalone) | 31.1 K |
| Proposed (all 5 codecs—shared) | 19.6 K |

As compared to the elements in the original intramatrix in Figure 2, the elements in (8) are smaller which helps to decrease the size of the RAM. Once MF is obtained, in the first step this MF is multiplied with the 4 bits left shifted transform coefficient as the value of $r$ is 4 in this case. However, second step is not applicable to this standard and as a result the output of the first step is directly right shifted by $(n + qs\_bit) = (8 + 5) = 13$ bits in the third step.

TABLE 6: Comparison of decoding capability of the multiquantizer schemes.

| Arch. | 1920 × 1080 | | 1280 × 720 | | Comments |
|---|---|---|---|---|---|
| | Time to transmit 1 frame (msec) | Frame per second (fps) | Time to transmit 1 frame (msec) | Frame per second (fps) | |
| [2] | 23.3 | 43 | 10.2 | 97 | Supports only H.264 |
| [7] | 28.8 | 34 | 12.8 | 78 | Supports only H.264 |
| [8] | 33.1 | 30 | 14.7 | 67 | Supports only H.264 |
| Proposed | 16.6 | 60 | 7.4 | 135 | Supports five codecs |

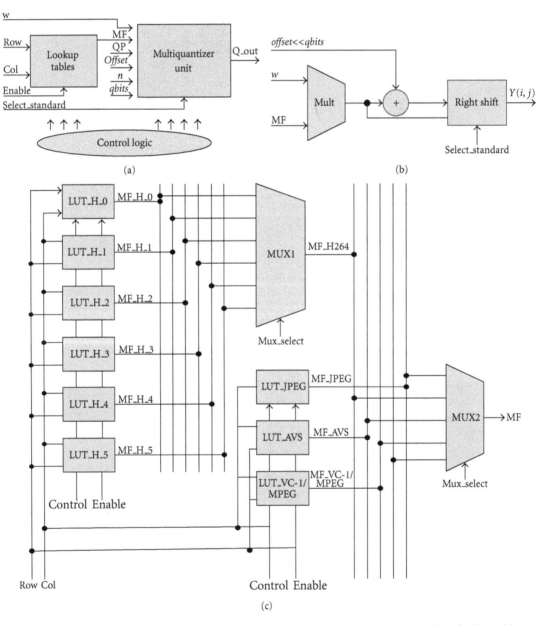

FIGURE 4: (a) Overall block diagram of the proposed architecture, (b) core unit with a multiplier, and (c) lookup tables and data flow diagram.

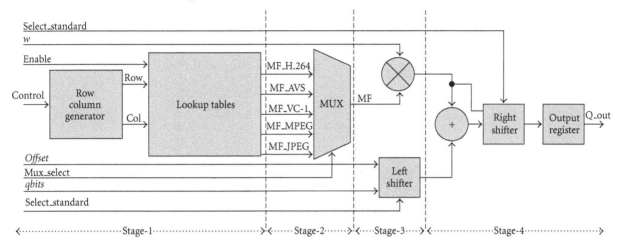

FIGURE 5: Detailed block diagram of the entire operation with all the pipelining boundaries.

TABLE 7: Performance measure using standard images for different standards.

| Sample images | PSNR (dB) | | | |
|---|---|---|---|---|
| | H.264 | VC-1/MPEG-2/4 | JPEG | AVS |
| Peppers | 38.62 | 32.09 | 34.81 | 50.64 |
| House | 38.97 | 33.36 | 35.51 | 50.64 |
| Girl | 38.67 | 33.03 | 35.56 | 50.64 |
| Mandrill | 36.20 | 27.46 | 28.91 | 50.69 |
| Tree | 36.78 | 29.09 | 31.11 | 50.60 |
| Lena | 38.81 | 31.73 | 34.14 | 50.65 |
| Lake | 37.28 | 29.47 | 31.74 | 50.64 |
| Mean | 37.91 | 30.89 | 33.11 | 50.64 |

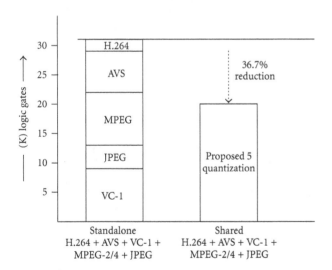

FIGURE 6: Comparison in terms gate count.

### 2.4. DFQA Applied to JPEG.

Similarly for JPEG codec, we calculate MFs for each of the coefficients of the quantization matrix. The JPEG standard does not define any fixed quantization matrix. It is the prerogative of the user to select a quantization matrix. There are two quantization matrices provided in Annex K of the JPEG standard for reference. Here we focus only on the Luminance quantization matrix shown in Figure 3.

The following matrix shows the MFs for the corresponding quantization matrix of Figure 3:

$$
MF = \begin{bmatrix}
16 & 22 & 25 & 16 & 10 & 6 & 5 & 4 \\
20 & 20 & 18 & 14 & 10 & 4 & 4 & 5 \\
18 & 20 & 16 & 10 & 6 & 4 & 4 & 4 \\
18 & 15 & 11 & 8 & 5 & 3 & 3 & 4 \\
14 & 11 & 7 & 4 & 4 & 2 & 2 & 3 \\
10 & 7 & 5 & 4 & 3 & 2 & 2 & 3 \\
5 & 4 & 3 & 3 & 2 & 2 & 2 & 2 \\
4 & 3 & 3 & 3 & 2 & 2 & 2 & 2
\end{bmatrix}. \tag{9}
$$

Again the elements in (9) are smaller than those of the original Luminance matrix in Figure 3, which reduces the size of the RAM. After we calculate the MF, each of them is directly multiplied by the corresponding transform coefficient in the first step. Similar to VC-1 and MPEG-2/4 codecs, the second step is not applied to the JPEG standard. Finally, in third step of the proposed DFQA, the multiplied output of the initial step is right shifted by 8 bits which gives the desired quantized level. To reduce the quantization error in VC-1, MPEG-2/4, and JPEG, we also calculate MF with different amount of right shift operation. But that approach increases the hardware cost and cannot reduce the quantization error significantly. Hence we implement the quantization by using the MF with fixed 8 bit right shift.

## 3. Hardware Implementation of DFQA

The overall architecture of the proposed cost-sharing algorithm is shown in Figure 4(a). It can perform the $8 \times 8$ quantization of any of the five different standards as selected by the user (or another master system) using the select_standard pin. The proposed architecture contains three main blocks with four-stage pipelining: (1) lookup tables to hold the multiplying factors (MF), (2) one multiquantization unit (composed of only one shared multiplier), and (3) one finite

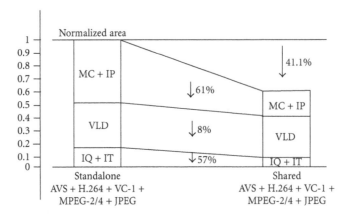

FIGURE 7: Cost reduction map of a decoder using the proposed architecture.

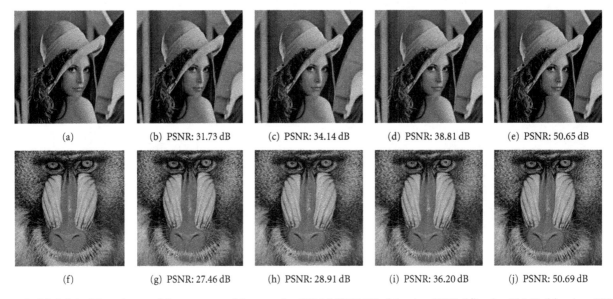

FIGURE 8: (a) Original Lena image; (b) reconstructed image using VC-1/MPEG-2/4; (c) using JPEG; (d) using H.264; (e) using AVS; (f) original Mandrill image; (g) reconstructed using VC-1/MPEG-2/4; (h) using JPEG; (i) using H.264; (j) using AVS.

state machine to control all the standards. The description of these blocks and their operations are described below. However, QP processing is not necessary for hardware implementation as it does not process data but calculates parameters used for data processing in the quantization block. Hence we assume that QP processing is previously done by software.

The core unit of the multiquantizer unit, as shown in Figure 4(b), contains one general-purpose multiplier, adder and shared right shifter. Right shift operation depends on the select_standard pin. The look-up tables in Figure 4(c) contain all the MF matrices for five standards. However, one look-up table is used at a time based on the specified standard. The multiplexer is used to select the valid data from the look-up tables. To reduce the power consumption, only one look-up table is activated at a time by the enable pin. Once the standard is chosen by the user, the desired look-up table is activated by the controller and all the other look-up tables go into the sleep mode. The control logic

assigns the enable signal as well as the MUX selection signals accordingly.

For H.264 standard according to Figure 4(c), there are six look-up tables—LUT_H_0, LUT_H_1, LUT_H_2, LUT_H_3, LUT_H_4, and LUT_H_5 for QP = 0, 1, ..., 5. If QP is greater than 5 even then the same look-up tables will be used, only the $q$bits will be changed. For example, with QP = 6 and QP = 7, LUT_H_0 and LUT_H_1 will be used, respectively. Similarly the rest of the look-up tables will be reused as the value of QP is being increased. MUX1 selects the desired MF for H.264 standard from these six look-up tables based on QP. LUT_AVS, LUT_VC-1/MPEG, and LUT_JPEG contain MFs for AVS, VC-1/MPEG-2/4, and JPEG, respectively. The detailed block diagram of the entire operation with all the pipelining boundaries is shown in Figure 5.

According to Figure 5, the proposed architecture operates in four stages of pipeline, which consists of a row-column-generator to point the row and column of the look-up tables, several multiplexers to select the valid path, a shared multiplier for all five standards, a shared adder, and shared shifter. Here quantization is performed by multiplication and right shift operation rather than the division operation. In the first stage of pipelining, the value of row and col is generated to point to the row and column of the look-up table by the Row-Column-Generator with the help of the controller. This row and col is used to get the Multiplication Factor, MF from look-up table. After that in second stage of the pipeline operation the multiplexer selects the valid MF. Next in stage 3 the multiplier multiplies the transform coefficient $w[i, j]$ coming from the transform unit with the desired MF$[i, j]$. Moreover, at the same time in this stage the *offset* value is left shifted by $q$bits by the left shifter only for H.264 and AVS standards. For VC-1, MPEG-2/4, and JPEG, this left shifter involved in stage 3 is not used. The output of the multiplier and the left shifter are added and finally right shifted in the fourth and final stage of the pipeline operation and the output register gives the quantized output. However, for VC-1, MPEG-2/4, and JPEG, the output of the multiplier is directly right shifted in this final stage and the output register returns the final quantized level. The left shift and right shift operation for AVS, H.264, VC-1, MPEG-2/4, or JPEG is chosen by the select_standard pin. In addition to the logic shown in Figure 5, there are pipelining registers between each stage of pipelining.

The design of the shared multiplier along with the shifter instead of the divider is the key part of the entire process. Although quantization is defined as the division operation, the AVS and H.264 standards define quantization as the multiplication and the right shift operation. To integrate the old standards like MPEG-2/4 and JPEG with AVS and H.264, we propose the whole architecture as a shared multiplication and right shift operation. Due to this strategy, the proposed architecture needs only a shared multiplier rather than both the multiplier (for AVS and H.264) and the divider (for VC-1, MPEG-2/4, and JPEG), which reduces the hardware complexity as well as the cost. Moreover, the whole design shares only one control circuit rather than using specific control circuit for each standard, which makes the design more cost effective.

## 4. Hardware Comparison

*4.1. Performance Comparison in FPGA.* The proposed architecture is implemented in Verilog HDL, and the operation is verified using Xilinx Vertex4 LX60 FPGA. The design is later synthesized using 0.18 $\mu$m CMOS technology. The proposed architecture costs 553 LUTs and 298 slices with a maximum operating frequency of 187.1 MHz. In Table 3, we summarize the performance (FPGA only) of our proposed multiquantizer supporting five standards in terms of hardware count, maximum working frequency, and supporting standards with other designs. The design in [2] has lesser hardware count than ours but supports only one standard, H.264.

For better evaluation, we have integrated the multi-transform design (for five codecs) in [1] with the proposed multiquantization scheme. The combined design is implemented in Xilinx FPGA (Vertex4 LX60) and the results are shown in Table 4. This combined architecture costs 1722 LUTs (4-input), 972 slices, and 1036 registers with a maximum operating frequency of 187 MHz. Note that, the operating frequency of the multitransform design in [1] is 194 MHz. In Table 4, we compare the performance (FPGA only) of this combined multi-DCT and multiquantizer with the existing designs; those include both DCT and quantization block. The designs in [6] and [10] can support only one standard, H.264, and hence has lesser hardware than ours. Compared to the existing designs, our design has higher frequency of operation with comparable hardware count. Thus, it can be seen from the Tables 3 and 4 that the proposed design can support the highest number of popular and widely used video standards (i.e., AVS, H.264/AVC, VC-1, JPEG, and MPEG-2/4) and still consumes relatively lesser hardware cost and runs at higher operational frequency.

*4.2. Performance Comparison in VLSI.* The proposed design is synthesized in CMOS 0.18 $\mu$m technology using Artisan library cells. It consumes 176,911 $\mu$m$^2$ silicon area, 19.6 K gates, and 6.8 K standard cells. The frequency of operation is 88.5 MHz. As seen here, the operational frequency of our design is much higher in FPGA because of the use of optimized LUTs that are inherent to the type of FPGA chosen.

In Table 5, we compare the VLSI implementation of the proposed DFQA scheme with that of the estimated cost of the existing designs. Since, as of today, we have not come across to any design that can support all five codecs, we show an estimate of the projected cost. The costs of the standalone quantization units are added together to find the total estimated cost of five standalone codecs which is 31.1 K logic gates. The cost of the proposed circuit shared quantizer architecture is 19.6 K logic gates, which saves up to 36.7% than the estimated cost of five codecs. Figure 6 illustrates the comparison showing the percentage of reduction based on Table 5.

*4.3. Estimated Area Saving in a Multicodec Design.* In order to better assess the saving in hardware for the entire decoder, we have done a cost analysis as presented in Figure 7 where the costs of standalone and shared design are shown. The cost of a decoder for four codecs (H.264, VC-1, AVS, MPEG2/4) is taken from [14]. The cost of JPEG codec is taken from [24] and added with the previous to calculate the total cost for all five codecs. Here, MC is motion compensation, IP is intra prediction, VLD is variable length decoder, IQ is inverse quantization, and IT is inverse transform. To calculate the hypothetical cost of shared implementation, we have used the implementation cost for MC, IP, and VLD units from the shared design presented in [14]. Then the cost for IT (for shared design taken from our previous work [1]) and the cost for IQ (taken from the current work) are added. Thus, we can see that the shared design (that includes the proposed multicodec DFQA scheme) is estimated to save overall 41.1% area of a decoder compared to standalone design for five codecs.

In Table 6, we compare the decoding capability of the proposed multiquantization approach with other quantization only designs. While working at maximum capacity on Virtex4 LX60 FPGA, the proposed multiquantizer can achieve a frame rate of 60 fps (with $4:2:0$ luma-chroma sampling, $187 \times 10^6/(1{,}920 \times 1{,}080 + 2 \times 960 \times 540) = 60.1 \approx 60$). The decoding capability of other designs is also calculated using $4:2:0$ sampling. It is seen in Table 6 that the proposed scheme achieves the highest decoding capacity.

*4.4. Performance Evaluation Using Standard Images.* In order to verify the functional correctness, in this section, we present the performance evaluation of the proposed algorithm using several standard gray-scale images. The images are first coded with transform (used in [1]) and quantization (presented here) operations, followed by a decoding (inverse) process. The quantization parameter (or quality factor) is set to 10 in all cases. The results are shown in terms of peak-signal-to-noise-ratio (PSNR) and presented below in Table 7. Figure 8 presents the original and reconstruction images of "Lena" and "Mandrill" for all five codecs.

# 5. Conclusion

In this paper, we present a high performance circuit shared architecture to perform the $8 \times 8$ quantization operation for five different multimedia codecs. The architecture replaces the hardware costly division operation with addition and shift operations. In addition only one control circuit is designed to control the entire architecture for all five standards. These strategies of using shared multiplier and shared control circuit result in a much lower hardware cost. The performance analysis shows that the proposed design satisfies the requirement of all codecs and achieves the competitive decoding capability. The scheme is later verified for functional correctness using standard images. Overall, the architecture is suitable for real-time application in modern multicodec systems.

# References

[1] K. A. Wahid, M. Martuza, M. Das, and C. McCrosky, "Efficient hardware implementation of 8x8 integer cosine transforms for multiple video codecs," *Journal of Real-Time Image Processing.* In press.

[2] R. C. Kordasiewicz and S. Shirani, "ASIC and FPGA implementations of H.264 DCT and quantization blocks," in *Proceedings of the IEEE International Conference on Image Processing (ICIP '05)*, pp. 1020–1023, September 2005.

[3] S. P. Jeoong and T. Ogunfunmi, "A new hardware implementation of the H.264 8x8 transform and quantization," in *Proceedings of the IEEE International Conference on Acoustics, Speech, and Signal Processing (ICASSP '09)*, pp. 585–588, April 2009.

[4] I. Amer, W. Badawy, and G. Jullien, "A high-performance hardware implementation of the H.264 simplified 8x8 transformation and quantization," in *Proceedings of the IEEE International Conference on Acoustics, Speech and Signal Processing (ICASSP '05)*, pp. II1137–II1140, March 2005.

[5] G. Pastuszak, "Transforms and quantization in the high-throughput H.264/AVC encoder based on advanced mode selection," in *Proceedings of the IEEE Computer Society Annual Symposium on VLSI: Trends in VLSI Technology and Design (ISVLSI '08)*, pp. 203–208, April 2008.

[6] X. T. Tran and V. H. Tran, "Cost-efficient 130nm TSMC forward transform and quantization for H.264/AVC encoders," in *Proceedings of the 14th IEEE International Symposium on Design and Diagnostics of Electronic Circuits and Systems (DDECS '11)*, pp. 47–52, April 2011.

[7] R. Husemann, M. Majolo, V. Guimaraes, A. Susin, V. Roesler, and J. V. Lima, "Hardware integrated quantization solution for improvement of computational H.264 encoder module," in *Proceedings of the 18th IEEE/IFIP International Conference on VLSI and System-on-Chip (VLSI-SoC '10)*, pp. 316–321, September 2010.

[8] R. Kordasiewicz and S. Shirani, "Hardware implementation of the optimized transform and quantization blocks of H.264," in *Proceedings of the Canadian Conference on Electrical and Computer Engineering (CCECE '04)*, vol. 2, pp. 0943–0946, May 2004.

[9] O. Tasdizen and I. Hamzaoglu, "A high performance and low cost hardware architecture for H. 264 transform and quantization algorithms," in *Proceedings of the 13th European Signal Processing Conference*, pp. 4–8, September 2005.

[10] C. P. Fan and Y. L. Cheng, "FPGA implementations of low latency and high throughput 4x4 block texture coding processor for H.264/AVC," *Journal of the Chinese Institute of Engineers*, vol. 32, no. 1, pp. 33–44, 2009.

[11] K. Zhang, Y. Zhu, and L. Yu, "Area-efficient quantization architecture with zero-prediction method for AVS encoders," in *Proceedings of the Picture Coding Symposium (PCS '07)*, p. 4, November 2007.

[12] K. Suh, K. Y. Min, K. Kim, J. S. Koh, and J. W. Chong, "Design of DPCM hybrid coding loop using single 1-D DCT in MPEG-2 video encoder," in *Proceedings of the IEEE International Symposium on Circuits and Systems (ISCAS '99)*, pp. V-279–V-282, June 1999.

[13] H. Osman, W. Mahjoup, A. Nabih, and G. M. Aly, "JPEG encoder for low-cost FPGAs," in *Proceedings of the International Conference on Computer Engineering and Systems (ICCES '07)*, pp. 406–411, November 2007.

[14] C. C. Ju, Y. C. Chang, C. Y. Cheng et al., "A full-HD 60fps AVS/H.264/VC-1/MPEG-2 video decoder for digital home applications," in *Proceedings of the International Symposium on VLSI Design, Automation and Test (VLSI-DAT '11)*, pp. 1–4, April 2011.

[15] Silicon Image Inc., 2011, http://www.siliconimage.com/products/index.aspx.

[16] CCITT recommendation T. 81, digital compression and coding continuous-tone still images, 1992.

[17] ISO/IEC, Information technology—generic coding of moving pictures and associated audio information: video, 13818-2:1995.

[18] Standard for television: VC-1 compressed video bitstream format and decoding process, SMPTE 421 M, 2006.

[19] ITU-T Rec. H. 264/ISO/IEC, 14496-10 AVC, 2003.

[20] GB/T, 20090. 1 Information technology—advanced coding of audio and video Part 1: system, Chinese AVS standard.

[21] S. Srinivasan, P. Hsu, T. Holcomb et al., "Windows media video 9: overview and applications," *Signal Processing*, vol. 19, no. 9, pp. 851–875, 2004.

[22] A. Vetro, C. Christopoulos, and H. Sun, "Video transcoding architectures and techniques: an overview," *IEEE Signal Processing Magazine*, vol. 20, no. 2, pp. 18–29, 2003.

[23] I. Ahmad, X. Wei, Y. Sun, and Y. Q. Zhang, "Video transcoding: an overview of various techniques and research issues," *IEEE Transactions on Multimedia*, vol. 7, no. 5, pp. 793–804, 2005.

[24] C. J. Lian, L. G. Chen, H. C. Chang, and Y. C. Chang, "Design and implementation of JPEG encoder IP core," in *Proceedings of the Asia and South Pacific Design Automation Conference*, pp. 29–30, 2001.

[25] L. Yu, F. Yi, J. Bong, and C. Zhang, "Overview of AVS-video: tools, performance and complexity," in *Visual Communications and Image Processing*, vol. 5960 of *Proceedings of SPIE*, pp. 679–690, July 2005.

[26] J. B. Lee and H. Kalva, *The VC-1 and H.264 Video Compression Standards for Broadband Video Services*, vol. 32, Springer, Florida, Fla, UDA, 1st edition, 2008.

# 12

# Multitarget Tracking of Pedestrians in Video Sequences Based on Particle Filters

**Hui Li, Shengwu Xiong, Pengfei Duan, and Xiangzhen Kong**

*School of Computer Science and Technology, Wuhan University of Technology, Wuhan 430070, China*

Correspondence should be addressed to Hui Li, lipeilin1984xyz@163.com

Academic Editor: Weidong Cai

Video target tracking is a critical problem in the field of computer vision. Particle filters have been proven to be very useful in target tracking for nonlinear and non-Gaussian estimation problems. Although most existing algorithms are able to track targets well in controlled environments, it is often difficult to achieve automated and robust tracking of pedestrians in video sequences if there are various changes in target appearance or surrounding illumination. To surmount these difficulties, this paper presents multitarget tracking of pedestrians in video sequences based on particle filters. In order to improve the efficiency and accuracy of the detection, the algorithm firstly obtains target regions in training frames by combining the methods of background subtraction and Histogram of Oriented Gradient (HOG) and then establishes discriminative appearance model by generating patches and constructing codebooks using superpixel and Local Binary Pattern (LBP) features in those target regions. During the process of tracking, the algorithm uses the similarity between candidates and codebooks as observation likelihood function and processes severe occlusion condition to prevent drift and loss phenomenon caused by target occlusion. Experimental results demonstrate that our algorithm improves the tracking performance in complicated real scenarios.

## 1. Introduction

Video target tracking is an important research field in computer vision for its wide range of application demands and prospects in many industries, such as military guidance, visual surveillance, visual navigation of robots, human-computer interaction and medical diagnosis [1–3], and so forth. The main task of target tracking is to track one or more mobile targets in video sequences so that the position, velocity, trajectory, and other parameters of the target can be obtained. Two main tasks needs to be completed by moving target tracking during the processing procedure: the first one is target detection and classification which detects the location of relevant targets in the image frames; the second one is the relevance of the target location of consecutive image frames, which identifies the target points in the image and determines their location coordinates, thus to determine the trajectory of the target as time changes. However, automated detection and tracking of pedestrians in video sequences is still a challenging task because of following reasons [4]. (1) Large intraclass variability which refers to various changes in appearance of pedestrians due to different poses, clothing, viewpoints, illumination, and articulation. (2) Interclass similarities which are the common likeness between pedestrians and other background objects in heavy cluttered environment. (3) Partial occlusions, which may change frequently in a dynamic scene, of pedestrians which are caused by other interclass or intraclass targets.

Considering the difficulties mentioned above in pedestrians detection and tracking tasks, pedestrians tracking has been studied intensively and a number of elegant algorithms have been established. One popular tracking method is mean shift procedure [5], which finds the local maximum of probability distribution in the direction of gradient. Comaniciu and Ramesh [6] gave a strict proof of the convergence of the algorithm and proposed a mean shift based on tracking method. As a deterministic method, mean shift keeps single hypothesis and is thus computationally efficient. But it may run into trouble when similar targets are presented in background or occlusion occurs. Another common approach is the use of the Kalman filter [7]. This approach is based on the assumption that the probability distribution of the target state is Gaussian, and therefore the mean and covariance, computed recursively by the Kalman filter equations, can fully characterize the behavior of the tracked target. However, in video target tracking, tracking targets in real world rarely satisfy Gaussian assumptions required by the Kalman filter in that background clutter may resemble a part of foreground features. One promising category is sequential Monte Carlo approach, which is also known as particle filter [8], which recursively estimates target posterior with discrete sample-weight pairs in a dynamic Bayesian framework. Due to particle filters' non-Gaussian, non-linear assumption and multiple hypothesis property, they have been successfully applied to video target tracking [9].

## 2. Previous Work

Various researchers have attempted to extend particle filters to target tracking. Among others, one of the most successful features used in target tracking is color. Nummiaro et al. [10] proposed a tracking algorithm that considered color histograms, as a feature, that were tracked using the particle filter algorithm. Despite the algorithm being more robust to the partial blocked target and the target shape changes, the algorithm exhibits high sensitivity to illumination changes that may cause the tracker to fail. Vermaak et al. [11] introduced a mixture particle filter (MPF), where each component was modeled with an individual particle filter that formed part of the mixture. The filters in the mixture interacted only through the computation of the importance weights. By distributing the resampling step to individual filters, the MPF avoids the problem of sample depletion. Okuma et al. [12] extended the approach of Vermaak et al. and proposed a boosted particle filter. The algorithm combined the strengths of two successful algorithms: mixture particle filters and adaboost. It is a simple and automatic multiple target tracking system, but it is easy to fail in tracking when the background image is complex.

Therefore, a more effective method for target recognition is needed. Superpixel has been one of the most promising representations with demonstrated success in image segmentation and target recognition [13–15]. For this reason, Ren and Malik [16] proposed a tracking method based on superpixel, which regards tracking task as a figure/ground segmentation across frames. However, as it processes every entire frame individually with Delaunay triangularization and conditional random field (CRF) for region matching, the computational complexity is rather high. Further, it is not designed to handle complex scenes including heavy occlusion and cluttered background as well as large lighting change. Wang et al. [17] proposed a tracking method from the perspective of mid-level vision with structural information captured in superpixel. The method is able to handle heavy occlusion and recover from drifts. Thus in this paper, the observation model adopts superpixel which is combined with the LBP to extract the target feature.

In recent years, bag of features (BoF) representation has been successfully applied to object and natural scene classification owing to its simplicity, robustness, and good practical performance. Yang et al. [18] proposed a visual

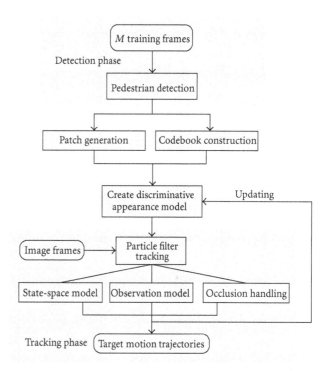

FIGURE 1: The flowchart of algorithm.

tracking approach based on BoF. The algorithm randomly samples image patches within the object region in training frames to construct two codebooks using RGB and LBP features instead of only one codebook in traditional BoF. It is more robust in handling occlusion, scaling and rotation, but it can only track one target. Based on the advantages of BoF in target tracking, the paper employs BoF to establish discriminative appearance model, which converts high-dimensional feature vector into low-dimensional histogram comparison, overcoming high computational complexity due to superpixel in the observation model.

Therefore, to achieve automated and robust tracking of pedestrians in complex scenarios, we present multi-target tracking of pedestrians in video sequences based on particle filters. The algorithm uses BoF algorithm to create discriminative appearance model which is then used to be combined with particle filter algorithm to achieve target tracking. In order to improve the efficiency and accuracy of the detection, firstly, background subtraction and the HOG detection methods are combined to get the target motion regions in the training frames. And then the discriminative appearance model established by the target regions is used to discriminate the candidate targets. During the process of tracking, severe occlusion condition is handled to prevent drift and loss phenomenon due to pedestrians' mutual occlusion. Figure 1 shows the entire algorithmic flowchart.

The paper is organized as follows: Section 3 introduces detection of pedestrians; Section 4 describes our particle filter algorithm; Section 5 presents the experimental results and the performance evaluation and conclusion work is given in Section 6.

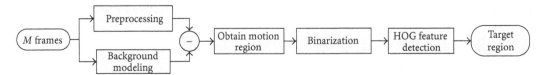

FIGURE 2: Flow diagram of target regions extraction of $M$ frames.

# 3. Detection of Pedestrians

There are mainly two parts in this section, one is target regions extraction, and the other is the construction of the discriminative appearance model. The former aims to determine the target regions of video sequence in the first $M$ frames, the latter aims to do sampling, feature extraction in the target region when these target regions are seen as a training set, and eventually establish the discriminative appearance model.

*3.1. Target Regions Extraction.* Before tracking, we need to detect the targets in the first $M$ frames and get the target regions in each frame for later trainings. Figure 2 shows the whole flow diagram of target regions extraction of the first $M$ frames.

We can see from Figure 2 that, first of all, in order to get motion region, a simple and fast approach is to perform background subtraction, which identifies motion targets from the portion of video sequences that differ significantly from a background model, as shown in Figure 3. Then we use the HOG descriptors [19] and Support Vector Machines (SVMs) to build a pedestrian detector. Since the method has been proved to be capable but time-consuming, we only detect motion regions which have been acquired by background subtraction and $M$ frames. This not only reduces the HOG detection region, but also improves the efficiency and the accuracy of the detection. Figure 4 shows that adopting the HOG detection after background subtracting improves the accuracy of pedestrian detection, whereas using the HOG directly can lead to false detection.

*3.2. Discriminative Appearance Model.* During this stage, discriminative appearance model is created by target regions extraction of the first $M$ frames to distinguish targets from cluttered backgrounds. The $k$th pedestrian in the $t$th frame is $p_t^k$ ($t = 1, 2, \ldots, M; k = 1, 2, \ldots, F_s$), where $M$ is the number of training frames, $F_s$ is the number of target pedestrians in the training frames. According to all $M$-frame regions in which pedestrian $k$ appears, we draw the pedestrian's discriminative appearance model (We assume that the number of targets in the training frames is invariable.), and therefore we need get $F_s$ discriminative appearance models.

*3.2.1. Patch Generation.* In the training stage, some patches with a constant scale are randomly sampled within the region of the pedestrian $p_t^k$. For pedestrian $k$, $M$ image patches are collected and represented by superpixel descriptor and LBP descriptor, respectively, in each training frame. Superpixel descriptor and LBP descriptor extraction process in training frames is illustrated in Figure 5.

FIGURE 3: Background subtraction result.

(a)

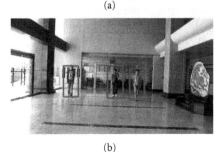

(b)

FIGURE 4: The HOG detection result. (a) Detection results of using the HOG directly. (b) Detection results of adopting the HOG after background subtracting.

The superpixel segmentation method we adopt in this paper is SLIC [15] (Simple Linear Iterative Clustering) that clusters pixels in the combined five-dimensional color and image plane space to efficiently generate compact, nearly uniform superpixel. For superpixel descriptor, we segment target region in $t$th training frame into $S_t$ superpixels, as shown in Figure 5. As the superpixel does not have a fixed shape, and its distribution is often irregular, it is unsuitable for extracting the local template information; in addition, due to the similarity of the superpixel's internal pixel texture as well as the similarity of color characteristics, more stable superpixel information can be obtained by extracting the color space histogram. However, RGB color space distribution does not accord with human's vision distribution, and it is not robust enough for illumination

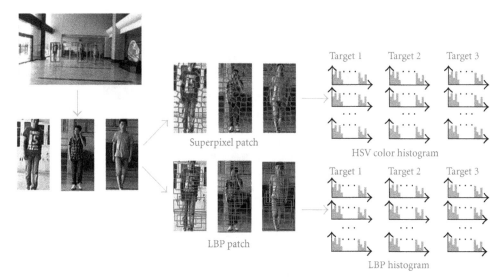

FIGURE 5: Extraction process of superpixel descriptor and LBP descriptor in training frames.

changes, therefore we only use the normalized histogram of HSV color space which is simple and accords with human's vision as a feature for all superpixels.

LBP is vastly used for texture description which has good performance in texture classification, fabric defect detection and moving region detection. LBP is an illumination invariant descriptor which is not sensitive to the intensity change caused by the light changes. The LBP descriptor is stable as long as the differences among the image pixel values do not change a lot. In addition, there are certain complementary between LBP and color features, so we adopt LBP descriptor as a feature. The LBP descriptor is defined as follows:

$$\text{LBP}(P_c) = \sum_{n=0}^{p-1} s(g_n - g_c) 2^n,$$

$$s(x) = \begin{cases} 1, & x \geq 0 \\ 0, & x < 0, \end{cases} \tag{1}$$

where $g_c$ is the intensity value of center pixel $P_c$ and $g_n$ is the intensity of neighboring pixels.

The image histogram obtained from the computation of LBP is defined as follows:

$$H_i = \sum_{x,y} I(f(x,y) = i), \quad i = 0,\dots,n-1,$$

$$I(f(x,y) = i) = \begin{cases} 1 & f(x,y) = i \\ 0 & f(x,y) \neq i, \end{cases} \tag{2}$$

where $n = 2^p$ represents the length of the encode bit generated by the LBP operator, $p$ represents the number of pixels in the neighborhood, $f(x,y)$ is the LBP value at $(x,y)$, in this way, $H_i$ represents the number of pixels which have the LBP value of $i$, the histogram can reflect the distribution of the LBP values.

*3.2.2. Codebook Construction.* As frames slip, patches accumulate. For extracted collections of sample features

$\text{Sample}_k = \{S_n\}_{n=1}^M$, features are gathered into a number of clusters by performing mean shift clustering, and cluster centers $C = \{C_{cl}\}_{cl=1}^{cl\_num}$ compose the codebook. Here cl _num is the number of cluster centers as well as the size of the codebook. Cluster centers which represent the most typical features are regarded as the keywords in the codebook and used to create bags. In this way, a large collection of sample characteristics is converted into a comparatively small codebook. Figure 6 shows the process of codebook construction.

After codebook construction, for each characteristic of a set of features $\text{Sample}_k$ in each training sample image, find the codeword which has the nearest Euclidean distance from it, then count the appearance times of all features corresponding nearest codeword to acquire the final histogram. Repeat the above steps to $M$ training sample images, a set of training images will be converted into a set of histograms called bags. A bag is equivalent to the occurrence frequency of codewords in an image and can be represented as a histogram. $M$ training images are converted to a set of bags $\{B_m\}_{m=1}^M$ by raw counts.

Here the discriminative appearance model has been established for subsequent classification decisions.

*3.2.3. Updating.* Since appearance and pose changes of a target occur all the time, updating is necessary or even crucial. After $M$ frames, a new collection of patches $\{P_i\}_{i=1}^{fp}$ is obtained. We then perform mean shift clustering again on $\{P_i\}_{i=1}^{fp}$ and the old codebook $\{C_{cl}\}_{cl=1}^{cl\_num}$ using

$$C_{\text{new}} = \{C_{cl}\}_{cl=1}^{cl\_num} = \text{meanshift}\left(\{P_i\}_{i=1}^{fp}, \mu\{C_{cl}\}_{cl=1}^{cl\_num}\right). \tag{3}$$

Here, $C_{\text{new}}$ denotes the new codebook. $\mu$ $(0 < \mu < 1)$ is a forget factor imposed on the old codebook to reduce its importance gradually so that the newly-constructed codebook pays more attention to the latest patches.

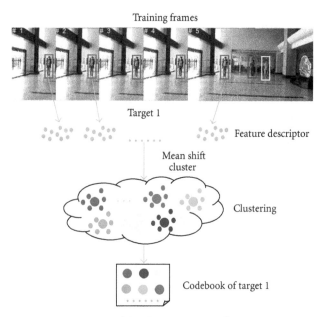

Training frames

Target 1

Feature descriptor

Mean shift cluster

Clustering

Codebook of target 1

FIGURE 6: Codebook construction of target 1.

# 4. Particle Filter Tracking

The particle filter [8] is a Bayesian sequential importance sampling technique, which recursively approximates the posterior distribution using a finite set of weighted samples. It consists of two essential steps: prediction and update. We use $X_t = [x_{1,t}, \ldots, x_{F_t,t}]$ to express the set of states of the target system at moment $t$. In the set of states $X_t$, $F_t$ stands for the target's states number at moment $t$; $x_{j,t}, j = 1, \ldots, F_t$ stands for the state of the $j$th target at moment $t$.

Given all available observations $Z_{1:t-1} = \{Z_1, \ldots, Z_{t-1}\}$, up to time $t - 1$, the prediction stage uses the probabilistic system transition model $p(X_t \mid X_{t-1})$ to predict the posterior at time $t$ as

$$p(X_t \mid Z_{1:t-1}) = \int p(X_t \mid X_{t-1}) p(X_{t-1} \mid Z_{1:t-1}) dX_{t-1}. \quad (4)$$

At time $t$, the observation $Z_t$ is available, the state can be updated using Bayesian's rule:

$$p(X_t \mid Z_{1:t}) = \frac{p(Z_t \mid X_t) p(X_t \mid Z_{1:t-1})}{p(Z_t \mid Z_{1:t-1})}, \quad (5)$$

where $p(Z_t \mid X_t)$ is described by the observation equation.

*4.1. State-Space Model.* In the video scene, the movement of each target can be considered as an independent process, and therefore state-space model can be regarded as the joint product form of a single-target motion model:

$$p(X_t \mid X_{t-1}) = \prod_{i=1}^{F} p(x_{i,t} \mid x_{i,t-1}). \quad (6)$$

Suppose the target state number of both moment $t$ and $t - 1$ are $F(F \geq \max\{F_{t-1}, F_t\})$, $X_t = [x_{1,t}, x_{2,t}, \ldots, x_{F,t}]$, $F_t$ is the state number in $X_t$, $F_{t-1}$ is the state number in $X_{t-1}$, $x_{j,t}$ is the state of the $j$th video target at moment $t$, $x_{j,t} = [x_j, y_j, w_j, h_j]$, $x_j$ and $y_j$ are respectively the rectangle center's position in the direction of $x$ and $y$ in the image, $w_j$ and $h_j$ are the length and width of the rectangle.

To get the state transition density function of the $j$th target at moment $t$, random perturbation model is used to describe the state transition of the $j$th target from momet $t - 1$ to moment $t$, that is,

$$p(x_{j,t} \mid x_{j,t-1}) = N(x_{j,t}; x_{j,t-1}, \Sigma), \quad (7)$$

where $N(x_{j,t}; x_{j,t-1}, \Sigma)$ is the normal density function whose covariance is $\Sigma$. $\Sigma$ is a diagonal matrix, and the variances of the four parameters in $\Sigma$'s diagonal elements corresponding state $x_{j,t}$ are $\sigma_x^2, \sigma_y^2, \sigma_w^2, \sigma_h^2$. Random perturbation model is used to describe the motion of each target mainly in the condition that the tracking targets of the video are pedestrians who have movement randomness, thus it is difficult to predict the state of motion for the next moment by using constant-velocity model or constant acceleration model.

*4.2. Observation Model.* When a new frame arrives, for target $k$, firstly, according to its location at the last frame, state-space model is used to randomly sample $T$ candidate targets, as illustrated in Figure 7.

Secondly, each candidate target is handled as follows:

(1) extract $N$ superpixel patches.

We adopt superpixel segmentation to each candidate target and obtain $N$ superpixels. Then extract each superpixel's HSV color histogram and normalized them.

(2) extract $N$ LBP patches.

Extract $N$ patches from each candidate target, and then calculate each patch's LBP histogram and normalize them.

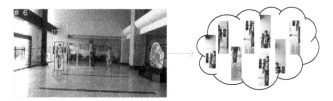

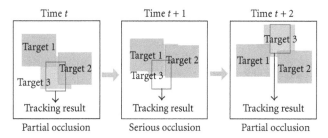

FIGURE 7: Collection of $T$ candidate targets.

FIGURE 8: Tracking result in severe occlusion condition.

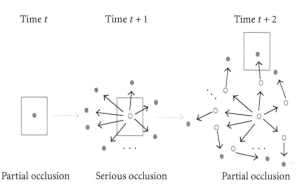

FIGURE 9: Particles' movements in severe occlusion condition.

Then calculate the color histogram and the LBP histogram of $N$ patches (each superpixel is also referred to as a patch) separately according to the following process:

We calculate the patches' similarities with codewords, so a similarity function is defined as follows:

$$\text{sim}^i = \frac{1}{\sqrt{2\pi\sigma^2}} \exp\left(-\frac{d^2\left[S_i, C_j\right]}{2\sigma^2}\right), \quad (j = 1, \ldots, \text{cl\_num}),$$

(8)

where $\text{sim}^i$ denotes the similarity between patch $i$ and each codeword $j$, $i = 1, \ldots, N$; $S_i$ denotes the eigenvector of the test patch $i$, $C_j$ denotes the eigenvector of the codeword $j$ in the codebook, $d^2[S_i, C_j]$ denotes the histogram intersection distance between the two histogram images.

Thus, the patches in each candidate target all have their most similar codewords. Make a statistics of the occurring frequency of codewords in each candidate target $T$ as a bag of features, $B_T$, which is illustrated in the following formula:

$$B_T = \sum_{i=1}^{N} I\left(\operatorname*{argmax}_j\left(\text{sim}^i\right) = j\right), \quad j = 1, \ldots, \text{cl\_num},$$

$$I\left(\operatorname*{argmax}_j\left(\text{sim}^i\right) = j\right) = \begin{cases} 1 & \operatorname*{argmax}_j\left(\text{sim}^i\right) = j \\ 0 & \operatorname*{argmax}_j\left(\text{sim}^i\right) \neq j. \end{cases}$$

(9)

Then we compute the similarity of bags to get the weight of each candidate target:

$$w = \frac{1}{\sqrt{2\pi\sigma^2}} \exp\left(-\frac{d_t^2[B_T, B_m]}{2\sigma^2}\right),$$

(10)

where $B_m$ denotes the eigenvector of the test sample, $B_T$ denotes the eigenvector of the template, $d_t^2[B_T, B_m]$ denotes the bag of features intersection distance between the two patches.

The observation likelihood function is defined as follows:

$$p(Z_t \mid X_t) = \max\left(\frac{1}{\sqrt{2\pi\sigma^2}} \exp\left(-\frac{d^2\left[S_i, C_j\right]}{2\sigma^2}\right)\right),$$

$$(i = 1, \ldots, N; j = 1, \ldots, \text{cl\_num}; ).$$

(11)

In this way, we get $w_{\text{superpixel}}$, $p_{\text{superpixel}}(Z_t \mid X_t)$, $w_{\text{LBP}}$, and $p_{\text{LBP}}(Z_t \mid X_t)$, respectively. In the condition that $X_t$ is the

given target state, the total observation likelihood function of the target is defined as follows:

$$p_{\text{all}}(Z_t \mid X_t) = a \cdot p_{\text{superpixel}}(Z_t \mid X_t) + b \cdot p_{\text{LBP}}(Z_t \mid X_t)$$

$$a = \frac{w_{\text{superpixel}}}{w_{\text{superpixel}} + w_{\text{LBP}}}, \qquad b = \frac{w_{\text{LBP}}}{w_{\text{superpixel}} + w_{\text{LBP}}},$$

$$a + b = 1,$$

(12)

where $p_{\text{superpixel}}(Z_t \mid X_t)$, $p_{\text{LBP}}(Z_t \mid X_t)$ are the observation likelihood functions of superpixel and LBP features respectively, $0 \leq a, b \leq 1$ are the weights of the two characteristics information in the fusion. The feature weights can be dynamically calculated through the weight distribution of the particle sets.

*4.3. Occlusion Handling.* The above procedure can be used to handle partial occlusion of the target. However, when there is severe or complete occlusion, the total observation likelihood value of the target becomes extremely small. As to that situation, when the total observation likelihood value is smaller than certain threshold, we keep the target's last tracking state unchanged and the particles continue state transition. Tracking result and particles' movements in severe occlusion condition are illustrated in Figures 8 and 9, respectively.

*4.4. The Algorithmic Process.* The entire algorithmic process can be summarized as in Algorithm 1.

Table 1: Parameters of our algorithm.

| Parameters | Value |
| --- | --- |
| Number of training frames | 5 |
| Size of codebook | 20 |
| Number of LBP patches | 50 |
| Number of superpixel patches | 200 |
| Forget factor | 0.9 |
| Number of particles | 300 |

## 5. Experimental Verification and Analysis

To verify performance of our algorithm, we evaluate our algorithm on some video sequences. These sequences are acquired from our own dataset, PETS 2012 Benchmark data and CAVIAR database where the target pedestrians move in different conditions which include complex background, severe occlusion, illumination and changes of walking speed, and so forth.

In our algorithm, parameter settings are shown in Table 1. These parameters are fixed for all video sequences.

*5.1. Comparison with Other Trackers.* For comparison purposes, these sequences are utilized to evaluate the performance of superpixel tracking, boost particle filter (BPF) and our algorithm under the situation of occlusion.

The video parameters in the evaluation are shown in Table 2.

First of all, sequence "three pedestrians in the hall" is tested, in which three pedestrians are walking in the hall from our own dataset. In Figure 10, the first row and the second row represents the outcomes of the algorithm which are contrasted with those of superpixel tracking and BPF respectively. We can see from these frames that BPF tracker leads to drifts under the situation of the pedestrian's occlusion and the pedestrian's distraction in that BPF tracker constructs proposal distribution using a mixture model that incorporates information from the dynamic models of each pedestrian and the detection hypotheses generated by Adaboost. However, when partial occlusion occurs, BPF tracker cannot get enough pedestrian feature descriptions, which leads to the failure. By contrast, both superpixel tracking and our algorithm track the targets because they require only part of the feature to track targets, and they are able to handle severe occlusion and recover from drifts. Therefore, both superpixel tracking and our algorithm can track the targets accurately, but the latter has better tracking accuracy and robustness than the former.

The pedestrians' weight variation curves of superpixel weight and LBP weight in the process of tracking are illustrated in Figure 11. Because occlusion does not occur in the tracking process to pedestrian 3, there is no obvious fluctuation of superpixel weight and LBP weight. Superpixel weight begins to decline after the 107th frame in which the occlusions between pedestrians emerge and LBP weight begins to increase. As the targets move, the interferences of the occlusions between pedestrians move away after the 123th frame, therefore superpixel weight regains the state of being higher than LBP weight.

Figure 12 shows three pedestrians' position error respectively in the process of target tracking. For each pedestrian, the position error is defined as follows:

$$\text{PositionError}_t = \sqrt{(x'_t - x_t)^2 + (y'_t - y_t)^2}, \quad (13)$$

where $(x'_t, y'_t)$ denotes the estimation value of target position at moment $t$, $(x_t, y_t)$ denotes the real position at moment $t$, $\text{PositionError}_t$ denotes the mean-square-root error at moment $t$.

We can see that the our algorithm has better accuracy than any of the other two in that using the superpixel tracking and the BPF tracking. It can be seen that the robustness of tracking is improved by using our algorithm.

Figure 13 shows target motion trajectories from the first frame to the last by using our algorithm. The different colors represent different pedestrian trajectories. The points in the graph constitute target motion trajectory, and each point represents the target location of each frame.

Secondly, sequence "five pedestrians in the corridor" is tested from CAVIAR database, in which there are twice severe occlusions. Figure 14 shows that our algorithm has better tracking accuracy and robustness, although the pedestrians' severe mutual occlusion occurs. Figure 15 shows target motion trajectories from the first frame to the last by using our algorithm.

Thirdly, sequence "sparse crowd" is tested from PETS 2012 Benchmark data. It can be seen from Figure 16 that there are failures in tracking when either the superpixel tracking or the BPF tracking is used. However, our algorithm can track all the targets in the condition of severe occlusion, pose variation, or changes of walking speed. Figure 17 shows target motion trajectories from the first frame to the last by using our algorithm.

Finally, sequence "two pedestrians in the square" is tested, in which one pedestrian was severely obscured by another pedestrian at a time. It differs from the first group of videos in that certain changes happen to pedestrians' walking environment illumination, that is, from the strong illumination into the weak illumination environment. Figure 18 shows our algorithm has better tracking accuracy and robustness. Although the pedestrians' walking illumination changes and severe mutual occlusion occurs, they are tracked out with accurate location. Figure 19 shows target motion trajectories from the first frame to the last by using our algorithm.

The quantitative evaluations of the superpixel tracking, BPF, and our algorithm are presented in Table 3. It can be seen from the table that our algorithm has smaller average errors of center location in pixels than the other two algorithms, thus it has better tracking accuracy. For each pedestrian, the average position error is defined as follows:

$$\overline{\text{PositionError}} = \frac{1}{\text{Frames}} \sum_{i=1}^{\text{Frames}} \text{PositionError}_i, \quad (14)$$

where Frames denotes the total frame numbers of the tracked video sequence, $\overline{\text{PositionError}}$ denotes the average mean-square-root error which measures the experiment results

(1) Extract target regions in the first $M$ frames
    (1.1) Perform background subtraction and get motion region.
    (1.2) Building a pedestrian detector using HOG descriptors and SVM.
    (1.3) Detect $F$ pedestrians in each frame.
(2) Build up the discriminative appearance model
    For $t = 1, 2, \ldots, M$
        (2.1) Randomly sample patches
            Generate superpixel patches and LBP patches for each target.
            Extract superpixel descriptor and LBP descriptor for all patches.
    End For
    For target $= 1, 2, \ldots, F$
        (2.2) Construct Codebook
            perform meanshift clustering for all superpixel descriptor, cluster centers $C_{\text{superpixel}} = \{C_{\text{cl}}\}_{\text{cl}=1}^{\text{cl\_num}}$
            compose the superpixel codebook.
            perform meanshift clustering for all LBP descriptor, cluster centers $C_{\text{LBP}} = \{C_{\text{cl}}\}_{\text{cl}=1}^{\text{cl\_num}}$ compose
            the LBP codebook.
            For $t = 1, 2, \ldots, M$
                Find its nearest keyword and make statistics of the appearance times of the keyword.
            End For
            Compose trained bags $\{B_m\}_{m=1}^{M}$.
    End For
(3) Tracking
    For target $= 1, 2, \ldots, F$
        (3.1) Initialize particle state distribution $\{X_M^{(i)}\}_{i=1}^{T}$ using the center of specifying region.
        (3.2) Set initial weight value of feature information $a = b = 0$.
    End For
    For $t = M + 1, M + 2, \ldots$
        For target $= 1, 2, \ldots, F$
            (3.3) Important sampling step
                Propagate $\{X_M^{(i)}\}_{i=1}^{T}$ and get new particles $\{X_{M+1}^{(i)}\}_{i=1}^{N}$ using (7).
            (3.4) Update the weights
                Compute the observation likelihood function $p_{\text{superpixel}}(Z_t \mid X_t)$ and $p_{\text{LBP}}(Z_t \mid X_t)$ for each
                particle using (11).
                Update weights value of features information using (12).
                If $p_{\text{all}}(Z_t \mid X_t) < TH$
                    $X_t = X_{t-1}$
                End if
        End For
    End For
    (3.5) Update codebook
        For each $M$ frames
            Perform mean shift clustering again on $\{P_i\}_{i=1}^{fp}$ and the old codebook $\{C_{\text{cl}}\}_{\text{cl}=1}^{\text{cl\_num}}$ using (3).
        End For
    (3.6) State estimation
        Estimate the state $X_t = E(X_t \mid Z_{1:t}) \approx \sum_{i=1}^{N} \widetilde{w_t^{(i)}} \widetilde{X_t^{(i)}}$

ALGORITHM 1: Our algorithm.

TABLE 2: Video parameters in simulation.

| Sequences | Frame size | Total frames | fps (frames per second) |
|---|---|---|---|
| (1) Three pedestrians in the hall | $800 \times 450$ | 131 | 30 |
| (2) Five pedestrians in the corridor | $384 \times 288$ | 238 | 25 |
| (3) Sparse crowd | $768 \times 576$ | 74 | 30 |
| (4) Two pedestrians in the square | $640 \times 360$ | 151 | 30 |

FIGURE 10: Sequence 1: tracking results. The results by our algorithm, superpixel tracking, and BPF methods are represented by solid line, dashed line, and dotted line rectangles. Rectangles in different colors denote the tracking results of different pedestrians.

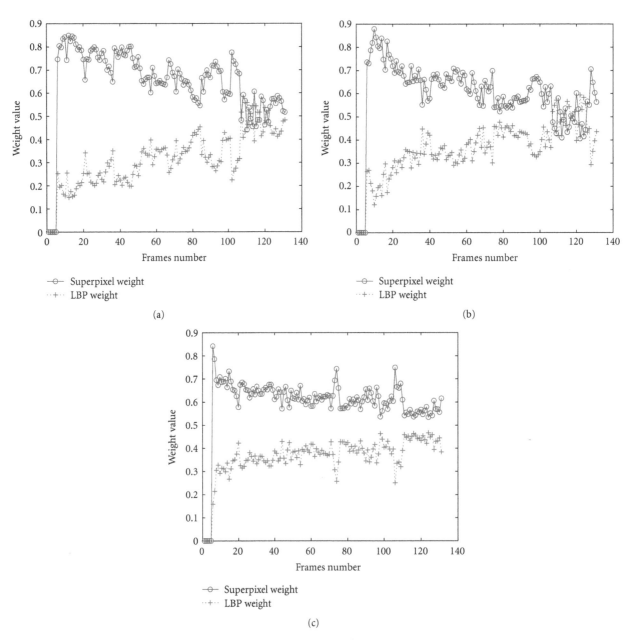

FIGURE 11: Sequence 1: pedestrians' weight variation curves. (a) pedestrian 1, (b) pedestrian 2, and (c) pedestrian 3.

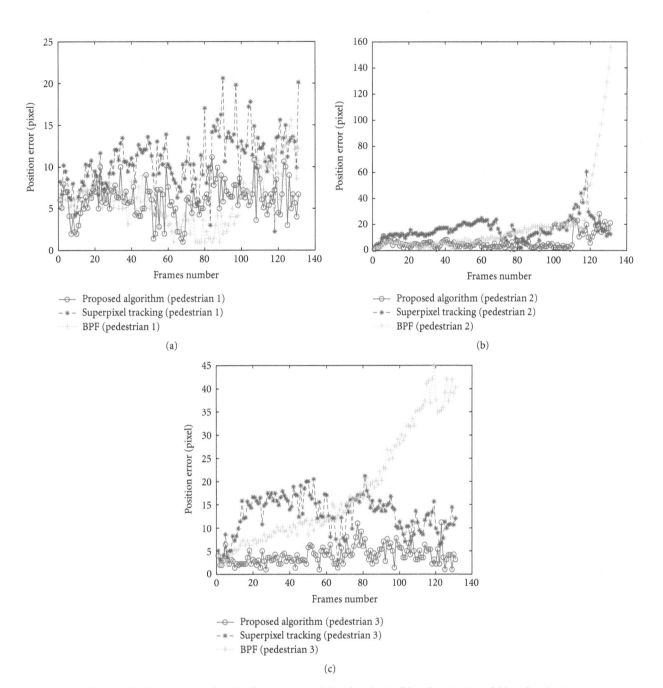

FIGURE 12: Sequence 1: pedestrians' error curves. (a) pedestrian 1, (b) pedestrian 2, and (c) pedestrian 3.

FIGURE 13: Sequence 1: target motion trajectories.

FIGURE 14: Sequence 2: tracking results. The results by our algorithm, superpixel tracking, and BPF methods are represented by solid line, dashed line, and dotted line rectangles. Rectangles in different colors denote the tracking results of different pedestrians.

FIGURE 15: Sequence 2: target motion trajectories.

FIGURE 16: Sequence 3: tracking results. The results by our algorithm, superpixel tracking, and BPF methods are represented by solid line, dashed line, and dotted line rectangles. Rectangles in different colors denote the tracking results of different pedestrians.

error; the smaller the $\overline{\text{PositionError}}$, the better the tracking effect.

*5.2. More Tracking Results.* Our algorithm is tested in more sequences which are acquired from our own dataset, PETS

2012 Benchmark data and CAVIAR database. Tracking results are showed in Figure 20.

It can be seen from the test results of the above three groups of video sequences, the our algorithm has better tracking performances in dealing with complex situations

FIGURE 17: Sequence 3: target motion trajectories.

FIGURE 18: Sequence 4: tracking results. The results of our algorithm, superpixel tracking, and BPF methods are represented by solid line, dashed line, and dotted line rectangles. Rectangles in different colors denote the tracking results of different pedestrians.

FIGURE 19: Sequence 4: target motion trajectories.

such as the target's translation, severe occlusion, illumination, and changes of walking speed, as well as analogue interference, and so forth.

## 6. Conclusions

In this paper, we propose multi-target tracking of pedestrians in video sequences based on particle filters. The contribution of our work can be listed as the following: (1) we apply background subtraction and HOG to getting target regions in training frames rapidly and accurately. (2) Our algorithm builds discriminative appearance model to collect training samples and construct two codebooks using superpixel and LBP features. (3) We integrate BoF into particle filter to get better observation results, and then automatically adjust the weight value of each feature according to the current tracking environment. Our algorithm was tested on a pedestrian tracking application in campus environment. In that case the algorithm can reliably track multiple targets and targets' motion trajectories in difficult sequences with dramatic illumination changes, partial or severe occlusions, and background clutter edges. Experimental results demonstrate the effectiveness and robustness of our algorithm.

TABLE 3: Tracking average error. The numbers denote average errors of center location in pixels.

| Sequences | Superpixel tracking | BPF | Our algorithm |
| --- | --- | --- | --- |
| (1) Three pedestrians in the hall | 11, 17, 13 | 6, 19, 18 | 6, 6, 4 |
| (2) Five pedestrians in the corridor | 51, 15, 23, 5, 14 | 48, 7, 6, 3, 8 | 8, 6, 10, 4, 3 |
| (3) Sparse crowd | 9, 34, 67, 11, 4, 6 | 35, 31, 102, 3, 4, 3 | 4, 3, 5, 3, 6, 6 |
| (4) Two pedestrians in the square | 17, 38 | 7, 23 | 6, 9 |

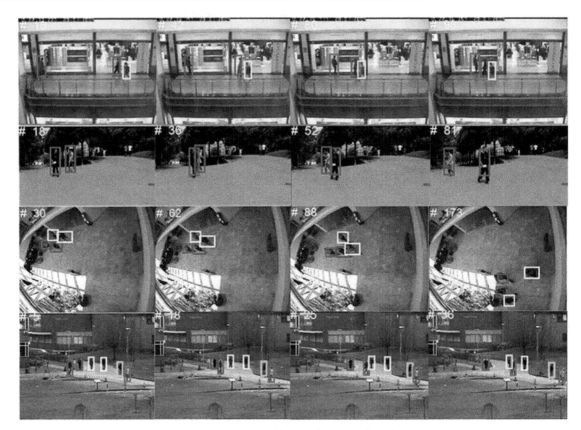

FIGURE 20: More tracking results of our algorithm.

## Acknowledgments

This work was supported in part by the National Science Foundation of China under Grant no. 61170202 and Wuhan Municipality Programs for Science and Technology Development under Grant no. 201210121029.

## References

[1] B. Babenko, S. Belongie, and M. H. Yang, "Visual tracking with online multiple instance learning," in *Proceedings of the IEEE Computer Society Conference on Computer Vision and Pattern Recognition Workshops, CVPR Workshops 2009*, pp. 983–990, June 2009.

[2] J. Kwon and K. M. Lee, "Visual tracking decomposition," in *Proceedings of the IEEE Computer Society Conference on Computer Vision and Pattern Recognition (CVPR '10)*, pp. 1269–1276, June 2010.

[3] A. Makris, D. Kosmopoulos, S. Perantonis, and S. Theodoridis, "A hierarchical feature fusion framework for adaptive visual tracking," *Image and Vision Computing*, vol. 29, no. 9, pp. 594–606, 2011.

[4] B. Leibe, E. Seemann, and B. Schiele, "Pedestrian detection in crowded scenes," in *Proceedings of the IEEE Computer Society Conference on Computer Vision and Pattern Recognition (CVPR '05)*, pp. 878–885, June 2005.

[5] H. Zhou, Y. Yuan, and C. Shi, "Object tracking using SIFT features and mean shift," *Computer Vision and Image Understanding*, vol. 113, no. 3, pp. 345–352, 2009.

[6] D. Comaniciu and V. Ramesh, "Mean shift and optimal prediction for efficient object tracking," in *Proceedings of the International Conference on Image Processing (ICIP '00)*, pp. 70–73, Vancouver, Canada, September 2000.

[7] B. O. S. Teixeira, M. A. Santillo, R. S. Erwin, and D. S. Bernstein, "Spacecraft tracking using sampled-data Kalman filters," *IEEE Control Systems Magazine*, vol. 28, no. 4, pp. 78–94, 2008.

[8] M. S. Arulampalam, S. Maskell, N. Gordon, and T. Clapp, "A tutorial on particle filters for online nonlinear/non-Gaussian Bayesian tracking," *IEEE Transactions on Signal Processing*, vol. 50, no. 2, pp. 174–188, 2002.

[9] S. L. Tang, Z. Kadim, K. M. Liang, and M. K. Lim, "Hybrid blob and particle filter tracking approach for robust object tracking," in *Proceedings of the 10th International Conference on Computational Science (ICCS '10)*, pp. 2559–2567, June 2010.

[10] K. Nummiaro, E. Koller-Meier, and L. Van Gool, "An adaptive color-based particle filter," *Image and Vision Computing*, vol. 21, no. 1, pp. 99–110, 2003.

[11] J. Vermaak, A. Doucet, and P. Pérez, "Maintaining multi-modality through mixture tracking," in *Proceedings of the 9th IEEE International Conference on Computer Vision*, pp. 1110–1116, October 2003.

[12] K. Okuma, A. Taleghani, N. De Freitas et al., "A boosted particle filter: Multitarget detection and tracking," in *Proceedings of the European Conference on Computer Vision*, pp. 28–39, 2004.

[13] A. Vedaldi and S. Soatto, "Quick shift and kernel methods for mode seeking," in *Proceedings of the European Conference on Computer Vision*, pp. 705–718, 2008.

[14] A. Levinshtein, A. Stere, K. N. Kutulakos, D. J. Fleet, S. J. Dickinson, and K. Siddiqi, "TurboPixels: fast superpixels using geometric flows," *IEEE Transactions on Pattern Analysis and Machine Intelligence*, vol. 31, no. 12, pp. 2290–2297, 2009.

[15] R. Achanta, A. Shaji, K. Smith, A. Lucchi, P. Fua, and S. Susstrunk, "Slic superpixels," EPFL Technical Report 149300, 2010.

[16] X. Ren and J. Malik, "Tracking as repeated figure/ground segmentation," in *Proceedings of the IEEE Computer Society Conference on Computer Vision and Pattern Recognition*, pp. 1–8, June 2007.

[17] S. Wang, H. C. Lu, F. Yang, and M. H. Yang, "Superpixel tracking," in *Proceedings of the IEEE International Conference on Computer Vision*, pp. 1323–1330, 2011.

[18] F. Yang, H. Lu, and Y. W. Chen, "Bag of features tracking," in *Proceedings of the International Conference on Pattern Recognition (ICPR '10)*, pp. 153–156, August 2010.

[19] N. Dalal and B. Triggs, "Histograms of oriented gradients for human detection," in *Proceedings of the IEEE Computer Society Conference on Computer Vision and Pattern Recognition (CVPR '05)*, pp. 886–893, June 2005.

# 13

# A Novel Anonymous Proxy Signature Scheme

**Jue-Sam Chou**

*Department of Information Management, Nanhua University, Chiayi 622, Taiwan*

Correspondence should be addressed to Jue-Sam Chou, jschou@mail.nhu.edu.tw

Academic Editor: Joonki Paik

Recently, several studies about proxy signature schemes have been conducted. In 2009, Yu et al. proposed an anonymous proxy signature scheme attempting to protect the proxy signer's privacy from outsiders. They claimed that their scheme can make the proxy signer anonymous. However, based on our research, we determined that this was not the case and the proxy signer's privacy was not anonymous. Hence, in this paper, we propose a new anonymous proxy signature scheme that truly makes the proxy signer anonymous while making it more secure and efficient when compared with Yu et al.'s scheme. Our proxy signature scheme consists of two contributions. First, we mainly use random numbers and bilinear pairings to attain the anonymous property. Secondly, we increase the security and efficiency of our proxy in the design.

## 1. Introduction

Proxy signature schemes can be used in many business applications such as signing important documents when the original signer is not present. For example, an important document needs to be signed by the CEO, but the CEO is out of the office or not immediately available. At this time, the CEO can use the proxy signature scheme to designate the general manager or business executive to sign the document on his or her behalf. The signed document will be valid and can be verified by everyone without the CEO actually signing it. Any proxy signature scheme has to meet the identifiability, undeniability, verifiability, and unforgeability security requirements. It may be necessary to protect the proxy signer's privacy from outsiders or third parties. In 1996, Mambo et al. [1] first proposed the concept of proxy signature. In their proposal, there are three parties: a user also called *original signer*, a *proxy signer* whom is delegated to sign a message on behalf of the original signer, and a *verifier* who verifies whether a signed message is legal or not.

Since Mambo et al.'s 1996 scheme, many proxy signature schemes have been proposed [1–27] (some other schemes though are signature schemes whereas not proxy signatures such as [28–33]). Generally speaking, there are two main categories of proxy signature schemes, the first category is

one-to-one and the other is *one-to-many*. In the former, there is one original signer and one proxy signer, but in the latter, except for the original signer, there are a group of proxy signers. The *one-to-one* schemes are [4, 7, 10, 12, 13, 15–17, 25–27] and the proxy blind signature [2], which is based on a special digital signature scheme first introduced by Chaum [34] in 1983. In the *one-to-many*, there are two subsets, one is the proxy multisignature and the other is the $(t, n)$ threshold proxy signature. In the proxy multisignature [5, 6, 9, 19–22], the original signer has an authorized proxy signer group, each proxy signer has to generate a partial proxy signature. If all partials of signatures are correct, the proxy signature will be generated by summation or multiplication operations of the partial proxy signatures. In the $(t, n)$ threshold proxy signature [3, 11, 18, 23, 24], the original signer can choose the threshold and a proxy signing key is shared by $n$ proxy signers. Any $t$ of proxy signers can cooperatively derive the proxy signing key to sign the message.

In any proxy signature, the following four security properties are required.

*(i) Unforgeability.* Only a designated proxy signer can create a valid proxy signature for the original signer. In other words, nobody can forge a valid proxy signature without the delegation of the original signer.

*(ii) Verifiability.* After checking and verifying the proxy signature, a verifier can be convinced that the received message is signed by the proxy signer authorized by the original signer.

*(iii) Undeniability.* The proxy signer cannot repudiate the signature he produced.

*(iv) Identifiability.* Anyone including the original signer can determine the corresponding proxy signer's identity from the proxy signature. That is, from the proxy signature any verifier can determine the proxy signer's identity.

Although proxy signatures incorporate the above-mentioned security functions, they still face many threats such as man-in-the-middle, replay, frame, and public-key substitute attacks. In frame attacks [23], the malicious original signer can forge a signature after intercepting sent information and the forged signature can be accepted by the verifier. In public-key substitute attacks [24], the attacker can be either the original signer or any proxy signer. By changing their public keys, he can forge a valid proxy signature [11]. This indicates that when designing a proxy signature scheme, care should be taken to avoid these kinds of attacks.

Researchers, Shum and Wei's [26] and Yang, and Peng [10], presented two *one-to-one* anonymous proxy signature (APS) schemes. They point that an APS scheme should possess not only the security features of unforgeability, verifiability, and undeniability, but also the properties of anonymity and anonymity revocation. The anonymity means that only one of the proxy signers can sign the message in the proxy signer group, other proxy signers cannot know who the signer is. And the anonymity revocation indicates that once required, the proxy signer can assure the others that he is the real signer. However, N. Y. Lee and M. F. Lee [27] indicate that Shum and Wei's scheme [26] violates the property of the unforgeability. Yang and Peng [10] therefore proposed a modified one-to-one APS scheme. In 2009, Yu et al. [8] first proposed a *one-to-many* APS scheme. In their scheme, there is a group of proxy signers, but only one proxy signer can anonymously signs the message. By using a group of signers, Yu et al. want to provide privacy and anonymous protection for the real proxy signer. They claim that their scheme is provably secure. However, based on our research by just using some of the transmitted data along with public information, we were able to isolate and identify the proxy signer. More details of the analysis are described in Section 3.2.

The rest of the paper is organized as follows. In Section 2, we present the basic concepts of bilinear pairings and some related mathematical problems. In Section 3, we review and show the weakness of Yu et al.'s scheme. Section 4 shows the proposed scheme, and Section 5 makes comparison of computation efficiency between Yu et al.'s scheme and ours. Finally, a conclusion is given in Section 6.

## 2. Background

In this section, we describe the concept of bilinear pairings which is used as the mathematical basis for this design.

Let $G_1$ be a cyclic additive group of order $q$ generated by a base point $P$ on Elliptic curve and $G_2$ a cyclic multiplicative group with the same order. It is assumed that solving the Elliptic curve discrete logarithm problem (ECDLP) in $G_1$ and discrete logarithm problem (DLP) problem in $G_2$ is difficult. A bilinear map $e$ is defined as $e : G_1 \times G_1 \rightarrow G_2$, which has the following properties:

(1) bilinearity: $e(aP, bQ) = e(P, Q)^{ab}$, where $P, Q \in G_1$ and all $a, b \in Z_q^*$;

(2) nondegeneracy: there exists $P, Q \in G_1$ such that $e(P, Q) \neq 1$; in other words, the map does not send all pairs in $G_1 \times G_1$ to the identity in $G_2$;

(3) computability: there is an efficient algorithm to compute $e(P, Q)$ for all $P, Q \in G_1$.

## 3. Review of Yu et al.'s Scheme

In this section, we review Yu et al.'s APS scheme [8] and demonstrate that the original APS cannot satisfy the anonymous property in Section 3.2.

*3.1. Yu et al.'s APS Scheme.* There are six phases in Yu et al.'s APS scheme: (1) the parameter generation phase, (2) the key generation phase, (3) the delegation signing phase, (4) the delegation verification phase, (5) the APS generation phase, and (6) the APS verification phase. We describe them as follows.

(1) In the parameter generation phase, on input of security parameter k, a system parameter generation algorithm outputs a cyclic additive group $G_1$ of order $q$, a multiplicative group $G_2$ of the same order, a bilinear map $e : G_1 \times G_1 \rightarrow G_2$, and a generator $P$ of $G_1$. This algorithm also outputs two cryptographic hash functions: $H_0 : \{0,1\}^* \times G_1 \rightarrow Z_q^*$ and $H_1 : \{0,1\}^* \rightarrow G_1$.

(2) In the key generation phase as shown in Figure 1, the original signer *Alice* selects $x_o \in Z_q^*$ as her private key and computes her public key as $Y_o = x_o P$. Each proxy signer $u_i \in \mathcal{U}$ randomly selects $x_i \in Z_q^*$ as his/her private key and sets the corresponding public key as $Y_i = x_i P$.

(3) In the delegation signing phase, *Alice* firstly generates a warrant $m_w$ which contains some explicit descriptions about the delegation relation such as the identities of both *Alice* and the proxy signers, the expiration time of the delegation, and the signing power in the warrant. Then, *Alice* randomly picks a number $r \in Z_q^*$ and computes $R = rP$ and $s = r + x_o H_0(m_w, R) \bmod q$. Finally, *Alice* sends $(m_w, R, s)$ to the proxy signers in set $\mathcal{U} = \{u_1, \ldots, u_n\}$.

(4) Upon receiving $(m_w, R, s)$, each proxy signer $u_i$ checks if the equation $sP = R + H_0(m_w, R)Y_o$ holds. If it does not, the delegation will be rejected. Otherwise, it will be accepted and each proxy signer $u_i$ computes his/her proxy secret key as $psk_i = s + x_i H_0(m_w, R) \bmod q$.

<table>
<tr><td></td><td>Original signer Alice</td><td>Proxy signer $u_i$</td></tr>
</table>

Key generation
$x_o \in Z_q^*$ (private key)           $x_i \in Z_q^*$ (private key)

$Y_o = x_o P$ (public key)              $Y_i = x_i P$ (public key)

Delegation signing   $m_w$ (warrant)

$r \in Z_q^*$

$R = rP$

$s = r + x_o H_0(m_w, R) \bmod q$

$\xrightarrow{(m_w, R, s)}$

Delegation
verification

Checks $sP = R + H_0(m_w, R) Y_o$

$psk_i = s + x_i H_0(m_w, R) \bmod q$

FIGURE 1: Key generation, delegation signing, and delegation verification phases of Yu et al.'s scheme.

(5) In the APS generation phase as shown in Figure 2, proxy signer $u_s \in \mathcal{U}$ signs on a message $m$ with his proxy secret key $psk_s$ on behalf of the original signer, Alice, in an anonymous way. $u_s$ first chooses random numbers $r_i \in Z_q^*$, where $i \in \{1, 2, \ldots, n\}$ and $i \neq s$, computes both $\sigma_i = r_i P$ and $\sigma_s = (1/psk_s)(H_1(m\|m_w) - \sum_{i \neq s} r_i(R + H_0(m_w, R)(Y_o + Y_i)))$, and sends $\sigma = (\sigma_1, \sigma_2, \ldots, \sigma_n, m, m_w, R)$ to the verifier.

(6) In the APS verification phase, given public keys $Y_o, Y_1, \ldots, Y_n$ and a received anonymous proxy signature $\sigma$, the verifier can examine the validity of the signature $\sigma$ by checking whether the following expression holds:

$$\prod_{i=1}^{n} e(R + H_0(m_w, R)(Y_o + Y_i), \sigma_i)$$

$$= \prod_{i=1, i \neq s}^{n} e(R + H_0(m_w, R)(Y_o + Y_i), \sigma_i)$$

$$\cdot e(R + H_0(m_w, R)(Y_o + Y_s), \sigma_s)$$

$$= \prod_{i=1, i \neq s}^{n} e(r_i(R + H_0(m_w, R)(Y_o + Y_i)), P)$$

$$\cdot e\left(R + H_0(m_w, R)(Y_o + Y_s), \frac{1}{psk_s}\right.$$

$$\left.\times \left(H_1(m\|m_w) - \sum_{i \neq s} r_i(R + H_0(m_w, R)(Y_o + Y_i))\right)\right)$$

$$= \prod_{i=1, i \neq s}^{n} e(r_i(R + H_0(m_w, R)(Y_o + Y_i)), P)$$

$$\cdot e\left(P, H_1(m\|m_w) - \sum_{i \neq s} r_i(R + H_0(m_w, R)(Y_o + Y_i))\right)$$

$$= e(P, H_1(m\|m_w)). \tag{1}$$

*3.2. Weakness of Yu et al.'s Scheme.* After reviewing Yu et al.'s scheme above, we now explain the violation of the scheme's anonymous property which they emphasized as follows.

Since $R$, $H_0(m_w, R)$, and $(Y_o + Y_s)$ are public, we can obtain $psk_s P$ by deducing $psk_s P = R + H_0(m_w, R)(Y_o + Y_s)$ because

$$psk_s P = (s + x_i H_0(m_w, R))P$$

$$= (r + x_o H_0(m_w, R) + x_i H_0(m_w, R))P$$

$$= (r + (x_o + x_i)H_0(m_w, R))P$$

$$= (rP + ((x_o + x_i)H_0(m_w, R)P))$$

$$= R + H_0(m_w, R)(Y_o + Y_s). \tag{2}$$

Next, we define an inspector **X** to be $e(psk_x P, \sigma_j)$, where $psk_x$ is $u_x$'s secret proxy key, $\sigma_j$ is a specific subsignature in $\sigma$, and $x, j \in \{1, \ldots n\}$. In addition, we define **Y** to be $\prod_{i=1, i \neq x}^{n} e((R + H_0(m_w, R)(Y_o + Y_i)), \sigma_i)$. Then, if there exist some $x$ and $j$ satisfying **X** $\cdot$ **Y** $= e(P, H_1(m\|m_w))$, we can determine that $x$ should be equal to $j$, and $u_j$ is then the right proxy signer. This is because if $u_j$ is the right proxy signer, then the corresponding subsignature $\sigma_j$ must have the factor $1/psk_j$, and therefore only applying the right $psk_x P$, that is, $x = j$, can cancel the factor result in the holing of the end. Otherwise, we continue to examine next possible $x$ or $j$. By

| | Proxy signer $u_s$ | Verifier |
|---|---|---|
| Proxy signature generation | $r_i \in Z_q^*$ | |
| | $\sigma_i = r_i P$ | |
| | $\sigma_s = \frac{1}{\mathrm{psk}_s}((H_1(m \,\|\, m_w)) - \sum_{i \neq s} r_i(R + H_0(m_w, R)(Y_o + Y_i)))$ | |
| | $\sigma = (\sigma_1, \sigma_2, \ldots, \sigma_n, m, m_w, R)$ | |
| | $\xrightarrow{\sigma}$ | Checks |
| | | $\prod_{i=1}^{n} e(R + H_0(m_w, R)(Y_o + Y_i), \sigma_i) = e(P, H_1(m \,\|\, m_w))$ |

Figure 2: APS generation phase and the APS verification phase of Yu et al.'s scheme.

doing this way, we can deduce the right proxy signer at most $n^2$ times.

For more clarity, we take three proxy signers, $u_1$, $u_2$, $u_3$, as an example. Suppose $u_2$ is the real proxy signer, then $\sigma_1 = r_1 P$, $\sigma_2 = (\mathrm{psk}_2)^{-1}(H_1(m\|m_w) - \sum_{i=1,i\neq 1}^{3} r_i(R + H_0(m_w, R)(Y_o + Y_i)))$ and $\sigma_3 = r_3 P$.

If we first try $\sigma_1$ with different $x = 1, 2, 3$, then we have three tries as in the following.

(1.1) When $x = 1$ and thus $\mathbf{X} = e(\mathrm{psk}_1 P, \sigma_1)$, the value $\mathbf{X} \cdot \mathbf{Y}$ should be

$$\begin{aligned} & e(\mathrm{psk}_1 P, \sigma_1) \cdot \prod_{i=1,i\neq 2}^{3} e(r_i(R + H_0(m_w, R)(Y_o + Y_i)), P) \\ & = e(P, \mathrm{psk}_1 \sigma_1) \cdot \prod_{i=1,i\neq 2}^{3} e((R + H_0(m_w, R)(Y_o + Y_i)), r_i P) \\ & = e(P, \mathrm{psk}_1 \cdot r_1 P) \cdot e((R + H_0(m_w, R)(Y_o + Y_1)), \sigma_2) \\ & \quad \cdot e((R + H_0(m_w, R)(Y_o + Y_3)), \sigma_3) \\ & \neq e(P, H_1(m\| m_w)). \end{aligned} \tag{3}$$

(1.2) When $x = 2$ and thus $\mathbf{X} = e(\mathrm{psk}_2 P, \sigma_1)$, the value $\mathbf{X} \cdot \mathbf{Y}$ should be

$$\begin{aligned} & e(\mathrm{psk}_2 P, \sigma_1) \cdot \prod_{i=1,i\neq 2}^{3} e(r_i(R + H_0(m_w, R)(Y_o + Y_i)), P) \\ & = e(P, \mathrm{psk}_2 \sigma_1) \cdot \prod_{i=1,i\neq 2}^{3} e((R + H_0(m_w, R)(Y_o + Y_i)), r_i P) \\ & = e(P, \mathrm{psk}_2 \cdot r_1 P) \cdot e((R + H_0(m_w, R)(Y_o + Y_1)), \sigma_2) \\ & \quad \cdot e((R + H_0(m_w, R)(Y_o + Y_3)), \sigma_3) \\ & \neq e(P, H_1(m\| m_w)). \end{aligned} \tag{4}$$

(1.3) When $x = 3$ and thus $\mathbf{X} = e(\mathrm{psk}_3 P, \sigma_1)$, the value $\mathbf{X} \cdot \mathbf{Y}$ should be

$$\begin{aligned} & e(\mathrm{psk}_3 P, \sigma_1) \cdot \prod_{i=1,i\neq 2}^{3} e(r_i(R + H_0(m_w, R)(Y_o + Y_i)), P) \\ & = e(P, \mathrm{psk}_3 \sigma_1) \cdot \prod_{i=1,i\neq 2}^{3} e((R + H_0(m_w, R)(Y_o + Y_i)), r_i P) \\ & = e(P, \mathrm{psk}_3 \cdot r_1 P) \cdot e((R + H_0(m_w, R)(Y_o + Y_2)), \sigma_2) \\ & \quad \cdot e((R + H_0(m_w, R)(Y_o + Y_1)), \sigma_3) \\ & \neq e(P, H_1(m\| m_w)). \end{aligned} \tag{5}$$

Secondly, if we try $\sigma_2$ with different $x = 1, 2, 3$, then we have three tries as in the following.

(2.1) When $x = 1$ and thus $\mathbf{X} = e(\mathrm{psk}_1 P, \sigma_2)$, the value $\mathbf{X} \cdot \mathbf{Y}$ should be

$$\begin{aligned} & e(\mathrm{psk}_1 P, \sigma_2) \cdot \prod_{i=1,i\neq 2}^{3} e(r_i(R + H_0(m_w, R)(Y_o + Y_i)), P) \\ & = e(P, \mathrm{psk}_1 \sigma_2) \cdot \prod_{i=1,i\neq 2}^{3} e((R + H_0(m_w, R)(Y_o + Y_i)), r_i P) \\ & = e(P, \mathrm{psk}_1 \cdot r_2 P) \cdot e((R + H_0(m_w, R)(Y_o + Y_1)), \sigma_1) \\ & \quad \cdot e((R + H_0(m_w, R)(Y_o + Y_3)), \sigma_3) \\ & \neq e(P, H_1(m\| m_w)). \end{aligned} \tag{6}$$

(2.2) When $x = 2$ and thus $\mathbf{X} = e(\text{psk}_2 P, \sigma_2)$, the value $\mathbf{X} \cdot \mathbf{Y}$ should be

$$e(\text{psk}_2 P, \sigma_2) \cdot \prod_{i=1, i \neq 1}^{3} e(r_i(R + H_0(m_w, R)(Y_o + Y_i)), P)$$

$$= e(P, \text{psk}_2 \sigma_2) \cdot \prod_{i=1, i \neq 1}^{3} e(r_i(R + H_0(m_w, R)(Y_o + Y_i)), P)$$

$$= e\left( P, \text{psk}_2 \cdot \frac{1}{\text{psk}_2}\left( H_1(m\| m_w) - \sum_{i \neq s} r_i(R + H_0(m_w, R)(Y_o + Y_i)) \right) \right)$$

$$\cdot \prod_{i=1, i \neq 1}^{3} e(r_i(R + H_0(m_w, R)(Y_o + Y_i)), P)$$

$$= e\left( P, H_1(m\| m_w) - \sum_{i \neq 1} r_i(R + H_0(m_w, R)(Y_o + Y_i)) \right)$$

$$\cdot \prod_{i=1, i \neq 1}^{3} e(r_i(R + H_0(m_w, R)(Y_o + Y_i)), P)$$

$$= \frac{e(P, H_1(m\| m_w))}{e(P, r_1(R + H_0(m_w, R)(Y_o + Y_1))) \cdot e(P, r_3(R + H_0(m_w, R)(Y_o + Y_3)))}$$

$$\cdot e(P, r_1(R + H_0(m_w, R)(Y_o + Y_1)))e(P, r_3(R + H_0(m_w, R)(Y_o + Y_3)))$$

$$= \frac{e(P, H_1(m\| m_w))}{e(\sigma_1, (R + H_0(m_w, R)(Y_o + Y_1))) \cdot e(\sigma_3, (R + H_0(m_w, R)(Y_o + Y_3)))}$$

$$\cdot e(\sigma_1, (R + H_0(m_w, R)(Y_o + Y_1)))e(\sigma_3, (R + H_0(m_w, R)(Y_o + Y_3)))$$

$$= e(P, H_1(m\| m_w)).$$

(7)

(2.3) When $x = 3$ and thus $\mathbf{X} = e(\text{psk}_3 P, \sigma_2)$, the value $\mathbf{X} \cdot \mathbf{Y}$ should be

$$e(\text{psk}_3 P, \sigma_2) \cdot \prod_{i=1, i \neq 2}^{3} e(r_i(R + H_0(m_w, R)(Y_o + Y_i)), P)$$

$$= e(P, \text{psk}_3 \sigma_2) \cdot \prod_{i=1, i \neq 2}^{3} e((R + H_0(m_w, R)(Y_o + Y_i)), r_i P)$$

$$= e(P, \text{psk}_3 \cdot r_2 P) \cdot e((R + H_0(m_w, R)(Y_o + Y_1)), \sigma_1)$$

$$\cdot e((R + H_0(m_w, R)(Y_o + Y_3)), \sigma_3)$$

$$\neq e(P, H_1(m\| m_w)).$$

(8)

From the above demonstration, for inspector $\mathbf{X} = e(\text{psk}_x P, \sigma_j)$, only when the subscript $x = j = 2$, the result of $\mathbf{X} \cdot \mathbf{Y}$ is $e(P, H_1(m\| m_w))$. Therefore, we determined that $u_2$ is the right proxy signer and the anonymous property that they emphasized is broken.

## 4. Proposed Scheme

In this section, we propose a new *one-to-many* APS scheme to correct the anonymous flaw as discovered in Section 3. Our scheme is the same as theirs in the first two phases. The differences are in the last four phases, the delegation signing, delegation verification, APS generation, and APS verification phase. More details of our APS are shown in Section 4.1. Its correctness is demonstrated in Section 4.2 and the APS requirements are analyzed in Section 4.3. Before describing our protocol, we define some basic notations listed in Table 1.

*4.1. The New Proposed APS Scheme.* In our APS scheme, there also exist an original signer *Alice* and a proxy signer

TABLE 1: The definitions of used notations

| Notations | Definitions |
| --- | --- |
| $G_1$ | A cyclic additive group on an Elliptic Curve with order $q$ generated and a base point $P$ |
| $G_2$ | A cyclic multiplicative group with order $q$ |
| $e$ | A bilinear map which is defined as $e : G_1 \times G_1 \rightarrow G_2$ |
| $\{\mathcal{P}_1, \mathcal{P}_2, \ldots, \mathcal{P}_n\}$ | A proxy signer group |
| $m$ | A message to be signed |
| $m_w$ | A warrant which contains the original signer's and proxy signer's identities, delegation, authorization period, valid period, and so forth |
| $\mathcal{P}_i$ | A proxy signer in the proxy signer group $\{\mathcal{P}_1, \mathcal{P}_2, \ldots, \mathcal{P}_n\}$ |
| $\mathcal{P}_s$ | The real signer in the proxy signer group $\{\mathcal{P}_1, \mathcal{P}_2, \ldots, \mathcal{P}_n\}$ |
| $(x_0, Y_0)$ | The private/public key pair of the original signer |
| $(x_i, Y_i)$ | The private/public key pair of $\mathcal{P}_i$ |
| $\text{psk}_s$ | The proxy secret key computed by $\mathcal{P}_s$ |
| $r_i$ | A random integer in $Z_q{}^*$ |
| $\|$ | A concatenation of two strings |
| $H_0(\cdot)$ | A hash function mapping from $\{0,1\}^* \times G_1$ to $Z_q{}^*$ |
| $H_1(\cdot)$ | A hash function mapping from $\{0,1\}^*$ to $Z_q{}^*$ |
| $H_2(\cdot)$ | A hash function mapping from $\{0,1\}^* \times G_1 \times G_1$ to $Z_q{}^*$ |
| $\sigma_i$ | The random point $(= r_i V)$ constructed by $\mathcal{P}_s$ to stand for the signatures as if they were really made by $\mathcal{P}_i$, where $s \neq i$, correspondingly |
| $\sigma_s$ | The signature generated by $\mathcal{P}_s$, where $s \neq i$ |
| $p\sigma$ sum | $= (\sum_{i(\neq s)=1}^{n} \sigma_i) + \sigma_s$ (the summation of partial proxy signatures) |
| $A, B, C, D, L, U, V, R$ | The points in $G_1$ |

group $\{\mathcal{P}_1, \mathcal{P}_2, \ldots, \mathcal{P}_n\}$, and only one proxy signer in the proxy signers group can sign the message. For more clarity, we show our scheme in detail as follows. The proposed scheme consists of six phases: (1) the parameter generation phase, (2) key generation phase, (3) delegation signing phase, (4) delegation verification phase, (5) APS generation phase, and (6) APS verification phase. Phases (1) and (2) are the same as in Yu et al.'s scheme, which has been delineated in Section 3.1. We omit these phases in the following but show phases (3) and (4) in Figure 3 and phases (5) and (6) in Figure 4.

(3) In the delegation signing phase, as shown in Figure 3, the original signer randomly selects a number $r \in Z_q^*$ and uses $r$ to compute $R = rP$ and $v = r + x_0 H_0(m_w, R)$. Then, the original signer sends $(m_w, R, v)$ to each proxy signer $\mathcal{P}_i \in \{\mathcal{P}_1, \mathcal{P}_2, \ldots, \mathcal{P}_n\}$ with warrant $m_w$, where warrant contains the records of the original signer's and proxy

signer's identities, delegation, authorization period, valid period, and so forth.

(4) In the delegation verification phase, after receiving $(m_w, R, v)$ the proxy signer $\mathcal{P}_i$ first checks whether the equation $vP ? = R + H_0(m_w, R)Y_0$ holds. If it does not, stop the protocol, otherwise, he stores $(m_w, R)$. Second, when signing message $m$, $\mathcal{P}_i$ chooses random numbers $r_i \in Z_q^*$, $i = 1$ to $n$, and $V = vP$ computes $c = H_1(r_1 \| \cdots \| r_n)$, $U = cP$, and the proxy secret key, $\text{psk}_i = r_i^{-1} * x_i^{-1} * H_2(m_w \| m, V, U)$.

(5) In the APS generation phase, as shown in Figure 4, let $\mathcal{P}_s$ be the real proxy signer. He computes $\sigma_i = r_i V$, where $i \in \{1, 2, \ldots, n\}$ and $i \neq s$ and computes $L = c * x_s^{-1} * V$, then sets $Y, \sigma_s, p\sigma$ sum $= \sum_{i=1}^{n} \sigma_i, A, B, C$, and $D$, as $Y = \sum_{i=1}^{n} Y_i$, $\sigma_s = \text{psk}_s * Y = r_s^{-1} * x_s^{-1} * H_2(m_w \| m, V, U)^* Y$, $A = r_s * c * \text{psk}_s P$, $B = r_s \sigma_s$, $C = r_s * p\sigma$ sum, and $D = r_s * c * V$, respectively. Finally, $\mathcal{P}_s$ outputs

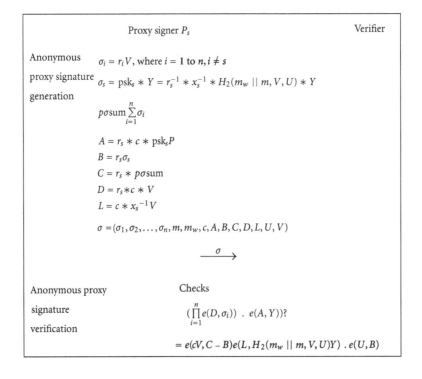

Original signer                     Proxy signer $P_i$

Key generation       $x_o \in Z_q^*$ (private key)             $x_i \in Z_q^*$ (private key)

                   $Y_o = x_o P$ (public key)           $Y_i = x_i P$ (public key)

Delegation signing    $m_w$ (warrant)

                   $r \in Z_q^*$

                   $R = rP$
                   $v = r + x_o H_0(m_w, R)$

$$\xrightarrow{(m_w, R, v)}$$

Delegation verification                    Checks

                   $vP? = R + H_0(m_w, R)Y_o$

                   If it holds, $P_i$ stores $(m_w, R)$.

                   When signing on $m$, he computes
                   $V = vP$
                   $r_i \in Z_q^*, i = 1$ to $n$
                   $c = H_1(r_1 \| \cdots \| r_n)$
                   $U = cP$
                   $\mathrm{psk}_i = r_i^{-1} * x_i^{-1} * H_2(m_w \| m, V, U)$

FIGURE 3: The delegation signing and delegation verification phases of our scheme.

Proxy signer $P_s$                    Verifier

Anonymous     $\sigma_i = r_i V$, where $i = 1$ to $n, i \neq s$

proxy signature   $\sigma_s = \mathrm{psk}_s * Y = r_s^{-1} * x_s^{-1} * H_2(m_w \| m, V, U) * Y$

generation

         $p\sigma\mathrm{sum} \sum\limits_{i=1}^{n} \sigma_i$

         $A = r_s * c * \mathrm{psk}_s P$
         $B = r_s \sigma_s$
         $C = r_s * p\sigma\mathrm{sum}$
         $D = r_s * c * V$
         $L = c * x_s^{-1} V$

         $\sigma = (\sigma_1, \sigma_2, \ldots, \sigma_n, m, m_w, c, A, B, C, D, L, U, V)$

$$\xrightarrow{\sigma}$$

Anonymous proxy         Checks

signature              $(\prod\limits_{i=1}^{n} e(D, \sigma_i)) \cdot e(A, Y))?$

verification

             $= e(cV, C - B)e(L, H_2(m_w \| m, V, U)Y) \cdot e(U, B)$

FIGURE 4: Anonymous proxy signature generation phase and the verification phase of our scheme.

$\sigma = (\sigma_1, \sigma_2, \ldots, \sigma_n, m, m_w, c, A, B, C, D, L, U, V)$ as the anonymous proxy signature and sends $\sigma$ to the verifier.

(6) In APS verification phase, upon receiving the proxy signature the verifier computes $\sum_{i=1}^{n} Y_i = Y$ and checks whether the equation $e(D, \sum_{i=1}^{n} \sigma_i) \cdot e(A, Y)? = e(cV, C-B) \cdot e(L, H_2(m_w \| m, V, U)Y) \cdot e(U, B)$ holds. If it holds, the verifier accepts the signature, otherwise rejects it.

*4.2. Correctness.* In the delegation verification phase, each proxy signer can check whether the equation $vP? = R + H_0(m_w, R)Y_o$ holds as follows.

*Proof (first proof).*

$$vP? = R + H_0(m_w, R)Y_o$$

$$vP = (r + x_o H_0(m_w, R))P$$

$$= rP + x_o H_0(m_w, R)P \qquad (9)$$

$$= R + H_0(m_w, R)Y_o. \qquad \square$$

If it holds, the proxy signer can know that the message is sent from the original signer. Because in the verification equation, he use the original signer's public key $Y_o$ to examine it. If any adversary intercepts the message and modify it, it cannot pass the verification equation.

In the proxy signature verification phase, the following equation gives the correctness of the verification.

*Proof (second proof).*

$$\left( \prod_{i=1}^{n} e(D, \sigma_i) \right) \cdot e(A, Y)?$$

$$= e(cV, C - B) \cdot e(L, H_2(m_w \| m, V, U)Y) \cdot e(U, B)$$

$$\left( \prod_{i=1}^{n} e(D, \sigma_i) \right) \cdot e(A, Y)$$

$$= \left( \prod_{i=1, i \neq s}^{n} e(cr_s V, \sigma_i) \cdot e(cr_s V, \sigma_s) \right) \cdot e(r_s * c * \mathrm{psk}_s P, Y)$$

$$= \prod_{i=1, i \neq s}^{n} e(cr_s V, \sigma_i) \cdot e(cr_s V, r_s^{-1} * x_s^{-1} * H_2(m_w \| m, V, U)$$

$$* Y) \cdot e(cP, r_s \mathrm{psk}_s Y)$$

$$= \prod_{i=1, i \neq s}^{n} e(cr_s V, \sigma_i) \cdot e(cr_s V, r_s^{-1} * x_s^{-1} * H_2(m_w \| m, V, U)$$

$$* Y) \cdot e(cP, r_s \sigma_s)$$

$$= \prod_{i=1, i \neq s}^{n} e(cr_s V, \sigma_i) \cdot e(x_s^{-1} * cV, H_2(m_w \| m, V, U) * Y)$$

$$\cdot e(U, B)$$

$$= \prod_{i=1, i \neq s}^{n} e(cr_s V, \sigma_i) \cdot e(L, H_2(m_w \| m, V, U)Y) \cdot e(U, B)$$

$$= e\left( cr_s V, \sum_{i=1, i \neq s}^{n} \sigma_i \right) \cdot e(L, H_2(m_w \| m, V, U)Y) \cdot e(U, B)$$

$$= e(cr_s V, p\sigma \operatorname{sum} - \sigma_s) \cdot e(L, H_2(m_w \| m, V, U)Y)$$

$$\cdot e(U, B)$$

$$= e(cV, r_s(p\sigma \operatorname{sum} - \sigma_s)) \cdot e(L, H_2(m_w \| m, V, U)Y)$$

$$\cdot e(U, B)$$

$$= e(cV, r_s(p\sigma \operatorname{sum} - \sigma_s)) \cdot e(L, H_2(m_w \| m, V, U)Y)$$

$$\cdot e(U, B)$$

$$= e(cV, C - B) \cdot e(L, H_2(m_w \| m, V, U)Y) \cdot e(U, B). \qquad (10)$$

$\square$

*4.3. Security Analyses.* In this section, we demonstrate that our APS scheme can satisfy the security properties as discussed in Section 1 for (1) verifiability, (2) unforgeability, (3) undeniability, (4) anonymity, and (5) anonymity revocation. Now, we demonstrate why our scheme can satisfy these five security properties as follows.

*(1) Verifiability.* In APS verification phase, after checking and verifying the proxy signature $\sigma$, where $\sigma = (\sigma_1, \sigma_2, \ldots, \sigma_n, m, m_w, c, A, B, C, D, L, U, V)$, the verifier can calculate to check whether the verification equation $(\prod_{i=1}^{n} e(D, \sigma_i)) \cdot e(A, Y)? = e(cV, C - B) \cdot e(L, H_2(m_w \| m, V, U)Y) \cdot e(U, B)$ holds. If it does, the verifier can be convinced that the received message is signed by one of the proxy signer members authorized by the original signer because $Y(= \sum_{i=1}^{n} Y_i)$ and $V(= vP = R + H_0(m_w, R)Y_o)$ are used in the verification equation.

*(2) Unforgeability.* It means that any entity (other than the real proxy signer $\mathcal{P}_s$), including the original signer, cannot generate a valid proxy signature. Only an authorized proxy signer $\mathcal{P}_s$ can create a valid proxy signature $\sigma$. If any attacker wants to forge a proxy signature, he must be authorized by the original signer signing on a warrant $m_w$ and use the proxy signer's proxy secret key $\mathrm{psk}_s$ to compute $\sigma_s$. However, this is impossible since the identity of the attacker wasn not in $m_w$ signed by the original signer. Not to mention, he does not know $\mathrm{psk}_s$. Under this situation, even if he want to (1) fake the proxy signer key as $\mathrm{psk}_s'$, (2) change value $c$ to $c'$, or (3) randomly select $r_s' \in Z_q^*$, trying to counterfeit the proxy

TABLE 2: Comparison of computational costs of our scheme and Yu et al.'s scheme.

| | Key generation | Generation and verification of psk | APS generation | APS verification |
|---|---|---|---|---|
| Yu et al.'s scheme | Same | $(2n+1)\text{Pm} + n\text{Pa}$ | $(3n-2)\text{Pm} + (n+1)\text{Pa}$ | $(n+1)e + n\text{Pm} + 2n\text{Pa}$ |
| Our scheme | Same | $(2n+1)\text{Pm} + n\text{Pa}$ | $(n+6)\text{Pm} + (2n-1)\text{Pa}$ | $5e + 2\text{Pm} + (2n-1)\text{Pa}$ |

signature, we demonstrate that his attempt deems to fail. We demonstrate the reasons for the failures of these three cases in the following.

*Case 1.* If an attacker does not know the proxy secret key $\text{psk}_s$, he cannot generate valid $\sigma_s(= \text{psk}_s * Y)$, $p\sigma$ sum$(= \sum_{i=1}^{n} \sigma_i)$, $A(= r_s * c * \text{psk}_s P)$, $B(= r_s \sigma_s)$, and $C(= r_s * p\sigma \text{ sum})$. Even if he uses a random $\text{psk}'_s$ to sign the message, since $\text{psk}_s = r_s^{-1} * x_s^{-1} * H_2(m_w \| m, V, U)$, he cannot evaluate the right value $x_s^{-1}$ for computing $L$ to be successfully verified in the verification equation.

*Case 2.* Because $c$ is changed to $c'$, this results in at least one of the random numbers $r_i$ should also be modified. Without loss of generality, we let $r_i = r_1 \neq r_s$. Accordingly, all the parameters $U(= cP)$, $\text{psk}_s(= r_s^{-1} * x_s^{-1} * H_2(m_w \| m, V, U))$, $\sigma_s(= \text{psk}_s * Y)$, $p\sigma$ sum$(= \sum_{i=1}^{n} \sigma_i)$, $A(= r_s * c * \text{psk}_s P)$, $B(= r_s \sigma_s)$, $C(= r_s * p\sigma \text{ sum})$, $D(= r_s * c * V)$, and $L(= c * x_s^{-1} * V)$ are changed as well. That is $\sigma' = (\sigma'_1, \sigma_2, \dots, \sigma'_s, \sigma_{s+1}, \dots, \sigma_n, m, m_w, c', A', B', C', D', L', U', V)$. Apparently, the verification equation $(\prod_{i=1}^{n} e(D, \sigma_i)) \cdot e(A, Y) = e(cV, C - B) \cdot e(L, H_2(m_w \| m, V, U)Y) \cdot e(U, B)$ cannot hold. Below, we only show the inequality of portion of the verification equation $e(A', Y) = e(U', B')$:

$$
\begin{aligned}
e(A', Y) &= e(r'_s * c' * \text{psk}'_s P, Y) \\
&= e(c'P, r'_s \text{psk}'_s Y) \\
&= e(c'P, r'_s \sigma_s) \\
&\neq e(U, B).
\end{aligned}
\tag{11}
$$

*Case 3.* In this case, if any attacker randomly selects $r'_s \in Z_q^*$, trying to generate the valid proxy signature $\sigma'$. Accordingly, the parameters $U(= cP)$, $\text{psk}_s(= r_s^{-1} * x_s^{-1} * H_2(m_w \| m, V, U))$, $\sigma_s(= r_s^{-1} * x_s^{-1} * H_2(m_w \| m, V, U) * Y)$, $p\sigma$ sum$(= \sum_{i=1}^{n} \sigma_i)$, $A(= r_s * c * \text{psk}_s P)$, $B(= r_s \sigma_s)$, $C(= r_s * p\sigma \text{ sum})$, $D(= r_s * c * V)$, and $L(= c * x_s^{-1} * V)$ are all changed. Therefore, the signature now becomes $\sigma' = (\sigma'_1, \sigma'_2, \dots, \sigma'_s, \sigma_{s+1}, \dots, \sigma'_n, m, m_w, c', A', B', C', D', L', U', V)$. As in Case 1, the verifier checks whether $e(A', Y) = e(U', B')$ holds or not. Apparently, it cannot pass the verification.

*(3) Undeniability.* As in Section 4.2 proof (second proof), the verifier uses the verification equation: $(\prod_{i=1}^{n} e(D, \sigma_i)) \cdot e(A, Y) = e(cV, C - B) \cdot e(L, H_2(m_w \| m, V, U)Y) \cdot e(U, B)$ to check whether the proxy signature comes from one of the members in the proxy signer group. Since the equation $V(= vP = R + H_0(m_w, R)Y_o)$ includes the original signer's public key $Y_o$ and $Y = \sum_{i=1}^{n} Y_i$, it means the original signer and the

proxy signer group cannot repudiate their participations in the signature generation.

*(4) Anonymity.* In the APS generation phase, all the parameters $A$, $B$, $C$, $D$, and $L$ have to be multiplied by $r_s \in Z_q^*$ to make the proxy signature $\sigma$ anonymous. If any attacker wants to know who is the real proxy signer, he must know the value $r_s$ to use $r_s^{-1}$ for unrandomizing all parameters to get $A'(= c' * \text{psk}'_s P)$, $B(= \sigma'_s)$, $C'(= p\sigma \text{ sum}')$, $D'(= c' * V)$, and $\sigma'_s(= x_s^{-1} * H_2(m_w \| m, V, U) * Y)$. But now $\sigma_i = r_i V, i \neq s$, even the attacker knows $r_s$, without the knowledge of $r_i$ and $x_s$, he cannot know who the real signer is. Not to mention, he cannot know the value of $r_s$. It means that anyone cannot know who signs the signature. Hence, the anonymity holds.

*(5) Anonymity Revocation.* In our scheme, only the proxy signer knows $r_s^{-1}$ and the secret $x_s^{-1}$. He can convince the others that he is the real proxy signer by just showing them $r_s^{-1}$ and the holdness of the equation $r_s * x_s * \sigma_s = H_2(m_w \| m, V, U) * Y$ without revealing $x_s$ in polynomial time.

## 5. Comparisons

In this section, we compare the computational cost between Yu et al.'s APS scheme and ours and summarize the result in Table 2. We denote by $e$ the pairing operation, $Pm$ and $Pa$ the point multiplication and point addition on $G_1$ respectively, and by $n$ the number of proxy signers. In Yu et al.'s APS scheme, the generation and verification of psk should be $(2n+1)\text{Pm} + n\text{Pa}$ instead of $(n+1)\text{Pm}$ operations. Because in Yu et al.'s scheme, the generation and verification of psk are $R = rP$ and $sP = R + H_0(m_w, R)Y_0$, the $sP$ should be computed by $n$ proxy signers. The APS verification should be $(n+1)e + n\text{Pm} + 2n\text{Pa}$ rather than the original $(n+1)e + n\text{Pm} + (n+1)\text{Pa}$ as listed in the table of [8]. From Table 2, we can see that our scheme is more efficient than Yu et al.'s protocol.

## 6. Conclusions

In 2009, Yu et al. first proposed a *one-to-many* APS scheme attempting to protect the proxy signer's privacy while maintaining secrecy to outsiders. However, after analyses, we determined that Yu et al.'s original protocol could not satisfy the anonymous property. Accordingly, we proposed a novel *one-to-many* APS scheme to reach the goal. Our construction makes use of a random number $r_s$, one-way hash function and bilinear pairings to make the proxy signature anonymous. After comparisons, we conclude that our new protocol is a significant improvement against attackers trying to reveal the identity of the real signer and is more efficient in computational cost as demonstrated in Table 2.

# References

[1] M. Mambo, K. Usuda, and E. Okamoto, "Proxy signature: delegation of the power to sign messages," *IEICE—Transactions on Fundamentals of Electronics*, vol. E79-A, no. 9, pp. 1338–1354, 1996.

[2] R. Lu, Z. Cao, and Y. Zhou, "Proxy blind multi-signature scheme without a secure channel," *Applied Mathematics and Computation*, vol. 164, no. 1, pp. 179–187, 2005.

[3] H. F. Huang and C. C. Chang, "A novel efficient (t, n) threshold proxy signature scheme," *Information Sciences*, vol. 176, no. 10, pp. 1338–1349, 2006.

[4] B. Kang, C. Boyd, and E. Dawson, "Identity-based strong designated verifier signature schemes: attacks and new construction," *Computers and Electrical Engineering*, vol. 35, no. 1, pp. 49–53, 2009.

[5] K. L. Wu, J. Zou, X. H. Wei, and F. Y. Liu, "Proxy group signature: a new anonymous proxy signature scheme," in *Proceedings of the 7th International Conference on Machine Learning and Cybernetics (ICMLC'08)*, pp. 1369–1373, Kunming, China, July 2008.

[6] Z. Shao, "Improvement of identity-based proxy multi-signature scheme," *The Journal of Systems and Software*, vol. 82, no. 5, pp. 794–800, 2009.

[7] Z. H. Liu, Y. P. Hu, X. S. Zhang, and H. Ma, "Secure proxy signature scheme with fast revocation in the standard model," *Journal of China Universities of Posts and Telecommunications*, vol. 16, no. 4, pp. 116–124, 2009.

[8] Y. Yu, C. Xu, X. Huang, and Y. Mu, "An efficient anonymous proxy signature scheme with provable security," *Computer Standards and Interfaces*, vol. 31, no. 2, pp. 348–353, 2009.

[9] F. Cao and Z. Cao, "A secure identity-based proxy multi-signature scheme," *Information Sciences*, vol. 179, no. 3, pp. 292–302, 2009.

[10] A. Yang and W. P. Peng, "A modified anonymous proxy signature with a trusted party," in *Proceedings of the 1st International Workshop on Education Technology and Computer Science (ETCS'09)*, pp. 233–236, Wuhan, China, March 2009.

[11] J. H. Hu and J. Zhang, "Cryptanalysis and improvement of a threshold proxy signature scheme," *Computer Standards and Interfaces*, vol. 31, no. 1, pp. 169–173, 2009.

[12] Y. Yu, C. X. Xu, X. S. Zhang, and Y. J. Liao, "Designated verifier proxy signature scheme without random oracles," *Computers and Mathematics with Applications*, vol. 57, no. 8, pp. 1352–1364, 2009.

[13] J. H. Zhang, C. L. Liu, and Y. I. Yang, "An efficient secure proxy verifiably encrypted signature scheme," *Journal of Network and Computer Applications*, vol. 33, no. 1, pp. 29–34, 2010.

[14] B. D. Wei, F. G. Zhang, and X. F. Chen, "ID-based ring proxy signatures," in *Proceedings of the IEEE International Symposium on Information Theory (ISIT'07)*, pp. 1031–1035, Nice, France, June 2007.

[15] T. S. Wu and H. Y. Lin, "Efficient self-certified proxy CAE scheme and its variants," *The Journal of Systems and Software*, vol. 82, no. 6, pp. 974–980, 2009.

[16] S. Lal and V. Verma, "Identity based Bi-designated verifier proxy signature schemes," Cryptography Eprint Archive Report 394, 2008.

[17] S. Lal and V. Verma, "Identity based strong designated verifier proxy signature schemes," Cryptography Eprint Archive Report 394, 2006.

[18] C. Y. Yang, S. F. Tzeng, and M. S. Hwang, "On the efficiency of nonrepudiable threshold proxy signature scheme with known signers," *The Journal of Systems and Software*, vol. 73, no. 3, pp. 507–514, 2004.

[19] H. Xiong, J. Hu, Z. Chen, and F. Li, "On the security of an identity based multi-proxy signature scheme," *Computers and Electrical Engineering*, vol. 37, no. 2, pp. 129–135, 2011.

[20] Y. Sun, C. Xu, Y. Yu, and Y. Mu, "Strongly unforgeable proxy signature scheme secure in the standard model," *The Journal of Systems and Software*, vol. 84, no. 9, pp. 1471–1479, 2011.

[21] Y. Sun, C. Xu, Y. Yu, and B. Yang, "Improvement of a proxy multi-signature scheme without random oracles," *Computer Communications*, vol. 34, no. 3, pp. 257–263, 2011.

[22] Z. Liu, Y. Hu, X. Zhang, and H. Ma, "Provably secure multi-proxy signature scheme with revocation in the standard model," *Computer Communications*, vol. 34, no. 3, pp. 494–501, 2011.

[23] H. Bao, Z. Cao, and S. Wang, "Improvement on Tzeng et al.'s nonrepudiable threshold multi-proxy multi-signature scheme with shared verification," *Applied Mathematics and Computation*, vol. 169, no. 2, pp. 1419–1430, 2005.

[24] J. G. Li and Z. F. Cao, "Improvement of a threshold proxy signature scheme," *Computer Research and Development*, vol. 39, no. 11, pp. 1513–1518, 2002.

[25] Y. Yu, Y. Mu, W. Susilo, Y. Sun, and Y. Ji, "Provably secure proxy signature scheme from factorization," *Mathematical and Computer Modelling*, vol. 55, no. 3-4, pp. 1160–1168, 2012.

[26] K. Shum and V. K. Wei, "A strong proxy signature scheme with proxy signer privacy protection," in *Proceedings of the 11th IEEE International Workshops on Enabling Technologies: Infrastructure for Collaborative Enterprises (WETICE'02)*, pp. 55–56, Pittsburgh, Pa, USA, 2002.

[27] N. Y. Lee and M. F. Lee, "The security of a strong proxy signature scheme with proxy signer privacy protection," *Applied Mathematics and Computation*, vol. 161, no. 3, pp. 807–812, 2005.

[28] S. Saeednia, "An identity-based society oriented signature scheme with anonymous signers," *Information Processing Letters*, vol. 83, no. 6, pp. 295–299, 2002.

[29] C. L. Hsu, T. S. Wu, and T. C. Wu, "Group-oriented signature scheme with distinguished signing authorities," *Future Generation Computer Systems*, vol. 20, no. 5, pp. 865–873, 2004.

[30] C. Y. Lin, T. C. Wu, F. Zhang, and J. J. Hwang, "New identity-based society oriented signature schemes from pairings on elliptic curves," *Applied Mathematics and Computation*, vol. 160, no. 1, pp. 245–260, 2005.

[31] Z. Shao, "Certificate-based verifiably encrypted signatures from pairings," *Information Sciences*, vol. 178, no. 10, pp. 2360–2373, 2008.

[32] J. Zhang and J. Mao, "A novel ID-based designated verifier signature scheme," *Information Sciences*, vol. 178, no. 3, pp. 766–773, 2008.

[33] Y. F. Chung, Z. Y. Wu, and T. S. Chen, "Ring signature scheme for ECC-based anonymous signcryption," *Computer Standards and Interfaces*, vol. 31, no. 4, pp. 669–674, 2009.

[34] D. Chaum, "Blind signatures for untraceable payments," in *Advances in Cryptology: Proceedings of CRYPTO '82*, pp. 199–203, Springer, New York, NY, USA, 1983.

# 14

# Reversible Data Hiding Using Two Marked Images Based on Adaptive Coefficient-Shifting Algorithm

**Ching-Yu Yang**

*Deptartment of Computer Science and Information Engineering, National Penghu University of Science and Technology, No. 300, Liu-Ho Road, Magong 880, Taiwan*

Correspondence should be addressed to Ching-Yu Yang, chingyu@npu.edu.tw

Academic Editor: Dimitrios Tzovaras

This paper proposes a novel form of reversible data hiding using two marked images by employing the adaptive coefficient-shifting (ACS) algorithm. The proposed ACS algorithm consists of three parts: the minimum-preserved scheme, the minimum-preserved with squeezing scheme, and the base-value embedding scheme. More specifically, each input block of a host image can be encoded to two stego-blocks according to three predetermined rules by the above three schemes. Simulations validate that the proposed method not only completely recovers the host medium but also losslessly extracts the hidden message. The proposed method can handle various kinds of images without any occurrence of overflow/underflow. Moreover, the payload and peak signal-to-noise ratio (PSNR) performance of the proposed method is superior to that of the conventional invertible data hiding schemes. Furthermore, the number of shadows required by the proposed method is less than that required by the approaches which are based upon secret image sharing with reversible steganography.

## 1. Introduction

Due to ubiquitous broadband services and high-speed networks provided by Internet service providers (ISPs), along with mass production of high-capacity and low-cost multimedia devices, individuals and organizations can easily share their information on the Internet. Moreover, thanks to the portability and mobility provided by such wireless communications as intelligent mobile systems, wireless fidelity (Wi-Fi), and worldwide interoperability microaccess (WiMax), people can exchange/retrieve resources anywhere and anytime. Preventing data from being eavesdropped, tampered with, and falsified during transmission has become an important goal. In addition to the use of cryptographic systems, one can use data hiding to achieve this result. Primary applications of data hiding can be found in proof of ownership, content authentication, copyright protection, and covert communications. In general, data hiding can be divided into two categories: digital watermarking and steganography [1, 2]. In digital watermarking, the embedded message (or watermark) is often related to the medium and

conveys additional information about the medium. Robust performance is a key feature of the watermarking schemes [3–5]. In steganography, the hidden message often has nothing to do with the host media; however, both hiding capacity and perceived quality are the two areas of concern pursued by the authors [6–8]. One of the major issues of the steganographic approach is that the marked images are susceptible to manipulation. In this scenario, the embedded message cannot be extracted if even a slight alteration is imposed on the marked images. Note that the two above mentioned data hiding techniques are irreversible. Since host media such as medical and military images, geographic systems, and satellite resources can be valuable or even priceless, it is undesirable that the host media be at all damaged after data extraction. Recently, several researchers [9–15] have presented lossless data hiding in an effort to address this issue.

Tian [9] used a difference expansion (DE) technique to derive a high-capacity and low-distortion form of reversible watermarking. An image was first divided into pairs of pixels. A secret message was then embedded into the difference of the pixels in each of the pairs that were not expected to cause

TABLE 1: Three rules of data embedment for each host block.

| Input block | Output (two) blocks | | |
| --- | --- | --- | --- |
| | Rule 1* (BV < $\tau$/3) | Rule 2$^+$ ($\tau$/3 ≤ BV ≤ $\tau$) | Rule 3$^\dagger$ (BV > $\tau$) |
| H | S1-A | S1-A | S1-C |
| | S2-A | S2-B | S2-C |

* Both S1 and S2 were introduced by embedding data bits into H via the minimum-preserved scheme (A).
$^+$ S1 was introduced by embedding a secret message into H via the minimum-preserved scheme, and S2 was introduced by the BV embedding scheme (B).
$^\dagger$ Both S1 and S2 were introduced by embedding data bits into H via the minimum-preserved with squeezing scheme (C).

an overflow or an underflow. For a single-layer embedding, the payload size of the technique was less than 0.5 bits per pixel (bpp). Alattar [10] extended Tian's algorithm using a DE of vectors, instead of pairs, to improve the performance of the algorithm. In a single pass, Alattar's algorithm can embed several bits in every vector. In addition to grayscale images, the algorithm can effectively be applied to color systems. Lin et al. [11] proposed a multilayer scheme for reversible data hiding based on the modification of the difference histogram. By combining the peak point of a difference image with a multilevel hiding strategy, the scheme maintained high capacity while keeping distortion low. In the fifteenth-level embedding, the optimal payload surpassed $5 \times 10^5$ bits with a peak signal-to-noise ratio (PSNR) value of 25.39 dB. To obtain a reversible watermarking technique, Zeng et al. [12] used adjacent pixel difference and multilayer embedding techniques on a scan path. Specifically, they employed nine predetermined scan paths to dig out space for hiding bits. The multilayer embedding technique did increase the hiding capacity. To improve the performance of the conventional difference expansion methods, Wu et al. [13] presented a high-capacity reversible data hiding scheme based on the JPEG-LS predictive technique and the multiple-base notational system. In using the JPEG-LS predictive technique, the distortion of the marked images can be significantly reduced. Moreover, the multiple-base notational system can effectively increase the hiding storage capacity. Simulations indicate that their method can provide a high embedding capacity while preserving the quality of the perceived results. Yang and Tsai [14] suggested a reversible (multilevel) data hiding method based upon an interleaving prediction. All predictive values were transformed into a histogram to generate high peak values and improve the hiding capacity. For each pixel, the difference in value between the original image and the marked one remained within ±1. This guaranteed that the PSNR of the marked image was around 48 dB. Moreover, in the twelfth-level embedding, the optimal payload surpassed $3.5 \times 10^5$ bits with a PSNR value of 29.26 dB. Yang and Hu [15] proposed a lossless data hiding method based on the minimum/maximum preserved with overflow/underflow avoidance (MMPOUA) algorithm. First, the MMPOUA algorithm kept the minimum (or maximum) pixel of a host block unchanged. A difference block was introduced by subtracting the pixels remaining in the block from the minimum (or maximum) one. Following pixel adjustment, data bits were embedded in the difference blocks. Simulations showed that the MMPOUA algorithm not only generated good hiding capacity but also high perceived quality, especially at a moderate rate of embedding.

To enlarge the hiding storage, the idea of a secret sharing scheme, namely, the $(t, n)$ threshold scheme invented by Shamir [16], was employed and extended to image hiding and authentication [17–23]. Moreover, to fully recover the host image and losslessly extract the hidden message, researchers [24, 25] presented reversible secret image sharing with steganography. However, a $(t, n)$ threshold of secret image sharing with steganography often requires $t \leq n$ and $n \geq 3$. As result, a large size of storage is an inevitable requirement.

In this paper, we present the adaptive coefficient-shifting (ACS) algorithm to losslessly embed a secret message into a host image. The ACS algorithm requires less number of shadows than the techniques based upon reversible secret image sharing with steganography. In addition, both the payload and the PSNR for the ACS algorithm are far larger than that of the existing invertible data hiding schemes. The rest of the paper is organized as follows. Section 2 describes the ACS algorithm, including the minimum-preserved scheme, the minimum-preserved with squeezing scheme, the base-value (BV) embedding scheme, and the prevention of overflow/underflow. Section 3 presents the simulation results and also includes performance comparisons. Section 4 offers the conclusions.

## 2. Proposed AdaptiveCoefficient-Shifting (ACS) Algorithm

The proposed ACS algorithm consists of three parts: the minimum-preserved scheme, the minimum-preserved with squeezing scheme, and the base-value embedding scheme. Namely, each input (host) block can be encoded to two stego-blocks according to the three predetermined rules listed in Table 1. For example, the two blocks stego-block 1 (S1) and stego-block 2 (S2) can be generated by embedding data bits into a host block (H) via the minimum-preserved scheme, when the BV of the block is less than $\tau$/3. The term $\tau$ is a control parameter. The details of the ACS algorithm are specified in the following subsections. In addition, the BV of the block will be defined later in Section 2.3.

*2.1. The Minimum-Preserved Scheme.* Table 1 indicates that both S1 and S2 can be generated by the minimum-preserved scheme when the BV of the host block is less than $\tau$/3. In addition, a stego-block S1 can be generated by the minimum-preserved scheme if the BV of the host block satisfies $\tau$/3 ≤ BV ≤ $\tau$. The details of the minimum-preserved scheme are described in the following sections.

*2.1.1. Bit Embedding.* Let $P = \{p_{ij}\}_{i=0}^{n \times n - 1}$ be the $j$th non-overlapping block of size $n \times n$ that is divided from an input image. A difference block $\{\hat{p}_{ij}\}_{i=0}^{n \times n - 1}$ can be obtained by

$$\left\{\hat{p}_{ij}\right\}_{i=0}^{n \times n - 1} = \left\{p_{ij}\right\}_{i=0}^{n \times n - 1} - m_j, \tag{1}$$

where $m_j = \text{Min}\{p_{ij}\}_{i=0}^{n \times n - 1}$ indicates the minimum pixel value of the $j$th block. To maintain low levels of distortion, an isolation process can be subsequently conducted to $\hat{p}_{ij}$ to obtain a new value $\widetilde{p}_{ij}$ according to the following criteria:

$$\widetilde{p}_{ij} = \hat{p}_{ij} + \left(2^k - 1\right)\beta \quad \text{if } \hat{p}_{ij} \geq \beta. \tag{2}$$

The term $\beta$ is a control parameter and $k$ is an integer. Namely, no data bits would be carried by the isolated coefficients. After adjustment, data bits are ready to be embedded into $\hat{p}_{ij}$ with $0 \leq \hat{p}_{ij} < \beta$, by multiplying $\hat{p}_{ij}$ by $2^k$ to obtain $\widetilde{p}_{ij}$ and adding an input data to $\widetilde{p}_{ij}$. Finally, a stego-block is formed by adding $m_j$ to $\widetilde{p}_{ij}$ and $\widetilde{p}_{ij}$, respectively.

*2.1.2. Bit Extraction.* Let $Q = \{q_{ij}\}_{i=0}^{n \times n - 1}$ be the $j$th hidden block of the stego-image and $m_j = \text{Min}\{q_{ij}\}_{i=0}^{n \times n - 1}$ the minimum pixel value of the block. The coefficients of the $j$th difference block $\{\hat{q}_{ij}\}_{i=0}^{n \times n - 1}$ are acquired using $\{\hat{q}_{ij}\}_{i=0}^{n \times n - 1} = \{q_{ij}\}_{i=0}^{n \times n - 1} - m_j$. Then, data bits can be extracted from a difference block. If $0 \leq \hat{q}_{ij} < 2^k\beta$, then the data bits are obtained by applying modulo-$2^k$ operation. Subsequently, the pixels $\hat{q}_{ij}$ which hid the data bit can be restored by computing $\hat{q}_{ij} = \lfloor \hat{q}_{ij}/2^k \rfloor$. The pixels $\hat{q}_{ij}$ which satisfy $\hat{q}_{ij} \geq 2^k\beta$ were subtracted from $(2^k - 1)\beta$ in order to recover the pixels which contained no data bits. Notice that $\lfloor x \rfloor$ is the floor function. Finally, a host block can be restored by adding $m_j$ to all the coefficients except the minimum pixel of the difference block.

*2.2. The Minimum-Preserved with Squeezing Scheme.* To provide even further capacity, the minimum-preserved with squeezing scheme can be used to embed data bits into the blocks classified by Rule 3 of Table 1. A major distinction between the minimum-preserved scheme and the minimum-preserved with squeezing scheme is that the latter scheme employs a squeezing technique which can effectively dig out extra hiding space. The minimum-preserved with squeezing scheme is summarized in the following subsections.

*2.2.1. Bit Embedding and Extraction.* As a difference block was obtained by $\{\hat{p}_{ij}\}_{i=0}^{n \times n - 1} = \{p_{ij}\}_{i=0}^{n \times n - 1} - m_j$, the squeezing process adjusted $\hat{p}_{ij}$ to a new value $\widetilde{p}_{ij} = \hat{p}_{ij} - \gamma$ if $\hat{p}_{ij} > \gamma$, where $\gamma$ is a control parameter. Note that a bitmap was used here to flag whether or not a coefficient of the block had undergone adjustment. To help the decoder to later extract the data bits, overhead information can be losslessly compressed and sent by an out-of-band transmission to the receiver. After the squeezing process, the isolation process and bit embedding mentioned in Section 2.1.1 can be sequentially performed on the difference block.

The bit extraction of the minimum-preserved with squeezing scheme that uses the bitmap as a look-up table is similar to that of the minimum-preserved scheme (see Section 2.1.2). After bit extraction, to restore the original difference coefficients which had undergone adjustment, the term $\gamma$ has to be added to the temporary difference block if the corresponding flag in the bitmap was set at 1. Subsequently, the original pixels can be recovered by adding $m_j$ to all the coefficients except the minimum pixel of the difference block.

*2.2.2. Overhead Information Analysis.* The number of bits for the bitmap is $s \times n^2$ with $s$ denoting the occurrence of the blocks encoded by the minimum-preserved with squeezing scheme. The overhead information can be significantly reduced if $(s/\lfloor M/n \rfloor \times \lfloor N/n \rfloor) \times 100\% \leq 40\%$, where the image size is $M \times N$. This can be achieved by adjusting the value of $\tau$ during data embedding.

*2.3. BV Embedding Scheme.* According to Rule 2 of Table 1, the minimum-preserved scheme and the BV embedding scheme can be used to generate stego-blocks 1 and 2, respectively, when the BV of the host block satisfies $\tau/3 \leq \text{BV} \leq \tau$. Let $b_j$ be the BV of the $j$th block. The term $b_j$ is defined by

$$b_j = C_{\max} - C_{\min} + 1, \tag{3}$$

where $C_{\min} = \text{Min}\{p_{ij}\}_{i=0}^{n \times n - 1}$ and $C_{\max} = \text{Max}\{p_{ij}\}_{i=0}^{n \times n - 1}$ represent the minimum and maximum pixel value of the block. A difference block $\{\hat{p}_{ij}\}_{i=0}^{n \times n - 3}$ can be obtained by

$$\left\{\hat{p}_{ij}\right\}_{i=0}^{n \times n - 3} = \left\{p_{ij}\right\}_{i=0}^{n \times n - 3} - C_{\min}. \tag{4}$$

Note that the minimum and the maximum pixel values of the block remain intact. The main idea of the BV embedding scheme is the addition of the difference block $\{\hat{p}_{ij}\}_{i=0}^{n \times n - 3}$ to an input bit stream. More specifically, let the binary bit stream with the length of $L$ to be embedded into $\{\hat{p}_{ij}\}_{i=0}^{n \times n - 3}$ be $B = \{\phi_i\}_{i=0}^{L-1} = \sum_{i=0}^{L-1} \phi_i 2^i$. Transform $B$ into $B = \sum_{i=0}^{n^2-3} \eta_i b_j^i = (\eta_{n^2-3}, \ldots, \eta_1, \eta_0)_{b_j}$ with BV of $b_j$. The resulting $j$th stego-block $\{\widetilde{p}_{ij}\}_{i=0}^{n^2-3}$ is obtained by

$$\left\{\widetilde{p}_{ij}\right\}_{i=0}^{n^2-3} = \left\{\hat{p}_{ij} + \eta_i + C_{\min}\right\}_{i=0}^{n^2-3}. \tag{5}$$

Notice that the locations of both the minimum and the maximum pixels must be adjusted to the top-left of the block before the addition of data ($\eta_i$) and restored to their original locations after the addition of the minimum pixel ($C_{\min}$).

At the receiver, instead of retrieving the BV from the stego-block 2, we compute the BV $b_j' = D_{\max} - D_{\min} + 1$, where $D_{\max}$ and $D_{\min}$ represent the maximum and minimum pixel values of the host block. These values have been previously restored by the minimum-preserved scheme from the stego-block 1. Let $Q = \{q_{ij}\}_{i=0}^{n \times n - 1}$ be the $j$th hidden block which is derived from stego-image 2. The difference pixels of the $j$th block can be acquired using

$$\left\{\hat{q}_{ij}\right\}_{i=0}^{n \times n - 3} = \left\{q_{ij}\right\}_{i=0}^{n \times n - 3} - D_{\min}. \tag{6}$$

| 115 | 115 | 118 |
|---|---|---|
| 115 | 115 | 118 |
| 115 | 115 | 118 |

(a)

| 115 | 0 | 118 |
|---|---|---|
| 0 | 0 | 3 |
| 0 | 0 | 3 |

(b)

| 115 | 118 | 0 |
|---|---|---|
| 0 | 0 | 3 |
| 0 | 0 | 3 |

(c)

| 115 | 118 | 2 |
|---|---|---|
| 3 | 0 | 4 |
| 3 | 0 | 4 |

(d)

| 115 | 118 | 117 |
|---|---|---|
| 118 | 115 | 119 |
| 118 | 115 | 119 |

(e)

| 115 | 117 | 118 |
|---|---|---|
| 118 | 115 | 119 |
| 118 | 115 | 119 |

(f)

FIGURE 1: Example of data embedment with an input data digits of $(103\ 103\ 2)_4$. (a) A host block, (b) a difference block; (c) adjust the maximum pixel value (118) to the top-left of the block; (d) add each data digit to the coefficients of the block in reverse order, (e) a hidden block, and (f) the resultant stego-block 2.

| 115 | 117 | 118 |
|---|---|---|
| 118 | 115 | 119 |
| 118 | 115 | 119 |

(a)

| 115 | 118 | 117 |
|---|---|---|
| 118 | 11 | 119 |
| 118 | 11 | 119 |

(b)

| 115 | 118 | 2 |
|---|---|---|
| 3 | 0 | 4 |
| 3 | 0 | 4 |

(c)

| 115 | 115 | 118 |
|---|---|---|
| 115 | 115 | 118 |
| 115 | 115 | 118 |

(d)

| 115 | 0 | 118 |
|---|---|---|
| 0 | 0 | 3 |
| 0 | 0 | 3 |

(e)

| 115 | 118 | 0 |
|---|---|---|
| 0 | 0 | 3 |
| 0 | 0 | 3 |

(f)

FIGURE 2: Example of data extraction. (a) The stego-block 2, (b) after the adjustment of the maximum pixel value, (c) the difference block, (d) the host block restored from the stego-block 1, (e) the difference block of (d), and (f) after adjustment the maximum pixel value. The hidden digits can be extracted by subtracting the coefficients in (c) from those in (f); respectively, the extracted digits was $(103\ \ 103\ \ 2)_4$.

Then treat the $n^2$-3 digit number

$$\left\{\eta'_{ij}\right\}_{i=0}^{n^2-3} = \left\{\widehat{q}_{ij} - \widehat{p}_{ij}\right\}_{i=0}^{n^2-3} \qquad (7)$$

as a BV of $b'_j$ number, and convert the number $\{\eta'_{ij}\}_{i=0}^{n^2-3}$ to the expected number with BV of 2. Note that the coefficients $\{\widehat{p}_{ij}\}_{i=0}^{n^2-3}$ have been previously obtained from the stego-block 1 by the minimum-preserved scheme. Notice as well that the number of bits hidden in the block is $L = \lfloor (n^2 - 2)\log_2 b_j \rfloor$. This implies that the length of bits to be embedded into a host block is determined by the BV of $b_j$.

Figures 1 and 2 present examples of data embedding and extraction by the BV embedding scheme. A host block was shown in Figure 1(a) with the minimum and maximum pixel value of the block denoted by the gray highlighted numbers. The BV of the block is $118 - 115 + 1 = 4$. Figure 1(b) shows the difference block which was introduced by subtracting all the pixels except the minimum and maximum ones in Figure 1(a) from 115. Figure 1(c) was obtained by adjusting the maximum pixel value of 118 to the top-left of the block. Note that the corresponding adjusted coefficient in Figure 1(c) was marked by a rectangle. Assume that the secret bit stream $(0100110\ 1001101)_2$ is the 14-bit stream to be embedded in Figure 1(c). Figure 1(d) was acquired by adding the input digits $(0100110\ 1001101)_2 = (4942)_{10} = (1031032)_4$ to the coefficients in Figure 1(c) in a raster scan with a reverse order. The hidden block, as shown in Figure 1(e), was generated by adding 115 to each of the coefficients in Figure 1(d). Finally, the stego-block 2 in which the maximum pixel was restored, is shown in Figure 1(f). The mean square error (MSE) computed from Figures 1(a) and 1(f) was 2.67. To extract the hidden data and recover

the host block, a similar reverse procedure can be conducted to Figure 1(f). An example of data extraction is given in Figure 2.

2.4. *Overflow/Underflow Discussion.* Since the minimum pixel value of the block is preserved by the minimum-preserved (with squeezing) scheme, an underflow issue can be prevented. As for the blocks encoded by the BV embedding scheme, the underflow issue could be avoided by adjusting the value of parameter $\tau$. However, if there is a pixel of the block where the value is equal to (or a little less than) 255, an overflow issue can occur during bit embedding. A block skipped policy can be used to solve the issue. Alternatively, the maximum-preserved (with squeezing) scheme, which preserves the maximum pixel value of the block, can be employed in the proposed ACS algorithm to overcome the overflow issue; more precisely, the minimum-preserved (with squeezing) scheme can be replaced by the maximum-preserved (with squeezing) scheme when (1) the host images were incapable of recovering from the stego-images by the former scheme or (2) the number of skipped blocks lies beyond a predefined threshold. Since the process of data embedment and the extraction procedure for the maximum-preserved (with squeezing) scheme is similar to that of the minimum-preserved (with squeezing) scheme, they are skipped here.

## 3. Experimental Results

Several $512 \times 512$ gray-scale images, as shown in Figure 3, are used as the host images. One of the host images, *Baboon*, is used as the test data. The size of block is $3 \times 3$, and the

(a) *Lena*   (b) *Jet*   (c) *Peppers*   (d) *Baboon*   (e) Goldhill

(f) Scene   (g) Man   (h) *Boat*   (i) *Tiffany*

FIGURE 3: The host images.

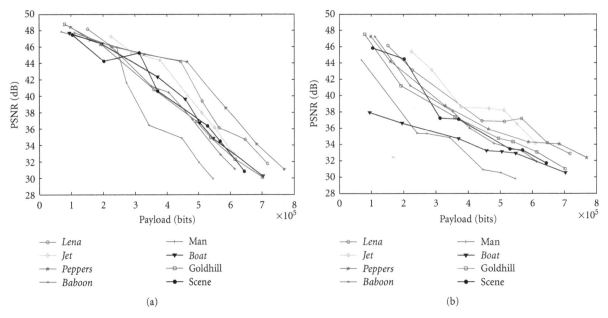

FIGURE 4: The relationship between PSNR and payload for the proposed method on test images. (a) Stego-image 1 and (b) stego-image 2.

integer $k$ is set to 1. A tradeoff between the PSNR (dB) and the payload (in bits) for the stego-images 1 and 2 generated by the proposed method using various $\beta$ is drawn in Figure 4. Figure 4(a) shows that the payload exceeds $6 \times 10^5$ bits for all images except *Baboon*. The optimal PSNRs for the stego-image 1 (Figure 4(a)) and stego-image 2 (Figure 4(b)) are 30.98 dB and 31.78 dB, respectively, with an average payload size of 662,861 bits. Moreover, Figure 4 reveals that the average PSNR value of stego-image 2 is nearly 2 dB below that of stego-image 1 if the payload size is less than $5 \times 10^5$ bits. Notice that a block skipped policy was employed on the image *Boat*; however, only 5 blocks were skipped. In addition, two stego-images generated by the proposed method

from the images *Lena* and *Baboon*, respectively, are depicted in Figure 5. It can be seen that the perceived quality of these images is acceptable. The average PSNR/payload for the images *Lena* and *Baboon* are 33.73 dB/690,233 bits and 30.36 dB/546,688 bits, respectively. The PSNR is defined by

$$\text{PSNR} = 10 \times \log_{10} \frac{255^2}{\text{MSE}}, \qquad (8)$$

where MSE $= (1/MN) \sum_{i=1}^{N} \sum_{j=1}^{M} (\hat{x}(i,j) - x(i,j))^2$ if the image size is $M \times N$. Here $x(i,j)$ and $\hat{x}(i,j)$ denote the pixel values of the original image and the marked image, respectively. Notice as well that the relation between two

FIGURE 5: Two stego-images generated by the proposed method. (a) Stego-image 1 of *Lena* (33.19 dB), (b) stego-image 2 of *Lena* (34.25 dB), (c) stego-image 1 of *Baboon* (30.41 dB), and (d) stego-image 2 of *Baboon* (30.78 dB).

control parameters $\beta$ and $\gamma$ is $\gamma = \beta - 1$. Figure 6 indicates that the payload size varied by a different combination of the parameters $\beta$, $\gamma$, and $\tau$ on the images *Lena* and *Baboon*. The payload is gradually increased as $\beta$ (or $\tau$) is enlarged. Figure 6 also reveals that the maximum hiding storage provided by the image *Lena* is approximately $2 \times 10^5$ bits larger than that provided by the image *Baboon*. To demonstrate the capability of handling the overflow issue, the proposed maximum-preserved (with squeezing) scheme was applied to the image *Tiffany*, which is a typical image often used to test the occurrence of overflow by several existing methods. Simulations confirm not only that the proposed method can losslessly extract the secret message but also that the host image can be fully recovered. Figure 7 presents the experimental results. Figure 7(a) displays the relationship between PSNR and payload. We can see that the performance of stego-image 1 is better than that of stego-image 2 when the payload size is lower than $6.5 \times 10^5$ bits. Moreover, Figure 7(b) shows the variations of payload versus the parameters of $\beta$, $\gamma$, and $\tau$. It presents a similar performance to that of Figure 6(a).

To evaluate our scheme's performance, this subsection compares our scheme with various approaches [11, 13, 14, 20, 22, 24]. Since the PSNR value of Yang and Tsai [14] is better than those of Zeng et al. [12] and Yang and Hu [15] when the payload approaches 1 bpp, the performance comparison does not include both methods. Figure 8 illustrates the comparison between various methods in two test images, *Lena* and *Boat*. Figure 8(a) shows that our method provides the best PSNR with the largest hiding capacity when the payload is larger than $1.70 \times 10^5$ bits. Note that the larger the payload, the larger the leading gap. Similarly, Figure 8(b) reveals the superiority of the proposed method when the payload is larger than $1.25 \times 10^5$ bits. Table 2 compares our method with the conventional reversible data hiding techniques [11, 13, 14] when the average payload size is larger than $3 \times 10^5$ bits with the PSNR around 30 dB. Table 2 indicates that the payload generated by the proposed method is far larger than that generated by the rest of the techniques, while our PSNR is the best among them. Table 2 also implies that it is difficult for the reversible data hiding techniques [11–15] to provide

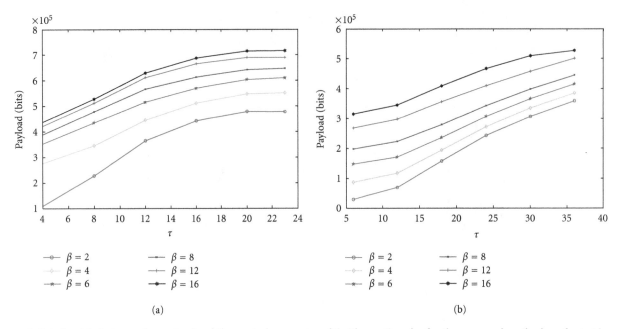

FIGURE 6: Relationship between the payload and the control parameters $\beta$ (with $\gamma - 1$) and $\tau$ for the proposed method on the test images. (a) *Lena* and (b) *Baboon*.

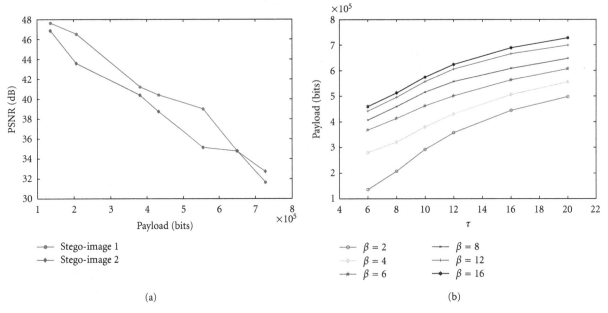

FIGURE 7: Simulations of the image *Tiffany*. (a) Tradeoff between PSNR and payload and (b) the relationship between the payload and the parameters $\beta$ (with $\gamma - 1$) and $\tau$.

TABLE 2: Payload/PSNR performance comparison between various methods (under PSNR value above 30 dB).

| Methods | Images | | | | |
|---|---|---|---|---|---|
| | *Lena* | *Jet* | *Peppers* | *Boat* | *Average* |
| Lin et al. [11] | 346,568/30.19 | 362,847/30.19 | 342,175/30.19 | 314,196/30.19 | 341,447/30.19 |
| Wu et al. [13] | 319,816/30.30 | 411,566/31.35 | 322,437/31.54 | 306,708/31.01 | 340,132/31.05 |
| Yang and Tsai [14] | 385,519/31.65 | 364,951/31.65 | 341,202/31.65 | 280,285/31.65 | 342,989/31.65 |
| Our method† | 716,596/32.29 | 610,269/33.58 | 769,364/31.71 | 702,811/30.60 | 699,760/32.05 |

†The average PSNR of stego-image 1 and stego-image 2 was displayed here.

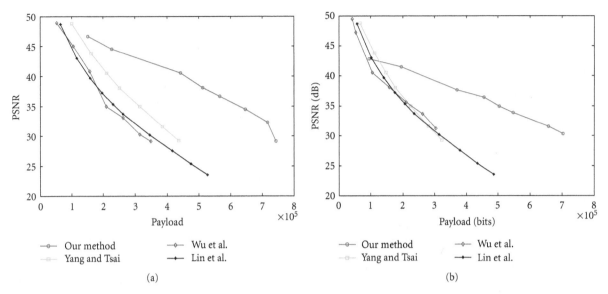

FIGURE 8: Performance comparison between various methods on two test images. (a) *Lena* and (b) *Boat*.

TABLE 3: Comparisons of the related secret image sharing schemes.

| Functionality | Methods | | | | |
| --- | --- | --- | --- | --- | --- |
| | Yang et al. [20] | Chang et al. [21] | Chang et al. [22] | Lin et al. [24] | Our method |
| Meaningful shadows | Yes | Yes | No | Yes | Yes |
| PSNR | 40 dB | 40 dB | ~34 dB | 43 dB | ~35 dB |
| Lossless secret image | Yes | Yes | Yes | Yes | Yes |
| Lossless cover image | No | No | No | Yes | Yes |
| Max. payload (bytes) | $(M \times N)/4$ | $(M \times N)/4$ | $(M \times N)/8 \leq$ | $((t-3)M \times N)/3$ | $>(M \times N)/4$ |
| Number of shadows | 3 | 3 | 2 | >3 | 2 |

a payload of a size approaching $7 \times 10^5$ bits with a PSNR value above 32 dB. For example, if one tried to embed a secret message of the above size into two host images using one of the other approaches, the PSNR value would be around 31 dB. Since a secret message can be separately embedded into two stego-images using the proposed method, third parties (or malicious users) would be incapable of extracting the hidden message (and recovering the original host image) when they are only dealing with one of the stego-images.

Table 3 compares our method with the secret image sharing schemes. All of the methods except for Chang et al.'s technique [22] have the capability of generating meaningful stego-images, which can be an important feature for a secret image sharing (with steganography). In addition, however, the three schemes, Yang et al. [20], Chang et al. [21], and Chang et al. [22], are incapable of recovering the host image without distortion. Although the PSNR of our method is not better than that of the other schemes [20, 21, 24], the maximum capacity provided by our method is larger than that provided by Yang et al. [20] and Chang et al. [21]. However, both the PSNR and the payload of our method are superior to that of Chang et al. [22]. Finally, the last row of Table 3 reveals that the number of shadows needed to implement the proposed method is less than that required by the other three schemes [20, 21, 24].

## 4. Conclusions

This paper presents an effective reversible data hiding method using two marked images via the adaptive coefficient-shifting (ACS) algorithm. According to the three predetermined rules, two target blocks, stego-block 1 (S1) and stego-block 2 (S2), are generated by embedding secret digits into the host block via the ACS algorithm. More specifically, both S1 and S2 are generated by either the minimum-preserved scheme (or the minimum-preserved with squeezing scheme) when Rule 1 (or Rule 3) is satisfied. S1 and S2 are generated by the minimum-preserved scheme and the BV embedding scheme, respectively, if Rule 2 fits the case. Simulations validate that the ACS algorithm not only completely recovers a host medium but is also able to obtain a distortion-free extracted message. The ACS algorithm is capable of handling various kinds of images without any occurrence of overflow/underflow. Moreover, the payload and PSNR performance of the proposed method is superior to that of the conventional invertible data hiding schemes. Since a secret message is spread into two stego-images by the proposed method, third parties with one stego-image cannot extract the hidden message nor can the original host image be recovered. Furthermore, the number of shadows required by the proposed method is less than that required by the existing $(t, n)$-threshold schemes of secret image sharing with steganography.

## Acknowledgment

The author would like to thank the editors and anonymous reviewers for providing valuable comments that helped to improve the content of the paper.

## References

[1] I. J. Cox, M. L. Miller, J. A. Bloom, J. Fridrich, and T. Kalker, *Digital Watermarking and Steganography*, Morgan Kaufmann, Massachusetts, Mass, USA, 2nd edition, 2008.

[2] F. Y. Shih, *Digital Watermarking and Steganography: Fundamentals and Techniques*, CRC Press, Florida, Fla, USA, 2008.

[3] C. Y. Yang, W. C. Hu, W. Y. Hwang, and Y. F. Cheng, "A simple digital watermarking by the adaptive bit-labeling scheme," *International Journal of Innovative Computing, Information and Control*, vol. 6, no. 3, pp. 1401–1410, 2010.

[4] C. C. Lin and P. F. Shiu, "High capacity data hiding scheme for DCT-based images," *Journal of Information Hiding and Multimedia Signal Processing*, vol. 1, no. 3, pp. 220–240, 2010.

[5] K. Yamamoto and M. Iwakiri, "Real-time audio watermarking based on characteristics of PCM in digital instrument," *Journal of Information Hiding and Multimedia Signal Processing*, vol. 1, no. 2, pp. 59–71, 2010.

[6] S. Zhou, Q. Zhang, and X. Wei, "An image encryption algorithm based on dual DNA sequences for image hiding," *ICIC Express Letters*, vol. 4, no. 4, pp. 1393–1398, 2010.

[7] S. Wang, B. Yang, and X. Niu, "Secure steganography method based on genetic algorithm," *Journal of Information Hiding and Multimedia Signal Processing*, vol. 1, no. 1, pp. 28–35, 2010.

[8] Z. G. Qu, X. B. Chen, X. J. Zhou, X. X. Niu, and Y. X. Yang, "Novel quantum steganography with large payload," *Optics Communications*, vol. 283, no. 23, pp. 4782–4786, 2010.

[9] J. Tian, "Reversible data embedding using a difference expansion," *IEEE Transactions on Circuits and Systems for Video Technology*, vol. 13, no. 8, pp. 890–896, 2003.

[10] A. M. Alattar, "Reversible watermark using the difference expansion of a generalized integer transform," *IEEE Transactions on Image Processing*, vol. 13, no. 8, pp. 1147–1156, 2004.

[11] C. C. Lin, W. L. Tai, and C. C. Chang, "Multilevel reversible data hiding based on histogram modification of difference images," *Pattern Recognition*, vol. 41, no. 12, pp. 3582–3591, 2008.

[12] X. Zeng, L. Ping, and Z. Li, "Lossless data hiding scheme using adjacent pixel difference based on scan path," *Journal of Multimedia*, vol. 4, no. 3, pp. 145–152, 2009.

[13] H. C. Wu, C. C. Lee, C. S. Tsai, Y. P. Chu, and H. R. Chen, "A high capacity reversible data hiding scheme with edge prediction and difference expansion," *Journal of Systems and Software*, vol. 82, no. 12, pp. 1966–1973, 2009.

[14] C. H. Yang and M. H. Tsai, "Improving histogram-based reversible data hiding by interleaving predictions," *IET Image Processing*, vol. 4, no. 4, pp. 223–234, 2010.

[15] C. Y. Yang and W. C. Hu, "High-performance reversible data hiding with overflow/underflow avoidance," *ETRI Journal*, vol. 33, no. 4, pp. 580–588, 2011.

[16] A. Shamir, "How to share a secret," *Communications of the ACM*, vol. 22, no. 11, pp. 612–613, 1979.

[17] M. Naor and A. Shamir, "Visual cryptography," in *Advances in Cryptology, Workshop on the Theory and Application of Cryptographic Techniques (EUROCRYPT '94)*, vol. 950 of *Lecture Notes in Computer Science*, pp. 1–12, Perugia, Italy, May 1994.

[18] C. C. Lin and W. H. Tsai, "Secret image sharing with steganography and authentication," *Journal of Systems and Software*, vol. 73, no. 3, pp. 405–414, 2004.

[19] Y. S. Wu, C. C. Thien, and J. C. Lin, "Sharing and hiding secret images with size constraint," *Pattern Recognition*, vol. 37, no. 7, pp. 1377–1385, 2004.

[20] C. N. Yang, T. S. Chen, K. H. Yu, and C. C. Wang, "Improvements of image sharing with steganography and authentication," *Journal of Systems and Software*, vol. 80, no. 7, pp. 1070–1076, 2007.

[21] C. C. Chang, Y. P. Hsieh, and C. H. Lin, "Sharing secrets in stego images with authentication," *Pattern Recognition*, vol. 41, no. 10, pp. 3130–3137, 2008.

[22] C. C. Chang, C. C. Lin, T. H. N. Le, and H. B. Le, "Sharing a verifiable secret image using two shadows," *Pattern Recognition*, vol. 42, no. 11, pp. 3097–3114, 2009.

[23] Z. Eslami, S. H. Razzaghi, and J. Z. Ahmadabadi, "Secret image sharing based on cellular automata and steganography," *Pattern Recognition*, vol. 43, no. 1, pp. 397–404, 2010.

[24] P. Y. Lin, J. S. Lee, and C. C. Chang, "Distortion-free secret image sharing mechanism using modulus operator," *Pattern Recognition*, vol. 42, no. 5, pp. 886–895, 2009.

[25] P. Y. Lin and C. S. Chan, "Invertible secret image sharing with steganography," *Pattern Recognition Letters*, vol. 31, no. 13, pp. 1887–1893, 2010.

# 15

# High-Definition Video Streams Analysis, Modeling, and Prediction

**Abdel-Karim Al-Tamimi,[1] Raj Jain,[2] and Chakchai So-In[3]**

[1] *Computer Engineering Department, Yarmouk University, Irbid 21163, Jordan*
[2] *Department of Computer Science and Engineering, Washington University in St. Louis, St. Louis, MO 63130, USA*
[3] *Department of Computer Science, Khon Kaen University, Khon Kaen 4002, Thailand*

Correspondence should be addressed to Abdel-Karim Al-Tamimi, altamimi@yu.edu.jo

Academic Editor: Marios C. Angelides

High-definition video streams' unique statistical characteristics and their high bandwidth requirements are considered to be a challenge in both network scheduling and resource allocation fields. In this paper, we introduce an innovative way to model and predict high-definition (HD) video traces encoded with H.264/AVC encoding standard. Our results are based on our compilation of over 50 HD video traces. We show that our model, simplified seasonal ARIMA (SAM), provides an accurate representation for HD videos, and it provides significant improvements in prediction accuracy. Such accuracy is vital to provide better dynamic resource allocation for video traffic. In addition, we provide a statistical analysis of HD videos, including both factor and cluster analysis to support a better understanding of video stream workload characteristics and their impact on network traffic. We discuss our methodology to collect and encode our collection of HD video traces. Our video collection, results, and tools are available for the research community.

## 1. Introduction

Web-based video streaming websites facilitate the creation and distribution of digital video contents to millions of people. Websites like YouTube [1] are now considered to be among the most accessed websites by Internet users. Such websites are now accounting for 27 percent of the Internet traffic, rising from 13 percent in one year [2]. Internet video traffic is expected to amount to 50% of consumer Internet traffic in 2012 [3].

This surge in traffic percentage can be explained by the latest surveys that show that the percentage of US Internet users watching streaming videos has increased from 81% to 84.4%, and the average time spent per month increased from 8.3 to 10.8 hours/month in just three months period July–October of 2009 [4, 5]. Additionally, several websites, for example, Hulu [6] and Netflix [7], have started offering access to TV shows and selected movies that has increased the reliance of the daily Internet users on such websites and augmented their expectations of the level of services and quality of delivery.

Resource and bandwidth allocation schemes for video streaming are dependent on their ability to predict and manage the time variant demand of video streams. Existing dynamic resource allocation schemes [8–10] utilize video traffic prediction to offer better accommodation for existing video traffic, and allow higher admission rates. The traffic predictor is the most important part in dynamic bandwidth allocation. It is can be based either on traffic characteristics or on the video content. Video-content-based traffic predictors have shown their superiority over their traffic-based counterparts [10].

Therefore, it essential to analyze and model video traffic to allow better quality of service (QoS) support. In this paper, we present the results of our model-based predictor and discuss its video traffic prediction capabilities.

Modeling video streams is a challenging task because of the high variability of video frame sizes. Such variability has increased with the introduction of MPEG4-Part10/advanced video codec (AVC)/H.264 high-definition video codec standard. AVC provides better compression rate (i.e., lower mean values) than its predecessors. Yet at the same time, it results in higher frame size variability [11].

In this paper, we present our work to analyze, model, and predict high-definition (HD) video traces encoded with the H.264/AVC codec. We present results based on over 50 HD video traces. We compare three modeling methods: autoregressive (AR) [12], autoregressive integrated moving average (ARIMA) [12] using the approach proposed in [13], and our Simplified Seasonal ARIMA Model (SAM) that was developed for the less resource demanding mobile video traces [14, 15]. In addition we compare these models in their prediction accuracy.

There have been several contributions that aimed to achieve a better understanding of the relationship between the statistical characteristics of video traces and their impact on data networks. In [16], the authors presented a statistical and factor analysis study of 20 MPEG1 encoded video traces and their impact on ATM networks. Similar approaches were presented in [17] with emphasis on video trace frame size distribution. The author in [18] performed a statistical analysis on four MPEG4-AVC encoded video traces demonstrating the quantization effects over several statistical measurements, including the intercorrelation between video frames. In [11], the authors compared the statistical characteristics of AVC standard versus its predecessor, namely, MPEG4-Part2 in terms of bit rate distortion performance, bit rate variability, and long-range dependence (LRD).

In this paper, we present our work of analyzing and modeling over 50 HD video traces from YouTube HD videos section. We aim through this contribution to investigate the main statistical characteristics that define an HD video trace. This identification is important for two main reasons: it helps in clustering video traces depending on certain statistical criteria to help choose the correct traffic workload, or in other possible data mining processes [16]. Additionally, it helps define the main statistical attributes of HD video traces that should be considered to achieve a valid statistical model [19].

One of the main challenges in developing a valid video workload model is the availability of an adequate number of traces to test the proposed model. The available traces on the web are scarce and do not represent all the different types of videos. Thus, one of the aims of this contribution is to provide researchers with a sufficient number of traces to support their future studies. All our tools, results, and video traces are available through our website [20].

In addition to analyzing and modeling these video traces, we provide several tools: a trace generator based on our model that can be used to generate user-defined traces with the desired statistical characteristics, and a simple GUI interface to provide the essential statistical analysis and comparison graphs for HD video traces. The trace generator can also be used to produce a new movie trace that represents a blend of different video characteristics. Figure 1 summarizes the main steps taken in analyzing and modeling the selected videos and shows each step's corresponding outputs.

Our encoding process starts with an HD YouTube video in *mp4* format, which is then converted to a YUV (4:2:0) raw video format. Such format allows video frames to be much more compressible [21]. The raw video is consequently encoded with AVC, and the process produces the following: an encoded movie file, its encoding statistics file, and a full verbose description of the encoding process. The verbose output is then parsed using our analysis tool to get the video trace information, which is then modeled using AR, ARIMA, or SAM. The video trace is used also to produce the video frames autocorrelation function (ACF) and the partial autocorrelation function (PACF) graphs. ACF plots are commonly used tools to check for randomness in a data series by plotting the data set values over several time lags [22]. Given a data series $X_t$, PACF for a lag $k$ is the autocorrelation between $X_t$ and $X_{t-k}$ that is not accounted for by lags 1 to $k-1$ inclusive.

The SAM parameters for each video can be used in either video traffic prediction analysis, or in generating video traces. SAM frame generator uses these parameters to generate a movie trace that is statistically close to the original movie trace.

This paper is organized as follows: Section 2 discusses the methodology of obtaining and encoding our collection of HD videos. Section 3 shows the results of our statistical analysis, including both factor and cluster analysis. In Section 4, we compare the results of modeling the video traces and provide a simple introduction to SAM. Section 5 discusses the approach to evaluate the prediction accuracy of the compared models and the comparisons results. Section 6 illustrates our tools design and their implementations. Finally, we conclude the paper and give some insights to the impact of our results and our future work.

## 2. Encoding YouTube HD Videos

To represent real life video traffic load, we chose YouTube website as our source. YouTube is currently the most popular video streaming website on the Internet [23]. Our first step in selecting the candidate videos from YouTube was to make sure that we have a good variety of both texture/details and motion levels. To select a representative group of the available videos, we started our selection process with 9 videos of the most visited videos in YouTube HD section [1]. Then, we increased our collection by selecting three random videos from each of the 15 subcategories available for YouTube website's users. In total we have collected 54 video files in *mp4* format.

Then, we analyzed the collected videos using *MediaInfo* [24] to determine the encoding parameters for the various videos and to select the most commonly used parameter values. We made sure that the parameter values we selected were consistent with those recommended in [25, 26] for YouTube video encoding. Our next step was to convert all these videos to raw or YUV (4:2:0) format. This step is important to ensure unified encoding parameters for all the collected videos to allow objective comparisons. We performed the conversion process using the open source coding library FFMPEG [27].

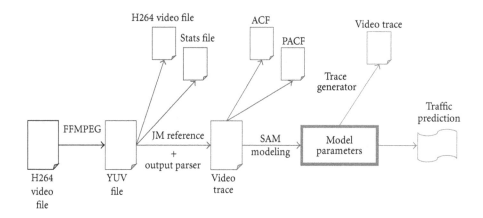

FIGURE 1: Modeling, analyzing, and generating video traces processes.

TABLE 1: Encoding parameters for the selected YouTube video collection.

| Encoding parameter | Value |
| --- | --- |
| FrameRate | 24 |
| OutputWidth | 1280 |
| OutputHeight | 720 |
| ProfileIDC | 100 (High) |
| LevelIDC | 40 (62914560 samples/sec) |
| NumberBFrames | 2 |
| IDRPeriod | 24 |
| NumberReferenceFrames | 3 |
| QP (quantization parameter) | $I = 28, P = 28, B = 30$ |

To convert YUV files to the H.264/AVC format, we tested two publically available encoding libraries: x264 [28] and JM reference software [29]. Though x264 is significantly faster than JM reference software, it provided us with less information about the encoding process. Table 1 lists the main encoding parameters used with JM reference software.

These parameters were chosen to represent the majority of the videos we have collected. We used in our encoding process Instantaneous Decoding Refresh (IDR) frames [25]. IDR frames are special type of I frames that allow better seeking precision and thus enhance the user's experience. We used *closed-GOP* setting [26] to ensure that all I frames are IDR frames, hence improving the user's online experience. The majority of the collected videos have a frame rate of 24 fps. *IDRPeriod* defines the periodicity of IDR frames.

The *ProfileIDC* parameter defines the video profile, which, in this case, is set to high. This parameter, along with the *LevelIDC* parameter, specifies the capabilities that the client decoder must have in order to decode the video stream. Parameter *NumberBFrames* specifies the number of B slices or frames between I, IDR, and P frames. The quantization parameters used are the default values for the encoder. The parameter *NumberReferenceFrames* sets the maximum number of reference frames stored in the decoder buffer, and it is set to three frames. All other encoding parameters are set

to the default values of JM reference software. In the course of our analysis and encoding processes, we used two versions of JM reference software: v15.1 and v16.0.

The encoding procedure is both time and resource consuming process. The encoding of a single video file took on average 37 hours, with an average encoding rate of 0.02 fps. The average size of a raw YUV (4 : 2 : 0) video file is around 4 GB. The encoding was done using a 2.8 GHz Core i7 machine with 6 GB of DDR3 RAM. These figures support our conviction of the necessity to have a valid trace model and generator. The output of the encoding process is then run through our parser to extract the video trace frame size information needed for the next steps of our analysis and modeling.

## 3. Factor and Cluster Analysis of Video Traces

In this section we discuss the steps taken to perform a full statistical analysis of the collected video traces in order to achieve a better understanding of the main factors that can be used to represent a video trace in order to develop a representative statistical model.

Multivariate analysis is used to reveal the full structure of the collected data, and any hidden patterns and key features [30]. Multivariate analysis is used especially when the variables are closely related to each other, and there is a need to understand the underlying relationship between them. We have computed the following statistical quantitative values for traces frame sizes: mean, minimum, maximum, range, variance, standard deviation, the coefficient of variance, and the median value. In addition, we computed the Hurst exponent value, as shown in (4), which indicates the video sequence's ability to regress to its mean value, with higher values indicating a smoother trend, less volatility, and less roughness. Its value varies between 0 and 1. This is also an indication of the strength of the long-range dependence (LRD) among video frames [19]. The Hurst exponent can be computed by first calculating the mean adjusted series $Y$:

$$Y_i = x_i - \overline{x}, \quad i = 1, 2, \ldots, N, \tag{1}$$

TABLE 2: Range of statistical values for the collected video traces.

|  | Mean | Range | Variance | Hurst | Coefficient of variance | Median | Skewness | Kurtosis |
|---|---|---|---|---|---|---|---|---|
| Max | 83340.43 | 1198416 | 13767760363 | 0.902836 | 3.9860815 | 62748 | 6.58066 | 61.34631 |
| Min | 9782.01 | 65576 | 154362485 | 0.498937 | 0.6875022 | 448 | 0.2287191 | 1.643709 |

where $x_i$ is the frame size at index $i$, $\bar{x}$ is the mean frame size over the trace length $N$, then we calculate the cumulative deviate vector $S$:

$$S_t = \sum_{j=1}^{i} Y_j, \quad i = 1, 2, \ldots, N. \tag{2}$$

The next step is to calculate the range value $R$, and we divide it over the standard deviation value denoted by $\sigma$:

$$R = \frac{\max(S) - \min(S)}{\sigma}, \tag{3}$$

$$\text{Hurst Index} = \frac{\log(R)}{\log(N) - \log(2)}, \tag{4}$$

where $x_i$ is the frame size at index $i$, $\bar{x}$ is the mean frame size, and $N$ is the number of frames in the trace. We also computed the skewness value that represents the symmetry of the observed distribution around its center point [19]:

$$\text{Skewness} = \frac{\sum_{i=1}^{N} (x_i - \bar{x})^3}{(N - 1) \times \text{std}^3}. \tag{5}$$

Here std is the standard deviation of the frames sizes. Additionally, we computed the kurtosis value, which is an indication whether the observed video trace distribution is peaked or flat relative to a normal distribution [19]. The kurtosis equation is illustrated below

$$\text{Kurtosis} = \frac{\sum_{i=1}^{N} (x_i - \bar{x})^4}{(N - 1) \times \text{std}^4}. \tag{6}$$

As Table 2 shows, the collected videos represent a statistically diverse data samples. And as we mentioned before, the video frame size variance of HD videos is considerably substantial. The table shows the most important variables that have been collected. We noticed through our preparation analysis that min variable does not contribute to the total variance significantly, and thus it was disregarded. Both max and range, and variance and standard deviation pairs are almost identical. We picked range and variance to represent the two pairs, respectively. In the next subsections, we will discuss the methodology and results of performing both factor and cluster analysis.

*3.1. Principal Component Analysis.* One of the most common factor analysis methods is principal component analysis (PCA) [16], where a group of possibly related variables are analyzed and then reduced to a smaller number of uncorrelated factors. These factors accounts for most of the variance in the observed variables. By performing this process, we aim

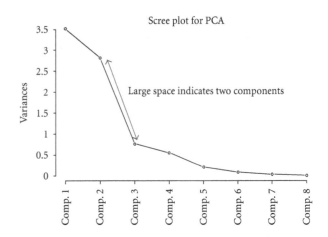

FIGURE 2: Scree plot for the HD video collection data based on the eight selected variables which indicates two principal components.

to minimize the number of variables to represent a video trace without much loss of information [30].

Our first step is to determine the smallest number of variables to represent each video trace. Table 3 shows the correlation between the selected variables. These variables collectively represent the majority of the samples variation.

The importance of each factor is represented by its eigenvalue. To determine the number of factors to extract we used Kaiser-Guttman rule [31]. By following this rule, we excluded the factors with eigenvalue less than 1. We supported our selection by performing the Scree test [32] as shown in Figure 2, where we plotted the relationship between the number of factors and their cumulative contribution to the total variance of the data set, and we looked for either large spaces between the plotted variables or a knee in the graph to determine the number of factors to be considered.

Our analysis resulted in choosing two factors with the following eigenvalues: $\lambda_1 = 3.51$, and $\lambda_2 = 2.82$. These factors account for 79% $[(\lambda_1 + \lambda_2)/8]$ of the total standardized variance. We confirmed that the number of factors is sufficient to explain the intercorrelations among variables by performing several nongraphical tests [33].

To simplify the factor structure and spread out the correlations between the variables and the factors (their loadings values) as much as possible, we performed both orthogonal and oblique rotations on the factors [34]. We chose *varimax* orthogonal rotation as it gave the best results. As shown in Figure 3, the two significant groups are the mean and skewness groups. Table 4 shows the loadings values for both varimax rotated and unrotated factors.

As can be noticed, the rotated factors are better spread out and simpler to interpret. From Table 4 we can note that the first factor $F_1^*$ defines mainly mean and variance values.

TABLE 3: Correlation between the selected variables.

|  | Mean | Range | Var | Hurst | c.var | Median | Skew | Kurt |
|---|---|---|---|---|---|---|---|---|
| Mean | 1 | 0.48 | 0.73 | 0.48 | −0.40 | −0.9 | −0.36 | −0.23 |
| Range | 0.48 | 1 | 0.74 | 0.34 | 0.19 | 0.25 | 0.51 | 0.6 |
| Var | 0.73 | 0.74 | 1 | 0.36 | 0.13 | 0.41 | 0.13 | 0.14 |
| Hurst | 0.48 | 0.34 | 0.36 | 1 | −0.44 | 0.41 | 0.25 | 0.17 |
| c.var | −0.40 | 0.19 | 0.13 | −0.44 | 1 | −0.56 | 0.71 | 0.51 |
| Median | −0.9 | 0.25 | 0.41 | 0.41 | −0.56 | 1 | −0.49 | −0.33 |
| Skew | −0.36 | 0.51 | 0.13 | 0.25 | 0.71 | −0.49 | 1 | 0.93 |
| Kurt | −0.23 | 0.6 | 0.14 | 0.17 | 0.51 | −0.33 | 0.93 | 1 |

TABLE 4: Estimated and rotated factors loadings.

|  | Estimated | | Rotated (varimax) | |
|---|---|---|---|---|
|  | $F_1$ | $F_2$ | $F_1^*$ | $F_2^*$ |
| Mean | 0.84 | 0.46 | **0.93** | — |
| Range | — | 0.95 | 0.73 | 0.62 |
| Variance | 0.39 | 0.80 | 0.84 | — |
| Hurst | 0.62 | — | 0.64 | — |
| C. Var | −0.75 | 0.35 | — | 0.77 |
| Median | 0.87 | — | 0.77 | −0.46 |
| Skewness | −0.75 | 0.62 | — | **0.97** |
| Kurtosis | −0.62 | 0.67 | — | **0.91** |

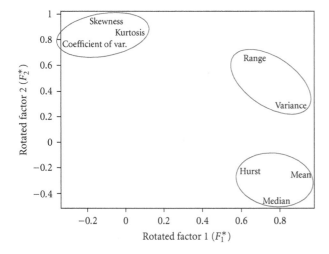

FIGURE 3: Scatter plot of varimax rotated factors $F_1^*$ and $F_2^*$ in the space of the two principal components.

The second factor defines mainly skewness and kurtosis values. We chose *mean* to represent the first factor since it has the highest load. We chose kurtosis as a representative of $F_2^*$ since it has the lowest correlation between it and the mean (−0.23). This analysis shows the importance of skewness and kurtosis in HD videos traces. These two variables were considered irrelevant in previous video analysis [16]. This realization can be explained by the dependence of these variables on the standard deviation that accounts for a significant proportion of the total variance of HD videos traces.

*3.2. Cluster Analysis Using k-Means Clustering.* We have demonstrated that the selected two factors, or principal components, are sufficient to characterize a HD video trace. The second step of our analysis is to group the collected video traces into clusters. We used one of the most popular clustering methods: *k-means* clustering algorithm [35]. *k*-means algorithm achieves clustering by minimizing the within-cluster sum of squares as shown in

$$\arg\min_s \sum_{i=1}^{k} \sum_{x_j \in S_i} \left\| x_j - \mu_i \right\|^2, \qquad (7)$$

where $x_i$ is the video trace at index $i$, $k$ is the number of sets ($k < n$, $n$: number of video traces), $S_i$ is the $i$th set, and $\mu_i$ is the mean of $S_i$.

Our next step is to estimate the number of clusters or groups to consider for $k$-means clustering. PCA helps give an insight of how many clusters the video traces can be grouped into [36]. In our case, PCA suggests that we need two clusters. In order to verify the analysis results from PCA, we proceeded with computing the within-cluster sum of squares for different number of clusters. Our aim is to select the minimum number of clusters that allows the minimal possible value for the within-cluster sum of squares. By plotting these values to represent a graph similar to the previously shown *scree* test in Figure 2, the large spaces between the plotted variables and the graph *knee* values indicate the possible values are two, three, and four clusters as shown in the Figure 4(a). To further investigate the best possible number of clusters to use, we performed a hierarchical clustering to identify the number of clusters using *Ward's*

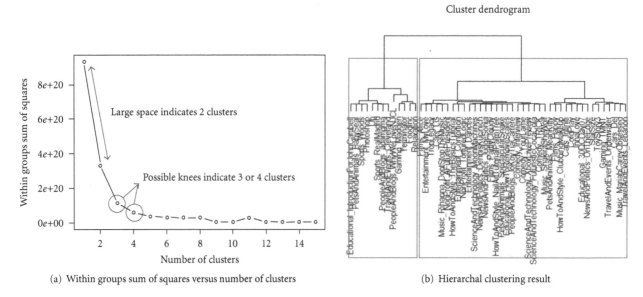

(a) Within groups sum of squares versus number of clusters    (b) Hierarchal clustering result

FIGURE 4: Determining number of clusters using scree test and hieratical analysis.

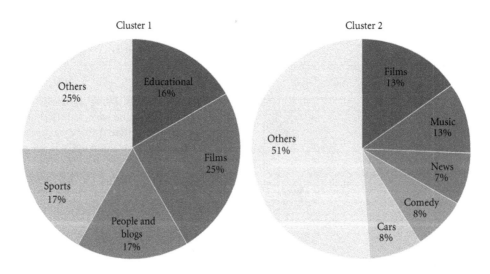

FIGURE 5: Distribution of movie groups over the two clusters.

method [35]. As shown in Figure 4(b), the video traces are divided into two main clusters. Our choice of grouping the video traces into two clusters was further verified by performing *silhouette* validation method [37].

By performing $k$-means clustering we grouped the video traces into 2 clusters. Table 5 shows the two chosen principal components corresponding to the centroids of the two clusters, and the two clusters main members. Figure 5 shows the distribution of video groups over the two clusters.

In summary, video traces that belong to cluster 2 have significantly lower mean values and have considerably low peaks compared to normal distribution, and lighter tails as indicated by their low Kurtosis values.

We also notice that films category video traces are spread across both clusters. Most blogs and sport category videos are characterized as peaky video traces because of their content.

News and comedy videos are less peaky and have lower means than other movies.

To summarize, in this section, we demonstrated our results of performing both factor and cluster analysis on our collection of video traces. Both methods of analysis give us a better understanding of the distribution of the movie traces and their key statistical attributes.

## 4. Modeling HD Video Traces

In this section, we discuss and compare three statistical models to represent HD video traces. Several models to represent VBR (Variable Bit Rate) MPEG traffic have been proposed in the recent years. Some of the models proposed are based on Markov chain models, which are known for their inefficiency

TABLE 5: Clustering results using $k$-means clustering.

| Variables | Cluster 1 | Cluster 2 |
|---|---|---|
| Mean | 59,251 | 32,582 |
| Kurtosis | 12.028829 | 9.099512 |
| No. of elements | 13 | 39 |
| Main video groups | Films, people and blogs, sports, educational | Films, music, news, comedy, cars |

in representing the long-range dependence (LRD) characteristics of MPEG traffic [38, 39]. Due to the high influence of LRD, multiplicative processes have been considered like Fractional ARIMA (FARIMA), which have been shown to be accurate, but also computationally demanding and provide marginal improvements over ARIMA [12]. Wavelet-based prediction has been shown to require more computation resources, and to provide less accurate results than ARIMA [40]. Our aim is to select a simple to implement, accurate, and applicable model for all video traces without the need of significant statistical background.

The chosen model should not require video-specific, complex, and tedious steps. The model should be able to not only represent video frame size distribution, but also the correlation between the frames. These attributes are important to achieve the desired results and to allow the analysis of our large collection of video traces. Our pre-analysis step resulted in choosing three modeling methods: autoregressive (AR) model, autoregressive integrated moving average (ARIMA) model using the approach proposed in [13], and SAM model [14, 15]. All these models use maximum likelihood estimation to determine the model terms coefficients and consider Akaike's Information Criterion (AIC) as their optimization goal. AIC is defined as

$$\text{AIC} = 2k + n\left[\ln\left(\frac{\text{RSS}}{n}\right)\right], \qquad (8)$$

here $k$ is the number of parameters, $n$ is the number of the video frames, and RSS is the residual sum of squares. AIC defines the goodness of fit for the models, considering both their accuracy and complexity defined by their number of parameters. Lower AIC values indicate better models in terms of their validity and simplicity. Each of the modeling methods is described briefly below.

*4.1. AR Modeling.* Autoregressive fitting takes into consideration the previous values of the fitted trace. An autoregressive model of order $p$ can be written as

$$X_t = \sum_{i=1}^{p} \varphi_i X_{t-i} + \varepsilon_t, \qquad (9)$$

where $\varphi_i$ is the $i$th model parameter and $\varepsilon_t$ is white noise.

We used maximum likelihood estimation (MLE) to estimate the model parameters of the AR model. Using AR to fit the video traces is a considerably simple process, but it does not always yield accurate results. Additionally, each video trace has its own set of parameters in terms of their numbers and their coefficients values.

*4.2. ARIMA Modeling.* Autoregressive integrated moving average model is a mathematical class model with both autoregressive and moving average terms. Moving average (MA) terms describe the correlation between the current value of the trace with the previous error terms. The integrated or differencing part of the model can be used to remove the nonstationarity of the trace.

ARIMA is usually referred as ARIMA $(p, d, q)$ where $p$ is the order of the autoregressive part, $q$ is the order of the moving average part, and $d$ is the order of differencing part. ARIMA model can be written as

$$\left(1 - \sum_{i=1}^{p} \phi_i L^i\right)(1 - L)^d X_t = \left(1 + \sum_{i=1}^{q} \theta_i L^i\right)\varepsilon_t, \qquad (10)$$

where $L$ is the lag operator and $\theta_i$ is the $i$th moving average parameter. We used the automatic ARIMA estimation algorithm proposed in [13], which implements a unified approach to specify the model parameters using a stepwise procedure. It also takes into consideration the seasonality of the trace to allow representing seasonal data series. This approach also results in a separate set of parameters for each video trace in terms of their numbers and their values. For the rest of this paper we will refer to this approach simply as ARIMA.

*4.3. SAM Model.* SAM is a mathematical model based on Seasonal ARIMA (SARIMA) models [12]. SARIMA models aim to achieve better modeling by identifying both nonseasonal and seasonal parts of data traces. SARIMA is described as

$$\text{SARIMA} = (p, d, q) \times (P, D, Q)^s, \qquad (11)$$

where $P$ is the order of the seasonal autoregressive part, $Q$ is the order of the seasonal moving average part, $D$ is the order of seasonal differencing, and $s$ denotes the seasonality of the time series. SAM as SARIMA model can be written as

$$\text{SAM} = (1, 0, 1) \times (1, 1, 1)^s, \qquad (12)$$

where $s$ is the video trace seasonality, in our case this is equal to the frames rate.

SAM provides a unified approach to model video traces encoded with different video codec standards using different encoding settings [14, 15]. The model was developed to model mobile video traces, and we investigate in this paper its ability to model more resource-demanding HD video traces with higher resolutions and different encoding settings. Seasonal ARIMA modeling can be represented by two main steps: defining the model order, by selecting the order of *p*, *d*, *q*, *P*, *D*, and *Q* terms, and then estimating the order coefficients using methods like maximum likelihood estimation. SARIMA models require a considerable degree of analysis and statistical background to identify the model terms order. SAM, on the other hand, has only four parameters, and therefore each model is represented with only four coefficient values, while achieving similar results to the SARIMA models calculated for each video trace [14, 15]. The values the parameters are determined using maximum likelihood estimation and optimized using *Nelder-Mead* method [41]. The four parameters are the coefficients of autoregressive, moving average, seasonal autoregressive, and seasonal moving average parts. Therefore, using SAM simplifies the analysis process that is usually required for seasonal series and removes manual processing and expert analysis requirements.

*4.4. Modeling Results.* After performing the modeling analysis on 54 HD video traces, we evaluated the achieved results first by simply comparing the sum of the AIC values for all the modeled video traces. We also calculated the number in which each model scored the best AIC, that is, lowest value, for a certain video trace. Additionally, we compared the three models using three statistical measures to evaluate how close the models values are to the actual traces: the mean absolute error (MAE) as shown in (13), mean absolute relative error (MARE) as shown in (14), and normalized mean square error (NMSE), as shown in (15)

$$ \text{MAE} = \frac{1}{N} \sum_{i=1}^{N} |e_i|, \tag{13} $$

$$ \text{MARE} = \frac{1}{N} \sum_{i=1}^{N} \frac{|e_i|}{x_i}, \tag{14} $$

$$ \text{RMSE} = \sqrt{\frac{1}{N} \sum_{i=1}^{N} (e_i)^2}, \tag{15} $$

where $N$ is number of frames, $e_i$ is the modeling error at the $i$th frame, and $x_i$ is the $i$th frame size. The results are shown in Table 6. It can be noted that SAM achieved the best results, while AR and ARIMA came in second and last place, respectively. The achieved results demonstrate two main points: SAM is superior to the other two modeling methods, and that the automated approach used with ARIMA modeling does not always yield the expected results.

Additionally, we performed several graphical comparisons for all the video traces by comparing the original video traces, their autocorrelation function (ACF) plots, and their empirical cumulative distribution function (ECDF) plots to ones achieved by the different models. Figure 6 shows an example of one of the compared video traces. As we can notice, SAM has better results and represents the traces statistical characteristics better than the other

TABLE 6: Comparison between AR, ARIMA, and SAM using AIC.

|                 | AR      | ARIMA   | SAM     |
|-----------------|---------|---------|---------|
| Total MAE       | 830753  | 894700  | 641897  |
| Total MARE      | 200.12  | 220.47  | 126.28  |
| Total RMSE      | 1583607 | 1644015 | 1114846 |
| Total AIC       | 3473929 | 3492401 | 3344490 |
| No. of Best AIC | 6       | 3       | 43      |

two models. For this example, modeling using AR required 12 parameters, using ARIMA required 7 parameters (two AR parameters and five MA parameters), and using SAM required only 4 parameters.

The results show that SAM has a significant advantage over the other two modeling methods especially on the seasonal transition of the video trace. This advantage is also apparent in ACF and ECDF plots comparisons. All graphical comparison results for all the HD video traces are also available through our website [20].

# 5. Forecasting HD Video Traffic

Because of the variability exhibited in video traffic and especially in AVC encoded videos, static bandwidth allocation is considered not suitable for providing high utilization of the network resources. Thus, dynamic bandwidth allocation has been considered as an alternative approach [42]. The heart of the dynamic bandwidth allocation schemes is the traffic predictor that helps in making decisions for future bandwidth allocations.

In order to evaluate the different prediction methods, we characterized different requirements for the predictor in which to operate. These requirements are set to test the abilities of these models to operate under different network traffic scenarios. The first criterion is the model's ability to correctly predict traffic to achieve long-term prediction. The prediction process itself consumes network resources. Thus, it is preferable to run the predictor as few times as possible. On the other hand, we do not need the prediction interval to be too large, because the video frame sizes change frequently and do not follow a certain pattern for a long period of time that may result in severe prediction errors. Prediction errors results in either in inefficient use of network resources, or result in an increased rate of dropped packets due to insufficient space in the receiving network buffers. We evaluated this criterion by comparing the three modeling methods using four different prediction interval lengths: 48, 72, 96, and 120 frames that translate to 2, 3, 4, and 5 seconds, respectively.

The second criterion is the ability of the predictor to capture the statistical characteristics of the movie trace by analyzing as few video frames as possible. We evaluated this criterion by comparing the prediction accuracy in the cases where the predictor has already processed 250, 500, 1000, and 1500 video frames. This translates to around 10, 20, 40, and 60 seconds, respectively.

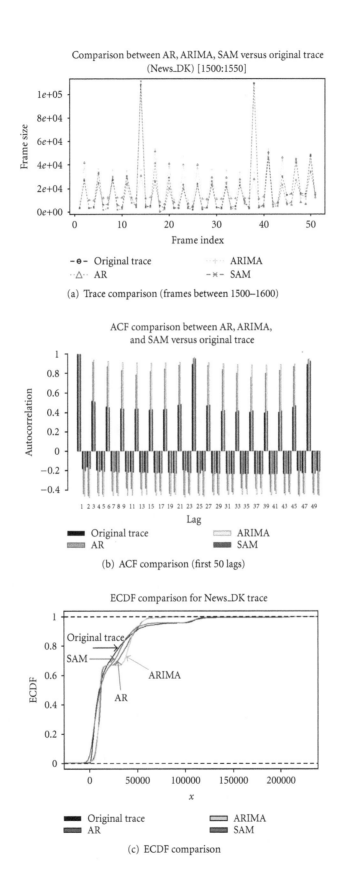

(a) Trace comparison (frames between 1500–1600)

(b) ACF comparison (first 50 lags)

(c) ECDF comparison

FIGURE 6: Graphical comparisons between AR, ARIMA, and SAM.

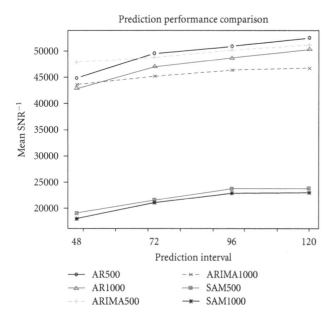

FIGURE 7: Comparisons between AR, ARIMA, and SAM SNR$^{-1}$ values.

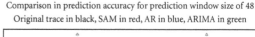

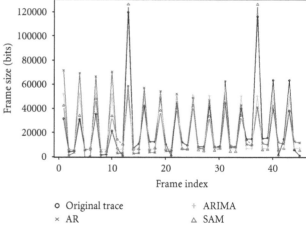

FIGURE 8: Prediction comparison between AR, ARIMA, and SAM.

Evidently, we seek out the best predictor that can achieve the best prediction accuracy for the longest prediction window with the least number of frames to be analyzed. We chose the commonly used noise to signal (SNR$^{-1}$) ratio as our prediction accuracy metric. SNR$^{-1}$ computes the ratio between the sum of squares of the prediction errors, and the sum of squares of the video frame size. SNR$^{-1}$ can be depicted as

$$\text{SNR}^{-1} = \frac{\sum (e)^2}{\sum (\text{size})^2}, \qquad (16)$$

where $e$ is the prediction error, and *size* is the video frame size.

Figure 7 shows a summary of the main results. As seen in this figure, the prediction error is directly related to the increase of the prediction window size. It also shows that the increase of the predictor knowledge, as represented in the number of frames processed, provides better prediction accuracy. It is obvious from the figure that SAM provides significant improvements over the other two methods. Table 7 shows the improvements SAM provides over AR and ARIMA when 1000 frames are processed. SAM improves up to 55% over AR, and 53.3% over ARIMA.

To better understand the reasons behind the observed improvement, we plot the three models predictions for a prediction window of 48 after processing 1000 of video frames. As shown in Figure 8, SAM not only manages to predict the video frames accurately, it is the only one that can predict the significant transitions of the frame sizes. SAM can also provide accurate results with relatively fewer numbers of frames. For instance, SAM results with 1500 preprocessed frames have only 4.7% improvement over SAM with 250 preprocessed frames [19].

TABLE 7: SNR$^{-1}$ comparison between AR, ARIMA, and SAM.

|                        | AR 1000 | ARIMA1000 | SAM 1000 |
|------------------------|---------|-----------|----------|
| SNR$^{-1}$ (avg)       | 47180   | 45457     | **21220** |
| Improvement over AR    | —       | 3.6%      | **55%**  |
| Improvement over ARIMA | −3.6%   | —         | **53.3%** |

We further investigated the possibility of using SAM with even fewer numbers of frames. Theoretically, SAM needs a minimum of 29 frames as suggested in [43]. Our results showed that we need at least 100 frames to achieve the desired accuracy. With SAM, using 1500 frames provided only 1% improvement over using 100 frames on average. Thus, based on our results, we recommend using SAM with 100 frames (~4 seconds) to predict the subsequent 120 frames (5 seconds). This means that a dynamic bandwidth allocation scheme needs only to negotiate the allocation once every 5 seconds.

In this section we compared three possible models that can be used to achieve the desired prediction accuracy with HD video traces. Our results showed that SAM has a clear edge over the two other models. In the next section we discuss some of the developed tools.

## 6. SAM-Based Developed Tools

In this section we demonstrate the design and implementation of two SAM-based tools: SAM-based traffic generator that can be used to generate HD video traces for video streaming simulations, and GUI interface to facilitate the analysis of video traces.

*6.1. SAM-Based Trace Generator.* As we have mentioned before, SAM allows researchers to represent the video traces using only four parameters. In addition to that we need a fifth parameter to help initialize the simulation process needed for the traffic generation. The fifth parameter is the standard deviation of the modeling error.

In *R* [44], there are two functions that can be used to generate time-series points based on ARIMA models: *arima.sim* and *garsim* included in the *gsarima* package [45]. Unfortunately, these two functions can only simulate ARIMA models and not work with SARIMA (seasonal ARIMA) models. To overcome this obstacle, we converted SARIMA model to an infinite series of AR coefficients [12, 46]. The *gsarima* package provides a function "*arrep*" that is capable of such conversion. From our experience, we found that 250 AR coefficients are sufficient to provide good results. We implemented the SAM-based generator using C#. The generator is based on the equation developed in [47].

Figure 9 shows a CDF comparison between the trace obtained from our trace generator and the actual trace. The provided trace generator implementation is also available for the research community to improve and adjust to different simulation setups.

*6.2. SAM-Based Video Trace Analyzer.* To ease the analysis of video traces and the comparison of SAM model against the original trace, we developed a simple GUI, shown in Figure 10, that allows the users to load the video trace frame size information from a text file. SAM analyzer then processes the information and calculates the seasonality of the trace, its SAM parameters, and its AIC value.

The user can plot the ACF and PACF graphs of the video trace. In addition, the user can plot original video trace versus SAM generated trace comparison graphs for ACF and ECDF. Figure 11 shows an example an example of the comparison graphs generated by SAM trace analyzer. Additional comparisons can be added upon user needs. SAM trace analyzer is implemented using C#. Our implementation provides an interface to *R* compiled code to allow full utilization of its capabilities.

In this section we illustrated the usage of two of our developed tools. In the next section we discuss the importance of our contribution and conclude the paper.

# 7. Conclusions

In this paper, we presented our work of encoding, analyzing, and modeling over 50 HD video traces that represent a wide spectrum of statistical characteristics.

We can summarize the key contributions of this paper in the following points.

(1) We collected over 50 HD video traces from YouTube website that represents a wide variety of video traces. We encoded these traces using AVC standard with the most common settings supported by experts' recommendations. These traces provide the research community with the means to test and research new methods to optimize network resources, and especially using dynamic bandwidth allocation. All the video traces and the developed tools are available to the research community through our website [20].

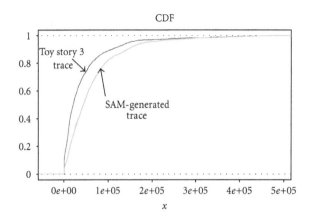

FIGURE 9: CDF comparison between SAM-generator and actual trace.

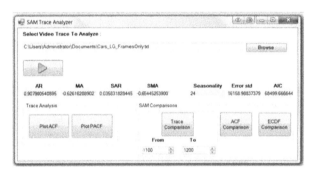

FIGURE 10: SAM-based video trace analyzer GUI.

(2) We performed a full statistical analysis to show the variance of the collected video traces using the most common quantitative measures.

(3) We performed a factor analysis to determine the principal components that define a HD video trace. We concluded that both Mean and Kurtosis values can be considered as the two main principal components. Our analysis has shown that both Kurtosis and Skewness values are important in defining a HD video trace, contrary to what has been considered before for MPEG1 encoded videos.

(4) We performed a cluster analysis on our collection of HD videos using *k*-means clustering. Our results showed that we can group these movies into two main clusters. We supported our results using different graphical and nongraphical methods.

(5) We compared three modeling methods in their ability to model our collection of HD video traces. Our results showed that SAM has a clear advantage over both AR and ARIMA models in both accuracy and simplicity as represented in its AIC values.

(6) We have also compared these methods in their ability to forecast video traffic. Our prediction analysis was based on several factors to ensure that the chosen model is capable of providing the best results under the lowest requirements. Our results showed once

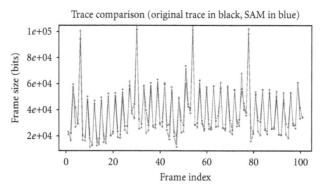

(a) Trace Comparison (frames between 1100–1200)

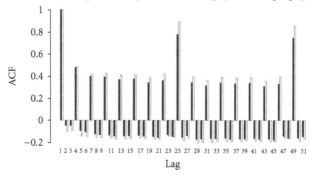

(b) ACF Comparison (first 50 lags)

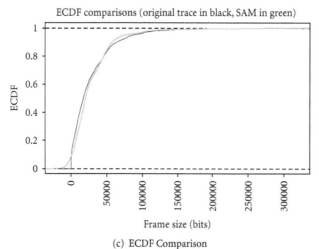

(c) ECDF Comparison

FIGURE 11: An example of SAM trace analyzer generated comparison plots.

again that SAM has a significant improvement over both AR and ARIMA, where it provided at least 50% better $SNR^{-1}$ values.

(7) Finally we illustrated the implementation of two of our developed tools. We showed the ability of the SAM-based generator of generating HD video traces that can be configured and used in different simulation scenarios.

This contribution provides the initial steps to achieve a better dynamic bandwidth allocation schemes designed to optimize bandwidth utilization with the presence of the high-demanding HD video streams.

## References

[1] Google, "YouTube HD video section," June 2010, http://www .youtube.com/HD.

[2] C. Albrecht, "Survey: Online Video Up to 27% of Internet Traffic," October 2009, http://tinyurl.com/yzpzoew.

[3] Cisco, "Cisco VNI: Forecast and Methodology, 2010–2015," February 2012, http://tinyurl.com/3p7v28.

[4] Comscore Press Release, http://tinyurl.com/l4o3rs.

[5] Comscore Press Release in November 2009, http://news.web-sitegear.com/view/149267.

[6] Hulu, "Hulu Website," June 2011, http://www.hulu.com.

[7] Netflix, "DVD Rental and HD video streaming service," June 2011, http://www.netflix.com.

[8] A. Adas, "Supporting real time VBR video using dynamic reservation based on linear prediction," in *Proceedings of 15th Annual Joint Conference of the IEEE Computer and Communications Societies (INFOCOM '96)*, pp. 1476–1483, March 1996.

[9] M. Wu, R. A. Joyce, H. S. Wong, L. Guan, and S. Y. Kung, "Dynamic resource allocation via video content and short-term traffic statistics," *IEEE Transactions on Multimedia*, vol. 3, no. 2, pp. 186–199, 2001.

[10] Y. Liang and M. Han, "Dynamic bandwidth allocation based on online traffic prediction for real-time MPEG-4 video streams," *EURASIP Journal on Advances in Signal Processing*, vol. 2007, Article ID 87136, 2007.

[11] G. van der Auwera, P. T. David, and M. Reisslein, "Traffic characteristics of H.264/AVC variable bit rate video," *IEEE Communications Magazine*, vol. 46, no. 11, pp. 164–174, 2008.

[12] C. Chatfield, *The Analysis of Time Series: An Introduction*, Chapman & Hall/CRC, 6th edition, 2003.

[13] R. J. Hyndman and Y. Khandakar, "Automatic time series forecasting: the forecast package for R," *Journal of Statistical Software*, vol. 27, no. 3, pp. 1–22, 2008.

[14] A. K. Al Tamimi, R. Jain, and C. So-In, "Modeling and generation of AVC and SVC-TS mobile video traces for broadband access networks," in *Proceedings of the 1st Annual ACM SIGMM Conference on Multimedia Systems (MMSys '10)*, pp. 89–98, February 2010.

[15] A. Al Tamimi, C. So-In, R. Jain et al., "Modeling and resource allocation for mobile video over WiMAX broadband wireless networks," *IEEE Journal on Selected Areas in Communications*, vol. 28, no. 3, pp. 354–365, 2010.

[16] P. Manzoni, P. Cremonesi, and G. Serazzi, "Workload models of VBR video traffic and their use in resource allocation policies," *IEEE/ACM Transactions on Networking*, vol. 7, no. 3, pp. 387–397, 1999.

[17] O. Rose, "Statistical properties of MPEG video traffic and their impact on traffic modeling in ATM systems," in *Proceedings of the 20th Conference on Local Computer Networks*, no. 16–19, pp. 397–406, October 1995.

[18] L. L. Laetitia, *MPEG-4 AVC traffic analysis and bandwidth prediction for broadband cable networks*, M.S. thesis, Georgia Tech, 2008.

[19] A. K. Al Tamimi, R. Jain, and C. So-In, "Modeling and prediction of high definition video traffic: a real-world case study," in *Proceedings of the 2nd International Conferences on Advances in Multimedia (MMEDIA '10)*, pp. 168–173, Athens, Ga, USA, 2010.

[20] A. Al-Tamimi and R. Jain, "SAM model Traces website," June 2011, http://www.cse.wustl.edu/~jain/sam/index.html.

[21] K. Jack, *Video Demystified*, HighText, 2nd edition, 1996.

[22] G. E. P. Box and G. Jenkins, *Time Series Analysis: Forecasting and Control*, Holden-Day, 1976.

[23] The Top 5 video streaming websites, March 2010, http://www.techsupportalert.com/top-5-video-streaming-websites.htm.

[24] MediaInfo, "MediaInfo supplies technical and tag information about your video or audio files," June 2011, http://mediainfo.sourceforge.net/en.

[25] J. Ozer, "Producing H.264 Video for Flash: An Overview," March 2010, http://www.streaminglearningcenter.com/articles/producing-h264-video-for-flash-an-overview.html.

[26] Digital Rapids, April 2012, http://dr6.sitesystems.ca/downloads/docs/DR_Studio_AVC.pdf.

[27] FFMPEG Coding Library, Cross-platform solution to record, convert and stream audio and video, http://ffmpeg.org.

[28] x264 Encoder, March 2010, http://www.videolan.org/developers/x264.html.

[29] JM Reference Software, March 2010, http://iphome.hhi.de/suehring/tml/.

[30] B. S. Everitt, *An R and S-Plus® Companion to Multivariate Analysis*, Springer, 2007.

[31] H. T. Kaiser, "The application of electronic computers to factor analysis," *Educational and Psychological Measurement*, vol. 20, pp. 141–151, 1960.

[32] R.B. Cattel, "The scree test for the number of factors," *Multivariate Behavioral Research*, vol. 1, no. 2, pp. 245–276, 1966.

[33] G. Raîche, M. Riopel, and J. Blais, "Non graphical solutions for the cattell's scree test," in *Proceedings of the Annual Meeting of the Psychometric Society*, Montreal, Canada.

[34] G. Kootstra, "Project on exploratory Factor Analysis applied to foreign language learning," 2004.

[35] M. Norusis, *SPSS 17.0 Statistical Procedures Companion*, Prentice Hall, 2009.

[36] C. Ding and X. He, "K-means clustering via principal component analysis," in *Proceedings of the 21t International Conference on Machine Learning (ICML '04)*, vol. 69, 2004.

[37] Cluster Validity Algorithms, October 2009, http://tinyurl.com/yj8jz9w.

[38] A. M. Dawood and M. Ghanbari, "Content-based MPEG video traffic modeling," *IEEE Transactions on Multimedia*, vol. 1, no. 1, pp. 77–87, 1999.

[39] Y. Sun and J. N. Daigle, "A source model of video traffic based on full-length VBR MPEG4 video traces," in *Proceedings of IEEE Global Telecommunications Conference*, vol. 2, p. 5, 2005.

[40] H. Feng and Y. Shu, "Study on network traffic prediction techniques," in *Proceedings of the International Conference on Wireless Communications, Networking and Mobile Computing (WCNM '05)*, pp. 1041–1044, September 2005.

[41] J. A. Nelder and R. Mead, "A simplex algorithm for function minimization," *Computer Journal*, vol. 7, pp. 308–313, 1965.

[42] H. Zhao, N. Ansari, and Y. Shi, "Efficient predictive bandwidth allocation for real time videos," *IEICE Transactions on Communications*, vol. 86, no. 1, 2003.

[43] R. Hyndman and A. Kostenko, "Minimum sample size requirements for seasonal forecasting models," *Foresight*, vol. 6, pp. 12–15, 2007.

[44] The project R of statstical computing, June 2011, http://www.r-project.org.

[45] O. Briet, "Gsarima: Two functions for Generalized SARIMA time series simulation," June 2011, http://cran.fyxm.net/web/packages/gsarima/index.html.

[46] D. Montgomery, *Forecasting and Time Series Analysis*, McGraw-Hill, 1990.

[47] A. K. Al-Tamimi, R. Jain, and C. So-In, "Dynamic resource allocation based on online traffic prediction for video streams," in *Proceedings of IEEE 4th International Conference on Internet Multimedia Services Architecture and Application (IMSAA '10)*, Bangalore, India, December 2010.

# 16

# Optimal Resource Allocation and VCG Auction-Based Pricing for H.264 Scalable Video Quality Maximization in 4G Wireless Systems

**Shreyans Parakh and Aditya K. Jagannatham**

*Department of Electrical Engineering, Indian Institute of Technology, Kanpur 208016, India*

Correspondence should be addressed to Aditya K. Jagannatham, adityaj@iitk.ac.in

Academic Editor: Raouf Hamzaoui

We present novel schemes for optimal OFDMA bitrate allocation towards video quality maximization in H.264 scalable video coding (SVC)-based 4G wireless systems. We use the rate and quality models for video characterization of the SVC extension of the H.264/AVC and develop the framework for optimal scalable video transmission. Subsequently, we derive the closed form solution of the optimal H.264 scalable video quantization parameter for sum video quality maximization in unicast and multicast 4G WiMAX adaptive modulation and coding (AMC) scenarios. We also formulate a Vickrey-Clarke-Groves (VCG) auction-based time-frequency (TF) resource pricing scheme for dynamic bitrate allocation and simultaneous prevention of video quality degradation by malicious users for H.264-based scalable video transmission. Simulation results demonstrate that application of the proposed optimal 4G OFDMA schemes for unicast/multicast video quality maximization yield significantly superior performance in comparison to fixed rate video agnostic allocation.

## 1. Introduction

The rapid rise in the demand for ubiquitous mobile broadband wireless access has spurred the development of 4G wireless standards such as LTE and WiMAX. These technologies provide high data rates and reliable wireless services to the users. A significant component of the 4G wireless traffic comprises of video and multimedia-based rich applications such as surveillance, multimedia streaming, mobile TV, and video conferencing. A typical 4G wireless communication scenario for the above-described applications is shown in Figure 1. The key challenge in 4G cellular networks in the context of video transmission is to support reliable video streaming over the erratic fading wireless channels. This fading nature can potentially result in intolerable jitter and latency resulting in poor end-user experience for the highly sensitive multimedia applications. The fading nature of the wireless channel can be successfully mitigated using orthogonal frequency division multiplexing (OFDM) [1, 2], thus ensuring inter-symbol interference free transmission across

frequency-selective wireless channels. orthogonal frequency division for multiple access (OFDMA) is the multiple access technology based on OFDM in which different users (unicast) or groups of users (multicast) are allocated a fraction of the total subcarriers over a period of time. This is also known as time-frequency resource allocation in OFDMA systems.

Supporting video applications on wireless links necessitates the development of sophisticated multimedia codecs tailored for applicability in the erratic mobile wireless environment. A unique challenge for video transmission in 4G wireless systems is to ensure quality of video transmission over the time-varying fading wireless channel to mobile users with devices of disparate capabilities and QoS requirements. This has lead to the development of the scalable video coding (SVC) profile of the H.264/AVC [3, 4] which can be readily adopted for video transmission in unicast and multicast wireless scenarios. Scalable video coding enables the video content to be coded and stored at its highest fidelity levels, from which partial bit streams of lower fidelity can be extracted dynamically and adapted to meet the requirements

Optimal Resource Allocation and VCG Auction-Based Pricing for H.264 Scalable Video Quality Maximization in 4G Wireless Systems

189

of the users and the wireless links. The bitrate and video quality of the coded video stream depend on the combination of frame rate, spatial resolution, and quantization parameter [5]. Hence, it is essential to judiciously choose the coded video parameters to maximize the end user video quality and experience. Further, this has a direct impact on the end user quality of service (QoS) aspects such as jitter and latency. Compared to the spatial and temporal modes of scalability, the quantization parameter of a video stream can be adapted on a much finer scale and allows for greater flexibility towards optimal time-frequency resource allocation. The allocated bitrate and quality of video depends critically on the intrinsic video motion parameters. In this context, we consider a framework for optimal H.264-coded video rate-based time-frequency resource allocation at the 4G wireless Base Station (BS) for video quality maximization. In this paradigm, the users request the videos either individually or in multicast groups, and the server allocates time/frequency resources in the OFDMA system.

Previous works such as in [6] consider scheduling and resource allocation based on priority and latency. However, most such previous approaches are not specialized to the context of video and do not take the scalable nature of video transmission into consideration. This leads to suboptimal resource allocation and a net decrease in the video quality delivered to the end users. The authors in [7] allocate the time/frequency resources for real-time layered video transmission in WiMAX assuming fixed bitrate allocation to each multicast group. The utility of each multicast group is assumed to be a concave function of the bitrate allocated. However, the considered rate dependent generic utility function is not an accurate representation of the video quality. In our work, we consider the true perceptual quality-based utility functions. Hence, our framework provides a better end user video experience since it optimizes the relevant video quality directly. In [8], a scheme is proposed for allocation of the time resources in a HSDPA cellular network. The proposed scheme therein requires users to request a video quality level, with video quality defined as a function of the number of enhancement layers and the cumulative data rate. However, this framework does not consider the dependence of video quality and bitrate on the quantization quality and frame rate. Further, it does not consider a realistic optimization framework as compared to the one illustrated in this work in the context of a practical 4G WiMAX system. Hence, the key to efficient resource allocation in 4G wireless systems lies in the interpretation of the characteristic video rate and quality parameters which lead to optimal bitrate allocation. This necessitates the development of optimal schemes for time-frequency resource allocation and management. The proposed optimal time-frequency resource allocation scheme computes the bitrate to be allocated to the video sequences in the physical layer for video quality maximization.

Therefore, we consider a framework for optimal OFDMA time-frequency resource allocation based on the characteristic video quality and bitrate models of the scalable video bit streams as functions of quantization parameter and frame rate. We compute the bitrate models of the H.264 SVC coded streams using the JSVM [9] reference codec and employ the standard video parameters from works such as [5, 10] to characterize the quality dependence on frame rate, quantization parameter of the coded videos. Based on these models, we formulate a constrained convex optimization problem for optimal OFDMA time-frequency resource allocation. We employ the robust framework of convex optimization [11] to present a closed form expression for computation of the optimal coded video parameters. The server can employ these parameters to compute the optimal resource allocation based on the requirements of the users and availability of the bandwidth. This efficient utilization of the available bandwidth results in maximizing the quality of the transmitted video and end user video experience. Our results demonstrate that optimization using the proposed model yields significant enhancement in the video quality as compared to the video agnostic equal bitrate allocation for unicast/multicast scenarios in the OFDMA system.

Further, in practical 4G systems, malicious users can distort the resource allocation scheme at the QoS enforcement points (such as base stations and service gateways in WiMAX) by misreporting the parameter values, thereby resulting in suboptimal resource allocation and disproportionate benefits to the malicious users. The optimal solution and the highest video quality is hence obtained only when the parameters are reported accurately by the unicast/multicast subscribers or service providers.

Game theory [12, 13] -based auctioning provides a framework to allocate resources in the presence of such distorting malicious users. This along with the optimization framework can be used to allocate bitrate to video sequences which discourages malicious users. Its applications have been recently extended to the field of wireless communication, especially in the context of resource optimization [14]. The authors in [15] define a utility function based on transmission rate and packet error probability and aim to achieve best quality of experience. In the context of 4G wireless video communication, game theory-based Vickrey-Clarke-Groves (VCG) auction procedure can be adapted for time-frequency (TF) resource allocation. The auctioned item in this context is the bitrate corresponding to the allotted TF resources, and the bidders/decision makers are the service providers or users themselves. The auctioneer is the QoS policy enforcer in the 4G wireless network. This interaction between various decision makers is akin to a strategic game, and the decision makers are also termed as players in the nomenclature of game theory. We assume that all the players are rational and are driven towards utility maximization. Each user reports the characteristic video parameter values to the policy enforcer to calculate the sum utility function. Unlike conventional utility-based exclusively on video quality, the VCG procedure employs the pricing-based net utility function, which prices the TF resources in accordance with the allocation. Therefore, knowledge of the characteristic video parameters is critical for optimizing the bitrate and quality of the streamed videos.

Some research regarding the use of game theory with malicious users has been considered in [16] in the context of peer-to-peer live streaming. The research in [17] proposes

FIGURE 1: A wireless communication scenario.

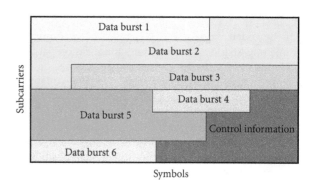

FIGURE 2: Rough schematic of OFDM frame in WiMAX.

a Vickrey scheme for computing the shortest path in a decentralized network. The authors in [18] present the application of a VCG procedure in mechanism design. In this paper, we are primarily concerned about misreporting of the quantizer-based rate and quality parameter values. The framework can readily be extended to VCG-based optimization for malicious users misreporting other parameter values.

In the simulation results, we specialize our proposed algorithm taking into account the different modulation and coding rates in a 4G WiMAX scenario and demonstrate that the proposed optimization scheme provides significant improvement in video quality over the content agnostic nonscalable equal symbol rate allocation scheme for unicast and multicast scenarios. We further consider that the parameters may be subverted to benefit a group of users. The proposed VCG procedure ensures that the users misreporting the parameters are punished by the QoS enforcer through higher resource pricing, in turn resulting in a reduced net utility for the malicious user. Hence, the VCG procedure naturally discourages users' malicious tendency towards misreporting and forces them to report accurate parameter values towards net utility maximization.

The rest of the paper is organized as follows. Section 2 describes the underlying framework for 4G WiMAX-based H.264 scalable video transmission considered in this paper and the rate and quality models of the videos. Subsequently, in Section 3 we describe the scheme for optimal video TF resource allocation in an OFDM frame. Section 4 describes the VCG procedure-based resource allocation to avoid misreporting of parameters by malicious users. In Section 5 we present the simulation results for the proposed optimal unicast/multicast video resource allocation schemes in 4G OFDMA wireless systems and a performance comparison with the existing schemes. Finally, we conclude the paper in Section 6.

## 2. System Model and 4G OFDMA WiMAX Framework

In OFDMA systems, the high data rate input stream is divided into a multitude of parallel low data rate streams which are subsequently loaded onto the orthogonal subcarriers. Each symbol in the time domain comprises of several orthogonal subcarriers. A few such subcarriers are designated as pilot and guard subcarriers which comprise an overhead in

the OFDMA system. Pilot subcarriers are employed to estimate the timing and frequency synchronization parameters so that the offset errors are minimized, while the guard subcarriers avoid overlap with adjacent OFDM bands. The OFDMA scheduler allocates the time/frequency resource blocks, which are characterized by the allotted OFDM symbols/subcarriers, respectively, to the users. The bitrate of the OFDMA system depends on the number of symbols in each OFDM frame, the number of subcarriers used in each symbol, the modulation, and channel coding formats employed. Figure 2 presents the rough schematic of an OFDMA frame in WiMAX.

In this context, the 4G wireless cellular standard WiMAX [19], which employs OFDMA in the physical layer for transmission of bits was designed to provide a high data rate broadband air interface to its users coupled with seamless data transfer under high speed mobility. WiMAX provides services such as unsolicited grants service (UGS) for constant bitrate VOIP applications, real-time polling service (rtPS) for real time applications such as video transmission, non real time polling service for large data transfers and best effort service for web applications. The scheduler present at the base station helps in optimally allocating the bandwidth resources, aimed at avoiding traffic congestion and data starvation. Thus, the DL scheduler has the critical tasks of optimal bandwidth allocation, choosing the modulation and coding schemes and data bursts depending on the service priority and wireless link quality determined from the channel quality indicator (CQICH) feedback channel. It then generates the UL/DL MAP containing the control information for users to access their bursts. Hence, our proposed model aims at optimally allocating the time-frequency resources in the UL and DL scheduler to maximize the net video quality.

2.1. Scalable Video Rate and Quality Models. The parametric models given in [5] can be conveniently employed to model the video bitrate. As proved in this work, we model the rate as a product of the normalized functions of the frame rate $t$ and quantization parameter $q$. We employ the JSVM reference codec to compute the rate parameters for quantization parameter in the range $15 \leq q \leq 40$ with intervals of $q = 5$, and frame rates $t = 15, 30$ fps. We employed four temporal layers and one quality layer in JSVM to obtain the bitrate for

Optimal Resource Allocation and VCG Auction-Based Pricing for H.264 Scalable Video Quality Maximization in 4G Wireless Systems

191

these layers. It is to be noted that quantization parameter and quantization step size ($q_s$) are related as $q = 4 + 6\log_2(q_s)$. The normalized rate functions $R_t(t), R_q(q)$ of the frame rate $t$ and quantization parameter $q$ respectively are given as

$$R_t(t) = \left(\frac{1 - e^{-ct/t_{max}}}{1 - e^{-c}}\right), \qquad R_q(q) = e^{d(1-q/q_{min})}. \qquad (1)$$

The video characteristic parameters $c$ and $d$ model the bitrate variation as a function of the frame rate and quantization parameter, respectively. The parameters $c$ and $d$ are higher for videos with low motion content. These video characteristic parameters $c$ and $d$ are obtained by minimizing the mean squared-error (MSE) between the measured rate obtained using the JSVM codec and the modeled video sequences for frame rates 15 fps and 30 fps. Frame rates lower than 15 fps result in noticeable artifacts due to persistence of the human visual system. Figure 3 demonstrates the plot of $R_q(q)$ versus quantization step size $q$ for the standard *Akiyo* test sequence. Hence, the resulting joint rate function $R(q, t)$ is given in terms of the normalized rate functions $R_t(t), R_q(q)$ as

$$R(q, t) = R_{max}R_t(t)R_q(q)$$
$$= R_{max}\left(\frac{1 - e^{-ct/t_{max}}}{1 - e^{-c}}\right)e^{d(1-q/q_{min})}, \qquad (2)$$

where $R_{max}$ is the bitrate of the highest quality video sequence corresponding to encoding at frame rate $t_{max}$ and quantization parameter $q_{min}$. The plot in Figure 4 demonstrates that the proposed rate model closely follows the observed rate. Videos coded at lower values of quantization parameter $q \in [1, 15]$ result in an exponential increase in bitrate and hence are not suitable for transmission in bandwidth constrained wireless scenarios. Further, we limit the quantization parameter to $q_{max} = 40$, as higher values lead to significant degradation of video quality.

Similarly, the normalized video quality functions $Q_t(t), Q_q(q)$ with respect to the frame rate $t$ and quantization parameter $q$, respectively can be modeled as

$$Q_t(t) = \frac{1 - e^{-at/t_{max}}}{1 - e^{-a}}, \qquad Q_q(q) = \beta q + \gamma. \qquad (3)$$

The quality function $Q_t(t)$ describes the variation in quality as a function of the frame rate $t$ and is characterized by the parameter value $a$. This value is higher in videos with lower motion content when compared to videos with higher degree of motion. The function $Q_q(q)$ is well approximated as a linear function of the quantization parameter $q$ as demonstrated in Figure 5. The parameters $\beta, \gamma$ are derived by fitting a linear model to video quality at the points $q = 15$ and $q = 35$ using the models specified in [5], while parameter values $a$ are given in [5] for CIF resolution and have been linearly extrapolated for the remaining videos of different resolutions with the values given in [10]. The resulting video quality is described by the product function:

$$Q(q, t) = Q_{max}Q_t(t)Q_q(q)$$
$$= Q_{max}\left(\frac{1 - e^{-at/t_{max}}}{1 - e^{-a}}\right)(\beta q + \gamma). \qquad (4)$$

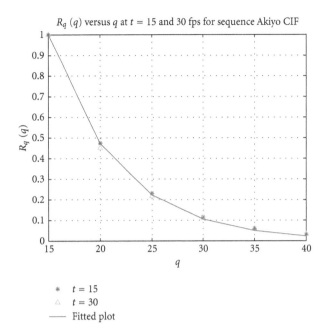

$R_q (q)$ versus $q$ at $t = 15$ and 30 fps for sequence Akiyo CIF

*    $t = 15$
△    $t = 30$
—— Fitted plot

FIGURE 3: Normalized rate $R_q(q)$ versus $q$ at $t = 15$, 30 fps for sequence Akiyo (CIF).

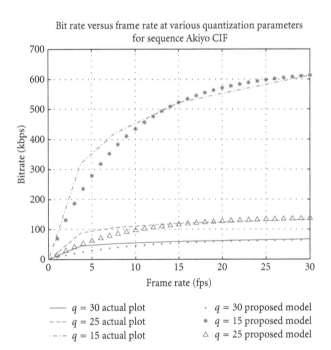

Bit rate versus frame rate at various quantization parameters for sequence Akiyo CIF

—— $q = 30$ actual plot     · $q = 30$ proposed model
--- $q = 25$ actual plot     * $q = 15$ proposed model
-·-· $q = 15$ actual plot     △ $q = 25$ proposed model

FIGURE 4: Plot showing proposed bitrate following actual bitrate at $q = 15, 25$, and 30.

The constant $Q_{max}$ is the quality when the video is coded at $t_{max}, q_{min}$ and can be normalized as $Q_{max} \triangleq 100$. For a fixed frame rate $t_f$ fps, the quality depends exclusively on the quantization parameter given by $Q_q(q)$. This function can then be employed as a handle to maximize the video quality.

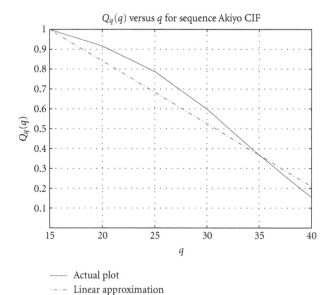

FIGURE 5: Video quality $Q_q(q)$ versus $q$ for the video sequence Akiyo (CIF).

## 3. Optimal Bitrate Calculation

Let $R_S$ denote the total symbol rate corresponding to all the subcarriers of the WiMAX OFDMA frame and $n_i, 1 \leq i \leq N$, the number of users corresponding to the $i$th multicast group. Let $Q^i(q_i, t_f)$, $R^i(q_i, t_f)$ represent the quality and rate of the $i$th video sequence corresponding to the quantization parameter $q_i$ for a given frame rate $t_f$. Let $m_i$ be the number of bits per symbol, that is, modulation order and $r_i$ the code rate of the $i$th user in the unicast scenario. Let $\xi_i$ denote the bit-error introduced resulting in a required bitrate $R^i(q_i, t_f)/(1 - \xi_i)$ for the $i$th video sequence. The optimization criterion for rate allocation towards video quality maximization can be formulated as

$$\text{max.} \quad \sum_{i=1}^{N} n_i Q^i\left(q_i, t_f\right)$$

$$\text{subject to} \quad \sum_{i=1}^{N} \frac{R^i\left(q_i, t_f\right)}{m_i r_i (1 - \xi_i)} \leq R_S \tag{5}$$

$$q_{\min} \leq q_i \leq q_{\max}, \quad 1 \leq i \leq N.$$

The Lagrangian $L(\overline{q}, \lambda, \overline{\mu}, \overline{\delta})$ of the above optimization problem can be expressed using the Lagrange multipliers $\lambda, \mu_i, \delta_i, 1 \leq i \leq N$ as

$$L\left(\overline{q}, \lambda, \overline{\mu}, \overline{\delta}\right) = \sum_{i=1}^{N} n_i Q_{\max} Q_t^i\left(t_f\right)\left(\beta_i q_i + \gamma_i\right)$$

$$+ \lambda\left(\sum_{i=1}^{N} k_i e^{d_i(1 - q_i/q_{\min})} - R_S\right) \tag{6}$$

$$+ \sum_{i=1}^{N} \mu_i\left(q_i - q_{\max}\right) + \sum_{i=1}^{N} \delta_i\left(q_{\min} - q_i\right),$$

where $k_i \triangleq (R_{\max}^i / m_i r_i (1 - \xi_i))((1 - e^{-c_i t_f / t_{\max}})/(1 - e^{-c_i}))$, and the quantity $R_{\max}^i$ is the maximum bitrate corresponding to the $i$th video. The KKT conditions for the above Lagrangian optimization criterion with $\overline{\mu}_i \succeq 0, \overline{\delta}_i \succeq 0$, can be formulated as follows:

$$n_i Q_{\max} Q_t^i\left(t_f\right)\beta_i - \lambda k_i\left(\frac{d_i}{q_{\min}}\right)e^{d_i(1 - q_i/q_{\min})} + \mu_i - \delta_i = 0,$$

$$\sum_{i=1}^{N} k_i e^{d_i(1 - q_i/q_{\min})} \leq R_S, \tag{7}$$

$$\lambda\left(\sum_{i=1}^{N} k_i e^{d_i(1 - q_i/q_{\min})} - R_S\right) = 0,$$

where the last condition above follows from the complementary slackness of the inequality constraint. Assuming $\mu_i = 0$ and $\delta_i = 0$, the expression for the optimal Lagrange multiplier $\lambda^*$ can be derived as

$$\lambda^* = \frac{q_{\min}}{R_S}\left(\sum_{j=1}^{N} n_j Q_{\max} Q_t^j\left(t_f\right)\frac{\beta_j}{d_j}\right). \tag{8}$$

Substituting the value of $\lambda^*$, $\mu_i$ and $\delta_i$ in the first KKT equation yields the closed form expression for the optimal quantization parameter $q_i^*$ given as

$$q_i^* = q_{\min}\left(1 - \frac{1}{d_i}\ln\left(\frac{Q_{\max} Q_t^i\left(t_f\right)q_{\min}\beta_i m_i r_i(1 - \xi_i)n_i}{R_{\max}^i R_t^i\left(t_f\right)\lambda^* d_i}\right)\right)$$

$$= q_{\min}\left(1 - \frac{1}{d_i}\ln\left(\frac{R_S}{k_i}\frac{n_i Q_t^i\left(t_f\right)\beta_i(d_i)^{-1}}{\sum_{j=1}^{N} n_j Q_t^j\left(t_f\right)\beta_j(d_i)^{-1}}\right)\right). \tag{9}$$

Substituting $q_i^*$ in (2) and (4) gives the required bitrate and maximum quality for each video. Figure 6 shows the optimal video quality versus bitrate plot for the video sequence *Akiyo* (CIF) as a function of the maximum rate $R_S$ at various frame rates. This corresponds to the unicast scenario in the above frame work with $N = 1$. As can be seen, the video quality is near 100% for bitrates in the range of 500–600 Kbps. At lower frame rates $t$, it can be seen from (4) that the quality $Q$ at higher bitrates is lower than 100% because the normalized quality function $Q_t(t) \ll 1$ for $t = 3.75, 7.5$ fps.

Based on the above analysis, we present an algorithm for fast computation of the optimal quantization parameters $q_i^*$ employing the closed form expression in (9). This algorithm has a very low computational complexity and hence can be employed for rapid computation of the optimal parameters. Algorithm 1 is described for the general case of multicast video transmission. This can be readily employed for the unicast scenario by substituting $n_i = 1$.

## 4. VCG-Based Video Resource Allocation

In this section, we present the VCG pricing- [12, 13] based TF resource allocation procedure for video quality

Optimal Resource Allocation and VCG Auction-Based Pricing for H.264 Scalable Video Quality Maximization in 4G Wireless Systems

193

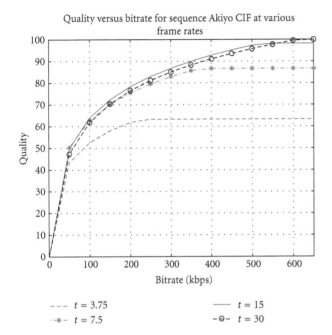

Quality versus bitrate for sequence Akiyo CIF at various frame rates

- - - $t = 3.75$       —— $t = 15$

-*- $t = 7.5$       -⊖- $t = 30$

FIGURE 6: Quality versus Bitrate for sequence Akiyo CIF at various frame rates.

maximization. We consider the variation of the net VCG-allocated utility as a function of the reported parameters $d$ and $\beta$ and demonstrate that its application in video rate and quality optimization leads to maximization of the net utility function. The utility function in this context of unicast/multicast video transmission, is the quality of video, which is given as a function of the quantization parameter in (4). The player/user might misreport the parameter values and subvert the allocation towards achieving disproportionate bitrate and therefore high-quality video at the cost of reduced quality to the other users. The overall utility and efficient allocation of bitrate to different videos is thus compromised. Such malicious users are penalized through the VCG auction-based TF resource pricing, which automatically leads to higher pricing and net utility reduction for the users misreporting the characteristic video parameter values. Let the actual and the reported utility functions of the $i$th user be denoted by $Q^i(q_i, t_f)$ and $M^i(q_i, t_f)$, respectively. The QoS enforcer determines the optimal allocation as per the reported utility functions $M^i(q_i, t_f)$. Let $\mathbf{q}^*$ denote the optimal quantization parameter allocation determined from the above convex optimization frame work. Also, let the quantity $Y_i(M_{-i}())$ for the $i$th user be defined as a function of the $N - 1$ utility functions $M^j(q_j, t_f)$ for all $j \neq i$ as

$$Y_i(M_{-i}()) = \max_{\underline{q}} \sum_{\substack{j=1 \\ j \neq i}}^{N} M^j(q_j, t_f). \qquad (10)$$

The VCG auction price $p_i$ of the allocated TF resources for video transmission to the $i$th user is given by the relation:

$$p_i = Y_i(M_{-i}()) - L_i(q^*), \qquad (11)$$

where the quantity $L_i(q^*)$ is defined as $L_i(q^*) \triangleq \sum_{\substack{j=1 \\ j \neq i}}^{N} M^j(q_j^*, t_f)$. It can be readily demonstrated that such a VCG auction-based pricing scheme results in serving appropriate retribution to the dishonest subscribers and service providers. Consider the net utility $Z_i$ of the $i$th player given as

$$Z_i \triangleq Q^i(q_i^*, t_f) - p_i, \qquad (12)$$

which is essentially the raw video quality adjusted for the price paid towards serving the users. The above net utility $Z_i$ can be expressed in terms of the true utility function $Q^i(q_i, t_f)$ and the reported utility function $M^i(q_i, t_f)$ as

$$Z_i = \underbrace{Q^i(q_i^*, t_f) + \sum_{\substack{j=1 \\ j \neq i}}^{N} M^j(q_j^*, t_f) - \max_{\underline{q}} \sum_{\substack{j=1 \\ j \neq i}}^{N} M^j(q_j, t_f)}_{U_i^*(\mathbf{q}^*)}. \qquad (13)$$

The last term $\max_{\underline{q}} \sum_{\substack{j=1 \\ j \neq i}}^{N} M^j(q_j, t_f)$ in the above expression is independent of the reported utility function of the $i$th user. Hence, it can be observed that $U_i(\mathbf{q}^*)$ for player $i$ is maximum for the allocated resource $\mathbf{q}^*$, calculated as per the optimization framework, only when the reported utility function $M^i(q_i^*, t_f)$ coincides with the true utility function $Q^i(q_i^*, t_f)$. Thus, the VCG procedure effectively punishes malicious users who deliberately misrepresent their video parameters. This TF resource allocation based on the VCG procedure is applied to all the $N$ players/service providers participating in the given scenario. We now present Algorithm 2 for computing the VCG parameters $q_i^*$ and $p_i$ below.

## 5. Simulation Results

We present simulation results to illustrate the performance of the proposed optimal schemes for OFDMA video transmission employing the DL/UL PUSC (partial usage of subcarriers) diversity permutation scheme used for subcarrier channelization in WiMAX. We consider the WiMAX profile with bandwidth $B = 20\,\text{Mhz}$, OFDMA frame time $T = 10\,\text{ms}$ (50% split for UL and DL traffic, i.e., 5 ms subframe for DL and UL) and number of subcarriers $N_S = 2048$ [19]. The number of data subcarriers is $N_d = 1440$ with each DL frame consisting of 44 OFDM symbols for data transmission out of the total available 48 symbols. Hence, the effective downlink symbol rate is $R_S = 44 \times 1440 \times (10 \times 10^{-3})^{-1} = 6.336\,\text{Msym/s}$. We assume that the distorting effects of interchannel interference and doppler effect are negligible to due robust signal processing at the physical layer.

### 5.1. Optimal 4G Video Resource Allocation. 
We consider the optimal time-frequency resource allocation for video transmission in the context of the WiMAX system described above. We begin with a unicast video transmission scenario, where each of the $N(= 9)$ standard video test sequences [20] of various spatial resolutions (QCIF, CIF, and 4CIF) listed

(1) **for** $i = 1 \to N$

(2) $\lambda^* = \dfrac{q_{\min}}{R_S}\left(\displaystyle\sum_{j=1}^{N} n_j Q_{\max} Q_t^j(t_f)\dfrac{\beta_j}{d_j}\right);$

(3) $q_i^* = q_{\min}\left(1 - \dfrac{1}{d_i}\ln\left(\dfrac{Q_{\max}Q_t^i(t_f)q_{\min}\beta_i m_i r_i(1-\xi_i)n_i}{R_{\max}^i R_t^i(t_f)\lambda^* d_i}\right)\right);$

(4) **if** $q_i^* < q_{\min}$ **then**

(5) 　　　$q_i^* = q_{\min};$

(6) **else if** $q_i^* > q_{\max}$ **then**

(7) 　　　$q_i^* = q_{\max};$

(8) **end if**

(9) $R^i(q_i^*, t_f) = R_{\max}^i\left(\dfrac{1 - e^{-c_i t/t_{\max}}}{1 - e^{-c_i}}\right)e^{d_i(1 - q_i^*/q_{\min})};$

(10) $R_S : R_S - R^i(q_i^*, t_f);$

(11) **end for**

(12) **if** $q_i^* = q_{\min}$ **then**

(13) 　　$R_S : R_S - \sum(R^i(q_{\min}^*, t_f));$

(14) 　　**repeat steps** (1) to (11) for the **remaining video sequences.**

(15) **end if**

ALGORITHM 1: Optimal quality.

(1) **compute** $R^i(q_i^*, t_f)$ and $Q^i(q_i^*, t_f)$ **employing** Algorithm 1;

(2) **set** $q_i^* = \hat{q}_i$ **using** $\{R^i, d_t\}$ **or** $\{Q^i, \beta_t\}$ **to avoid violation of constraints;**

(3) **compute** $Y_i(M_i()) = \max_q \sum_{\substack{j=1 \\ j \neq i}}^{N} M^j(q_j, t_f)$ **employing** (5);

(4) **compute** $L_i(q^*);$

(5) $p_i = Y_i(M_{-i}()) - L_i(q^*);$

(6) **repeat steps** (1) to (4) **with different** $d$ **or/and** $\beta.$

(7) **select minimum** $p_i.$

ALGORITHM 2: Algorithm for $q_i^*$ and $p_i.$

in Table 1 along with the associated values of the video characteristic parameters $a_i, c_i, d_i, \beta_i$, and $\gamma_i$ are streamed to individual users. Table 2 presents the symbol rate and quality for optimal and equal symbol rate allocation. The videos under consideration have different resolutions and varying degrees of motion. The values of the modulation index $m_i$ for each user are chosen randomly from the set $\{1, 2, 4, 6\}$ corresponding to the standard WiMAX modulation formats BPSK, QPSK, 16-QAM, and 64-QAM, respectively. The coding rates $r_i$ are similarly chosen randomly from the set $\{1/2, 2/3, 3/4, 5/6\}$ of standard WiMAX coding rates. The optimal video quality maximizing bitrate allocation and the associated quantization parameters $q_i^*$ are computed by solving the optimization problem in (5) employing the standard CVX based convex solver [21] and the closed form solution based scheme in Algorithm 1. The corresponding per video sequence normalized quality is listed in Table 1 for both the optimal and equal symbol rate allocation schemes at $t = 30$ fps from which it can be readily seen that the optimal resource allocation scheme outperforms the suboptimal equal resource allocation scheme. Figure 7 shows the comparison of these schemes for the above unicast scenario at various values of symbol rate $R_S$, clearly demonstrating the efficiency of the optimal allocation scheme described

in Section 3. Further, the optimal resource allocation computed employing the closed form solution in (9) and the associated fast algorithm described in Algorithm 1 achieve a performance close to that of the CVX solver, thereby verifying the theoretical analysis.

Figure 8 shows the comparison of these schemes for multicast scenarios with the number of multicast subscribers chosen randomly from the set $30 \leq n_i \leq 100$ at frame rate $t = 30$ fps. The bit-errors $\xi_i$ are assumed to be random in the interval $[10^{-3}, 10^{-5}]$. The parameters $m_i$ and $r_i$ for each multicast group are chosen randomly as described in the unicast scenario. Similar to the unicast scenario, it can be observed that optimal resource allocation results in progressively larger gains compared to the suboptimal equal resource allocation. Further, the net normalized video qualities for both the resource allocation schemes in the standard WiMAX multicast scenario described above with rate $R_S = 6.336$ Msym/s are given in Table 3 for each of the frame rates $t = 15$ and $t = 30$ fps. It can be clearly seen that the optimal allocation results in a significant enhancement of approximately 6.5% in the video quality over equal resource allocation. We schematically represent the optimal and equal allocation of time/frequency resources of the OFDMA symbol for unicast transmission in

Optimal Resource Allocation and VCG Auction-Based Pricing for H.264 Scalable Video Quality Maximization in 4G Wireless Systems

195

TABLE 1: Parameter values and $R_{\max}$.

| Sequence | $a_i$ | $c_i$ | $d_i$ | $\beta_i$ | $\gamma_i$ | $R_{\max}^i$ |
|---|---|---|---|---|---|---|
| Foreman CIF | 7.7000 | 2.0570 | 2.2070 | −0.0298 | 1.4475 | 3046.3 |
| Akiyo CIF | 8.0300 | 3.4910 | 2.2520 | −0.0316 | 1.4737 | 612.85 |
| Football CIF | 5.3800 | 1.3950 | 1.4900 | −0.0258 | 1.3872 | 5248.9 |
| Crew CIF | 7.3400 | 1.6270 | 1.8540 | −0.0393 | 1.5898 | 4358.2 |
| City CIF | 7.3500 | 2.0440 | 2.3260 | −0.0346 | 1.5196 | 2775.5 |
| Akiyo QCIF | 5.5600 | 4.0190 | 1.8320 | −0.0316 | 1.4737 | 139.63 |
| Foreman QCIF | 7.1000 | 2.5900 | 1.7850 | −0.0298 | 1.4475 | 641.73 |
| City 4CIF | 8.4000 | 1.0960 | 2.3670 | −0.0346 | 1.5196 | 20900 |
| Crew 4CIF | 7.3400 | 1.1530 | 2.4050 | −0.0393 | 1.5898 | 18021 |

TABLE 2: Allocation of symbols in an OFDM frame for unicast at $t = 30$ fps.

| Sequence | $m_i$ | $r_i$ | Equal symbol rate selction (ksps) | $Q_i/Q_{\max}$ | Optimal symbol rate allocation (ksps) | $Q_i/Q_{\max}$ |
|---|---|---|---|---|---|---|
| Foreman CIF | 1 | 5/6 | 704 | 0.666 | 685 | 0.660 |
| Akiyo CIF | 2 | 2/3 | 704 | 1.00 | 460 | 1.00 |
| Football CIF | 1 | 2/3 | 704 | 0.372 | 877 | 0.430 |
| Crew CIF | 1 | 5/6 | 704 | 0.362 | 1074 | 0.496 |
| City CIF | 1 | 2/3 | 704 | 0.602 | 754 | 0.618 |
| Akiyo QCIF | 4 | 1/2 | 704 | 1.00 | 70 | 1.00 |
| Foreman QCIF | 1 | 3/4 | 704 | 0.951 | 847 | 0.997 |
| City 4CIF | 4 | 2/3 | 704 | 0.471 | 741 | 0.482 |
| Crew 4CIF | 1 | 1/2 | 704 | 0.034 | 828 | 0.074 |

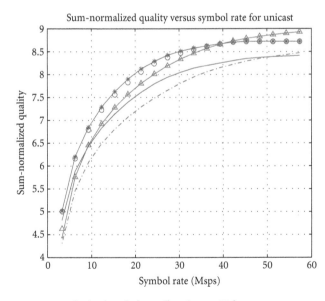

FIGURE 7: Unicast: sum-normalized quality versus symbol rate at $t = 15$ and 30 fps.

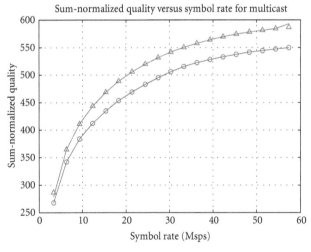

FIGURE 8: Multicast: sum normalized quality versus symbol rate at $t = 15$ and 30 fps.

Figures 9 and 10, respectively with each shade representing the portion of the DL subframe allocated to a particular video sequence belonging to the set under

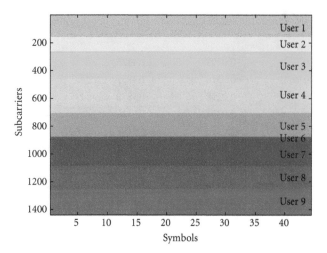

FIGURE 9: Allocation of symbols to videos with optimal allocation.

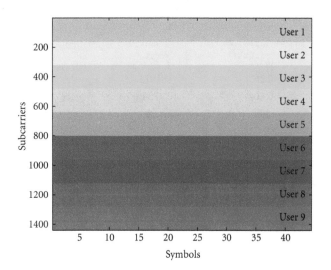

FIGURE 10: Allocation of symbols to videos with equal symbol rate allocation.

TABLE 3: Comparison of quality at frame rates for multicast $t = 15$ and $t = 30$ fps.

| Method | Sum $Q/Q_{max}$ at 15 fps | Sum $Q/Q_{max}$ at 30 fps |
|---|---|---|
| Optimal symbol rate | 395.5 | 364.9 |
| Equal symbol selection | 371.6 | 342.4 |

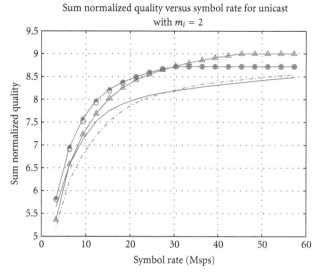

FIGURE 11: Unicast: sum normalized quality versus symbol rate at $t = 15$ and 30 fps with $m_i = 2$, for all $i$, and varying $r_i$.

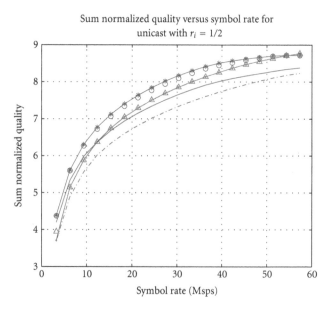

FIGURE 12: Unicast: sum normalized quality versus symbol rate at $t = 15$ and 30 fps with $r_i = 1/2$, for all $i$, and varying $m_i$.

consideration. Finally, we present the comparison of these schemes for unicast video transmission with $m_i = 2$, for all $i$ at various symbol rates $R_S$ and varying $r_i$ in Figure 11. Similarly, Figure 12 shows the comparison of these schemes for unicast with $r_i = 1/2$, for all $i$ at various $R_S$ and varying modulation order $m_i$. We conclude that higher modulation and coding rate provide higher net quality to the users. Overall, the optimal resource allocation algorithm proposed for OFDMA-based time-frequency resource allocation results in a significant improvement in the net video quality.

Optimal Resource Allocation and VCG Auction-Based Pricing for H.264 Scalable Video Quality Maximization in
4G Wireless Systems

197

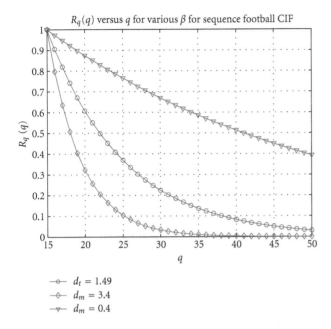

FIGURE 13: Rate versus quantization parameter at various $d$ for sequence football CIF: $d_t$ = true value, $d_m$ = misreprted value.

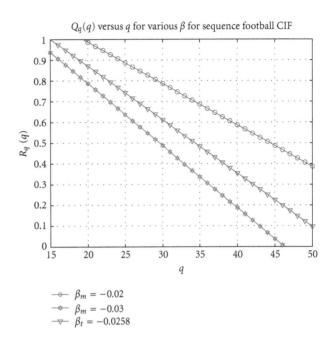

FIGURE 14: Quality versus quantization parameter at various $\beta$ for sequence football CIF: $\beta_t$ = true value, $\beta_m$ = misreprted value.

TABLE 4: Quantization parameter and bitrate for sequence football, Case I: $d = d_t$, Case II: $d < d_t$, and Case III: $d > d_t$.

| Case | I | II | III |
| --- | --- | --- | --- |
| $d_3$ | 1.49 | 0.4 | 3.4 |
| $q_3$ | 27.82 | 24.48 | 23.36 |
| $R^3$ | 1621.9 | 4076.6 | 789 |

### 5.2. VCG Auction-Based 4G Video Resource Allocation.

In this section, we study the impact of the parameters $d$ and $\beta$ on the bitrate and quality of the video. We then demonstrate the application of the proposed VCG procedure when the user misreports the parameter values. We consider $n_i = 1$, $r_i = 5/6$, and $m_i = 2$ for all $i$ to study the effect of misreporting $d$ and $\beta$. We consider the optimal allocation of TF resources in this scenario to the different groups and the net utility corresponding to accurate and misreporting of $d$, and $\beta$ parameters. We begin by specifically considering two separate cases in which a single subscriber of the standard test video sequence football CIF [20] misreports the parameter values $d$ (rate parameter) and $\beta$ (quality parameter). The scenario with multiple users misreporting multiple parameters is considered in the later simulations.

### 5.2.1. Behavior Corresponding to Misreporting d.

In this section we illustrate the effect of false reporting of parameter $d$ for the standard football video sequence on the overall bitrate allocation. Figure 13 depicts the bitrate of the sequence *Football* corresponding to $i = 3$, as a function of the quantization parameter $q$ for different values of the reported rate parameter $d$, where the true parameter $d_t = 1.49$. The curves corresponding to misreporting the $d$ parameter, that is, $d_m = 3.4 > d_t$ and $d_m = 0.4 < d_t$ can be seen

therein. Cases I, II and III in Table 4 demonstrate the allotted quantization parameter and corresponding bitrate when $d_m = d_t$, $d_m < d_t$ and $d_m > d_t$, respectively at $R_S = 6.336$ Msps for the standard football CIF sequence. Consider the adverse scenarios, where the user/service provider reports $d_m = 0.4 < d_t$ shown in case II. This results in suboptimal allocation of TF resources, with a disproportionate alloation of $R^3(q_3, t_f) = 4076.6$ Kbps. This is at the cost of decrease in video quality of the rest of the users. In the later simulations, it is shown that the application of the VCG procedure ensures that such malicious users are punished through a reduction in the net utility resulting from the VCG allocation. When $d_m = 3.4 > d_t$ as considered in case III, the allotted bitrate $R^3(q_3, t_f) = 789$ Kbps is much less than the rate 1621.9 Kbps (corresponding to case I). Hence, there is no incentive for the malicious user to misreport a lower value of the parameter $d$. However, the actual video encoded with this lower value of the allocated quantization parameter $q = 23.36$ will have bitrate $R^3(q_3, t_f) > 1621.9$ Kbps (corresponding to case I) and thus results in violating the overall bitrate constraint. Hence, the malicious user in this scenario is forced to compute the quantization parameter $\hat{q}_3$ corresponding to the allocated bitrate of 789 Kbps to ensure that the rate constraints are not violated. This results in lower quality $Q^3(\hat{q}_3, t_f)$.

### 5.2.2. Behavior Corresponding to Misreporting β.

We now consider the effect of misreporting of the parameter $\beta$ of a video sequence on the overall TF resource allocation. Figure 14 depicts the video quality as a function of the quantization parameter $q$ for the true value $\beta_t = -0.0258$ and misreported values $\beta_m = -0.03, -0.02$. Cases I, II, and III in Table 5 show the computed quantization parameters

TABLE 5: Quantization parameter and bitrate for sequence football Case I: $\beta = \beta_t$, Case II: $\beta_m < \beta_t$, and Case III: $\beta_m > \beta_t$.

| Case | I | II | III |
|------|-----|------|------|
| $\beta_3$ | $-0.0258$ | $-0.03$ | $-0.02$ |
| $q_3$ | 27.82 | 25.6 | 28.98 |
| $R^3$ | 1621.9 | 1832.2 | 1308.5 |

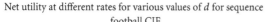

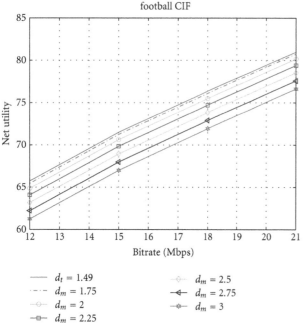

FIGURE 15: Net utility function versus rate at various values of parameter $d$ for sequence football. CIF: $d_t$ = true value, and $d_m$ = misreprted value.

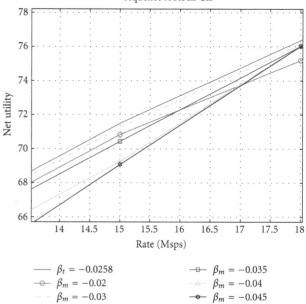

Net utility at different rates for various values of $\beta$ for sequence football CIF

Legend:
— $\beta_t = -0.0258$    —□— $\beta_m = -0.035$
—○— $\beta_m = -0.02$    —△— $\beta_m = -0.04$
—·· $\beta_m = -0.03$    —✳— $\beta_m = -0.045$

FIGURE 16: Net utility function versus rate at various values of parameter $\beta$ for sequence football. CIF: $\beta_t$ = true value, and $\beta_m$ = misreprted value.

and allotted bitrates of video sequences when $\beta = \beta_t$, $\beta_m = -0.03 < \beta_t$ and $\beta_m = -0.02 > \beta_t$, respectively at $R_S = 6.336$ Msps for the standard video sequence football CIF. When the misreported $\beta_m = -0.030 < -0.0258$ as in case II, the optimal bitrate allocation results in $R^3(q_3, t_f) = 1832.2 > 1621.9$ Kbps, and the difference $1832.2 - 1621.9 = 210.3$ Kbps is obtained by taking the share of bits from other videos. Hence, similar to reporting a lower value of $d$ as seen above, the malicious user has an incentive to report a lower value of the parameter $\beta$. For case III, corresponding to $\beta > -0.0258$, the bitrate obtained $R^3(q_3, t_f) = 1308.5 < 1621.9$ Kbps, as shown in Table 5. The quality $Q^3(q_3, t_f)$ is lower compared to the case when $\beta_t$ is reported. Hence, there is no incentive for the malicious user to report higher values of the quality parameter $\beta$.

*5.2.3. VCG Procedure Based TF Resource Allocation.* In this section, we illustrate the efficacy of the VCG procedure based resource allocation described in Section 4 towards punishing such malicious users and reducing their net utility, thereby discouraging false reporting of the video parameters. Similar to the scenarios presented above, we consider the video

streaming of $N = 9$ video sequences with $m_i \in \{1, 2, 4, 6\}$ and $r_i \in \{1/2, 2/3, 3/4, 5/6\}$. The TF resources are allocated as per the optimal solution corresponding to the reported utility function maximization in (5) at the VCG price $p_i$ computed in (11). Figures 15 and 16 show the net utility function as a function of the symbol-rate $R$ corresponding to the VCG procedure based TF resource allocation for the video sequence football. It can be seen therein that the net utility function is maximum when the true parameters $d = d_t = 1.49$ and $\beta = \beta_t = -0.0258$. Hence, the VCG procedure penalizes the users misreporting the video characteristic parameters by decreasing their net utility. In these scenarios we only consider false reporting of a single parameter (either $d$ or $\beta$, but not both) by a single user. Below, we consider the scenario where multiple users simultaneously misreport one or more characteristic video parameters.

We assume the following misreported parameter values $\beta_1 = -0.025$, $\beta_3 = -0.020$, $\beta_5 = -0.030$, $d_3 = 2.2$, $d_4 = 1.8$, $d_6 = 2.4$, with user 3 misreporting both $d$ and $\beta$ considered for simulations in Figures 17 and 18. In Figure 17 we plot the net utility of user 3 corresponding to misreporting $d_m = 2.2 > d_t = 1.49$ and several possible misreports of $\beta \neq \beta_t$ and $d \neq d_t$. It can be seen that, amongst all the net utility curves, the one corresponding to $\beta = \beta_t = -0.0258$ results in the maximization of net utility. Similarly, in Figure 18 we plot the net utility for the false reporting of $\beta_m = -0.020 > \beta_t$ and several possible misreports of the rate parameter $d$ and quality parameter $\beta$. Once again, it can be seen that reporting the true value of $d = d_t = 1.49$ results in net utility maximization for user 3. Thus, application of the VCG procedure results in penalizing the parameter misreporting

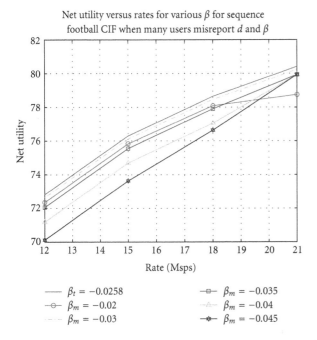

FIGURE 17: Net utility function versus rate at various values of parameter $\beta$ for sequence football CIF and other misreports: $\beta_t$ = true value; $\beta_m$ = misreprted value.

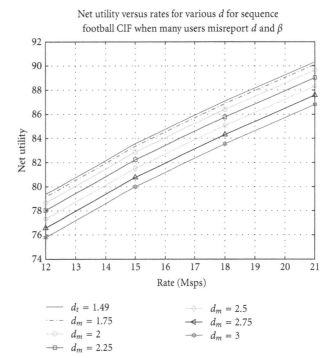

FIGURE 18: Net utility function versus rate at various values of parameter $d$ for sequence football CIF and other misreports: $d_t$=true value; $d_m$ = misreprted value.

malicious users, thereby encouraging users to report the true characteristic video parameters, thus resulting in optimal TF resource allocation.

## 6. Conclusion

We presented a novel scheme for time-frequency resource allocation in OFDMA-based 4G wireless systems aimed at video quality maximization. H.264-based scalable video models have been employed to characterize the video bitrate and quality as a function of the quantization parameter $q$. Based on these models, a constrained convex optimization framework has been presented for optimal OFDMA-based unicast/multicast resource allocation. A fast algorithm based on the closed form solution of the resource optimization problem has been presented to compute the optimal quantization parameters $q_i^*$. It has been observed in simulations that the proposed optimal scheme yields a considerable improvement in the video quality. Further, the performance gains increase progressively in multicast scenarios with increasing number of subscribers. For the specific case of PUSC WiMAX with $N_S$ = 2048 subcarriers and frame time $T$ = 10 ms, the proposed optimal scheme obtains a quality gain of about 6.5% over the suboptimal equal symbol rate allocation scheme.

We also presented a novel VCG procedure-based approach for optimal TF resource allocation towards scalable video transmission. In conventional 4G resource allocation based on sum quality maximization, there is an incentive for malicious users to misreport the video quality parameters towards disproportionately high-resource allocation, thus leading to suboptimality and subversion of the scheduler

operation at the base station. The proposed VCG procedure is effective for resource allocation in such scenarios, since it punishes malicious users through pricing-based optimal resource allocation, thereby discouraging false reports. Further, the incidental outcomes of the above VCG-based allocation are the price points for the allocated TF resources. Hence, the proposed scheme can also be used as an effective TF resource pricing algorithm for use in the OSS module of the core network, which in turn leads to overall optimal resource allocation.

## References

[1] D. Tse and P. Viswanath, *Fundamentals of Wireless Communication*, Cambridge University Press, New York, NY, USA, 2005.

[2] A. Goldsmith, *Wireless Communications*, Cambridge University Press, New York, NY, USA, 2005.

[3] H. Schwarz, D. Marpe, and T. Wiegand, "Overview of the scalable video coding extension of the H.264/AVC standard," *IEEE Transactions on Circuits and Systems for Video Technology*, vol. 17, no. 9, pp. 1103–1120, 2007.

[4] Y. Wang, Y.-Q. Zhang, and J. Ostermann, *Video Processing and Communications*, Prentice Hall PTR, Upper Saddle River, NJ, USA, 1st edition, 2001.

[5] Y. Wang, Z. Ma, and Y. F. Ou, "Modeling rate and perceptual quality of scalable video as functions of quantization and frame rate and its application in scalable video adaptation," in *Proceedings of the 17th International Packet Video Workshop (PV '09)*, pp. 1–9, Seattle, Wa, USA, May 2009.

[6] Y. N. Lin, C. W. Wu, Y. D. Lin, and Y. C. Lai, "A latency and modulation aware bandwidth allocation algorithm for

WiMAX base stations," in *Proceedings of the IEEE Wireless Communications and Networking Conference (WCNC '08)*, pp. 1408–1413, April 2008.

[7] S. Deb, S. Jaiswal, and K. Nagaraj, "Real-time video multicast in WiMAX networks," in *Proceedings of the IEEE 27th Conference on Computer Communications (INFOCOM '08)*, pp. 1579–1587, April 2008.

[8] J. Kim, J. Cho, and H. Shin, "Resource allocation for scalable video broadcast in wireless cellular networks," in *Proceedings of the IEEE International Conference on Wireless and Mobile Computing, Networking and Communications (WiMob '05)*, vol. 2, pp. 174–180, August 2005.

[9] JSVM, "Joint Scalable Video Model software, Joint Video Team, version 9.19.7".

[10] Y. F. Ou, T. Liu, Z. Zhao, Z. Ma, and Y. Wang, "Modeling the impact of frame rate on perceptual quality of video," in *Proceedings of the 15th IEEE International Conference on Image Processing (ICIP '08)*, pp. 689–692, October 2008.

[11] S. Boyd and L. Vandenberghe, *Convex Optimization*, Cambridge University Press, New York, NY, USA, 2004.

[12] N. Nisan, T. Roughgarden, E. Tardos, and V. Vazirani, *Algorithmic Game Theory*, Cambridge University Press, New York, NY, USA, 2007.

[13] "Lecture on VCG procedures," http://www.cse.iitd.ernet.in/rahul/cs905/lecture10/index.html.

[14] V. Srivastava, J. Neel, A. Mackenzie et al., "Using game theory to analyze wireless ad hoc networks," *IEEE Communications Surveys Tutorials*, vol. 7, no. 4, pp. 46–56, 2005.

[15] C. Sacchi, F. Granelli, and C. Schlegel, "A qoe-oriented strategy for ofdma radio resource allocation based on min-mos maximization," *IEEE Communications Letters*, vol. 15, no. 5, pp. 494–496, 2011.

[16] W. S. Lin, H. V. Zhao, and K. J. R. Liu, "Attack-resistant cooperation strategies in P2P live streaming social networks," in *Proceedings of the 42nd Asilomar Conference on Signals, Systems and Computers (ASILOMAR '08)*, pp. 1373–1377, October 2008.

[17] J. Hershberger and S. Suri, "Vickrey prices and shortest paths: what is an edge worth?" in *Proceedings of the 42nd Annual Symposium on Foundations of Computer Science*, pp. 252–259, October 2001.

[18] D. C. Parkes and J. Shneidman, "Distributed implementations of Vickrey-Clarke-Groves mechanisms," in *Proceedings of the 3rd International Joint Conference on Autonomous Agents and Multiagent Systems (AAMAS '04)*, pp. 261–268, July 2004.

[19] J. G. Andrews, A. Ghosh, and R. Muhamed, *Fundamentals of WiMAX: Understanding Broadband Wireless Networking*, Prentice Hall PTR, Upper Saddle River, NJ, USA, 2007.

[20] "Standard test video sequences," http://media.xiph.org/video/derf/.

[21] M. Grant and S. Boyd, "CVX: matlab software for disciplined convex programming, version 1.21," 2011, http://cvxr.com/cvx/.

# Permissions

The contributors of this book come from diverse backgrounds, making this book a truly international effort. This book will bring forth new frontiers with its revolutionizing research information and detailed analysis of the nascent developments around the world.

We would like to thank all the contributing authors for lending their expertise to make the book truly unique. They have played a crucial role in the development of this book. Without their invaluable contributions this book wouldn't have been possible. They have made vital efforts to compile up to date information on the varied aspects of this subject to make this book a valuable addition to the collection of many professionals and students.

This book was conceptualized with the vision of imparting up-to-date information and advanced data in this field. To ensure the same, a matchless editorial board was set up. Every individual on the board went through rigorous rounds of assessment to prove their worth. After which they invested a large part of their time researching and compiling the most relevant data for our readers. Conferences and sessions were held from time to time between the editorial board and the contributing authors to present the data in the most comprehensible form. The editorial team has worked tirelessly to provide valuable and valid information to help people across the globe.

Every chapter published in this book has been scrutinized by our experts. Their significance has been extensively debated. The topics covered herein carry significant findings which will fuel the growth of the discipline. They may even be implemented as practical applications or may be referred to as a beginning point for another development. Chapters in this book were first published by Hindawi Publishing Corporation; hereby published with permission under the Creative Commons Attribution License or equivalent.

The editorial board has been involved in producing this book since its inception. They have spent rigorous hours researching and exploring the diverse topics which have resulted in the successful publishing of this book. They have passed on their knowledge of decades through this book. To expedite this challenging task, the publisher supported the team at every step. A small team of assistant editors was also appointed to further simplify the editing procedure and attain best results for the readers.

Our editorial team has been hand-picked from every corner of the world. Their multi-ethnicity adds dynamic inputs to the discussions which result in innovative outcomes. These outcomes are then further discussed with the researchers and contributors who give their valuable feedback and opinion regarding the same. The feedback is then collaborated with the researches and they are edited in a comprehensive manner to aid the understanding of the subject.

Apart from the editorial board, the designing team has also invested a significant amount of their time in understanding the subject and creating the most relevant covers. They scrutinized every image to scout for the most suitable representation of the subject and create an appropriate cover for the book.

The publishing team has been involved in this book since its early stages. They were actively engaged in every process, be it collecting the data, connecting with the contributors or procuring relevant information. The team has been an ardent support to the editorial, designing and production team. Their endless efforts to recruit the best for this project, has resulted in the accomplishment of this book. They are a veteran in the field of academics and their pool of knowledge is as vast as their experience in printing. Their expertise and guidance has proved useful at every step. Their uncompromising quality standards have made this book an exceptional effort. Their encouragement from time to time has been an inspiration for everyone.

The publisher and the editorial board hope that this book will prove to be a valuable piece of knowledge for researchers, students, practitioners and scholars across the globe.

# List of Contributors

**R. Arockia Xavier Annie**
Department of Computer Science and Engineering, College of Engineering, Anna University, Chennai 600025, India

**P. Yogesh and A. Kannan**
Department of Information Science and Technology, College of Engineering, Anna University, Chennai 600025, India

**Mingfu Li**
Department of Electrical Engineering, Chang Gung University, 259Wen-Hwa 1st Road, Kwei-Shan, Tao-Yuan 33302, Taiwan

**Laith Al-Jobouri, Martin Fleury and Mohammed Ghanbari**
School of Computer Science and Electronic Engineering, University of Essex, Colchester CO4 3SQ, UK

**Vladislavs Dovgalecs, Rémi Mégret and Yannick Berthoumieu**
IMS Laboratory, University of Bordeaux, UMR5218 CNRS, Batiment A4, 351 cours de la Liberation, 33405 Talence, France

**Z. M. Parvez Sazzad and Y. Horita**
Graduate School of Science and Engineering, University of Toyama, Toyama 930-8555, Japan

**Roushain Akhter and J. Baltes**
Department of Computer Science, University of Manitoba, Winnipeg, MB, Canada R3T 2N2

**Shreyans Parakh, Vamseedhar R. Reddyvari and Aditya K. Jagannatham**
Department of Electrical Engineering, Indian Institute of Technology Kanpur, Kanpur 208016, India

**Francesco Cricri, Kostadin Dabov, Mikko J. Roininen and Moncef Gabbouj**
Department of Signal Processing, Tampere University of Technology, P.O. Box 553, 33101 Tampere, Finland

**Sujeet Mate and Igor D. D. Curcio**
Nokia Research Center, P.O. Box 1000, 33721 Tampere, Finland

**Yang Yang**
Key IC&SP Laboratory of Ministry of Education, Anhui University, Hefei 230039, China
MOE-Microsoft Key Laboratory of Multimedia Computing & Communication, University of Science and Technology of China, Hefei 230027, China

**Jun Ming**
Key IC&SP Laboratory of Ministry of Education, Anhui University, Hefei 230039, China

**Nenghai Yu**
MOE-Microsoft Key Laboratory of Multimedia Computing & Communication, University of Science and Technology of China, Hefei 230027, China

**Ivaylo Atanasov, Evelina Pencheva and Dora Marinska**
Department of Telecommunications, Technical University of Sofia, 1000 Sofia, Bulgaria

**Ismail A. Ali, Martin Fleury and Mohammed Ghanbari**
School of Computer Science and Electronic Engineering, University of Essex, Colchester CO4 3SQ, UK

**Mousumi Das, Atahar Mostafa and Khan Wahid**
Department of Electrical and Computer Engineering, University of Saskatchewan Saskatoon, SK, Canada S7N5A9

**Hui Li, Shengwu Xiong, Pengfei Duan and Xiangzhen Kong**
School of Computer Science and Technology, Wuhan University of Technology, Wuhan 430070, China

**Jue-Sam Chou**
Department of Information Management, Nanhua University, Chiayi 622, Taiwan

**Ching-Yu Yang**
Deptartment of Computer Science and Information Engineering, National Penghu University of Science and Technology, No. 300, Liu-Ho Road, Magong 880, Taiwan

**Abdel-Karim Al-Tamimi**
Computer Engineering Department, Yarmouk University, Irbid 21163, Jordan

**Raj Jain**
Department of Computer Science and Engineering, Washington University in St. Louis, St. Louis, MO 63130, USA

**Chakchai So-In**
Department of Computer Science, Khon Kaen University, Khon Kaen 4002, Thailand

Printed in the USA
CPSIA information can be obtained
at www.ICGtesting.com
JSHW051441221024
72173JS00006B/1539

9 781632 401281